THE LAST TRAIN FROM HIROSHIMA

THE LAST TRAIN FROM

HIROSHIMA

THE SURVIVORS LOOK BACK

CHARLES PELLEGRINO

A JOHN MACRAE BOOK

HENRY HOLT AND COMPANY NEW YORK

Henry Holt and Company, LLC
Publishers since 1866
175 Fifth Avenue
New York, New York 10010
www.henryholt.com

Henry Holt® and ® are registered trademarks of
Henry Holt and Company, LLC.

Library of Congress Cataloging-in-Publication Data

Pellegrino, Charles R.
  The last train from Hiroshima : the survivors look back / Charles
Pellegrino.—1st ed.
       p. cm.
  "A John Macrae book."
  Includes bibliographical references and index.
  ISBN 978-0-8050-8796-3
  1. Hiroshima-shi (Japan)—History—Bombardment, 1945—Personal narratives,
Japanese. 2. Atomic bomb victims—Japan—Hiroshima-shi—Biography.
3. Hiroshima-shi (Japan)—Biography. 4. Atomic bomb—Social aspects—Japan—
Hiroshima-shi—History—20th century. 5. World War, 1939–1945—Japan—
Hiroshima-shi. 6. Forensic archaeology—Japan—Hiroshima-shi. 7. Hiroshima-shi
(Japan)—History—Bombardment, 1945. I. Title.
  D767.25.H6P45 2010
  940.54'25219540922—dc22   2009030566

Henry Holt books are available for special promotions and
premiums. For details contact: Director, Special Markets.

First Edition 2010

Designed by Kelly S. Too

Printed in the United States of America
1 3 5 7 9 10 8 6 4 2

To Tomorrow's Child

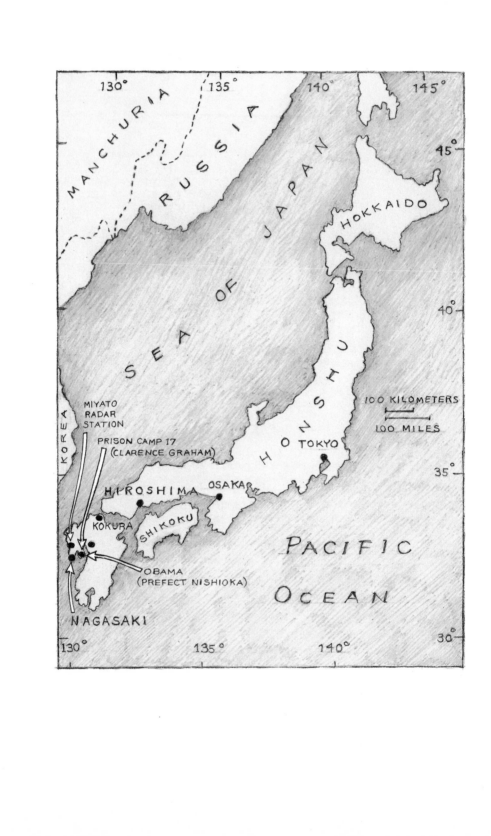

The question of whether the atomic bombs should have been exploded over Hiroshima and Nagasaki is a subject for another time, and for other people to debate.

This is simply the story of what happened to people and objects under the bombs, and it is dedicated to the slim hope that no one will ever die this way again.

As we move toward the precipice of runaway nuclear proliferation and even nuclear terrorism, we must remember that Hiroshima and Nagasaki represent the approximate destructive power of the weapons we are likely to see again. The hope that past is not prologue may indeed be slim, but I've never known the angel Hope when she was not looking a bit anorexic.

NOTE: Because many of the names encountered in this book are occasionally quite similar and may even appear to be the same, brief alphabetized biographical summaries of the major eyewitness participants in this history are included for reference, beginning on page 321. The term *Ground Zero* originated with Hiroshima and Nagasaki. It refers to the region where virtually all buildings are flattened, and where mortality is 85 percent or greater for unshielded persons standing outside. In Hiroshima, the radius of Ground Zero was more than a mile.

CONTENTS

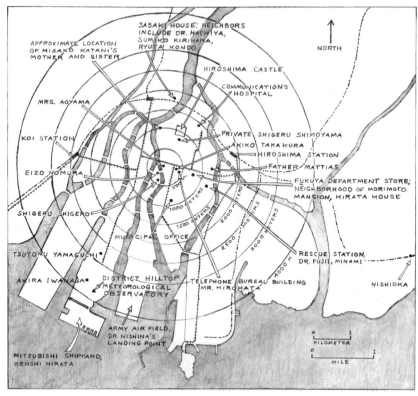

The city of Hiroshima, showing principal survivors and their locations at Moment Zero. Note that some names (including Kenshi Hirata, Misako Katani, and Tsutomu Yamaguchi) also appear on the Nagasaki map. These are people who, after surviving the first atomic bomb, departed from Hiroshima's Koi Station for Nagasaki, and became history's mysterious "double survivors" of the atomic bomb. (Patricia Wynne)

THE LAST TRAIN FROM HIROSHIMA

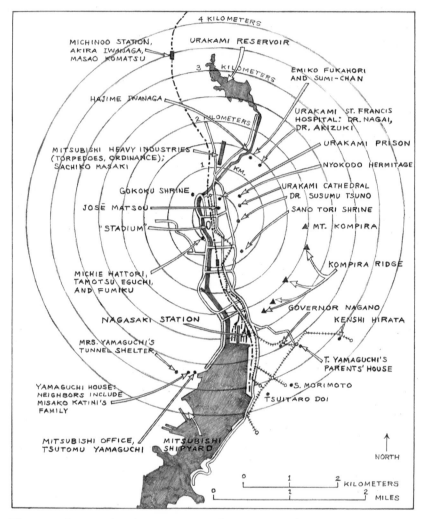

4 KILOMETERS

MICHINOO STATION, AKIRA IWANAGA, MASAO KOMATSU

URAKAMI RESERVOIR

3 KILOMETERS

EMIKO FUKAHORI AND SUMI-CHAN

HAJIME IWANAGA

2 KILOMETERS

URAKAMI ST. FRANCIS HOSPITAL: DR. NAGAI, DR. AKIZUKI

MITSUBISHI HEAVY INDUSTRIES (TORPEDOES, ORDINANCE); SACHIKO MASAKI

URAKAMI PRISON

1 KM.

NYOKODO HERMITAGE

GOKOKU SHRINE

URAKAMI CATHEDRAL DR. SUSUMU TSUNO

JOSÉ MATSOU

SANO TORI SHRINE

"STADIUM"

MT. KOMPIRA

KOMPIRA RIDGE

MICHIE HATTORI, TAMOTSU EGUCHI, AND FUMIKU

NAGASAKI STATION

GOVERNOR NAGANO

KENSHI HIRATA

MRS. YAMAGUCHI'S TUNNEL SHELTER

T. YAMAGUCHI'S PARENTS' HOUSE

S. MORIMOTO

YAMAGUCHI HOUSE; NEIGHBORS INCLUDE MISAKO KATINI'S FAMILY

TSUTARO DOI

NORTH

MITSUBISHI OFFICE, TSUTOMU YAMAGUCHI

MITSUBISHI SHIPYARD

0   1   2 KILOMETERS

0   1   2 MILES

The city of Nagasaki, showing principal survivors and locations at Moment Zero. (Patricia Wynne)

1

THE KILLING STAR

Had Mary Shelley or Edgar Allan Poe been born into the mid-twentieth century, they would never have had to invent horror.

For the Japanese scientists who first ventured into the still-radioactive hypocenters of Hiroshima and Nagasaki trying to understand what had occurred, the most fearsome deaths were the quickest. On a bridge located in central Hiroshima, a man could still be seen leading a horse, though he had utterly ceased to exist. His footsteps, the horse's footsteps, and the last footsteps of the people who had been crossing the bridge with him toward the heart of the city were preserved on the instantly bleached road surface, as if by an accidental new method of flash photography.

Only a little farther downriver, barely 140 steps from the exact center of the detonation, and still within this same sliver of a second, women who were sitting on the stone steps of the Sumitomo Bank's main entrance, evidently waiting for the doors to open, evaporated when the sky opened up instead. Those who did not survive the first half-second of human contact with a nuclear weapon were alive in one moment, on the bank's steps or on the streets and the bridges—hoping for Japan's victory or looking toward defeat, hoping for the return of loved ones taken away to war, or mourning loved ones already lost, thinking of increased food rations for their children, or of smaller dreams, or having no dreams at all—and then, facing the flash point, they were converted into gas and desiccated carbon and their minds and bodies dissolved, as if they had been merely the dream of something alien to human experience suddenly awakening. And yet the shadows of these people lingered behind their blast-dispersed carbon, imprinted upon the blistered sidewalks, and upon the bank's granite steps—testament that they had once lived and breathed.

On that sixth day of August 1945, no one who conceived, designed, or assembled the Hiroshima bomb knew where uranium nuclei came from, or what science had actually achieved. Not Oppenheimer or Urey, Alvarez, or even Einstein would have believed that they had resurrected something from the remote past, from a time and a place seldom encountered in human thought. Each of the uranium-235 atoms at the bomb's core had been forged more than 4.6 billion years earlier, in the hearts of supernovae. The core was assembled from the ash of stars that had lived and died long before the oldest mountains of the moon were born. Mined and refined to better than 83 percent purity, and brought together in precisely the right geometry, the primordial remnant of Creation was coerced to echo, after ages of quiescence, the last shriek of an imploding star. In all its barest quantum essentials, what happened above Hiroshima that morning—and three days later in Nagasaki, in a separate, plutonium cauldron, filled with the by-products of a uranium reactor—signified the brief reincarnations of distant suns.

None of the men who worked this strange alchemy understood yet that the carbon flowing within their veins was, like uranium, the dust of the stars. Nor did they know that the nuclei of carbon and uranium could possibly conceal anything much smaller than the diameter of a proton. Indeed, Einstein and Oppenheimer refused even to acknowledge that such quantum worlds existed. They therefore did not know what neutrons were made of or precisely how cracks in space-time—cracks in the universe itself—permitted matter to become energy. So primitive was their understanding that it might have been compared to the thought processes of a Neanderthal discovering napalm. In like manner, the scientists never suspected that the forces they unleashed bridged their day with the origin of the universe and bridged mega-time with the travel time of light across the diameter of a proton. Though they knew next to nothing about how their briefly created echo from the past worked, next to nothing was enough.

INEVITABLY, SOMEONE WAS BOUND to be standing below Point Zero. This peculiar distinction fell to a thirty-five-year-old widow and a half-dozen monks. Mrs. Aoyama had sent her son Nenkai away to school a half hour earlier than usual—which was why history was to claim the boy as the sole surviving resident from the neighborhood. The Aoyama home was attached on one side to a Buddhist temple with which the family shared and maintained a large vegetable garden. By 8:15, Mrs. Aoyama was probably working in the garden with her neighbors, just as she worked with them every morning. If so, no one was nearer the actual zero point, or more openly exposed, than Mrs. Aoyama and the monks.

Overhead, the Dome of Hiroshima's Industrial Sciences Building pointed straight up into the center of the detonation. The temple garden in which Mrs. Aoyama toiled was located immediately adjacent to what would become known to future generations as "the Peace Dome." During that final split second before Moment Zero, Mrs. Aoyama and the monks lived on the cusp of instantaneous nonexistence, on the verge of dying before it was possible to realize they were about to die. At the moment the bomb came to life, before a globe of plasma could belly down to ground level, the top millimeter of the Dome's metal cladding would catch the rays from the bomb and liquefy instantly, then flash to vapor. Bricks and concrete, too, were on the verge of developing a radiant, liquid skin.

Unlike the man leading a horse across the nearby "T" Bridge, Mrs. Aoyama could not possibly leave a permanent shadow on the ground. From the moment the rays began to pass through her bones, her marrow would begin vibrating at more than five times the boiling point of water. The bones themselves would become instantly incandescent, with all of her flesh trying simultaneously to explode away from her skeleton while being forced straight down into the ground as a compressed gas. Within the first three-tenths of a second following the bomb's detonation, most of the iron was going to be separated from Mrs. Aoyama's blood, as if by an atomic refinery. The top few millimeters of soil, as they converted to molten glass, would be shot through with such high concentrations of iron that, had the greenish-brown layer of glass been permitted to slowly cool, it would have been hidden beneath a sheet of carbon steel; but a slow and stately cooling was not to be. By the time the sound of the explosion reached her son Nenkai two kilometers away, all the substance of his mother's body, including blood-derived iron and calcium-enriched glass, would be ascending toward the stratosphere to become part of the strange radioactive thunderstorms that were to chase after Nenkai and the other survivors.

On the south side of town, about four city blocks beyond Mrs. Aoyama and the monks, Toshihiko Matsuda was about to leave his shadow on a wall in his mother's garden. He appeared to be bending down to pick a piece of fruit or to pull out a weed. During the next few milliseconds, the wall behind Toshihiko would be flash-printed not only with his shadow, but also with the ghost images of the plants that surrounded him (and which would provide his skin with some small measure of flash protection). On the wall print, at the moment of the bomb's awakening, could be seen the shadow of a leaf that had just detached from its vine and, though falling, would never reach the ground.

From the Aoyama and Matsuda households to the shrimp boats in the harbor, human nervous systems were simply not fast enough to register how quickly the dawn of atomic death burst toward them on that August morning. In the beginning, it had all unfolded from the realm of nanoseconds. Within the core of the reaction zone, approximately 560 grams (or 1.2 pounds) of uranium-235 began to undergo fission before the compressive, shotgun-like forces designed to start the reaction, and to hold it briefly together, were overwhelmed by forces pushing it apart. Three times heavier than gold (at the moment of compression), every ounce of the silvery, neutron-emitting uranium metal occupied three times less volume than gold. The active, business end of the bomb was therefore astonishingly small, occupying one-third of a golf ball's volume. The total volume of reacting uranium measured slightly more than two level teaspoons. Within that 1.2-pound, two-teaspoon volume, a sample of almost every element that had ever existed during the entire lifetime of the universe was instantly re-created, and many were just as quickly destroyed.

After only one-hundred-millionth of a second, the core began to expand and the fission reaction began to run down. During this ten-nanosecond interval, the first burst of light emerged with such intensity that even the green and yellow portions of the spectrum could be seen shining through the bomb's steel casing as if it were a bag of transparent cellophane. Five hundred and eighty meters (1,900 feet) below, no creatures on the ground could see this. During the first ten nanoseconds, light from the core traveled only three meters (about ten feet) in all directions. Fission reactions occurred within time frames so narrow that they bracketed the speed of light. Thus, to anyone located more than ten feet away, the bomb itself, though light was now shining through it, seemed to be hanging perfectly intact above the city. Directly below, Mrs. Aoyama was still alive and completely untouched by the flash.

One ten-millionth of a second later, a sphere of gamma rays, escaping the core at light speed, reached a radius of 33 meters (108 feet), with a secondary spray of neutrons following not very far behind. Between the gamma bubble and the newly formed neutron bubble, electrons were stripped from every atom of air and accelerated toward the walls of the larger gamma sphere. A plasma bubble began to form, producing a thermal shock that spiked hotter than the Sun's core and glowed billions of times brighter than the surface of the Sun.

Within this atomic flare, X-rays and gamma rays were repeatedly absorbed and scattered, polarized and reabsorbed, to such extent that the rays were as likely to reflect back toward the center of the bomb as away from it. A result of this was that by the time the light reached the ground, the gamma and X-ray bursts would be accompanied by a randomly scattering "sky shine" effect, by which a person shielded from the flash behind, for example, a solid brick wall, could still be pierced by rays emanating from all points of the compass.

During its first millionth of a second, the bubble of light grew to a radius of 300 meters—barely more than six city blocks wide. Though its own expanding dimensions had thinned and cooled the sphere's outer boundary to only a thousand times the boiling point of water, the temperature was more than three hundred times the number necessary to convert a human body to carbonized mist and incandescent bones. During this same first millionth of a second, and despite all that was happening, the light from the bomb still had not traveled far enough to reach the city. If either Toshihiko Matsuda or Mrs. Aoyama happened to be looking at the blast point at precisely this moment, and were their nervous systems equipped to register one-millionth of a second, the six-block-wide bubble would have appeared to them as an unexploded spear-point in the sky.

Above Matsuda and Aoyama—not merely unseen, but unseeable— the bomb's neutron surge, though traveling at a substantial fraction of light speed, lagged behind its flash and its gamma burst. From the place where the bomb had been—from its magnetic poles—nuclei of tungsten and iron shot ahead of the neutrons as a spreading shower effect, no longer behaving as if they had ever been part of the structure. Behind them, the outracing spray of neutrons (and to a lesser degree protons and short-lived anti-protons) now became a significant secondary source of prompt, and deadly, radiation.

After one ten-thousandth of a second, the air began absorbing the burst and responding to it. The surrounding atmosphere developed into an expanding gulf of near-perfect vacuum, snapping away from the place where the bomb had been, forming a cave of plasma. Along the cavern's walls, the neutron spray generated a second great burst of gamma rays. By now the initial flash had traveled to a radius of 30 kilometers (approximately 18 miles), and the light was just beginning to be registered by the rapidly firing nervous systems of mantis shrimps on the bottom of Hiroshima Harbor. Under the hypocenter, the blood in Mrs. Aoyama's brain was already beginning to vibrate, on the verge of flashing to vapor. What she experienced was one of the fastest deaths in all human history. Before a single nerve could begin to sense pain, she and her nerves ceased to be. Several city blocks away, Toshihiko Matsuda, and the plants that surrounded him, would live a while longer. At a radius of ten city blocks, koi and turtles swimming just below the surface of Hiroshima Castle's ponds would still be alive the next day—though before they could even begin to flinch or seek deeper water, they were going blind, with the scales and shells on their backs already searing.

Reaction rates were slowing down now—shifting from quantum time frames into the realm of biological time. During the next three milliseconds, a span in which a housefly could execute a single wing flap and start to alter course, the fireball began to form. Initially, it expanded at a hundred times the speed of sound, but by the time its lower surface neared the Hiroshima Dome and the roof of the Matsuda house, 97 milliseconds and 31 wing flaps later, it was down to only a fiftieth of its initial velocity. Near the periphery of the fireball, new fission-generated atoms with very short half-lives were undergoing rapid decay, sending forth a third gamma-ray burst. For all its capacity to cause harm, this third death ray was dwarfed by the heat ray that preceded it and by the gathering storm of a shock wave laced with lightning.

Throughout Hiroshima, one-tenth of a second after detonation, telephone wires and clothing began to send forth vertical columns of black vapor, yet all the buildings of the city still stood. Compared to its beginnings, the shockwave was now sluggish. This slowest of the three major atomic bubbles touched the earth at only twice the speed of sound, scarcely faster than human reflexes.

People required a full thirtieth of a second to register motion; a tenth of a second to flinch. The neural pathways of flies fired and reset, scanned and responded, almost fifty times faster than a human brain. From the fly's perspective, humans all but stood still, living in a universe of slowed time, much as humans viewed the time frames of garden-variety slugs and snails.

For miles in every direction, flies registered the initial pulse of light less than five milliseconds after it reached the ground, and they were capable of changing course and seeking shade a hundred milliseconds later, during the next thirty wing flaps, or within the average blink or flinch interval of human time.

After 300 milliseconds (or three-tenths of a second), the fireball had reached its maximum potential for inflicting flash burns at a distance; but by then most of Hiroshima's flies were already sheltering in the shadows of the nearest walls, or under the nearest leaves, or behind the nearest people. The gamma ray sky-shine effect scarcely mattered to them, because a fly's DNA repair systems were nearly two hundred times more efficient than a man's.

At three-tenths of a second, the bomb itself was long gone. Every-thing that followed, as events shifted from bullet-time and fly-time into the time frames humans knew best, signified nothing more than aftershocks.

Akiko Takakura and her friend Asami—though nearer to the bomb than Toshihiko Matsuda and his shadow garden—were lo-cated deep within the granite and concrete shell of the Sumitomo Bank when the gamma and infrared bursts started. Except for ran-dom shafts of sky shine that came in through windows in the build-ing's sides, the two women were more or less cocooned against the death rays.

Akiko would always remember how the clock in the main gallery stopped at a quarter past eight, the same time that the big clock atop the Hiroshima University tower had stopped three days earlier. Be-cause the war effort had drained almost all manpower and all spare metal parts, the resources to repair the city's main timepiece were lacking. During the past three days, Akiko and Asami had joked about how the broken clock tower, frozen seemingly forever at 8:15, underscored the futility of everything. For decades to come, their joke would be clothed in the mantle of prophecy, for in the end re-pairing the clock or leaving it unrepaired would have made no dif-ference at all. It would only have stopped again at a quarter past eight—like every other clock in Hiroshima.

Akiko and Asami were located only 250 meters (820 feet) from a hypocenter that originated more than twice as high—which placed the shock bubble's angle of approach almost directly overhead. Women sitting on the steps outside the bank were simultaneously ig-niting and carbonizing when, about one-tenth of a second before their nerves began to transmit pain, the blast wave intervened. Be-cause the shock-front came down from almost directly overhead, telephone poles and trees, and the vertical supports of the bank were able to resist and were largely bypassed by the forces of compression. Trees and poles and up-thrusting steel beams behaved much like the noses and fins of rocket bombs cutting through supersonic air. Akiko and her friend were spared much by an effect that needed to work only during the first two or three milliseconds of the shock-front's passage, in order to shield them through the entire five-second bypass of blast and turbulence that followed. The building had literally punched a hole through the advancing wave front, forming a shock cocoon for the two friends (and for a bank manager located in the basement) as the hammerhead of air rebounded outside, spreading away from them.

Akiko felt as if her lungs were being crushed by a surge of dense air. Asami was buffeted and tossed, struck in the back by decorative cladding from a wall that compressed like accordion skin and then erupted as granite shrapnel; but the two friends had been shielded within one of nature's strangest quirks. The shock-cocoon effect accompanied all major explosive events and tended not to occur where anyone acting on common sense alone would expect survival to be even remotely possible. Sometimes, the safest place to be was nearest the very heart of the explosion.

Like Akiko and Asami, Shigeyoshi Morimoto received a quick and intensive education in the physics of shock cocoons. Morimoto was one of Japan's four champion kite-makers, which was why he and three others had been drafted and transported to Hiroshima, to design high-altitude observation kites for ship convoys. At a quarter past eight on the morning of August 6, Morimoto was not much farther from the bomb than Akiko Takakura. Like Akiko, he recalled no sound accompanying the flash. The multitiered, heavily tiled mansion shook and compressed around Mr. Morimoto and his two cousins; but the combination of tiles and three layers of thick wooden beams overhead attenuated the gamma bursts by a factor of at least ten. Rooms filled floor-to-ceiling with shelves of books further attenuated the rays and absorbed the compression waves. In a sense, the three cousins were being safeguarded by culture. The compression of the upper three floors occurred as if the building had been designed with lifesaving crumple zones of wood and paper in mind, cocooning the Morimoto family so gently that they survived in the center of Hiroshima with only a few minor bruises.

At twice the Morimoto and Akiko radius, nearly six city blocks north of the hypocenter, Private Shigeru Shimoyama had just stepped into a concrete-reinforced warehouse—where, as he would recall later for historians, he was "shaded from the flash, but not from the bang." The hand of a vengeful giant seemed to have flung him toward the back wall, while in this same instant the roof was pushed down and the floor was pulled up. The walls, too, were yanked inward, toward the center of the room, and the rear wall stopped the flying private like a catcher's mitt. Outside, all of Shigeru's fellow draftees died instantly. When he discovered that the reason he appeared to be suspended almost a meter above the floor was that his shoulders were nailed to a wooden crossbeam, and when a never-ending silence made him feel as if he were the only living man in Hiroshima, he began to suspect that everyone else might have gotten away with a better deal.

Just beyond the Shigeru radius, at the edge of the army burial grounds, the sisters of a local girls' school were extracting oil from camphor trees when the sky ignited. The trees flew apart into thousands of flaming shreds. The granite tombstones nearby glowed cherry red, as if to herald the resurrection of the soldiers buried beneath, before the shockwave hurled them end over end off the top of Kyobashi Hill. Days later, Captain Mitsou Fuchida would arrive in the city center, searching for the nuns and their students. Finding the granite stones, and discovering that their outermost layers had boiled and turned to sand, he would understand that there was no point in looking for his friends. The stones would tell him everything he needed to know.

In the neighborhood of the Misasa Bridge, almost two kilometers upriver of the hypocenter, Sumiko Kirihara's family had been gathering for a portrait when the flash came. Sumiko was fourteen years old; she had seen the war draft cousins as young as sixteen out to sea, to be listed only weeks later as missing and presumed dead. Now her sixteen-year-old brother was being drafted to arsenal work, so the family came together from distant towns for what they believed might be a final reunion. Drawn now into the death zone, they had scheduled a photographer to arrive by eight, to pose them in a sunny, open-air garden; but for one reason or another he was delayed. And so, in a region where anyone standing outdoors and exposed to the flash from the bomb received lethal burns from the light alone, an unexpected change of schedule placed a family within the protective shadows of a tea room's wood and terra-cotta roof. When the heat ray flashed out from the direction of the Dome and the Sumitomo

Bank, the Kiriharas were safely indoors, reminiscing and playing music, and sipping cups of wartime tea so diluted that it might have been described as warm water sprinkled lightly with flakes of reused, dried leaves.

Outside, the garden vanished in a searing glare. Sumiko perceived the flash as a pale blue radiance that came from everywhere and seemed very hot, even indoors. At the same instant, she heard an electronic crackling, so loud that she believed it might split her eardrums. Her parents' two-story wooden house—along with the house of a neighbor—rode through the shockwaves almost completely undamaged, in a region where the only other buildings standing were a steel and concrete hospital and a cinder-block department store in flames. Mrs. Sasaki stepped out of her similarly shock-cocooned house with two-year-old Sadako in her arms. Like the Kirihara family, most of the Sasaki family appeared to have survived the *pika-don*—or "flash-bang"—completely unharmed, physically. Years later, little Sadako would insist that, though she was only age two at the time, she could still recall the radiance of a thousand suns bursting through the windows and a heat that pricked her eyes like needles. The false sunrise became her earliest memory.

The uranium fist was capricious, killing some and sparing others, even when people were within direct sight of one another. Mrs. Teruko Kono had kept her little boy home from school that day, and when the fist struck, she was watching him at play on his raft, from the second-story window of her riverside home within the Sadako zone, less than two kilometers from the hypocenter. Mrs. Kono was shielded from the heat ray, but her boy was fully exposed. She saw him flash out pallid white and send up a column of black smoke before her home was pitched on its side, hoisted into the air, then dropped into the river practically on top of her son.

On the bank of this same river, at this same radius and within sight of the Hiroshima Dome, Nobuo Tetsutani had been enjoying a peaceful respite at 8:14, a moment that would be burned into his memory by the strange circumstance of everything he loved being here one moment, gone the next.

The air was beautiful, filled with the sounds of cicadas and crickets rubbing their legs together, filled with the buzz of flower flies and the laughter of three-year-old Shin and his friend Kimi from next door, as they rode together on what Nobuo believed to be the last tricycle in Hiroshima to escape being melted down for the construction of steel hulls or artillery casings. Nobuo let out a laugh, and in the next 300 milliseconds he was spared, while the children were taken.

The tricycle's dark red paint caught the bright rays and held them, causing the outermost layers of steel on one side to flake apart, mixing explosively with the paint and igniting like iron filings on a birthday sparkler. The children's black hair caught the rays with equal efficiency, during the half-second before their world became deep rubble and glowing red coals. In a city fated to be rebuilt upon the ashes of "the disappeared," forty years would pass before Shin and Kimi were finally unearthed. Their little white bones would be found hand-in-hand, near a blistered brown pipe that turned out to be the handlebar of Shin's tricycle.

Some parents recalled premonitions, that morning, from children who only appeared to be trying to get out of school-based work details.

Etsuko Kuramoto was a fifth grader who had already stayed home for three days with a recurrent stomachache. She did not want to go to school again—insisting that something was about to happen and she did not want her mother to be lonely.

"Well then," Etsuko's mother said, "we'll die together when we die." She was laughing when she said this, and when she laid down the law that Etsuko would go to school even in a universal deluge, the child had insisted that she be allowed to wear her best outfit that morning. And when Sumi Kuramoto saw her daughter for the last time, her sacred, adored child was walking toward the National Elementary School in the direction of the hypocenter, wearing "her Sunday best," and crying.

Another fifth grader was more direct about his fears.

"Hiroshima will be totally destroyed today," Hiroshi Mori told his mother.

Yoshiko could not imagine where the child had heard such a horror. She warned him not to utter such words again, then ordered him away to school. And before he went away to a building whose steel beams were soon afterward stripped of their concrete shells and bent like blades of grass caught in a strong wind, the boy told his mother to take care of herself, and asked her not to pack any food into his canvas backpack, because he would not be needing lunch that day.

In another neighborhood school, at a radius of two kilometers, a teacher named Arai received an unforgettable lesson in the differential effects of black and white surfaces in absorbing light. When the flash came, she happened to be standing alone in her schoolroom, having decided to give the children a few minutes extra of playtime outdoors. Arai was hanging the best examples of her students' script in a window facing the hypocenter. One little girl, working her delicate calligraphy in India ink, had brushed her teacher's name onto white rice paper. The flash was so bright that Arai thought a thousand-pound bomb must have fallen right outside the window. In accordance with her air-raid training, she ducked instantly for cover, expecting nothing except "quick oblivion" from a bomb full of dynamite and phosphorus charges dropping so near. She was puzzled, therefore, when the light faded and the anticipated blast failed to come for what seemed many long seconds. She was on the verge of lifting her head for a peek outside when the window burst indoors and a thousand slivers of glass flew harmlessly over her back.

When Arai stood again, she beheld a giant volcanic cloud full of fireflies, shifting from gold to violet to a brilliant shade of green more dazzling than any emerald she could imagine. When the fireflies had risen out of sight and when a fly alighted on a cut in her forearm, she became aware of two new realities: the children outside were missing, as if something had spirited them silently away, leaving smoldering piles of rags in their place. Arai's second realization was that her arms, her face, and anything else that had not been shadow-shielded behind the papers on the window, felt badly sunburned.

In her hand, Arai still clutched the sheet of rice paper; but it had changed dramatically. The black Japanese characters had absorbed the light and flash-burned out of existence, whereas the surrounding white paper threw the light back from where it came and survived more or less intact. By the time the heat ray burned through the brush-strokes, the power of the bomb was all but fractionally spent and beginning to fade. A thin sheet of paper had shielded the teacher's

Throughout Hiroshima, walls and other still-standing structures preserved the shadows of people or objects. Each pointed in the direction of the flash. The creation of such images was similar to the pale shadow of a wristwatch after a day's sunburn on the beach. This telephone pole, located 1,300 meters from the hypocenter, after being seared by the flash, recorded the shape of a castor bush that had been flash-burned and then blown apart. Later, new shoots emerged below the shadow on the pole. The sharpness of the image's leaves indicates that the shadow was imprinted a second or two ahead of the blast wave's arrival. (Patricia Wynne)

eyes, sparing her from blindness, but even a dwindling fraction of the bomb's unspent fury was significant. Its light blazed through the missing letters like paint sprayed through a stencil. It struck Arai's face with the equivalent force of four or five full days under the August sun, stenciling the tender script of a child who was lost, permanently on her skin. All of this happened before Arai could even begin to duck—all of this, within four-tenths of a second.

Perception of the "flash-bang" seemed to change depending where one happened to be located. Akiko Takakura recalled that within a shock cocoon beneath the bomb, it had all begun for her with a white flash, in utter silence. At one kilometer, Yoshiko Mori saw a blue flash, accompanied almost instantly by a loud clattering noise. At almost two kilometers, Sadako Sasaki's mother remembered the flash as yellow, while her neighbor Sumiko was certain that the bomb had flashed blue. At this same distance, a shock-cocooned postal worker named Hiroko Fukada clearly recalled that it was yellow. Yasaku Mikami, one of only three firefighters who survived, saw the sky flash blue at a distance of 1.9 kilometers (1.2 miles). Five kilometers farther out, at a radius of 4.4 miles and in the bottom of a protected valley, photographer Seiso Yamada witnessed the whole spectrum of colors—"like rainbows and magnesium flashing overhead. Like ripples from a stone thrown into a pond, the rainbows came in waves"—and afterward he was shaken to the ground by the sound of a tremendous explosion.

Those witnesses nearest the hypocenter seemed never to have heard the blast. With increasing distance, the noise grew perceptible, then bone-rattling. At 1.8 to 1.9 kilometers, Sumiko heard a loud electronic buzz and crackle; but other survivors at this same radius, including the Sasakis, heard nothing. At three kilometers, ship designer Tsutomu Yamaguchi had been walking in a potato field, alongside a woman dressed in a black mompe, when something like a photographer's magnesium flashbulb blazed before his eyes. Responding instantly with his navy air-raid training, Mr. Yamaguchi dove to the ground and rolled into the nearest irrigation ditch, simultaneously flinging his hands to his head, locking fingers over his eyes, and jamming a thumb protectively into each ear. Even with his ears plugged by his thumbs, the sound that came to Yamaguchi was ear-shattering.

The ground roared and quivered, snapped and leaped, tossing Yamaguchi out of the ditch and nearly a meter into the air. As he fell, the fireball imploded overhead and began to rise at stupendous speed, creating a vacuum that for a second or two threatened to draw the engineer upward from the face of the earth; but instead it merely levitated him for what seemed an impossibly long time on a cushion of air and rushing dust, before finally dropping him face-first into one of the muddy furrows from which it had drawn him. He felt like a leaf on the wind.

When Yamaguchi regained his composure and peeked out of the ditch, a blizzard of burning paper and shreds of smoldering clothing were falling out of the sky, flickering like thousands of tiny lanterns and incense burners in the trees and on the leaves of the potato plants. It appeared to him that the contents of an entire office building had been hoisted into the heavens, then ripped up, blown apart, scorched, and strewn about.

Sitting in a mud pool, Yamaguchi became suddenly aware that one whole side of his body was intensely hot. The exposed skin on his left arm had been literally roasted brownish-black, like the skin of an overcooked chicken. Even then, before he knew anything about atomic bombs, the engineer began to suspect a heat ray of some sort; and he realized that his white shirt and his light-colored pants had spared him much. The woman in the black mompe had run toward the center of the field, where, standing upright, she exposed her entire body to the full fury of the flash, while clothed in the all-absorbing equivalent of India ink. She was nowhere in sight.

When Mr. Yamaguchi looked up, he noticed a solitary B-29 in the distance, headed out to sea toward some hidden air base that must surely have been still within range. He realized that the bomber might soon return. And all the burning in his body went away, to be replaced at once by the image of his wife and child alone at home. He contrived a plan, then, to find a train or an automobile that was still working, or a horse that was still alive and, by any means necessary, go home to Nagasaki.

Isao Kita was on a mountainside when the sky caught fire. He was the chief military weather forecaster for the District Bureau, and he remained at his post, recording and observing even after an unexplainable sense of dehydration and nausea took hold of him. The closer people were to the center of the storm, the less they could see of what was actually happening around them. At a distance of three kilometers, Mr. Yamaguchi had understood almost at once that he was witness to a high-energy device whose primary effect was a concussion of searing light. Nearer the hypocenter, all Shin's and Sadako's families could see were ruins, sheets of wind-driven dust, and rising seas of flame.

From the weather station, poised high above Hiroshima, more than a half-kilometer beyond Mr. Yamaguchi and just outside the bomb's radius of first-degree flash burns, Mr. Kita had a grandstand view. He was looking north across the city and the winds had been following their normal course for this time of the year—approaching from behind him. In the river basins below, the flash was partly obscured by brilliant white clouds that formed instantly around the hypocenter; they resembled the plain of Saturn's rings, viewed from a vantage point only slightly lower than edge-on, yet *this* cloudy layer of rings was in motion, rippling across the blue sky. Kita would always remember it as an amazingly colorful sight: "It was as if blue morning glories had bloomed in the sky." Then the air around him began to crackle and expand. Kita and the entire mountainside seemed to plunge suddenly into a hot oven. Like Yamaguchi, he realized immediately that something unusual had exploded over the city, and it appeared likely that a shockwave was already racing toward him.

Quickly estimating the seconds that had passed since the flash, Kita dove for cover and began to count. Two seconds later, a groaning sound reached him, building quickly to a rumbling roar that caused the observation deck to buck and kick. In one moment he was looking directly at the ground, believing he had successfully aimed his hands and feet protectively in the right direction. In the next instant, he glanced up in the direction where the sun and the fiery clouds should have been; but the heavens rushed down and struck him in the jaw. It seemed as unfair as it was disorienting that the sky should be paved with concrete instead of clouds; but Kita recovered quickly, and realized that the shock must have flipped him like a coin, two meters up into the air, then dropped him with toothcracking force onto the weather station's deck.

Pulling a piece of paper from his pocket, Kita jotted down the number five, representing the number of seconds between the flash and the bang. The distance from the center of the flash, near the "T" Bridge and the Dome, told him the speed of the shockwave: about 700 meters per second. Kita recorded that it must have been traveling at twice the speed of sound.

When the young scientist stood up and looked down upon the damage, only the word *unearthly* began ("and *only* began") to describe what happened.

Hiroshima no longer belonged in Kita's world. After the first five seconds, the whole city was converted to a lake of yellowish boiling dust, left behind by a billowing red cloud that rose at impossible speed. By the time Kita jotted the number 5, the cloud had already climbed more than five kilometers.

About five minutes later, the yellow lake of dust became stained with columns of inky black smoke; and two minutes after that, the layer of air above the dust was full of worms. After a while, Kita realized that the worms were whirling spouts of smoke and fire—sometimes moving off along separate paths and dying out, other times coalescing into actual tornadoes of flame orbited by uprooted masses of sheet metal and unrecognizable debris.

The wind at Kita's back seemed to be pushing all of the worms and the towers of smoke northwest toward Hiroshima Station and the Misasa Bridge, dividing the city into day and night. On Kita's side of the divide, the boiling dust layer settled or moved off and the ruins below were revealed as fields of broken wood and sparkles of glass, upon which the Sun was still shining brightly, during an otherwise normal summer morning. Everything in the south and east appeared to have turned into yellow desert sand. In the north, and upriver, the world was a darkness that even at a distance could be felt, broken only by lightning, and by glowing whirlwinds that sometimes towered five and ten stories tall. There were strange updrafts and downdrafts within the smoke; and through binoculars Kita was able to discern great sheets of black hail or snow, swooping down from on high.

"Noooo . . . ," he said. "Oh, no."

He could see that there were still people moving on the plain below. Thousands of people in open view, and probably thousands more trapped behind a black curtain.

2

GOJIRA'S EGG

For Nenkai Aoyama's mother and the man leading a horse across Hiroshima's "T" Bridge, life ceased so abruptly that it was as if nothing happened. Nothing at all.

Only beyond the zone of instant vaporization, or within the shock-cocooned gallery of the Sumitomo Bank, could people begin to wonder what had just occurred. Akiko Takakura, who would make her mark on history as the long-term survivor who had been nearest to the bomb, faded in and out of consciousness during the first three minutes. Her lungs ached from the sudden burst of compressed air, and from the equally fierce decompression that immediately followed. Several blocks north of Akiko's position, Private Shigeru contrived a plan to protect his lungs from a rising flood of soot and hot smoke by urinating into his shirt and using it as a filter, but the plan fell apart quickly, because it appeared to Shigeru that someone had nailed both arms and his right hand to a board while he lay unconscious. Only slightly nearer the hypocenter, kite-maker Shigeyoshi Morimoto noticed that all of his books had been knocked from the shelves and the ceiling was lower by more than a meter—which led him to conclude that he and his cousins must have survived a very close shave from a one-ton bomb landing on the front lawn. He could not imagine that most of the district that surrounded the mansion had disappeared.

Ship designer Tsutomu Yamaguchi climbed out of an irrigation ditch into a world that seemed to have turned instantly darker than a total eclipse of the sun. One side of Mr. Yamaguchi's face felt as if a thousand white-hot needles had pierced the skin, and he tried to soothe the heat with mud from the ditch. Three kilometers away, on the far side of Ground Zero, Sumiko Kirihara was coughing up yellow dust.

Scattered in random fashion throughout a city of a quarter-million people—a city in which survival appeared to be governed by random events—any two random survivors were all but guaranteed to be strangers. Despite a mathematics that rendered the survivors strangers, their lives tended to defy probability, becoming oddly connected.

The Sasaki and Ito families were examples of this. Although Masahiro Sasaki lived on the opposite side of the Misasa Bridge and more than ten kilometers away from ten-year-old Tsugio Ito, the two boys had already crossed paths at the State Middle School and College Complex's swimming pool, and they would eventually forge a lifelong friendship. Neither knew as yet that Tsugio's older brother Hiroshi and Masahiro's little sister Sadako were already drawing their families into a convergent path through history.

Only a few months before, Tsugio's brother Hiroshi had been accepted into one of Japan's most prestigious and competitive schools, from which the government typically recruited their top engineering students. Lately, twelve-year-old Hiroshi Ito's school had been converted from classrooms into makeshift factories supplying armaments for the soldiers of Hiroshima Castle. The older engineering students were being assigned to figure out how to manufacture triggers and other traditionally metal gun parts from more readily available hardwood—recovered from neighborhoods selected by the government to be flattened into firebreaks. In Hiroshi's classroom, brass shell casings were being substituted with a newer, clearly inferior alloy made mostly from demolished tin roofing. Bullets were being carved from mahogany—"for fighting at close range," a teacher had explained. Two-shot wooden handguns were being manufactured for distribution to children and their mothers. Everyone knew that the little guns would not be effective for very long if the Americans swarmed into the city, but the men who planned the final battle had decided that one or two shots from every citizen might work just long enough. In another classroom, the students were sharpening bamboo spears. *This is what happens to a nation that loses a war*, one observer said at the time. *Wooden bullets and bamboo spears.*

Five minutes after Moment Zero, Hiroshi Ito climbed out through the roof of his seventh-grade classroom, now reduced from a two-story building to less than a half-story. The Ito boy emerged completely unharmed into a mist of black water droplets whipped into motion by a combination of erupting fires and downpours of freezing black rain. The rain stung Hiroshi's skin and sent him running with thirty or forty other students into the swimming pool, crying for help. All of the other boys appeared to have been severely burned, and in every direction, Hiroshi Ito's world continued deteriorating into confusion. At the water's edge, schoolgirls, lying in rows, were dying one after another before his eyes. They had been wearing white blouses and black work pants. Most of them still wore only their white shirts, their dark pants having flashed into flame and ashes, removing all of the skin from the girls' legs. When Hiroshi looked in the opposite direction, toward the Misasa Bridge, a navy boat or a fuel tank greeted him with a huge explosion, from which something black and cylindrical rocketed up on streamers of flame. If it were possible, the sky became even darker after that, like a demonic pall drawn over the school and the river—a malediction.

At this moment, Hiroshi Ito's mother Hanako was running toward him from ten kilometers away in the eastern hill country. She knew that somewhere up ahead her son must be struggling for survival under the stem of the mushroom cloud. The initial flash had sunburned her face even at a distance of nearly seven miles; and she could not venture a guess at what the monstrosity might really be. Near the base of that same Ground Zero mushroom stem, Tsutomu Yamaguchi was trying to plan a way home to Nagasaki. He and Hanako Ito were now (like Tsugio Ito and Masahiro Sasaki) following convergent pathways. Both of them would be touched by Ground Zero a second time.

South of the stem, Yamaguchi's plan was almost thwarted by a whirlwind of brownish-yellow mist that descended suddenly from a great height and enveloped him. The mist was surprisingly cold, like frost, but it radiated an imperceptible heat, born of leaking neutrons and other exotic particles.

North of Yamaguchi, the Ito boy also felt the bite of freezing mist, from the moment he climbed out of the pool. By now Hiroshi Ito knew that he and only one other boy (a senior named Ryuso) had survived the destruction of their school without melted skin and crushed limbs. Their injured classmates moved in unearthly silence. There was no point in asking any of them for some clue or opinion about what had caused the blast and the burns. They seemed to have given up on everything; and so the two survivors set off to explore on their own, seeking answers.

Realizing that even their clothes were completely intact, the boys felt like intruders in a strange land where everyone else's eyes and lips had become blisters caked in black ash. Only a few minutes earlier, no one from this school had ever witnessed such injuries. Now, everyone else except Ito and Ryuso displayed the unusual wounds, as if what was normal became the rarity and what was abnormal reversed places with normal and became the majority. The reversal reminded them of stories their grandparents had told, about the prophesied breaking of the world.

"My God, my God," Ryuso said. "What just happened?"

Across the river, on the other side of the Misasa Bridge, Masahiro's and Sumiko's families were shadow-shielded and shock-cocooned—just like Hiroshi Ito and Ryuso. And, just like the two boys, they were initially unsuccessful at finding clues to the cause of the trouble. All they knew was that the phenomenon that converted idyllic backyard gardens glistening with morning dew into yellow dust and swirling black smoke had manifested like an instant dream. Mercifully, Masahiro's little sister Sadako would remember only the flash. Their mother wished never to add to those memories. Especially, she would never tell the girl about the tap dancer they saw.

Once the two families stepped outside, they discovered that all the people had gone away—except for a strange man who suddenly burrowed his way out of a wrecked house and began to run past them toward a curtain of whirling hot sparks. He flapped his arms like a bird's wings as he ran, and neither cried for help nor gave his onlookers any notice at all. The only sound he made was a rhythmic clicking on the road surface, as if he were dancing down the street with metal taps on his shoes. But he wore no shoes. In fact, his feet were gone and the bony stilts of two tibiae—chipping and fracturing with each step against the pavement—were the source of the tapping. No one saw what eventually happened to him. The tap dance in Dante's Hell was first muffled, then completely cut off by thick drifts of oily smoke—which enveloped both families in a gloomy quiet.

Beyond a radius of six or seven steps, their world became a silent and shadowy motion picture. After the tap dancer had passed, all that could be heard were the steady nearby pings of pebbles and grit from the sky, raining down upon sheets of corrugated zinc that had been blown into the neighborhood from somewhere far away. Sumiko Kirihara wondered if the instantaneous change in her world might actually have had no connection at all to the war, and might instead be connected to the final shattering of Earth itself, as had been prophesied for thousands of years. She began to believe this was the end of Hiroshima, of Japan, of humankind.

In a hospital near Ground Zero, a military physician had been recently reassigned, in preparation for the anticipated American assault on the mainland. His orders, issued to him at gunpoint, included the teaching of new soldiers—some as young as fourteen and fifteen—how to follow the latest procedures for strapping bombs to their bodies and throwing themselves under vehicles. The doctor now stood every bit as mystified as Sumiko by the silence of his surroundings. Decades would pass before anyone realized that he belonged to a very small coterie of shock-cocoon survivors. The riverside hospital in which he had been standing disappeared up to about the height of his waist. Everything was lifted away in a puff of dust, leaving him the only survivor, standing on the ground floor with not a single scratch. All the bomb had done to the doctor was snap the eyeglasses off his face. Looking down, he saw a little music box, also standing undamaged in this sudden purgatory of smoke and rising dust. The music box still played "Let Me Call You Sweetheart." Beyond that old Western tune everything else was silence, and everyone else seemed to have vanished.

The mystery deepened when, through occasional clearings in the dust, the physician began to see the true extent of the damage. And then he found his glasses, and discovered that he could no longer see clearly when he put them on . . . then discovered that everything came into sharp focus again when he took them off . . . became blurry again when he put them on. Some sort of pressure wave, he theorized, must have changed the shape of his eyeballs.

"But of course," he told a scientist years later, in a tone of genuine understatement, "I would not recommend nuclear detonations as a means of corrective eye surgery."

Elsewhere along Ground Zero's fringe, one of Mrs. Ito's conscripted co-workers had an equally remarkable story of survival to tell—owing to a precise combination of distance and obstacles, angles and forces, and luck. At Moment Zero, Mrs. Sumako Matsuyanagi's dark pants had ignited in the searing blue glare, but her long-sleeved white shirt protected the upper part of her body and the airburst instantly extinguished the flames of her pants before they could do any real harm. The hammerhead of air also scooped Mrs. Matsuyanagi off the sidewalk and flung her more than fifty meters—about halfway down a city block. She was farther away from the airburst than Akiko Takakura and the Sumitomo Bank, so the lower edge of the shock bubble did not bypass her. Instead it struck out laterally, and its bowl-shaped undersurface, spreading out along the flat anvil of the earth, compressed a precursor wave ahead of the outracing shock front—which was both a good thing and a bad thing in terms of survival. The precursor wave had shot several dozen meters ahead of Mrs. Matsuyanagi, gathering strength as it went. In this manner, the air, caught between shock front and anvil, became like a semi-fluid watermelon seed squirted between thumb and forefinger, with Mrs. Matsuyanagi cushioned in the center of the seed. Thus did the precursor wave, while propelling her at deadly speed, simultaneously perform the lifesaving service of clearing all the large windows of a house from Mrs. Matsuyanagi's flight path—which landed her in someone's sitting room, along with much of the room's ceiling.

Years later, Mrs. Matsuyanagi would recall, in a style of understatement exceeded only by the doctor whose vision was corrected by the bomb, that the people inside "were very surprised to see me."

"Where did you come from?" said an elderly woman.

"Are you hurt?" a kindly old man asked.

Mrs. Matsuyanagi looked around the demolished room in silence, not knowing what to say. The white-haired man pulled a broken chair out of the wreckage and asked her to rest. When she sat, her clothing began to crumble like brittle rice paper.

"What's causing *that*?" the man asked.

Mrs. Matsuyanagi answered absently, "Something seems to have happened." Her thoughts were only with her two boys, now. She thanked the couple and told them she had to go outside and find the school. *Had* to.

Thirteen-year-old Yoshitaka also survived the blast. He was attending one of the city's smaller schools, and the entire building seemed to have collapsed around him; yet some quirk of nature had sheltered him in an air pocket, from which he was able to push his way to the surface, quickly enough to witness the still-radiant cloud growing in the sky, almost directly overhead. The plasma within was still shockingly bright; Yoshitaka could feel its heat radiating against his face. It seemed to be catching the rays of the sun and throwing back every color of the rainbow—"And God forgive me," he would say later, "I could say that it was beautiful."

All around him, in the bricks and the rubble, other children were half buried and dying. Hands grabbed at Yoshi's feet and shins. He was horrified at the thought of so many hands trying to grab at him—the seemingly dead and the still-moving dead, trying to pull him down through the rubble—and all he could think of was to get away from them. So he kicked at the hands and ran away, continuing to look up at the beautiful apparition—to look anywhere but at the ground.

Had Yoshi stayed buried under even an ankle-deep layer of bricks for just a few seconds more, the rays might never have fallen upon him. The beauty he beheld in the cloud arose largely from the creation of secondary fission products, most of them with half-lives ranging from milliseconds to as long as three minutes. The decay of those isotopes, as pieces began to disappear from the universe, leaving bursts of energy in their place, fueled the third gamma ray surge—which diminished by more than 90 percent during the first ten seconds and continued to radiate the majority of its remaining power for a half-minute more.

When Mrs. Matsuyanagi found her two sons running aimlessly near the wreck of the school they appeared to have survived the flying glass and the collapsing walls without injury, but each had absorbed body-piercing gamma rays. Both had been granted only the briefest respite in which to presume they had escaped before succumbing by individual degrees to an epidemic no one had seen before. One boy had been shielded for only a few seconds inside a collapsing building, while his younger brother was shaded from the heat ray under a large tree whose thick trunk shielded him from the lateral slam of the shock wave. The blast forces must have diverged around the boy, but the bomb had unleashed an eerie menagerie of high-energy particles, some of them even deadlier than heat rays and blast waves. Among them were nuclei of iron—shotgunned from the bomb's interior along magnetic field lines, at up to 90 percent the speed of light. If a single uranium nucleus, chipped by a neutron bullet, releases enough power to make a grain of sand jump, an entire nucleus of iron shotgunned through a human body at relativistic velocity can deliver the force of a baseball squeezed through that same path at nearly 170 kilometers per hour. Along a path no wider than a human hair, flesh turns to ash, water explodes, and protein synthesis in the surrounding tissues is stopped dead. On that day, there existed rare, narrow kill zones where the bomb's magnetic field lines could guide *thousands* of such particles through a single body with an effect that was, in essence, nuclear machine-gun fire.

Both of Mrs. Matsuyanagi's children, as they wandered about the rubble pile that had been their school, were already feeling ill. The younger boy had gone to school hungry, but in the aftermath of the rays and the particle beams he lost all desire to eat. By the time his mother found him, he was overcome by dry heaves and seizures. Within minutes, the child's arms turned black-and-blue and he began to bleed despite the apparent lack of injuries. Hemorrhaging under the skin developed with such astonishing rapidity that scientists would one day wonder if the gamma burst was somehow lensed upon a specific child under a specific tree; or whether he was abnormally sensitive to doses of radiation that would have taken hours or days to sicken others; or whether Mrs. Matsuyanagi's memory of her child bleeding through the pores of his skin and dying only hours later, "like smoke fading away," was in reality a misremembered timing of events. A relativistic shotgun effect seemed just as likely, but no one would ever know for sure. On that day, Mrs. Matsuyanagi could not make even a bad guess at what had hurled her down a street and caused her clothes to fall apart like ancient parchment, or what manner of illness had pounced upon her two boys.

Before he left the house for the last time, the younger child cried because there had been no white rice available for many weeks, and he was allowed only a small portion of soybean mash for breakfast—which was anything but filling. Worse yet, in the near total absence of fresh fish or dried meat or other flavorings, the mash left an aftertaste like wet sawdust. For decades to come, Mrs. Matsuyanagi would pray for her child to visit with her in a dream, where she would take him in her arms and give him all the white rice and meat he could eat.

Mrs. Matsuyanagi's prayer reflected the emotions of many parents who remembered the ungranted wishes of their children. In the Peace Park that would one day occupy Ground Zero, one mother would leave a poem to the child who had asked for a tomato from the garden before he went to school. The boy's mother had told him that there was only one tomato left, and that it would stave off his usual bedtime hunger if he waited to eat it when he returned home. The poem spoke of the little shrine that would be constructed for him, on which she would leave a paper box covered with white cloth—and on top of the cloth, every day she would place a tomato.

LIKE EVERYONE ELSE in the city, Akiko Takakura did not know about gamma rays, neutron spray, or relativistic heavy ions. She could not define what was happening to her body, but what she wished she did not know now was a thirst she had never known before. She and Asami had filled air-raid helmets with water from a ruptured pipe in the Sumitomo Bank, but still their thirst intensified.

They were the only two souls inside the building's main gallery when the flash came, because by convention the cleaning chores were assigned exclusively to the female bank clerks and they were obligated to arrive a half-hour ahead of the managers and the customers. At 8:15, almost everyone else had been outside.

During the first half-minute after the flash, the air inside the bank had become unbearably hot. Akiko decided that it would be dangerous to stay indoors and any other location, in any other direction, must be safer. As it turned out, Asami's back was more badly injured than either of them had initially supposed; so it was not until 8:25— ten minutes past Moment Zero—that they were able to emerge into open air and see what happened. Then, of course, they wished they couldn't see at all.

The sun was gone. In the red glare of a fire whirlpool that appeared to be dancing itself out over the graves of buildings already reduced to flaming rubble, Akiko could see that the street was full of people turned to charcoal and piles of burning wax. At first glance the street had simply looked empty, but when she looked again it was easy to see how people who had been walking toward the bank were doubled up dead over one another, as far as she could peer through the smoke and the flames. Several people appeared to have flaked apart, like sacks of burned leaves spilled onto the ground. The red tornadoes—or fire worms—scattered the black leaf piles impartially, and the words "city of death" came quickly to her mind.

Akiko was among the first survivors to conclude that everything she saw had been wrought by a single, overpowering explosion. Stunned, and trying to comprehend, she crouched near something that had remained soft and fleshy. Its fingers were burning. Some sort of oil was being brought to the fingertips from the tissues below, and the five fingers burned like candles. She found it difficult to believe that fingers could burn like this—fingers that must once have held babies or turned pages. Akiko burst into tears, and then it began to rain.

For several minutes the two friends had forgotten about their thirst and were able to keep it at bay, but now the strange fever had returned and seemed to be paying them back with interest—which was why they began to drink the rain.

Some of the raindrops were as large as grapes—so large and falling with such force that they stung when they pounded down on Akiko's face. But she and Asami turned their faces toward the sky and drank the rain anyway, opening their mouths as wide as possible.

When she looked down at her arms, Akiko realized that the

water was staining her skin black. The rain was as dark as ink, but Akiko's thirst was so great that when her friend found an empty can, they used it to catch as much of the black rain as they could, and continued to drink.

The bomb had vaporized river water and pond water all across Hiroshima. Out to a radius of two kilometers, every leaf gave up a substantial portion of its moisture . . . as did every bird and cricket caught out in the open . . . and every blade of grass, every soldier, and every child. All the accumulated vapors of the city were hoisted up through the basement layers of the stratosphere, where they cooled and condensed, and began to fall.

The rain was black because it had coalesced around the stratospheric soot of Hiroshima and around the fission products of the cloud itself. Even with half-lives that lasted for only a few minutes, any mouthfuls of black rain ingested between 8:30 and 8:45 that morning were capable of delivering, during the next seven hours, at least half the DNA-scattering dose necessary to kill.

Akiko's body was evidently more resilient than her friend's. Asami succumbed quickly, but in 2005, Akiko tried to keep faith with the dead by keeping her friend's memory alive.

"She was a year younger than me," Akiko said. "I am nearly eighty years old now. She was only eighteen. Whenever I think of her, she is still eighteen years old. She was a very pretty, very gentle person."

LIKE AKIKO, MOST PEOPLE BELIEVED that anyplace except where they happened to be when the sky opened up had to be safer. From his post atop the weather station, Isao Kita arrived at the same conclusion as Akiko Takakura: a single stupendous explosive was the only explanation that made sense. Unlike Akiko, or anyone else below, Kita had a clear overview of what was happening on the ground. He was able to observe through binoculars how thousands of survivors on his side of the smoke and black rain, though reasonably safe, had begun a disorderly migration in random directions. Only gradually did they start to form strange, ant-like caravans zigzagging away from the fires and the darkness in the north.

Two of the wanderers, walking within Mr. Kita's ant trails, were a watchmaker and a surviving physician named Michihiko Hachiya. The watchmaker had merged, machine-like, into the first trail of victims who appeared to show any signs of organization. They were moving in one direction over a mound of yellow dust and broken roof tiles, so the watchmaker was taken more or less automatically into the movement and went along with them. The phrase he would use later was *muga-muchu*, which translated literally to "without self, without center." He felt that he could no longer make a decision on his own, so he followed the other people, losing himself in a hive mentality and being carried away by it.

Dr. Hachiya was completely naked when he fell in line. His clothes had been blown off before he joined the watchmaker and the rest of the ant-walkers, and he only half-realized that there was something remotely disturbing about the sudden desertion of his usual sense of modesty. Later, he would explain, "Those who were able walked silently toward the hills, their spirits broken, their initiative gone. When asked where they had come from, they pointed to the city and said, 'That way.' And when asked where they were going, pointed away from the city and said, 'This way.' They were so broken and confused that they—*we*—moved and behaved like automatons. Our reactions [would] astonish outsiders who reported with amazement the spectacle of long files of people holding stolidly to a narrow, rough path [over hills of jagged debris] when close by there was a smooth, easy road [to travel] going in the same direction. The outsiders could not grasp the fact that they were witnessing the exodus of a people who walked in the realm of dreams."

In this strange shock realm some of the survivors traded panic for an illusion of control by latching on to what became known (in the field of disaster psychology) as the Edith Russell Response: the tendency to focus on absurd details in the midst of horror or grave danger. One of the city's youngest military officers, who was normally stationed deep within Ground Zero, had been sent away on the morning of August 6 to a small town ten kilometers outside of Hiroshima. After receiving confirmation that all radio and telephone contact from Hiroshima had ceased, he packed his gear and headed back in the direction of the city.

The first flash-burn victim he encountered did not seem to be human. There was no face, only a swollen mass of charcoal above its shoulders that displayed an alligator-skin pattern reminiscent of burned wood. As he moved closer to the city, he encountered more creatures with the same burned-wood faces.

After more than an hour, the officer stopped, not knowing which road to take. The fire and the smoke and the charcoal people brought him to the point of bolting randomly in any direction, but a sudden thought about the military code book stopped his panic dead, and brought the young man back to self-control. He assigned himself the task of finding and securing the code book. As he walked, he firmed his resolve to recover the book and keep it away from the enemy even if nothing remained of it except flakes of blackened paper.

The officer walked past many ant trails along the outer-blast perimeter. Though his canteen was full, he ignored the ant people's pleas for water. He had to find the code book. Nothing else mattered. He quickened his pace as best he could, increasingly worried that when he finally arrived at the army camp, he would be severely reprimanded by his senior officers for having taken so long to return. When he arrived at his camp, however, there was no one left alive. Tents and buildings had either disappeared or been hammered flatly into the earth. Only the sturdier supply warehouses were recognizable.

A rectilinear depression in the ground led him to a flattened cabinet and, ultimately, to the ashes of the code book. The officer wrapped the book covers and the burned pages in a length of cloth he had torn and folded specifically for the recovery of documents. He then jogged away from the city, heading several kilometers upriver to military headquarters where, to his utter surprise, a senior officer reprimanded him for having obsessed on such an irrelevant detail as the disintegrated code book.

Meanwhile, inside one of the supply warehouses the obsessed officer had passed, Private Shigeru Shimoyama finally managed to pry himself free from the five nails that held his arms to a thick crossbeam. Somehow, through the explosion and through a process of de-crucifixion that had spattered blood in his eyes, Shigeru's glasses remained intact on his face. When he stepped out into daylight and thick swirling clouds of dust, the private realized that the glasses were not needed. In the manner of the physician who saw a music box on the ground and his glasses lying nearby and who was unable to see as clearly after he picked up his glasses and put them on, Shigeru's vision had improved enormously. Whatever force descended upon the city had simultaneously corrected his eyesight.

On the shore of the river, Private Shigeru observed, between gusts of smoke, that only a short distance away, near the outer fringe of the central "flat zone," Hiroshima Castle had burst apart. From that direction, a bureaucrat named Yasuda and four other men from the General Affairs Office were struggling toward him between burning piles of debris, holding high over their heads a life-size portrait of the Emperor. A second commotion drew Shigeru's attention to the river, where a naval boat was plying its way upstream through a field of shattered houses and floating bodies. The private watched, spellbound, as the boat slowed to a complete stop so that the crew could salute the Emperor's portrait. At the sight of this, even the burned and bleeding ant people saluted and bowed, and clasped their hands in prayer and wept. Dozens broke from their lines and joined the effort to rescue the painting, as smoldering telephone poles on either side of them ignited into torches. The Edith Russell Response and the culture lag—these were powerful distractions.

By now, Shigeru had seen enough. He was in possession of better information than the Sasakis and the Itos, than Akiko Takakura, Isao Kita, and the ant people.

Someone has been smashing atoms today, he concluded.

Shigeru's brother-in-law had informed him as early as 1943 that such bombs could be built, at least in theory. According to "the Professor," Yoshio Nishina, there was no reason to fear an actual race with the Americans or the British in developing a nuclear weapon because the electrical output of an entire country might not even be enough to refine the necessary few kilograms of rare neutron-emitting metals. Nishina and the other Tokyo scientists believed that an atomic bomb could be built if only Japan could obtain a pomegranate's volume of 90 percent pure uranium-235; but because they also believed that refining such material was technologically premature by about fifty years, they saw no point in racing toward development of the bomb.

All well and good, thought Shigeru, *so long as Nishina's fifty-year figure was not off by a factor of ten, and so long as the Americans had not bolted out of the starting gate five years ago.*

Only one grim chain of certainties obsessed Private Shigeru: *We were in a race all along and didn't know it. And we lost—which means that there can be many more of these things waiting to be dropped and I must get out of Hiroshima and return home to see my daughter one last time.*

Two others who thought of leaving were sixteen-year-old Misako Katani and her father. After the blast, strange whirlwinds of fire had come from the direction of the Sumitomo Bank and now stood between them and the wreckage of their house. As they watched, the flames spread like a tsunami over an area that surely included home, then spilled across a firebreak and overflowed the army stables.

"They're not home," Mr. Katani said. There was no emotion in his voice, no life. "They're gone." He was talking about Misako's mother and little sister, but all the younger Katani could think about were the screams of the horses as they broke free from the stables and ran toward her with flames leaping from their backs. They did not run very far; they all fell and died and sent forth a strange-colored smoke.

Father grabbed her by the hand and seemed to be running in no particular direction, except away from the flames.

"Where are we going?" Misako asked.

"Away from here," he said flatly. "I have relatives in a town three hundred K from here. Anyplace far away must be safer than Hiroshima. We must go to Nagasaki."

WITHIN THE FIRST TWENTY MINUTES, over vast areas of Hiroshima, the fire worms had begun merging into actual tornadoes that sent decks of corrugated metal cards flying with decapitating force and tore burning trolley cars from their track beds—while, behind them, nests of newborn fire worms rose from the ruins, like summoned spirits. Fire now raged everywhere, sending Sumiko Kirihara's and Sadako Sasaki's families fleeing to the river.

Two of the fire worms actually followed them to the shore, their approaching glare so intense that Sumiko's family had no choice but to run into the river. The surface was glutted with drifting wreckage. Entire neighborhoods of houses appeared to have been charred and mauled, then scattered in pieces over the water. On both banks, fire worms, rearing up and swirling more than five stories tall, seemed to take deliberate pause, as if surveying the scene, before deciding what action to take. Then one of the burning whirlwinds struck the river, converting at once from a column of fire to a column of foam and rushing water droplets—dashing a naval boat about and pausing threateningly near the place where Sumiko was wading.

Next, from the opposite bank, one fire worm followed another into the river, one after another turning into a waterspout before crossing over and drawing up new fire. Nearby, eighteen-year-old Hiroko Fukada tried to outswim one of the spouts but she was over-run by it and battered by drifts of wood, and spun about. Then, as the waterspout passed, huge chunks of black hail began to fall with bone-chipping force and Hiroko ducked beneath the water for shelter.

Surrounded by whirlwinds of fire and water—and by falling black ice—Sumiko wiggled free from her mother's grasp, ran out of the river, dug a shallow hole in the sand, and tried to crawl into it. At least two waterspouts followed her out of the river, raising clouds of sand that tore her shirt and pelted her back like a volley of little needles fired from a cannon. Finally, her mother grabbed her arm and she fled with the rest of the family to a ridge overlooking the river.

Everyone around them appeared to have been terribly burned. Sumiko would later recall feeling embarrassed about having survived the *pika-don* without injury, but she could easily see that her troubles were far from over. The heat from the landward side was becoming so great that she and her family were forced to reenter the river, where they were obliged to push corpses aside to drink the blackened water and quench a scorching thirst that seemed only to intensify with each passing minute.

The waterspouts and the whirlwinds of fire cost Hiroshi Ito the last of his courage. Looking around in panic and trying to find a way out, he lost sight of Ryuso. Along the opposite shore, people fleeing from the direction of the Sasaki house were falling into the river like swarms of insects. Riverside houses were also tumbling in—smashed in half with their rooms exposed and most of their furnishings curiously still in place, though in flames. Soon, the people in the water were pursued and overtaken by burning sticks and logs; and as a new picket of fire worms glared down at him, the Ito boy bolted in any random direction, then in another. A waterspout followed, eventually collapsing and blasting something slippery and sandy into his mouth. He spat it into his palm but could not see what he had almost swallowed because another gust of icy black rain overtook him and chased him slipping and stumbling over a pair of railroad tracks, which finally decided his direction.

He believed it likely that his mother might now be walking toward the city, searching for him, but against the black sky, the flames seemed to be strengthening everywhere, and especially in the direction of the school. Hiroshi Ito knew that his mother was smart enough not to come striding suicidally into this place. As he shook the rainwater from his hair and began following the tracks out of town, black hailstones started to fall, and the Ito boy found it impossible to believe that, less than twenty-five minutes before, the sky had been blue and clear.

SHIP DESIGNER TSUTOMU YAMAGUCHI, who was somehow spared while a woman in a black mompe disappeared nearby, realized, as the usual sensations of shock passed, that he was in severe pain. Ahead of him, the river offered the scent of death, but when Yamaguchi arrived at the river's edge he drank the water anyway. He had no choice. The flash burns on his arms and neck had brought dehydration and thirst.

The engineer did not have to look far to understand that he was luckier than most, including the grass boys. At first it had seemed to him that their burned and lacerated backs had grown strange mutant hair. Then he realized that the great wind had driven sharp blades of grass into their flesh, like nails. He helped them for a while; but all he could advise them to do was to pull out the blades one by one from each other's backs. This turned out to be easier done than advised, because they appeared to be weakening and dying before his eyes. Their thirst, like Yamaguchi's, was more overwhelming than their pain. Even hunger seemed not to matter anymore. The boys simply wandered away, one leading the others—apparently nowhere.

Yamaguchi had no intention of joining the ant-walkers. More sober concerns were driving him. He needed to get home to his wife and child, and home was a long way off. Ordinarily, as a precaution against the unexpected, and especially against the possibility of having to travel far without food or water, he always carried a canteen and an emergency ration of two small biscuits. Today, however, ordinary precautions did not seem to matter. After swallowing a bite from one biscuit, the engineer immediately vomited. From then on, he decided, he would only drink the water. Unlike Private Shigeru, he did not yet suspect that he might have absorbed radiation.

The bomb had created more abstract injuries than radiation sickness and the grass boys. "De-gloving" would become a polite, antiseptic term used by physicians to describe what happened when skin, whether or not it had been burned, was exposed to the ring of compressed supersonic air that formed between the central shock-cocoon zone of the Sumitomo Bank and the zone of grass nails. The skin was often pulled off by the wind—pulled off as if it had been bound to the body with all the adhesive quality of a leather glove, and could be stripped away just as easily.

Private Shigeru Shimoyama, having survived the peculiar horror of being nailed to a wooden beam by the bomb, now found a pinkish-white horse standing alone in his path. All of its skin and fur were gone. The sight fascinated more than horrified him, and it horrified him quite a lot. The animal did not appear to be in pain at all, and in fact it tried to follow the soldier as he moved on.

Every time the soldier looked back, the horse—its flesh de-gloved all the way down to layers of pale pink musculature—stared at him pleadingly and made faltering steps in his direction. Like Sumiko Kirihara and the Ito boy, Shigeru began to wonder if the end of the world might look something like this.

Shigeru was a Christian, and when he dreamed of the pink

horse—as every night for the rest of his life he would—he recalled a passage from the Revelation of Saint John:

> *And I heard the voice of the fourth beast say, "Come and see."*
> *And I looked.*
> *And I beheld a pale horse.*
> *And his name that sat upon him was Death.*
> *And hell followed with him.*

3

SETSUKO

By comparison with Hiroshima, the explosive detonations of Vesuvius or Krakatoa were relatively gentle upheavals, long and drawn out, releasing their energy over many, many seconds. Because the core of the atomic bomb was much more compact, its energy was released in one small part of a lightning bolt's life span, within a cauldron measured in cubic centimeters of metal, instead of across several dozen cubic kilometers of explosive, gas-saturated magma.

And for all its fury, the Hiroshima bomb had misfired. Though it would officially be listed with the Nagasaki bomb in the 22–30-kiloton range, it was in fact a 10-kiloton "dud." At a quarter-past eight, its energy had radiated from a spark scarcely wider than the tip of Setsuko Hirata's index finger. By the time the golden white plasma sphere had spread eighty meters wide—still within only one small part of a lightning bolt's life span—the spark had generated a short-lived but very intense magnetic field. Where the bomb had been, the metal rod and tamper system that ran down its center, from nose to fin, produced a cluster of dense metallic nuclei—stripped of their electrons, positively charged, and magnetically confined within forces that were trying to blow them apart at nearly the speed of light. The minds that conceived the bomb had accidentally created for an instant a predecessor to Brookhaven National Laboratory's relativistic heavy-ion collider. The bomb was an atomic accelerator whose magnetic shotgun barrels were aimed straight up and straight down. One stream of iron and tungsten nuclei went to the stars at up to 90 percent light speed, passing the orbit of the moon about a second and a half later. The other stream followed magnetic field lines to the ground.

Setsuko Hirata was seated in her living room, directly beneath the magnetic shotgun. Fast neutrons and heavy ions came down through tiles and roof beams and either stopped inside her body or kept going until stopped by several hundred meters of solid bedrock. Neutrinos also descended through the roof. Born of the so-called weak force, their interactions with the world were ghostly. They continued through Setsuko without noticing her, then traveled with the same quantum indifference through the earth itself. The very same neutrinos that passed through Setsuko sprayed up toward interstellar space a few hundred kilometers west of Brazil.

When Setsuko's neutrino spray erupted unseen, just off the coast of Ecuador, 134 milliseconds after detonation, she was still alive. Ceramic roof tiles, three meters above her head, were just then beginning to catch the infrared maximum from the flash—which peaked 150 milliseconds after the first atoms began to come apart. The tiles threw a small fraction of the rays back into the sky, but in the end they provided Setsuko with barely more protection than the silk nightgown her beloved Kenshi had bought her only two weeks earlier during their honeymoon at the Gardens of Miyajima.

Overhead, along the lower hemisphere of the blue-to-gold to blue-again globe, droplets of moisture had dissolved into a scatter of electron-stripped hydrogen and oxygen nuclei. A very small number of those hydrogen nuclei smashed together and fused, and collectively an amount of mass not quite equal to a grain of beach sand disappeared from the universe, adding a little kick of fusion to the fission power that burst down toward Setsuko. The instantaneous transformation of matter into energy produced a light so intense that if Setsuko were looking straight up she would have seen the hemisphere shining through the single layer of roof tiles and wooden planks as if it were an electric torch shining through the bones of her fingers in a darkened room. And within those first two-tenths of a second, she might have had time enough to become aware of an electronic buzzing in her ears, and a tingling sensation throughout her bones, and a feeling that she was being lifted out of her chair, or pressed into it more firmly, or both at the same instant—and the growing sphere in the sky . . . she might even have had time enough to perceive, if not actually watch, its expanding dimensions.

Setsuko's husband, Kenshi, had been working at the Mitsubishi Weapons Plant, slightly more than three kilometers away, when through a window came the most beautiful golden lightning flash he had ever seen, or imagined he would ever see. Simultaneously there was a strange buzzing in his ears, a sizzling sound, and a woman's voice cried out in his brain. He would suppose years later that maybe it was his grandmother's spirit—or more likely Setsuko's. The voice cried, "Get under cover!"

With all the speed of instinctive reflex, he dropped the papers he was carrying, dove to the floor, and buried his face in his arms. But three long seconds later when the expected shockwave had not arrived, he was left in adrenalized overdrive—with time to pray.

Outside, in utter silence, a giant red flower billowed over the city, rising on a stem of yellow-white dust.

Kenshi's prayers seemed to have been answered—yet again. He had walked away from the fire-bombing of Kobe without a single blister or bruise, initially thinking himself a bit unlucky because he should never have been there in the first place; and Kenshi *would* never have been there, had he not finished his work in Osaka a day early and departed for Kobe ahead of schedule. Two nights after surviving Kobe, he learned that Osaka, too, had been heavily bombed. Indeed, the very same hotel in which he should have been sleeping took a direct hit, with no survivors. At Hiroshima, Kenshi owed his survival to an instinct to obey an inner voice, and to the fact that the bomb had misfired, yielding a blast wave that was all but fractionally spent by the time it reached him.

Kenshi's next instinct did not serve him as well as his obedience to the voice. When he dropped to the floor, his initial impression was that huge incendiary bombs were exploding right on top of the building and that he would be cremated even before he could finish the first lines of a prayer. But nearly five full seconds followed the flash, and the light itself began to fade without a hint of concussion—

The bombs have not struck the building—

Kenshi raised his head to see what was happening around him. A young woman nearby had crept to a window and peeked outside. Whatever she saw in the direction of the city Kenshi would never know. She stood up, uttered something guttural and incomprehensible, and then the blast wave—lagging far behind the bomb's light waves—caught up with her. By the time the windowpanes traveled a half-meter, they had separated completely from their protective crosshatched net of air-raid tape, emerging as thousands of tiny shards. Like the individual pellets of a shotgun blast, each shard had been accelerated to at least half the speed of sound. The girl at the window took at least a quarter-kilogram of glass in her face and her chest before the wind jetted her toward the far wall.

Kenshi did not see where she eventually landed. Simultaneous with the window blast, the very floor of the building had come off its foundation and bucked him more than a half-meter into the air. He landed on his back, and when he stood up he discovered to his relief that he was completely unharmed, then discovered, to his horror, that he was the only one so spared. All of his fellow workers—all of them—looked as if they had crawled out of a blood pool.

We must have taken a direct hit after all, Kenshi guessed. He did not realize the full magnitude of the attack until he stepped outside. In the distance, toward home, the head of the flower was no longer silent. It had been rumbling up there in the heavens for more than a minute, at least seven kilometers high now, and it had dulled from brilliant red to dirty brown, almost to black. As he watched, the flower broke free from its stem and a smaller black bud bloomed in its place. It was, a fellow survivor would recall, like a decapitated dragon growing a new head.

A whisper escaped Kenshi's lips: "Setsuko . . ."

BEING IMMERSED IN DEATH, Father Mattias discovered, could be as bad as being counted among the dead. At the presbytery of the only Catholic church in the city, 1.3 kilometers east of the hypocenter, he and Father Hugo Lassalle had heard a plane moving overhead, revving its engines to full throttle and diving, as if trying to escape something. Overlooking a garden patio, they saw two parachutes drifting near the horizon and the otherwise empty sky suddenly strobed blue, then yellow—and then the ceiling dropped.

Mattias did not know what happened after that. His memory seemed to be recording only disjointed pieces. His first clear recollection was of walking toward the river; but time was playing tricks on him. All the usual reference points—the church and every other landmark—were gone. Some time ago—

A minute? An hour?—

—he had joined hundreds of other dazed, half-naked people and become one of the ant-walkers. The skin of the man in front of him flapped loosely from his back, like pieces of a tattered shirt; and all of the flesh on his forearm had been pulled off, as if it were a long glove. The priest followed the walking corpse aimlessly until it—and the scarecrow in front of it—bumped headlong into the frame of a charred and smoldering streetcar. When Father Mattias peered inside, he saw that the passengers' clothing and skin had been stripped off. Only one of them stirred: an unborn baby still struggling inside its dead mother.

He stumbled away, leaving the man who had led him to the streetcar gaping and swallowing on the ground, like a fish on dry land. Mattias did not know where he was going, but more than a dozen people fell in line behind him anyway, and began to follow.

Another ant-walker named Akihiro Takahashi staggered against the wrecked trolley. The only partly burned fourteen-year-old looked around and spotted the priest leading a new ant trail. Takahashi followed the priest, until he heard a friend calling his name. Then he veered off in the direction of his friend, and a new ant trail began to form behind him.

More than forty years later, Takahashi and Mattias would be seated together at a bus station in Washington, D.C., with an American chaperone and Paul Tibbets, the pilot of the plane that dropped the bomb. Mattias then told Tibbets how he had heard his plane's engines straining to get away from the bomb on this sunny August morning. Takahashi sat in silence for a very long time, knowing about Tibbets's reputation—about a willingness to reenact the bombing at air shows, and even to joke about his role in history by eating from birthday cakes shaped like mushroom clouds. Nervously, Takahashi told Tibbets that though it was amazing that a man could be close enough to have heard *Enola Gay*'s engines and to have survived, he had actually *spotted* Tibbets's airplane. And Tibbets remarked, "Yes, I could see all of Hiroshima below me." And then unexpectedly (and with apparent sincerity) he grabbed Takahashi's scarred right hand in both of his and said, "We should never let war happen again."

Far beyond the streetcar and the Takahashi ant trail, the corner wall of a brick apartment house—all that remained of the building— towered three stories above Father Mattias's head. Three children clung to the top of the tower, screaming. They were naked, and it registered somewhere in the back of the priest's mind that one of them appeared to be bleeding from his entire body.

At first grateful that he had been spared, now, as the unreality of the walking numb-state succumbed to clarities born of atrocity, he began slowly, surely, to blame himself for having survived. As he reached the river and the first rescue boats began plucking corpses out of the water and as he waded into the water himself and watched a woman carrying her child toward him—pleading with the infant to open its eyes—barely noticing that as she stepped into the water the skin and musculature began to fall away from her bones, the merciful numb-state began to crack. And he was touched by merciless guilt.

That's when he began thinking, truly thinking for the first time, about the three children he had seen at the brick tower. There were no familiar landmarks pointing the way back, and the fire worms had begun gathering themselves together into roving walls of flame. And he would wonder, every day for the rest of his life, whatever happened to the children on the tower. Each night, they would become the very last thing he thought about before he fell asleep. And he would dream about them. And they would be the first image that came to mind when he awoke.

AS KENSHI MADE HIS WAY toward the center of the city in search of his wife, the streets and fields sprouted what seemed to be thousands of tiny flickering lamps. He could not determine what the lamps

might actually be. Neither could any of the scientists who would hear
of this later. Each jet of flame was about the size and shape of a
doughnut. Kenshi knew that he could easily have extinguished any
"ground candles" in his path merely by stepping on them; but he was
"spooked" by an instinctive sense that it might somehow be dangerous to touch the fiery doughnuts, so he stepped around them instead.
He thought of Setsuko. He passed men and women whose backs had
been seared by the flash, but it was not the flash-burns that caught his
attention and stuck in his memory. The people appeared to be growing fresh green grass out of their roasted flesh. It occurred to Kenshi
only much later that thousands of grass blades must have been lifted
from the ground and driven through the air like miniature arrows. He
circumnavigated a giant column of flame in which steel beams could
be seen melting. He thought of Setsuko. Nearer the hypocenter, not
very far from the city's Municipal Office, he passed over a warm road
surface upon which a great fire must have risen, then inexplicably
died. All of the people simply disappeared here, and all of the wooden
houses, on either side of the road, were reduced to grayish-white ash.
He thought of Setsuko. The main street leading toward home seemed
more like a field than a road. In the middle of the field, he found two
blackened streetcars. Their ceilings and windows had vanished and
they were filled with lumps of charcoal that turned out to be passengers carbonized in their seats. The trolleys had apparently stopped on
either side of the street to pick up more passengers, and two people
were about to ascend the steps of one vehicle when the heat descended, and caught them, and converted them into bales of coal with
shirt buttons and teeth. He thought of Setsuko, now blaming himself
for their ill-omened honeymoon excursion two weeks earlier to the
Shrine Island of Miyajima.

There was a strange taboo in connection with the Miyajima Shrine.
It had been dedicated to a goddess who was believed by the older generations to become jealous if a newly married husband and wife
climbed the sacred steps together. If the taboo was violated, the old
people said, the wife would shortly die. But Kenshi's friend, a local
innkeeper who had arranged honeymoon lodgings for them near the
island's gardens, had scoffed at this and said it was pure superstition.
Since they had come all the way to Miyajima together, he advised,

then they should go at once to the famous shrine. So they did. And now, during the journey between his office and Ground Zero, Kenshi repented of it many times.

YOSAKU MIKAMI HAD MISSED the streetcar by only a few seconds, so he had to wait for another one, and he was therefore running nearly a quarter-hour behind his normal schedule when the next streetcar carried him by chance under the protection of the Miyuki Bashi Tunnel, and made him one of the few surviving firefighters in all of Hiroshima.

The first thing he noticed—after the blue flash from outside and after a blast of black smoke filled the car—was that the smoke had carried with it an awful smell. When he stepped outside, into the outermost fringe of Ground Zero, the familiar and dreadful scent became even stronger. As a firefighter, he understood at once what he was breathing. The smell that human flesh produced when it was burned happened to be quite similar to the scent of squid when it was grilled over hot coals—with a few pieces of sweet pork thrown alongside. The air was strong with the odor of squid and overdone pork, and so, as Yosaku ran toward the place where his firehouse had been, he knew what he was inhaling—tens of thousands of people.

No one had survived in the firehouse. Only the three fire trucks remained, in the place where Yosaku presumed the truck bay had been, though he couldn't be sure. Only the trucks and the building's foundations were recognizable, but the foundation lines were no longer straight. He found his captain scorched to death behind the wheel of Ladder 1. The man looked as if he must have been standing near the truck when the flash came, and had jumped into the cab and was about to start the engine so he could fight the fire—but then, of course, he could not.

THE STREETS OF HIROSHIMA were full of intriguing, seemingly impossible juxtapositions between the utterly destroyed and the miraculously unharmed. The roof tiles of Kenshi's home had boiled and cracked into thousands of tiny chips, and evidently the entire structure was simultaneously roasted and pounded nearly a half-meter into the earth. A few doors away, evidence of a gigantic shock bubble, in which the very atmosphere had recoiled at supersonic speed from the center of the explosion, could be seen in the evidence of the bubble's immediate aftereffect—the "vacuum effect" that had developed behind an outracing shock wave, pulling everything back again toward the center, toward the actual formation point of the mushroom cloud. The force of the imploding shock bubble had also pulled air-filled storm sewers up through the pavement. These manifestations only hinted at the forces unleashed when the low-density bubble, its walls shining with the power of plasma and super-compressed air, had spread and cooled to a point at which the press inward by the surrounding atmosphere started to become stronger than the heat and shock pushing away from the uranium storm. At this point, the shock bubble was only about 250 milliseconds old—just a quarter-second past Moment Zero and 400 meters in radius. When the bubble collapsed, less than two-tenths of a second later and nearly twenty blocks wide, the updraft experienced directly below, in Kenshi's neighborhood, was amplified by the almost simultaneous rise of the retreating plasma, which behaved somewhat like a superheated hot-air balloon. As it rose and lost power it had cooled from a fireball to an ominous black flower head, and had begun to shed debris the way a flower sheds pollen. Bicycles, bits of sidewalk, even half of a grand piano, fell out of the cloud, more than 800 meters away from the hypocenter.

And yet, amid all this havoc, pieces of bone china and jars of jellied fruit lay unbroken upon the ground. Kenshi discovered that trees, although dry roasted and stripped of their leaves, were still standing upright and unbroken in a 30-meter-wide area within his immediate neighborhood. A four-story house, too, appeared to have survived among the trees, suffering only a severe shaking and some compression, and a bit of searing. The owners were not there anymore, of course, but not for the reasons Kenshi would have expected.

Morimoto, the master kite-maker who happened to be visiting with two wealthy cousins in that house at Moment Zero, had walked away with only the most minor scrapes and bruises. The triple-tiered roof and the thick expensive wood, combined with the capricious nature of the bomb effects, rendered the house just strong enough to shield three men as they sipped tea on the ground floor. Morimoto and his cousins had simply walked away from the very eye of a nuclear detonation, and walked into the record books as members of one of history's most exclusive minorities. The large house, with its broad beams and layers of thick tiles, must have absorbed just enough of the gamma rays, X-rays, and neutron spray to spare their lives— and the near light-speed blasts of heavy nuclei had missed the Morimoto house entirely.

Still, as he climbed out of the steaming wood-and-clay pile in which the fire had been miraculously blown out, Morimoto walked into a dusty wilderness with an awareness that he had become very thirsty, and his skin felt as if every square centimeter had just become sunburned. His stomach and his intestines also ached, as if his insides, too, had been sunburned. He felt disoriented and confused, and by now Morimoto was beginning to suspect that even his brain must have been slightly sunburned. And after he stood atop a ridge of wreckage, and looked through breaks in the smoke, his disorientation multiplied. Normally, he would not have been able to see the mountains or the weather station's transmission tower from this location because there were tall buildings in the way. But the obstructions were all gone, now. The city was . . . *flat*. The whole thing. Amid sheets of shifting dust, he could recognize only burning sewing machines, concrete cisterns, blackened bicycles and streetcars, and piles of reddish-black flesh everywhere, a few vaguely in the shapes of human figures, or occasionally in the shapes of horses.

The thirst and the burning sensations intensified quickly, and Morimoto began to vomit—the first signs of gamma ray and neutron dosing, which blended undetectably with a shock state in which an unknowable interval of time had passed before the kite-maker realized that he had wandered off alone and could no longer see his cousins.

More than almost anyone else in the city this day, Morimoto would be able to tell future historians that his troubles were only beginning. He knew that Hiroshima, though overflown by bomber groups on their way to Osaka and other city targets, had been left unharmed. He had heard many rumors about why—including the ever-popular, "Hiroshima has too many gardens and shrines and is too beautiful to be bombed." But now Morimoto was among the first to conclude correctly that the Americans must have spared Hiroshima for something special—for how else could the designers of a new weapon hope to understand the damage wrought if the city were already carpeted with craters? If there were more of these special bombs to come, then they too would come to those cities intentionally left in pristine condition.

Most of Morimoto's family lived in one such city, Nagasaki—so it was from logic, and not from a superstitious dread, that he knew with a heartfelt certainty that his wife and children would be next, that the bomb was about to follow him home. But being followed did not matter to Morimoto.

If I am to die, he decided, *let me die with my family. So let me go back to Nagasaki.*

And from such logic, history was destined to receive two impossible shock-cocoon perspectives from the same person: nine kilotons directly overhead, and thirty kilotons 2.4 kilometers (a mile and a half) away.

ASSEMBLY PREFECT TAKEJIRO Nishioka had been completely shadow-shielded behind a tall ridge as his train approached Kaidaichi Station in the hilly suburbs of Hiroshima. The prefect had observed a glowing, reddish-yellow ring in the sky—huge and rocketing up from behind the hills in the direction of the city. As it faded into a cauliflower billow of multicolored vapor, soldiers on the train announced that an ammunition stockpile must have exploded. Nishioka knew better. No ammunition explosion had ever behaved like the cloud over Hiroshima. The prefect knew this, and more. He had been returning from Tokyo with instructions to withdraw publishing facilities, administrative barracks, and whatever great works from antiquity might be saved, into mountainside vaults.

During the past week, Nishioka had attended meetings with Professor Yoshio Nishina and his student Eizo Tajima, who had expressed bitter regrets that the late Third Reich never shared the fruits of its uranium refining facilities. The scientists estimated that given current production rates, working twenty-four hours a day, seven days a week, the country's two cyclotron accelerators might produce enough fissile material to assemble a single atomic bomb in about the year 2020. The plans for a heavy-ion relativistic shotgun weapon did not appear to be progressing much faster. Using power from the large dynamos at the Sakidaria plant, they had managed to prove that nuclei of gold were less easily scattered and more easily focused than iron nuclei—and in theory it was but a simple matter to aim relativistic kill weapons at B-29 bombers. But in practice, they would need a giant, ring-shaped accelerator nearly two kilometers in diameter, and the magnetic cannons would have to remain stationary, essentially anchored to the giant ring. The machines were therefore vulnerable to being neutralized even if the enemy chose not to attack the dynamos. All that the Americans, the British—and soon the Russians— needed to do was choose not to fly within range.

Young Tajima had asked if he should continue with his plans for the accelerator ring. The Emperor's representative did not answer.

And so it came to pass that Nishioka, unlike the officers on his train, understood at once what had probably happened to Hiroshima. The soldiers needed a little more time to surround the problem. As a precaution, they ordered the train to stop at Kaidaichi Station and to remain there until they made contact with the city. They shortly discovered that the phone lines were all dead, and even the usual daytime radio broadcasts had ceased. Then, from the direction of Hiroshima Station, came a train. All of the coaches had lost their windows, and apparently most of their passengers as well—save for a few stunned souls, looking out with blank expressions on their faces. The cars were all smoldering. Two were actually afire. The train did not stop. The engineer, looking more like a scarecrow than a man, leaned out the portside window and vomited streamers of bile and he either did not care or derived a perverse delight from the fact that he was picking up speed and fanning the flames as he passed.

The soldiers on Nishioka's side of the tracks immediately ordered the passenger coaches unhooked from their train. They took command of the locomotive and decided to proceed at once toward the stricken city. Nishioka, shaking the image of the scarecrow engineer out of his mind, ran after the crew, flashed his credentials, and ordered them to take him along in the cab of the engine. He did not know it yet, but he had just embarked upon one of history's most incredible journeys.

Within minutes of turning the curve of Kaidaichi Hill, Nishioka and the soldiers began to be confronted by lines of the walking wounded, following the railroad tracks away from the city. Pressing slowly and cautiously ahead—blowing the whistle to signal *Make way! Make way!*—they noticed that the burns on the refugees became progressively worse, and increasing numbers of the wounded were murmuring in low voices, "Water . . . Water . . ."

As they drew closer to the Cyclopean curtains of black smoke, the railroad tracks began shifting out of line and the locomotive was forced to stop.

The prefect decided to continue on foot, toward the appointment he had arranged two days earlier at the home of Field Marshal Hata. Nishioka had a reputation for punctuality, and neither tsunami warning nor typhoon had ever made him late before. He was not about to let an atomic bomb break his spotless record.

Even after Nishioka discovered that the ground between the trapped train and the field marshal's house was sprouting little flickering jets of strange fire, preserving his reputation obsessed him—no matter how disturbing those flames appeared to be. They emerged like miniature volcanic plumes, as if from burning bits of sulfur. They could have been extinguished easily by stepping on them as he passed, but he did not want to do that, believing later that merely by walking among the little jets he had exposed himself to radiation that caused his feet and shins to bleed beneath the skin.

For all of this, he was on time. The field marshal was late, despite the fact that his house had been shaded by a hill from the full effect of the *pika-don*. Nishioka expected that Hata would still have been inside at such an early hour, but he was met by an elderly officer whose face had first- and second-degree burns on one side and whose uniform had been torn apart. He asked for Hata, and the officer replied that he believed the field marshal to be dead.

The officer added, "I believe Hiroshima has been hit by an atomic bomb."

"I believe so, too," Nishioka said, and then decided to follow the tracks a little closer and see for himself.

A bridge stopped him. Its steel was sagging grotesquely and the wooden railway ties were on fire. No more survivors were crossing over from the city, but some of their cats had made it across. Six of them, their hair only slightly singed, were licking a ropy tangle of intestines hanging from a wounded horse that seemed not to notice.

Nishioka did not particularly like cats before Hiroshima. About the time Kenshi Hirata reached Ground Zero, the prefect was deciding he hated them. He also decided that there was nothing more he could accomplish in Hiroshima, and that he could better serve the empire by returning to his own regional headquarters at once with news of what he had seen.

Following the tracks away from the sea of smoke, he met a schoolboy who had been drafted into factory work by his teachers. The contours of the land—and especially Hiroshima Castle's moats and deflecting stone ramparts nearby—had somehow compressed the shock wave and focused it like a cannon shot through his building. The boy explained over and over again that he appeared to be the sole survivor. He was headed away from a zone Nishioka later learned was most heavily exposed to radioactive fallout (near the Misasa Bridge). The boy reportedly walked directly through the black rain zone, following a set of railroad tracks past Hiroshima's Communications Hospital and toward one of the suburban railroad stations—toward a place his family had arranged as a gathering point in the event of a severe air raid.

As they parted paths, the prefect gave the boy most of the provision of rice and water he had been carrying, and also a card with his name and the address of his headquarters, offering help and asking that his family contact him later. But he never did hear from the boy again, and he would wonder if this was because he and his family were to be counted among the dead or because they had counted him among the dead. The latter seemed just as likely as the former, because the address on Prefect Nishioka's card was the hypocenter of Nagasaki.

Historians would never be able to pin down the identity of the boy with any degree of certainty. And yet Hiroshima's Ito family would bear the distinction of a survivor's account that contained familiar congruences—which resounded hauntingly like the other side of Nishioka's story. Tsugio Ito's older brother Hiroshi was a schoolboy who emerged virtually a sole survivor from the Central School and who followed a set of railroad tracks eastward out of town, toward a prearranged family gathering place near the prefect's position. During a time in which food was so scarce that few if any people ever gave their rice away to strangers, the Ito boy reported to his family that a tall, authoritative stranger had given him food and offered him help.

During the hours that followed the encounter, nausea and weakness attacked Tsugio's brother Hiroshi, went away, then came after him more fiercely, causing him to vomit up the rice he had been given. Whether or not Hiroshi Ito was the same boy the prefect encountered, history had dealt the Ito and Nishioka families each an improbable hand, from the bottom of the deck. Heading off in opposite directions, it mattered little whether they eventually went to Nagasaki or to the Hiroshima suburbs. Nishioka would later record that the demon of atomic death seemed determined to stalk after them— for it was already deep within their flesh, sharpening its claws and waiting to pounce.

KENSHI HIRATA WOULD PROBABLY have escaped with no radiation injury at all had he not gone into the center of the blast area searching for Setsuko. Once he breathed the dry dust, then cleared the dust from his throat by drinking brownish-black water from a broken pipe, his cells were absorbing strange new variations on some very common elements. These new incarnations, or isotopes, tended to be so unstable that by the time he awoke in the morning most of them would no longer exist. Like little energized batteries, they were giving up their power. Unfortunately, they were discharging that power directly into Kenshi's skin and stomach, into his lungs and blood. The quirk that spared him a lethal dose was the initial collapse of the shock bubble and the rise of the hot cloud. A substantial volume of pulverized and irradiated debris had been hoisted up into the cloud, and most of the poisons had already fallen kilometers away as black rain. Even in terms of radiation effects, in its own, para-doxical way, Ground Zero was sometimes the safest place to be. It was all relative, naturally: Mr. Hirata's neighborhood was still hot with radioactivity; but places farther away were even hotter.

By nightfall of that first day, Kenshi had positively identified a particular depression in the ground as his home. Only a day before, the house and garden were surrounded by a beautiful tiled wall— and now, chips of those distinctive tiles were strewn through the embers. The large iron stove that had heated bathwater for Kenshi and his bride seemed to have been hammered into the ground, but it still appeared to be located in the right part of the house. Only a few steps away, he unearthed kitchen utensils, which though deformed by heat and blast looked all too painfully familiar. They were gifts from Setsuko's parents.

Kenshi had an odd instinctive feeling that the ground itself might be dangerous, and that he should leave the city immediately. The thought that stopped him was Setsuko: *If she is dead, her spirit may feel lonely under the ashes, in the dark, all by herself. So I will sleep with her overnight, in our home.*

Around midnight, he was awakened by enemy planes sweeping low, surveying the damage. The sky, in a wide, horizon-spanning arc from north to east, glowed crimson—reflecting the fires on the ground. Though there was little left to burn in what American fliers were al-ready calling Ground Zero, flames grew all around the fringes of the bomb zone, creeping outward and outward.

The planes circled and left. Kenshi put his head down again, upon the ashes of his home, and lay in the otherworldly desolation of the city center. The silence of Hiroshima was broken intermittently by more planes and by explosions near the horizon in the direction of the waterfront and the Syn-fuel gas works. As the ring of fire ex-panded to the gas tanks, there were no working fire hydrants or fire trucks, and only three firefighters left alive to prevent the tanks from igniting. Kenshi heard huge metal hulls rocketing into the air on jets of flame, crashing back to earth one by one, and shooting up again. But Ground Zero itself was deceptively peaceful, and the noises that reached Kenshi from the outside did not trouble him. He was too exhausted and too filled with worry about Setsuko's fate. If anything, the distant crackle of flames—even the occasional pops and bangs—lulled him into a deep slumber.

SUMIKO KIRIHARA'S AND SADAKO Sasaki's families tried desperately to get out of the city, but by midnight many of the people Prefect Nishioka had seen staggering away from Hiroshima were finding the roads blockaded by the residents of the outlying villages. In the countryside, during the space of only a few hours, the survivors had been transformed into fugitives, as localized councils made crystal clear through megaphones. By argument and by the occasional drawing of weapons, local authorities directed the walking wounded back toward the pyres and the places where black rain had fallen—and, though they did not know as yet that such poisons existed, toward the radioactivity.

Even before the bomb fell, city dwellers had found themselves unwelcome. After Osaka was cluster-bombed with incendiary weapons, no one wanted to live in any city. Children were sent off to relatives if they happened to have kin in the countryside. Satoko Matsumoto, another girl whose family had fled to the river with the Kirihara and Sasaki families, had hoped they could all cross together over a railroad bridge to the other side of a mountain, where some of her father's personal property had been sent a month earlier for storage. Then she remembered what her father had said at the time, that the townspeople were willing to accept luggage for safekeeping, but all refugees would be turned away. There were already food shortages in farming communities overtaxed by the military. Extra mouths to feed from the city, they had said, would push whole families over the edge from severe rationing and hunger into starvation.

Around the hour Kenshi Hirata laid his head down near his wife's grave, the first refugees returned to Hiroshima bearing unbelievable news of the "outlanders" turning them back with threats and even with lethal violence. So the three families decided to find an open space where they could spend the night.

Satoko Matsumoto's father would be stricken by "atomic bomb disease" in only a week. Developing huge purple bruises under his skin, losing his hair in large clumps, and bleeding cupfuls of blood through his nose, Mr. Matsumoto would stand up one evening, gaze at the setting sun, and without any warning or fuss, fall dead.

That first night, Satoko lay on her back and watched towers of smoke drifting up against the stars and blotting them out. Only at their bases did the towers dance with reflected light from the flames. Higher up they ceased to reflect anything at all; rather, they absorbed the light as if someone had spilled ink across the heavens. Like her father, she had suffered no visible injury; still, she found it painful to spend the interminable night lying on her back under that oppressive fried squid smell, listening to the fires consuming what was left of the city. Occasionally, the black shadows of American reconnaissance planes passed overhead. And when the smoke finally shifted to reveal more than half the sky, Satoko beheld more shooting stars than she had ever seen before.

Something managed to send a chill up her spine—during a night that had already been so full of fearful moments that just one more seemed bound to pass without notice—and yet Satoko was chilled to the bone when a woman mentioned that the unusual number of falling stars must mean that more people than they had already seen die were only now dying, or about to die.

THE FIRST SOLDIERS to reach the hypocenter came only an hour ahead of sunrise. The War Ministry had sent them in with stretchers—for what purpose, they could not understand. "There was not a living thing in sight," one of them would recall later. "It was as if the people who lived in this uncanny city had been reduced to ashes with their houses."

And yet there was a statue, standing undamaged in a place where not a single brick lay upon another brick. The statue was in fact a naked man standing with arms and legs spread apart—standing there, where everything else had been thrown down. The man had become charcoal—a pillar of charcoal so light and brittle that whole sections of him crumbled at the slightest touch. He must have climbed out of a shelter about a minute after the blast, chased perhaps by choking hot fumes from an underground broiler into the heart of hell. The fires killed him and carbonized him where he stood.

The next statue they found was covered in gray ashes. It appeared to have spent the last moment of its life trying to curl up into a fetal position. One of the soldiers probed it with a rod, expecting it to crumble apart. Instead, it opened its eyes.

The soldier flinched and asked, "How do you feel?" There seemed to be nothing else to say.

Instead of saying what he felt like saying—*How do you think I feel, you moron?*—the man replied that he was uninjured, and explained, "When I came home from my job, I found that everything was gone, as you see here now." The man insisted he needed no aid in leaving, nor did he wish to leave.

"This is the site of my house," he said. "My name is Kenshi."

DURING THAT FIRST NIGHT, Akira Iwanaga had taken shelter from the smoke and the fire worms only ten or twenty paces from his roommate and fellow ship-design engineer Tsutomo Yamaguchi, but neither man saw the other.

Akira had been standing outside Hiroshima's newest Mitsubishi plant when the *pika-don* was born. He was shielded from its full force by a low hill, at a distance of 3.7 kilometers. Even at a radius of slightly more than two miles, and behind a hill, Akira had felt a strong wave of heat in the air, followed quickly by a high wind and whirling dust. Overhead, the mushroom cloud's cap had seemed to glitter with flashes of bright golden lightning. And then had come black rain and a darkness that swallowed all the sounds of the world, and which seemed to know no end.

Sunrise now brought only the briefest respite. The winds—which had been drawn into the pyre like warm air drawn into the eye of a typhoon—were finally stalling and abating. The fire worms were dying. By now the arc of flame beyond the hypocenter burned with a steady, crackling roar, and Akira could begin to see clearly in the strengthening daybreak.

The river was still glutted with bodies and debris, just as he had seen it at sunset. In the outside world of countryside villages, the water-bloated bodies and the tide of ravenous black flies that seemed to be rising everywhere would have been shocking. But Akira now believed he was beyond the point at which he could be shocked. And then daylight continued to strengthen, revealing a young woman whose mind had clearly been wiped away. Only twenty-four hours before, her smile must have been absolutely beautiful. Even now there was something mournfully beautiful about her. She had apparently escaped without any flash burns and seemed completely uninjured . . . except for the huge slash across her abdomen. Having propped her back firmly against a wall, she must have spent much of the night carefully rearranging her intestines and trying to push them back inside, but the baby—which appeared to be only halfway to term—had come out with her insides and died and she did not seem to know quite what to do with it . . . whether to leave it outside her body or to continue pushing. She gave Akira a hideous grimace that became a smile, then flopped over to one side, dead.

Akira bolted, slipped on a loose brick pile, fell hard on a splintery shard of scorched wood, and screamed. He stood up and began running again, slipped on something soft, recovered his pace this time without falling, and continued running as fast and as far as he could, putting as much distance as possible between himself and that horrible beautiful girl.

DOZING NEARBY IN A half-sunk fishing boat, Yamaguchi dismissed the sudden scream and the scrabble of hands and feet over bricks as merely another anonymous mind that had snapped. He had not eaten for nearly twenty-four hours but had managed to keep dehydration in check by forcing himself to drink dirty water from broken pipes. The shipbuilder still carried most of his ration of two biscuits, but was having difficulty keeping down even a few sips of water. Appetite had failed him hours earlier.

During the night, a soldier told Yamaguchi that the local Mitsubishi plants appeared to be permanently out of action, and that any surviving engineering personnel should return to headquarters in Nagasaki. Yamaguchi had assumed that the rail services were every bit as dead as the Mitsubishi shipyard, but the soldier informed him that there were plans to send a train out of Koi Station to Nagasaki in the late afternoon.

After only two hours of rest in the ruins of the boat, Yamaguchi felt well enough to set out for Koi. Normally, he could make the trip in forty-five minutes. But now? Who knew if he would ever reach the station, much less Nagasaki.

The soldier had assured Yamaguchi that as a high-ranking naval engineer a priority seat would be available. The shipbuilder no longer cared very much about military priorities or the war effort. All he wanted was to get home to his wife and his infant son.

With nothing else in mind, he was able (with varying degrees of success) to harden his heart against all that the grim sunrise revealed: a mother singing a lullaby to her dead child, a horse's head burning like an oil lamp with an eerie, bluish-green flame. Yamaguchi came across a body that at first appeared to have been completely shielded from the searing rays, and then he realized that the shielding had only protected the man from his midsection down to his feet. The upper third of him was a carbonized corpse whose features had been eroded by the wind. The musculature and even the ribs were being carried away as soot on the morning breeze, revealing a blackened heart. Yamaguchi noted for future reference that whatever had shielded the man's lower body and turned his head and chest into loosely packed soot could easily have been worse the other way around—leaving the heart and eyes and brain intact while allowing the victim to see his bared pelvis and femurs before he died.

The engineer had to cross two rivers on his way to the station. The narrower of them no longer had a bridge, but in the shallows bodies were piled up like a natural dam that could also be crossed like a bridge. Even when he tried to keep his mind focused on nothing except the recollected faces of his wife and child, crossing that bridge pained him severely.

At the broader of the two crossings, he encountered an even more challenging bridge: a high railroad trestle whose iron frame was sagging ominously, as if on the verge of collapse. Almost all of its wooden ties had been burned, so he was obliged to belly-crawl and straddle and pull his way along a narrow steel track rail, as if he were a trainee in a high-wire act.

Near the train station, the engineer found several military officers gathered with Prefect Nishioka around a large aluminum cylinder.

The object was flash-burned on one side and appeared to have come crashing to earth like a meteorite. One of the officers told Yamaguchi that the cylinder had been dropped over the city by parachute, only seconds ahead of the flash. Inside the canister they had found a radio transmitter attached to atmospheric and scientific recording devices.

What they did not tell Yamaguchi—what only the prefect and one other officer knew at this stage—was that they had discovered an envelope among the pressure wave, gamma ray, and neutron sensors. The envelope contained an appeal addressed to Professors Ryokichi Sagane, Nishina, Tajima, and the rest of Japan's leading physicists. The appeal came from atomic bomb scientist Luis Alvarez, who four decades later would leave his mark on the history of nuclear arms reduction with the discovery of the "nuclear winter" effect.

"You have known for several years that an atomic bomb could be built," the letter began, "if a nation were willing to pay the enormous cost in preparing the necessary material." Alvarez continued, "Now that you have seen that we have constructed the production plants, there can be no doubt in your mind that all the output of these factories, working 24 hours a day, will be exploded in your homeland. . . . As scientists, we deplore the use to which a beautiful discovery has been put, but we can assure you that unless Japan surrenders at once, this rain of atomic bombs will increase many-fold in fury."

Alvarez was not telling the whole truth, of course. The end of World War II was more a game of poker than chess, and like any good poker player, the American dared not show all of his cards. The fact was that the factories alluded to could produce barely more than two troy ounces per day of the necessary material. Once the next bomb was dropped, another would not be available until September or October.

Whatever happened tomorrow or the day after really had very little to do with American behavior or with Japanese behavior. What it all came down to was that most of human history was fated to be forged by primal instincts, and not by civilized thought. The dawn of atomic death was a distinctly human story, told by tigers with uranium-and-plutonium-tipped claws.

Once upon a time there existed only three atomic bombs in all the world. The tigers tested one in the New Mexico desert, to be certain that the machine would work. Three weeks later the other two were dropped.

EVEN WHEN KENSHI REALIZED that the cloud had risen directly over his home, he prayed and held out hope that Setsuko might have somehow escaped harm. When he left the dockyard, he had packed a few extra biscuits for her. Now, a day later, he dug on all fours into the compressed ashes of his kitchen, descending nearly a half-meter—almost knee-deep. Whenever he paused to eat a biscuit or to sip water from a broken pipe, he sprinkled a share of the food and water ceremonially onto the ground—an offering to Setsuko.

As the August sun climbed higher and a snowfall of gray ashes blew through, the pipe stopped dripping. Kenshi was soon out of water as well as running low on biscuits, but he continued digging, hoping against knowledge that his failure to find any bones meant that Setsuko might not have been home when the flash came.

As exhaustion, thirst—and now hunger—began to compete with the first mild signs of radiation sickness, three women from his neighborhood returned to the ruins. Like Kenshi, they had been away, sheltered from the *pika-don*. The oldest of them, the head of their neighborhood association, had rediscovered the place where emergency rations were buried and had directed the excavation of three large sealed cans of dry rice. Seeing Kenshi, and hearing his pleas for anyone who might have encountered Setsuko, she went straight off to a nearby pit in the ground that was filled with glowing red coals of wood. She mixed some of her own water ration with rice and cooked a bowl of mildly radioactive gruel for Kenshi. He would recall later that he was moved to tears by the kindness of this woman. He never saw her again.

After he ate the bowl of rice soup, he felt reenergized despite slight waves of nausea and resumed his search for Setsuko.

He excavated the entire kitchen, knowing that his wife loved cooking more than almost anything in the world, and that she fancied herself a top chef who could turn even the most meager rations into the most subtle flavors by coaxing spices and herbs from what most people called termites and weeds and citrus ants. The kitchen, he decided, was where he would most likely have found her at 8:15 a.m.—planning how to bulk up a cup of stale soybeans and turn it into what she had promised to be "a taste like walking on a cloud."

When the dust of the kitchen had produced not the slightest trace of her, Kenshi began to grasp at hope. He was soon joined by ten men who worked in the city's sawmill and who knew the couple well, and had heard of Kenshi's distress.

They moved from the kitchen to the living room, excavating almost knee deep, and not a single trace of bone was found.

"She is not here," Kenshi said. "She is still alive somewhere."

"In order to make sure, we must dig a little deeper," one of his friends said.

Minutes later, hope died. His friend unearthed what seemed to Kenshi to be only a bit of seashell.

"We both love conches and giant clam shells," Kenshi insisted. "Setsuko uses them as table decorations!"

But already he knew in his heart that it was a fragment of human skull. The men quietly stepped back. Suppressing an uneasy feeling, Kenshi excavated gently with his fingertips, slowly widening and then deepening the area from which the "shell" had come. He touched little white scraps of spine, and found in them a pattern that indicated to him her final moment. She had been sitting when . . . it happened.

From the kitchen he excavated a metal bowl, singed but otherwise completely undamaged. Kenshi recognized it as the very same bowl he and Setsuko had brought with them from her parents' home on the train to Hiroshima, only ten days before . . . *Ten days*, he lamented, *and this poor girl's bones are to be put in this basin that she had brought with her from her native place.*

He was thirsty under the broiling sun of midsummer. Sweat had formed long streamers down his back and his trousers were soaked. He felt faint. His friend from the sawmill offered him water and he drank, then sprinkled some of the water over the basin—in the sense of giving his wife the last water to the end of her short life.

"The lumber mill is gone and there is no guessing what will become of us now," his friend said, then announced that he and his wife had been hoarding a small ration of fine white rice and dried fish, just in case the gradually worsening conditions came down to what westerners called "a rainy day."

"Well, it's been raining fire and black ice and horse guts," the mill owner said. "So, this must be the day."

He invited Kenshi home for a late but hardy lunch, and offered a place to stay until he decided where to go next.

Kenshi had already decided. As a surviving member of Mitsubishi management, he would be able to get priority seating on any trains still running. "If I can get to Koi or even all the way out to Kaidaichi Station," he said, cradling the bowl of bones close to his chest, "then I will be able to find a way to bring Setsuko home to her parents."

"Then all the more reason for you to have a good meal before you leave," his friend insisted.

On the outskirts of the city, the mill owner's house had survived behind a hill with only a few roof tiles dislodged. Nausea came and went, which made it easier for Kenshi to eat slowly and to keep his portions small. He did not want to take too much of the last good meal in town for himself, and away from his friends. All the while, the bowl from his own kitchen lay at his side. From the bones of his wife, isotopes of potassium and iodine were being liberated. They settled on Kenshi's trousers, and on his skin, and in his lungs.

While they ate, a young soldier came to the door with news that Hiroshima Station might never run again, and all of the high-priority seats at Koi Station were already taken for the afternoon of August 7. No trains were running out of Kaidaichi, owing to what the sixteen-year-old message-runner called "the most amazing train wreck ever!"

He explained excitedly how a train leaving Hiroshima during the flash had been fried so severely that even its deadman switches must have failed: "The thing shot right through Kaidaichi and just kept on flying. They say it was doing at least a hundred-and-fifty K when it finally hit a truck in a crossing and went off the rails!"

Kenshi merely thanked the boy for his report and asked him if any trains would be leaving Koi tomorrow.

"Yes," he said. "There's one leaving at 3 p.m., and you have pro-visional seating—which means you're on it, as long as you can get there."

Kenshi decided to make an early start. Many roads and bridges had ceased to exist, and how long the walk to Koi would take was anybody's guess. He filled his canteen and put two biscuits and a few grains of rice into his pants pocket, then cut some strings and wrapped a cloth tightly over the top of the basin so that Setsuko's bones would not spill if he tripped on the debris that filled the streets.

Before he left, Kenshi asked his friend for permission to pick a flower from his garden. Then, saying his thank-yous and good-byes, he went down to the river, where he threw offerings of a flower and rice grains into the water and bowed three times, in accordance with a Buddhist tradition that acknowledges a place of the dead.

Bodies were now being pulled from both sides of the river, and on the road ahead mass cremations had already begun.

How, Kenshi wondered, was he going to tell Setsuko's parents what happened to her? He could think of nothing else. He did not know yet that he would soon have much else to think about. It might even be said that his rendezvous with history these past two days had been merely the twilight before the dawn. Kenshi Hirata would reach Koi Station with time to spare; and at three o'clock on the afternoon of August 8, he would set out to bring Setsuko's bones home to her parents, aboard the last train to Nagasaki.

4

AND THE REST WERE NEUTRINOS

No one would have believed that the Hiroshima bomb was a "dud," or that it had come within bare millimeters of never even leaving the Isle of Tinian.

Before he climbed aboard the scientific observation plane *Great Artiste*, physicist Luis Alvarez had warned pilot Charles Sweeney that though he expected the bomb to detonate, it was, "to one degree or another," compromised. "At the very best," according to the physicist, "a third to one-half of a golf ball volume of uranium would react, instead of a whole golf ball's worth."

Flight engineer Joseph Fuoco did not know, even as he prepared for takeoff from the Tinian airstrip, the nature of the new incendiary bomb. Yet he already possessed enough clues to someday piece together the *"Little Boy* snafu."

For Fuoco, the past few days had been filled with enough strange history to last a lifetime. First, the military outposts at Guam and Tinian had begun swarming with civilian scientists who kept completely to themselves and said absolutely nothing. Then, on the evening of August 4, there had been an accident with what Charles Sweeney's crew and Dr. Luis Alvarez knew as "the gadget." One of the young civilians was already vomiting when they carried him away from the gadget's shed, where a preflight test of how to (or how not to) arm the weapon had gone terribly wrong.

Few besides Alvarez and Sweeney knew the true extent of worry and debate that had existed, over how ready for detonation the gadget's internal geometry really needed to be at the moment of takeoff. If already primed in *Enola Gay*'s bomb bay, the carefully divided uranium rings in the aft end of the bomb could all slam together at once and undergo partial fission if the plane crashed or even if it hit a very hard bump along the runway. The outcome of this scenario— which Dr. Alvarez called "an unscheduled energetic disassembly"— had five possible endings. None were good. The least of five worries would shoot tiny beads of molten uranium hundreds of feet in every direction, exhausting the greater portion of America's uranium supply and a threat to the health of anyone who happened to be within breathing distance. At the high end of Alvarez's five-point "Sphincter Scale," an unscheduled ring-slam could easily generate enough heat to trigger the bomb's detonators.

Luis Alvarez knew of the deadly (and now top secret) accident in the shed. The physicist knew of this, and much more. He was confident that the bomb could be dropped from the plane with its triggers and explosive charge completely absent when it hit the ground, and still it would lay waste to several city blocks—and this was the problem. In an attempt to construct a weapon guaranteed to fire under any circumstances, the scientists had produced a design so prone to accidental fission that the uranium shotgun method would never be used again. From what historian physicists would later learn about the Hiroshima bomb's structure, the nature of the Tinian accident involved only the uranium rings at the aft end of the weapon, beneath the fins, because any interaction between the rings and the cone-shaped uranium needle in the bomb's nose would likely have killed Luis Alvarez, Joseph Fuoco, and everyone else on the air base. Some portion of the aft ring assembly had surged long enough to reduce the weapon's efficiency but not long enough to melt the rings and cancel the mission; yet it was just long enough to place the young scientist conducting the test in the immediate presence of an atomic accelerator, without the benefit of shielding.

By the time he stopped the reaction and stepped away from the rings, he was technically dead already, with his DNA so thoroughly scrambled that all protein synthesis—life itself—must have shut down. The scientist's death had a second stage, a peculiar horror reserved for recipients of massive radiation doses. His nervous, circulatory, and respiratory systems had outlasted the rest of his body. He appeared alive—moving and weeping—almost until sunrise. A few others who had been near the particle surge were shielded to varying degrees by a combination of heavy equipment, thick file cabinets, and the outer walls of the shack. Sickened, they would survive, more or less.

After the accident, Alvarez and the pilots rewrote the mission profile. They had decided to lift off with the bomb assembly disarmed. Although this decision vastly reduced the possibility of another particle surge—or worse yet, an in-flight detonation—it also required a complex arming procedure while *Enola Gay* and its two scientific escort planes flew toward their target. Shortly before midnight on August 5, Dr. Alvarez had inserted three additional neutron "spark plugs" of polonium and beryllium into the core assembly. This action constituted a significant breach of protocol, because what Alvarez put into the bomb during that eleventh hour constituted almost all of the world's polonium supply. Normally, at Alvarez's discretion, only one polonium plug was to be inserted if he decided a fission insurance policy was needed. With all three inserted, no such policy remained in effect if another uranium bomb became available. The triple insertion was an indicator of just how weakened Alvarez believed the bomb had become.

About the time Luis Alvarez was providing his bomb with the nuclear equivalent of injecting nitrous oxide into a race car's engine, Colonel Costalati ordered Joseph Fuoco to be awakened and assigned him as a replacement flight engineer aboard one of the new, stripped-down B-29s. The officers told him nothing about the mission, beyond the fact that he was to take his usual post behind the co-pilot and carry out his usual job of monitoring fuel tanks and engine function and, whenever necessary, make his typically unconventional and even against the rule book in-flight repairs. Joseph had gained a reputation for being a quick-fire miracle worker during the fire-bombings of Tokyo, Osaka, and Kobe. The astonishing rapidity with which he once rigged a system of chains to drop a set of bombs that had jammed in the bomb bay during a mission—saving not only the plane but allowing the last-minute, impromptu bombing of an enemy ship that showed up on the horizon—had left little doubt in Costalati's mind whose name should rise to the top of the list when one of the Hiroshima mission's flight engineers, James Corliss, became suddenly ill. Thus was Joe Fuoco transferred from his beloved, battle-hardened plane, *Bad Penny*, to the Hiroshima mission's photographic airplane, *Necessary Evil*.

From the start, even before the planes were armed, nothing seemed usual about the mission profile. When the new bombers first arrived on the island, they had all been modified to carry heavier loads by removing all four guns from the turrets, along with the 20-millimeter aft cannon. Nothing remained except the two 50-caliber aft guns and a thousand rounds of ammunition.

"A few bursts and we'll be toothless," pilot Charles Sweeney observed, but Joseph Fuoco was not worried. If the enemy sent up a picket of fighter planes, the maximum velocity of a Japanese Zero was only 350 mph. The B-29s flew at up to 450 mph. They could never be chased down, and if a Zero dove at them from directly ahead it would only be capable of a single pass. Just the same, Joseph wanted every plane to scare off the interceptors from even attempting to make a second pass. True to his reputation for inventing solutions from whatever materials lay quickly at hand, he had made the B-29s look more heavily fortified than they actually were by mounting sections of two-inch steam pipe outside the turrets and painting them black, like 20-mm cannons.

During the past month, Joseph had overflown Hiroshima on photographic reconnaissance missions. Gunboats, battleships, and fishing boats seemed to remain anchored in the same places day after day, week after week. Except for trolley cars and the occasional military vehicle, all the traffic on the streets of the city had been reduced to people on horseback or on foot or bicycles. The fire-bombing of virtually every refinery and fuel depot that could be mapped had produced severe rationing throughout the land. Military ships were no longer going out on patrol, and even the fishing boats appeared to be out of fuel. (Down there in the city, a child named Keiji Nakazawa would live to tell how only now were the wealthy male citizens who had wanted the war and who had called for "a fight to the death"— though often it was the sons of their poorer neighbors who went off to war and died—only now were they beginning to feel the war's burdens.)

Paul Tibbets had selected as the aiming point for the bomb the Aioi Bridge, the "T" Bridge that crossed Hiroshima's Ota River, because it was a distinctive feature and could be immediately recognized by the bombardier, even at an altitude of nine kilometers (or 30,000 feet). The aiming point, like every other relevant fact, remained hidden from Joseph, even as he gathered his gear and was driven at 2:00 a.m. to one of three planes, each with its own runway—*three planes*, constituting less than one-fifteenth the normal contingent sent out on a firebombing. Half of the crew appeared to be civilians: tight-lipped scientist types, mostly.

Everything about the August 6 launch had a surreal aspect. Chaplain Downey stepped forward and beseeched God to bring an end to war. Flashbulbs popped in the chaplain's face as he spoke. Chuck Sweeney—who Joseph would learn later had sided with Costalati in recommending him for this mission—crushed out his cigar and offered a vise-grip handshake, along with his usual warm greeting, "Fuoco—what is a little guy like you doing in this big man's war?"

"It's just my job, I suppose," said the flight engineer, and looked around. His plane was Number 91, flown by Captain George Marquart. The plane had all of Runway C to herself. Runway B held Captain Sweeney's still unnamed *Great Artiste*. The next runway over, "A," was the center of some sort of commotion. Flashbulbs were igniting all around Paul Tibbets's *Enola Gay*. His was the only plane in the trio with a name painted behind its nose. Tibbets had named her after his mother.

After George Marquart, Joseph Fuoco, and the ground crew finished their walk-around of 91, searching for minute stress fractures or signs of leaking hydraulics, Captain Marquart handed Joseph a pair of black goggles, along with a tiny canvas bag containing an assortment of thick polarized lenses, each in a different color. The printed words on the bag instructed:

THESE LENSES FOR THE B-8 FLYING GOGGLE ARE MADE OF PLASTIC—
FLEXIBLE AND ARE SHATTER RESISTANT—REMOVE DUST AND FINGER-
PRINTS BY BREATHING ON THE LENS AND WIPING WITH A SOFT
CLOTH

The package contained more than thirty interchangeable goggle lenses, in colors ranging from blue and green to orange and red.

"What are these for?" Joseph asked.

"They weren't sure which ones we would really be needing," Marquart explained. "Like anything else, they just didn't know. But they went ahead and"—the captain pointed at the lens plate already inserted into the frame of Joseph's goggles—"they decided that this one, here, is about . . . not too bad."

The mission planners had selected the grayish-black lenses. The plastic was the color and thickness of welder's glass, and Joseph wondered if he was somehow expected to read his instruments through an "eye shield" that made the world look almost as dark as a mine shaft. Marquart stressed that he must wear the goggles when the order was given and under no circumstances was he to look directly at the source of the light.

"What light?"

"The light may be too bright for your eyes," Marquart warned. "They don't want you to hurt your eyes."

Joseph tried to imagine criteria for comparison to what his captain was attempting to explain. In recent weeks, during night raids on Kobe and Osaka involving whole squadrons of B-29s, waves of incendiary cluster bombs dropped at close range—barely more than a mile's altitude—had lit up the bottoms of the planes like search lamps. Maybe this was something similar to what they had already been using; except perhaps just a bit hotter and brighter.

"So, is this a new kind of firebomb, *or what?*" Joseph asked.

"You'll know soon enough," Captain Marquart said, and then said nothing more.

Joseph followed him up through the hatch in Number 91's nose-wheel well, and took his seat behind the co-pilot and above the bombardier. He stowed the goggles near his right leg for easy access and concluded that whatever he was flying into, the answer to his question was bound to involve mostly *or what*.

On Runway A, Paul Tibbets started *Enola Gay*'s run at 2:45 a.m. Three minutes later, Charles Sweeney flew *Great Artiste* off Runway B; and three minutes after that, George Marquart followed in Number 91, the *Necessary Evil*. The three planes remained staggered at sixteen-kilometer intervals throughout their three-hour flight to their first rendezvous point, during which members of the scientific team closed their eyes and attempted to take naps, reserving their energy for the business end of the mission.

At 5:45 a.m., Joseph became aware of a banking motion and saw the red hull of the sun emerging on the horizon. Directly below, the captured runways of Iwo Jima spread out before Mount Suribachi—already sanctuary for hundreds of B-29 crews returning from fire-bombings with half-crippled aircraft. Sweeney and Marquart drew in behind each of Tibbets's wings, circled Iwo with him, and set course for Japan.

Two hours later, Claude Eatherly's advance scout plane, *Straight Flush*, triggered a brief air-raid alert throughout Hiroshima while conducting weather reconnaissance. Because radar and ground observers judged the plane, correctly, to be just another flyover by a lone observer—just like Joseph Fuoco's previous photo-recon flights in *Bad Penny*—the alert was called off with an all-clear siren. The city's air defenses quickly returned to their usual stand-by status—just as Luis Alvarez and Paul Tibbets had planned. Joseph did not know as yet that one function of his previous Hiroshima flybys was to lull the target into a sense that flyovers by one or two B-29 "strays" were commonplace and, presumably, mostly harmless.

The tactic was cold and mathematical, cheerless and logical. Because "the gadget's" interior geometry needed to be machined so precisely that a single whack with a large hammer could knock the pieces out of line and degrade or disarm it, the idea of lulling ground-based flak gunners and fuel-poor fighter pilots into complacency was judged to be a "best defense." As Sweeney saw it, induced complacency reduced the probability that a bullet or a piece of shrapnel would pierce the plane's hull and "pooch" the bomb's delicate geometry. To Charles Sweeney, every one of Joseph Fuoco's flybys leading up to this day had been directed by the mathematics of probability theory mated to psychology. *Cold*, he acknowledged to himself. *But somewhere along the line, cold math became our new co-pilot. Logically, it had to.*

About 7:30 a.m., *Straight Flush* sent out a coded message: "C-1"— which translated as, "*Clear* weather, *primary* target." At that moment, Tibbets's three planes were crossing over from the ocean to the mainland of Japan, while ascending to their bombing altitude of nine kilometers. Joseph was mystified. Firebombers usually cruised in at only a fifth this altitude.

Three minutes from the Aioi Bridge, Captain Marquart ordered his crew to put on the goggles. Before his world went dark, all of Joseph's instrument readings were nominal; and according to the view through the forward dome, no one was sending up flak bursts. Nor, it seemed, were enemy planes being scrambled to intercept Tibbets's three "strays." As a handicap, the darkness of the goggles did not particularly worry Joseph. Whatever the purpose of this strange mission, it appeared that no one and nothing was going to interfere.

Starboard of *Necessary Evil*, aboard *Great Artiste*, Kermit Beahan and Luis Alvarez prepared to open the bomb-bay doors and release the three parachute-equipped scientific instrument cylinders. The plan called for *Enola Gay* and *Great Artiste* to drop their packages at precisely the same second. The bomb would free fall to an altitude of just under 579 meters (1,900 feet) before detonating, with the instruments deploying their chutes about twenty seconds earlier and 12,000 feet higher. The mirror-like canister surfaces and pure white chutes would, it was hoped, resist the flash effects and give the transmitters a second or two more of life before they were overcome by plasma and blast.

The planes would not be much farther away than the canisters. They were moving into a realm of total uncertainty. No one had ever tried flying away from a nuclear blast before, yet if unprecedented risk was the price of throwing open the doors to a nuclear frontier, then the planes and their crews would be expendable.

Planning for the worst, and hoping for the best, Joseph's captain was placing his bets on what he would later call "The Tibbets Maneuver," and what one critic, on first hearing of it, had already labeled

"The Bonehead Maneuver." It required a reversal of course and crash-dive acceleration—at one point straight toward the ground—during a time frame in which the bomb itself was also falling earthward.

The genesis of the maneuver was a question of simple spacial geometry. During the forty-three seconds between release of the bomb and detonation, how much space could a B-29 put between itself and the bomb so that the B-29 would still be?

Tibbets's maneuver was a variation on an ancient geometric formula he had learned in junior high school—"A gift from the Babylonians and Egyptians," he said, "with which we can calculate the distance from a point on a tangent to a semicircle." If the plane was traveling at a ground speed of 450 miles per hour (or 727 km/hr) at an altitude of 30,000 feet, then on release the bomb would start out with the same forward momentum as the plane, falling on a trajectory toward its target. The last thing in the world any pilot still taking in air and in his right mind wanted to do was what bomber pilots had been trained to do: stay in a tight formation into and away from the target—which amounted to flying in formation with their bombs.

Under the old rules, the Hiroshima formation would have traveled almost 5.5 miles by the time the bomb detonated below, and barely more than a mile behind. Tibbets saw immediately that if the planes simply shot off perpendicular to the line of trajectory, the bomb's forward momentum would carry it almost four miles downrange during the critical forty-three seconds; and if instead of fleeing at a mere 90-degree angle, he dove at the ground and used gravity to accelerate beyond his fastest cruising speed, in a direction exactly opposite the bomb's trajectory, he could take the plane more than nine slant-range miles away from the blast.

The tactic was totally unheard of by pilot George Marquart, and totally brilliant. Of course, no one had warned Joseph Fuoco about the maneuver. His first clue came after *Enola Gay* radioed a high-pitched warning signal to its companions. Thirty seconds later (at precisely 8:15:15), the signal stopped and four objects dropped simultaneously—one from *Enola Gay*, three from *Great Artiste*.

Joseph did not see this. All he could observe through his goggles were Earth's horizon out ahead and the braided outlines of Hiroshima's seven rivers below—he could scarcely read his instruments—when suddenly he was squeezed into his seat and the ground started rushing up to meet him. Joseph's initial impression was that either the pilot and co-pilot had *both* lost control of the plane, or they were trying desperately to escape something, by banking *Necessary Evil* into a sharp, high G-force, 155-degree turn. The extreme slant of the "deck" gave him a rare perspective. The horizon line was rising above Captain Marquart's head and shifting out of view until the city itself filled Joseph's entire forward field of vision. Looking down through the transparent floor of the forward dome, the engineer's gaze fell toward the center of Hiroshima. *Necessary Evil* was still diving and accelerating when the streets and the rivers blazed forth so fiercely that for a second or two Joseph squeezed his eyes shut—yet the light continued to bring a stab of pain, even through dark goggles and closed eyelids.

When he looked again, the engineer understood immediately that most of Hiroshima was now flying apart into ashes and dust. *That's it*, he thought, and all he could think about next was, *Climb ... Climb ... Get out of the way!*

From the tail, physicist Bernard Waldman began yelling inarticulately over the intercom. Joseph tried to warn Captain Marquart that something was gaining on him, but his words came out in the very same incomprehensible way as the scientist at the tail camera mount. Both men were trying to describe phenomena no one had seen before.

At the tail gunner's position, Waldman was positioned for a 180-degree wraparound view. Only he had witnessed how it all began, near the Aioi Bridge. The initial pinpoint of light was so intense that even in full obedience to Dr. Alvarez's warning to cover his eyes—even with both hands cupped tightly over his black goggles during the first three seconds—the light filled his head with a dazzling red glow. When he uncupped his hands, the fireball was already ascending at tremendous speed, dragging behind it a stem of roiling black dust in flames. During those first few seconds, Waldman snapped the only clear, top-to-bottom photograph of the Hiroshima fireball and its stem.

Even before the cloud began to form, during a part of a second too small to imagine, the lower-right corner of Waldman's film recorded an unusual halo. Evidently a heavy nucleus, traveling at a substantial fraction of light speed and following the bomb's short-lived but extremely powerful magnetic field lines, burned Waldman's negative. During that short chip of time, Joseph Fuoco's goggles developed a single linear scratch inside the plastic above the bridge of his nose. Each crew member was likely touched by one or two of these, for whenever a nucleus of iron is accelerated through a man's body at 30 to 90 percent the speed of light, it tends to shed an amount of energy roughly equivalent to the full force of a baseball thrown by a professional pitcher. Along a path narrower than a microscopic scratch, which in this case produced enough heat to melt the plastic, a "fossil" trace from the bomb's interior was preserved. Along a line of destruction only slightly wider than a few red corpuscles lined up side by side, flesh also melted, forming a microscopic line of cauterization all or most of the way through a human body. For several seconds afterward, veins and arteries in the line of fire would have been shooting clots of seared blood in random directions. Joseph Fuoco would recall later that he felt nothing—not even the rough equivalent of a bee sting or a pinprick—but of course, with all else that was happening around him, he supposed he just might not have noticed.

Three seconds after Bernard Waldman snapped his picture of the cloud, he was losing his composure. The scientist discovered that he was only able to describe in the language of gibberish how the air above Hiroshima was compressing into giant concentric rings and spreading outward from the hypocenter, and rushing toward him. Only the curses came out clearly.

Joseph Fuoco's vantage point was not as wide screen as Waldman's. Even so, the combination of steep dive angle and the B-29's broad hemisphere of front windows that reached down to the bombardier and the cockpit floor became a viewing port from which he could not turn his gaze and which pointed toward the heart of the city. From that direction, a huge circle of flame was swelling over the land. At one point, it appeared to be bursting up toward him. He thought of the 8,000 gallons of gasoline still in the B-29's tanks, and he wished again that Marquart would just pull up and get away from this place. As he watched, the flames became outracing streamers of

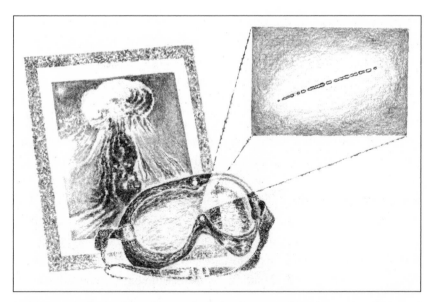

Necessary Evil, the Hiroshima mission's photographic plane, was showered with heavy ions that damaged photographic negatives and left marks on the men behind the cameras. A deep interior melt trail, half as wide as a human hair, can be seen above the bridge of flight engineer Joseph Fuoco's protective goggles. By the time *Necessary Evil* photographed the blast, pieces of the bomb (quantum artifacts) were already embedded in the crews' flesh. Fuoco did not recall feeling any sharp stings or burns, but nearby in *Enola Gay*, pilot Paul Tibbets reported that he heard and felt his teeth crackling, and simultaneously he became aware of a strange taste, "like an outflowing of lead." He concluded that something from the bomb had passed through, and interacted with, the fillings in his teeth. (CRP)

black, ground-hugging dust and sparkling debris, rolling over streets and factories like waves from a tsunami.

The airburst followed. It struck *Necessary Evil* with a force that Joseph Fuoco would record as being surprisingly gentle by comparison to what was happening on the ground. It amounted to a brief shaking of the aircraft, only slightly worse than ordinary storm turbulence.

Enola Gay and *Great Artiste* experienced a more violent buffeting, as if a giant had reached out and grabbed each plane by its tail, then given it a swift, hard yank. George Marquart drove *Necessary Evil* more steeply toward the earth, and this action might have put him in a location where the shock waves simply passed above and below him. Apparently, this maneuver also gave his team a much clearer, close-up view of what was happening to the city.

Joseph was able to discern individual buildings flying apart. Down there, a black tsunami plowed through a whole neighborhood, then parted unexpectedly in two directions, leaving a row of wooden structures untouched in the middle. A mile or two farther west, another set of waves appeared to be bunching together and gathering strength. Here and there, multi-storied structures of stone, concrete, and steel were struck laterally. Joseph watched them splash apart like water. He found it difficult to believe what his eyes were revealing: that solid buildings could become fluid and behave like crashing waterfalls. Fifty-six years later, and in a way the flight engineer could never have anticipated, the image would come back to haunt him.

In the cockpit of *Great Artiste*, Charles Sweeney had a less close-up and personal view. After he leveled out from the shock wave, Hiroshima lay to the west, on his starboard side. He looked down and saw a dirty brown stain on the earth, boiling over the city—spreading out horizontally and without detail. Out of it had emerged a vertical plume that contained every color imaginable, along with colors he had never imagined. He swore that, impossible as he knew this to be, he was seeing colors that simply did not exist in the electromagnetic spectrum—new colors, never before seen by human eyes. He circled once, so that the scientists could film the cloud, but much of the camera equipment and the film inside had been damaged.

The plume towered more than three miles overhead and was still growing when the B-29s turned back toward Tinian Island. They were nearly a half hour and 200 miles away from Hiroshima before the tail gunners lost sight of the mushroom cloud.

FAR BEHIND THE TIBBETS planes, in Tokyo, Dr. Yoshio Nishina and Eizo Tajima were already trying to convince War Minister Anami that the sudden, simultaneous cessation of all radio and telephone communication from Hiroshima was consistent with an atomic bomb. Even after Prefect Nishioka managed to patch a line through from the suburbs, and to confirm Dr. Nishina's assessment with his own eyewitness account and with Alvarez's letter in hand, Anami would not believe it. Even after the American president broke the secret to the whole world a few hours later—*"The world will note that the first atomic bomb was dropped on Hiroshima, a military base"*—the war minister refused to accept it.

Just the same, he decided that it would only be sound logic to discover what captive American airmen knew about their country's atomic bomb program. Anami was working under the dual certainty that everyone talked under torture and that the American program was as open a secret as Dr. Nishina's program.

The second "fact" was a myth. However, Tibbets and Alvarez, Sweeney and Marquart had been aware from the start that the first fact was true, and for this reason they carried already loaded sidearms during their mission—not for self-defense in the event of imminent capture but for self-silencing. One of the reasons Sweeney and Marquart had decided to keep the nature of their mission secret from their flight engineers was to give them at least some small chance at survival, if worse and worst ever came down to FUBAR.

The first pilots questioned by the War Ministry died without revealing anything. Anami was beginning to suspect that perhaps they really did know nothing at all—which enabled him to latch on to a hope that the atomic bomb might not exist—until, on the morning of August 7, the interrogators brought in Lieutenant Marcus McDilda, a fighter pilot who had been downed near Osaka. Marcus knew nothing about uranium or initiators, but as near as he could tell his interrogators seemed to have uranium on the brain, and they were telling him much more than he knew. Being a pilot, what he already did know, very well, were the mathematics of spatial geometry. Meanwhile, his interrogators already possessed one of the uranium bomb's biggest secrets: the business end of the bomb was all about spatial geometry—and childishly simple. Given enough of the highly refined neutron-emitting metal, there were many ways of skinning this particular mathematical cat; the truly difficult part was designing a bomb that would not surge when you did not want it to surge.

After a general cut off Marcus's lower lip with a sword and displayed for him the severed head of an airman who had "pretended" to know nothing about uranium, the pilot began designing a totally imaginary atomic bomb on short notice—having no real idea what he was doing but, rather, making it all up as he went along. Marcus described two uranium spheres separated at opposite ends of a lead shield, inside a bomb-shaped box small enough to fit inside a single B-29's fuselage. When the bomb was dropped from the plane, the shield was removed and two steel pedestals slammed the uranium spheres implosively together.

The general stood back, awestruck. What the airman described was consistent with an early version of the Nishina-Sagane design.

Marcus sensed that something unprecedented had just occurred. He had never heard of a prisoner striking awe and fear into a Japanese interrogator.

"What is the next target?" the general demanded.

Marcus grinned and spat blood. "Right here!" he said. "Tokyo will be bombed in the next few days. We're bringing it right down your throats!"

That evening, as Kenshi Hirata tossed a flower into a Hiroshima river and prepared to carry his wife's bones to Nagasaki, War Minister Anami assigned a pair of planes to Dr. Nishina and Lieutenant-General Seizo Arisue, with instructions to land in Hiroshima the next day and determine whether or not the bomb was indeed atomic.

Ahead of them, *Bad Penny* had already returned from Tinian for the first photographic reconnaissance of the ruins, dropping leaflets along its path into and out of Japan. Joseph Fuoco reported that over most of the city, only the physical geography remained recognizable—appearing much as it would have seemed ten thousand years ago, before city builders came to the river's edge. A few of the bridges were still there; but they were "bleached out"; and on that first day the shadow people on the Aioi "T" Bridge were much more distinct than they would appear to latecomers, two or three weeks after the first strong rains. In the middle of the "Flatland" known to the scientists as Ground Zero, the Dome and some of the municipal buildings and the telephone poles that surrounded them were still standing—and, farther off, Joseph saw the partly intact frame of a church.

Far beyond the church, amid a stand of mauled and dislodged

buildings, Tsutomo Yamaguchi boarded the second-to-last train to Nagasaki. He had developed a high fever and was suffering continually from dry heaves. There was no longer anything left in him to be vomiting up. By now he had discovered to his growing horror that he could not even keep down small sips of water, and thirst was tearing at his throat.

Prefect Takejiro Nishioka was aboard the same train, his only symptoms of radiation sickness a stinging and itching sensation in his legs, which he attributed to the strange "candle garden" through which he now wished he had never walked.

Engineer Akira Iwanaga was also aboard—thirsty and fending off mild bouts of nausea.

All three men were destined to become double atomic bomb survivors. A fourth passenger, Dr. Susumu Tsuno, dean of the Nagasaki Medical College, would meet a somewhat different destiny. He had escaped from the first bomb with scarcely a scratch, and was showing no symptoms at all of radiation sickness—yet, in less than forty-eight hours, he would be running an errand to a district about to disappear from history.

On Tinian, now that his own eyes and President Truman's announcement had rendered the weapon no longer a secret, Joseph Fuoco kept, as a souvenir, one of the multiple thousands of leaflets that had been dropped over Japan by *Bad Penny*, urging evacuation and "an honorable surrender" and warning about the accuracy of President Truman's statement—that the power now existed to completely destroy Japan's power to make war.

On one side of each bill-sized leaflet was printed a perfect counterfeit of Japanese currency; on the reverse, the message. Aware that civilians picking up and reading the leaflets might be punished by military police, they were disguised as currency to make concealment and private reading easier.

It seemed inexplicable to Joseph that in response to the bomb and to the president's message, and to the leaflets, there came only a desert of silence from Tokyo.

As the sun set on Hiroshima and Tinian, Curtis LeMay ordered 152 B-29s aloft, to inflict conventional firebombings upon Japan.

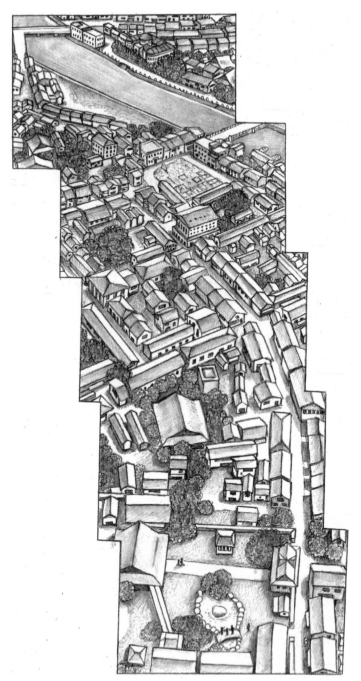

Hiroshima, 8:00 a.m., August 6, 1945: The "Atomic Dome" and the "T" Bridge are located at the top. The fish pond and arched bridge in the foreground are located approximately 500 meters from the hypocenter. (Patricia Wynne)

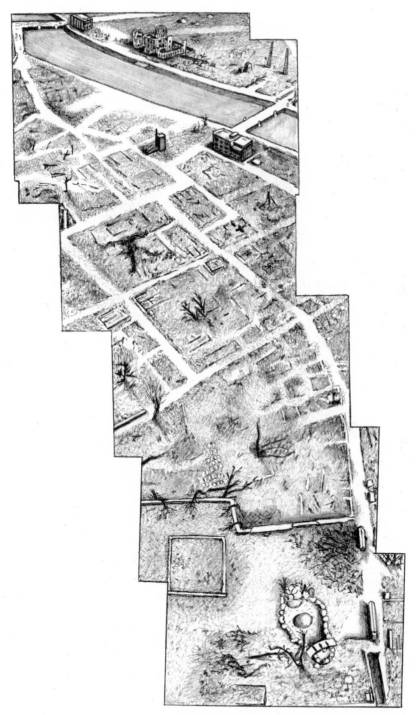

Hiroshima, 8:00 a.m., August 7, 1945, based on U.S. Bombing Survey photos taken during Joseph Fuoco's return flights. (Patricia Wynne)

The night of August 7 came and went, and still no response came from Tokyo.

As the dawn of August 8 approached Tinian, Charles Sweeney was called to the Intelligence hut. According to *Bad Penny*'s reconnaissance photographs, Hiroshima's activities as an industrial base had ceased. Preliminary casualty estimates were approaching 100,000 people.

Sweeney walked over to the air-conditioned compartment, called the Shed, and put his hands upon the hull of the plutonium bomb. Several of his fellow officers had already signed their names on its yellow-painted surface. Sweeney knew that plutonium emitted constant streams of alpha particles. The bomb's casing was warm to the touch—"as if it were a living thing," he would tell future historians.

The shape of things to come, Sweeney told himself. Luis Alvarez had just explained to him that this bomb was only a firecracker, compared to what would soon be on the drawing boards. Dr. Alvarez enthusiastically quoted a friend named Harold Urey, who had declared, "When humanity sees what science has done, they will see immediately that here is the end of war."

Sweeney did not believe that scientists understood humanity very well. "Still no word from Japan, I presume?" he asked.

"No," said the scientist. "It looks like we're going to have to do this again."

"Understood," Sweeney said, and walked out of the shed without saying anything more. He borrowed a Jeep and drove away from his own bombardment wing, the 509th, and toward the 313th. Captain Downey, the chaplain who had given the three Hiroshima crews a blessing on the morning of August 6, was a Lutheran. Sweeney was a Catholic. He needed to find a priest.

5

THE CRAZY IRIS

From Fukuyama to Hiroshima is 160 kilometers, and there, at a radius of nearly one hundred miles, the blast could be heard. Masuji Ibuse believed that had it not been for the surrounding wall of hills, he would certainly have seen and perhaps even felt the effects of the bomb.

He was thankful for the hills. In Mihara, a town only 49 kilometers nearer to Hiroshima and located on a hillside that gave everyone a grandstand view, the hill itself gave the shockwave a little boost of compression and reflection. Witnesses were knocked off balance by the concussion, and every window facing the city cracked.

Masuji was a writer and a poet who happened to be staying at a friend's house on the outskirts of Fukuyama, and who believed that the bomb had in some way been responsible for the beautiful purple iris he saw flowering suddenly and out of season. When he first noticed the iris from a window, he was not at all sure it could be a flower and must instead be a piece of colored paper floating near the edge of his friend's pond.

On this morning, only the suburbs of Fukuyama still existed, and it was conceivable to the poet that the paper had been carried aloft with the ashes of the city. During the night, incendiary bombers had flown over the valley like swarms of giant locusts. At daybreak, through a rift between the hills, Masuji could see a pillar of fire rising above the place where an ancient castle tower had stood. The pillar burned so brightly that, even in the daylight, a huge pinnacle of limestone nearby was bathed in the glow of the dying tower. The "paper," Masuji believed, had merely fallen out from the soot and the smoke of Fukuyama's dying.

Now, what is it really? Masuji wondered. The unexpected splash of color in a world that was becoming increasingly black, obsessed the poet, and it drew him down to the water's edge. And when finally he uncovered the source of the mystery, Masuji, who had always prided himself on remaining stoic and analytical in even the most distressing situations, drew his breath in horror and let out an involuntary wail.

The lady beneath the pond was wearing a beautiful nightgown tied with a red sash. Her long sleeves hovered near the surface like the fins of a large goldfish. She was lying on her back—and the purple object: it really was an iris bloom after all. The flower stalk had bent down along one side, toward the water's surface—as if, Masuji thought, the iris were trying to touch the girl's cheek.

Masuji Ibuse learned later that the woman was only twenty years old. Drafted into "volunteer service" by the Fukuyama Council, she had been sent to a munitions factory in Hiroshima; and except for a minor burn on one cheek, she had survived with no visible injuries, as she navigated a sea of the dead and the still moving dead on her way to Koi Station and the last train home to Fukuyama. The firebombing followed her arrival by a margin barely measurable in hours—and this, too, she appeared to have escaped without physical harm.

The police officer who came to examine the body found her sandals near the water's edge. She seemed to have run headlong from the burning town and, without any signs of struggle or hesitation, lay down and submerged herself by exhaling all of the air out of her lungs and then taking a deep, deliberate breath of water.

Even as the officer explained his theory of a young woman frightened into madness, the iris with the strangely twisted stem and the belated blossoming buds held Masuji spellbound.

"Do you think the iris was frightened into bloom?" the poet asked.

"It's extraordinary," came the reply. "I've never heard of an iris flowering this late. It must have gone crazy."

An apt analysis, Misuji told himself, and said, "The iris blooming in this pond is truly crazy, and belongs to a crazy age."

"THIS CANNOT BE," General Seizo Arisue told his pilot. The Chief of Intelligence's plane flew over the ruins ahead of Dr. Nishina—and even after he had circled twice, nothing below except the geography of the rivers seemed to make any sense.

General Arisue had seen Osaka, Kobe, and vast regions of Tokyo after carpet bombings with incendiaries, and in all three cases emergency shelters and kitchens were sprouting amid the ruins within forty-eight hours. Yet, below, little more than a grayish-yellow desert stretched across the missing military barracks, onward through the place where the castle and the Communications Center had been; and the ashes spread for kilometers beyond, with no signs at all of human activity.

"No, this cannot be," the general said again. "Where is Hiroshima?"

"Sir," the pilot said, "this is supposed to be Hiroshima."

The Dome and the "T" Bridge were down there in the center, somehow standing defiantly. All around the Dome, the trunks of trees—though stripped of their branches—were also standing defiantly, while for kilometers in every direction whole rows of trees appeared to be leaning away from the Dome. The general was reminded of the pictures he had seen of the forested area around Tunguska, Siberia. On June 30, 1908, a piece of solar driftwood had struck the atmosphere at more than 30 kilometers per second, burning high above Tunguska as a dazzling white fireball, and sending forth a series of concussions heard as far away as Kiev and London. When an expedition arrived at the point of impact more than a decade later, they found the trees standing vertically in the middle, while all the trees for kilometers and kilometers around had been plowed down, facing away from the hypocenter. To the general, the Hiroshima explosion looked strikingly like Tunguska.

When he touched down on a grassy field near the harbor, the similarity became undeniable. Individual blades of grass were apparently flash-grilled on one side until they turned the color of terracotta clay; and every blade was leaning—along with the trees of Hiroshima and just like the trees of Tunguska—away from the center of the explosion, as if pressed by a giant hot iron. Arisue and the pilot were met by a lieutenant colonel whose face, just like the grass, appeared to have been burned on one side.

"What happened to you?" Arisue asked.

"*Pika-don*," the young officer replied, and began to describe the flash and the blast that followed. The general interrupted him, wanting to know specifically whether the unharmed side of his face had been shaded from the *pika*, and whether his blistered flesh had been facing the center of the city when the flash occurred.

The officer confirmed Arisue's suspicions that the destruction of Hiroshima must indeed have begun with a single explosion, centered high above the Dome and the little cluster of trees standing near it.

The first thing Dr. Nishina did after he landed was to examine the pressed and burned grass. He then set his own very brisk pace in the direction indicated by the grass, seeming not to care whether the general or anyone else followed. Passing through the ruins of the Sumitomo Bank and tracing the hypocenter toward the Dome and the charcoal-encrusted tree trunks, Nishina discovered that even the thick bones of people's skulls and femurs had been converted into something like burned leaves and dust. Teeth were more resilient than bones, and at one intersection, where more than sixty individuals must have been standing fully exposed beneath the flash, the only evidence of their existence was a sidewalk strewn with teeth.

When Dr. Nishina brought a handful of blackened molars and canines close to his Geiger counter, the distinctive clicks told him beyond all serious dispute exactly what had happened.

"Human remains do not normally emit radiation," the physicist told Arisue.

"So, that's it?" the general said. "Just those few clicks tell it all?"

"That's it," Dr. Nishina said. "Just these little clicks, and it's over. We must make War Minister Anami understand: if the Americans have many more of these weapons, then take my word for it, General—there is no defense against this kind of power."

IN MOSCOW, Stalin was not nearly so skeptical as Tokyo's war minister. About the time Yoshio Nishina began filling an evidence vial with radioactive teeth, Japan's ambassador to Russia was called to the Kremlin, where he received an official declaration of war, to become effective at midnight—ostensibly in honor of a pledge to England and the United States that the Soviet Union would enter the Pacific War three months after the defeat of Germany.

Already, two Soviet armies were poised at the border of Japanese-occupied territory in Manchuria, and advance forces had begun to cross. After Ambassador Naotake Sato was escorted out of the Kremlin, the American ambassador, Averell Harriman, was escorted in for several toasts of vodka. Harriman found Stalin in an unusually jovial and talkative mood. On the surface, the most feared man in Russia congratulated the U.S. ambassador on his country's scientific triumph, and expressed gratitude to whatever gods may be that the universe had put him on the side of the people who discovered the atomic bomb.

Privately, the dictator had known about the American discovery months ahead of the Hiroshima event, and he had already put Lavrenti Beria, Commissioner of State Security, in charge of concentrating Russia's leading physicists and engineers in one laboratory and jump-starting the long-dormant nuclear program. Stalin told Beria that his program would have two great advantages over America's Manhattan Project.

First: Russia had captured nearly half of Germany's rocket scientists, and Stalin was confident in Beria's skills at persuading them to work toward building a missile able to drop an atomic bomb from orbit. The difficulty of refining fissionable metals and fashioning them into efficient bombs would be further simplified if Russian forces could penetrate quickly into the Japanese mainland and capture Drs. Sagane, Tajima, and Nishina.

A second and even more important advantage was that, when the

Americans started out, no one knew that the problem could actually be solved. "Now," Stalin told Beria, "the world knows that it can be done. That's the hardest part of the problem. Far, far more important than knowing *how* it can be done, is knowing that it *can* be done."

IN TOKYO, THE CODED RADIO message from Dr. Nishina was answered with defiance. Eizo Tajima confirmed for War Minister Anami that radioactive human remains and soil from the center of Hiroshima meant that atomic bombs must in fact exist. His confirmation changed nothing.

Dr. Ryokichi Sagane supported Nishina's findings, but he and a handful of colleagues underscored their report to Anami with an observation that if an ordinary American fighter pilot like Marcus McDilda was allowed to have even a crude understanding of how a uranium bomb functioned, then the Americans, for some reason, had *wanted* their "secret" to be known.

Sagane believed he had figured out the reason. He calculated that all of the American refining facilities and power plants that could be devoted exclusively to yielding fissionable materials—if allowed to operate twenty-four hours a day, seven days a week, for three years—might be able to produce two or three atomic bombs. He reasoned that the enemy would have tested one bomb, to make sure it would work; and he concluded that after Hiroshima, if they were not already out of atomic bombs, they only had one more left in the arsenal.

This was exactly what Anami wanted to hear. Sagane's calculation was based on sound reasoning and was only slightly off target. Nevertheless, he had not factored in the expanding nuclear industry already being devoted to plutonium production, or the booster shot given slightly more than two months earlier, by a ship arriving in New York Harbor with more than three hundred troy ounces of captured German uranium, refined to nearly 10 percent purity of U-235. Nor had Sagane figured in the inevitable FUBAR factor—which more or less balanced itself against plutonium and uranium gains. The latest ground-based plutonium trigger tests had misfired in lopsided fashion—instead of in accordance with their impossibly precise spherical implosion design—and they had fired prematurely, meaning that, if provided with a real plutonium core and dropped from a B-29, the triggers would have wrecked both the bomb and the plane. The latest uranium bomb casing and tamper fared no better. It met with misfortune when it (minus its priceless uranium) was dropped by mistake near a Chicago runway, and now a replacement would have to be built from square one.

A fourth atomic bomb would not be ready until mid-September, and perhaps not until October. Reality told it so. And the Sagane equation also told it so in spite of its defects: One bomb had been tested. Another bomb had been dropped. Only the third bomb remained.

War Minister Anami saw the proof of Sagane's math in the multiple firebombings of the previous night. "We only have President Truman's word for it that enough atomic bombs exist to strike down every one of our cities and ports," Anami told the rest of the warlords. "Certainly, if they possessed more of these weapons, they would not be wasting their time dropping ordinary incendiaries on our cities."

The war minister remained insistent on "staying the course," despite Foreign Minister Shigenori Togo's counterargument that the Americans were running out of Japanese target ships and there was precious little fuel left for what remained of Anami's navy and air force.

"Presently," Togo explained, "the Americans *own* the sea and the air. Even if Dr. Sagane's theory turns out to be correct and the enemy is running out of atomic bombs, the firebombings alone will destroy us all."

General Yoshijiro Umezu was every bit as insistent as War Minister Anami. Even with the navy now rendered impotent and even with cities aflame, he believed fanatically in making a major last stand in which the people of mainland Japan would either inflict unacceptable losses on the invading ground forces and repel them; or they would die in defeat and take the Americans down into hell with them.

Foreign Minister Togo realized that trying to guide these men toward the reality of the situation was like trying to guide a typhoon away from land. The Russian invasion of Manchuria had raised more concern in them than the bombing of Hiroshima, and if anything could be stated as a certainty in these times, it was that the Russian wound, if not Hiroshima's, had made Anami and Umezu more dangerous than ever.

Sooner or later—and sooner rather than later, the foreign minister decided, *we must forget about bravado and ask the Emperor to consider surrender, while there still exists a Japanese people to be saved.*

Shigenori Togo was now acutely aware that he and Dr. Nishina were trying to tread softly in a burning house—a task rendered all the more futile when the house was filled with wounded animals.

ON TINIAN ISLAND, news of the Russian invasion was received with consternation.

In the shed, Luis Alvarez was visited by an admiral who wanted to discuss concern about Russia's wholesale landgrab of formerly German-occupied Eastern Europe, including the annexation of East Berlin. During recent weeks, Wernher von Braun and his rocket team faced a choice between capture by the Russians and capture by the Americans, and most of the engineers had made a desperate and near-fatal mad dash toward the advancing Americans. Scientists from the German atomic bomb program faced the same choice and fled west, hoping that imprisonment across the Atlantic, in the States, would be better than in Siberia.

Not all of them reached the Americans, the admiral explained. The Russians had managed to capture about half of Germany's top scientists. Like silver and gold, and priceless works of art, they were considered by the survivors of Leningrad, Stalingrad, and the Cherkassy Pocket as merely the spoils of war.

The admiral was concerned about a coming nuclear arms race, but Alvarez started naming German scientists and asking which of them had made it to Eisenhower's and Patton's side, and which were trapped in the east and presumably now owned by the Russians. About two-thirds of the way through the list, the physicist put up a hand and said, "Don't worry. Our Germans are better than their Germans."

"And what do you think it will mean for us if the Russians or the Chinese take Japan before we do?"

"Then we must not let that happen," the physicist said. "By now, I hope Sagane and Nishina have received our message. If so, they're smart enough to know what a delayed surrender must mean for

Japan. If not, then letting them fall into any other nation's hands is simply not an option. We must get in there quickly, and pull those scientists out, dead or alive."

At the time, only Alvarez and a select handful of physicists and military commanders, along with President Truman, knew that just one atomic bomb remained in all the world.

Outside the shed, Fuoco and all the other B-29 crew members believed, as the Truman announcement had led them to believe, that at least a dozen more of the devices must already exist and only awaited delivery.

In the mess hall, Joseph Fuoco heard dismay and fear whenever the rapidly expanding Russian front—from Eastern Europe through Manchuria, and toward Japan—was discussed. The final agreement between Churchill, Roosevelt, and Stalin had specified reconstruction of vanquished nations, including a policy of returning ownership of all countries to their own people. The Russian takeover was seen as a terrifying act of betrayal.

The solution most frequently heard by Joseph Fuoco involved finishing off Japan as quickly as possible with nuclear force, and then moving on to Russia with the same force.

The Second World War was not quite over, yet the Cold War was already about to be born.

The second atomic bomb had not blazed over Nagasaki, and yet Joseph Fuoco was already witness to friends who cast their gaze beyond Japan toward Russia, and let loose with the very first use of the phrase, "Nuke them."

No one on or beyond Tinian knew, on August 8, 1945, what that phrase really meant. Not even the men who flew the first atomic mission and who watched the buildings splash apart could furnish criteria for detailed understanding. Only on the ground, in Hiroshima itself, did anyone truly understand.

WHEN HE GREW UP, seven-year-old Keiji Nakazawa would tell the world how a concrete wall at one end of a schoolyard had shadow-shielded him from the flash, and how a coin dropped at just the right instant made all the difference between life and death.

Keiji, who would later call himself "Barefoot Gen" of Hiroshima, bent down to pick up the coin. He was close enough never to hear the explosion—only to *see* what happened. At a radius of just over seven city blocks, the light came down at an angle of about 45 degrees. Except for a small spot at the back of his head, the wall completely shaded young Gen; but an older child with whom he had been talking caught the full force of the heat ray. During the first second or two, the glare blotted out everything, and Gen's whole neighborhood seemed simply to have disappeared. A second later the light was fading and details began coming back into his world. He felt as if he had momentarily vanished to a safe and featureless place and was suddenly being transported back again to a changed and changing Earth. The other child's face and arms had dissolved at the touch of the rays, and a column of dense black smoke was darting from her head. If she screamed, it was a silent scream. The blast wave was also eerily silent.

When Gen regained his senses and looked around again, the girl and the school were gone—along with most of Hiroshima, apparently. His only injury seemed to be a single burn on the back of his head. It stung only a little, but the burn was severe. The contrast between shadow and death-dealing heat had been knife-edge sharp, marking the only portion of Gen's body not shielded by the wall. His hair had vaporized along the line of exposure and the skin beneath was seared like carbonized leaves all the way down to the cap of his skull—as if by a clean slash from a saber of light.

Now, on the second day after the bomb, the wound was festering and Gen knew that his mother and baby sister were the only remnants of his family still surviving. On an expedition to a demolished army barracks behind what had once been Hiroshima Castle, Gen's self-assigned mission to find food for his mother was interrupted by sudden waves of nausea alternating with chills and flashes of fever. First Gen felt sick, then he *was* sick. When he reached up to rub a swarm of ravenous flies from his head, Gen discovered that his hair appeared to be falling out, and over the course of only a few minutes he was so overcome by radiation effects that he simply collapsed near a pile of bodies and was covered by flies.

A soldier saved him. While he lay unconscious, a cleanup detail passed through and piled all the bodies together for cremation, throwing little Gen onto the heap. The soldier, whom Gen would only know as "Sir," noticed that he was still breathing, and pulled him out of the pile before he was burned alive.

A few sips of water from a canteen seemed to revive Gen. Radiation sickness was capricious. It could strike like a thunderbolt and just as quickly ease. Sir gave Gen some food rations for his mother and decided to escort him to whatever passed for home in the ruins. But along the way, Sir became sick, and collapsed without warning. That quickly, their roles reversed. Now it was the boy propping the soldier up and helping him along, instead of the other way around.

Sir knew of the still-functioning Communications Hospital, just a short distance past the castle's foundations. They had barely sixty or seventy meters more to go, but it became an odyssey. The sun was blazing and the humidity was near 100 percent—and yet Sir's teeth were chattering and he claimed he was freezing to death. With thirty meters to go, the soldier lost control of his bowels, and ten meters after that, he began vomiting something black. Gen dragged him the last few meters, and the first doctor to arrive on the scene scolded the boy for bringing him a dead man.

"No," said Gen. "He can't be dead!"

"Did he have diarrhea?" the doctor asked. "And did he say he was cold?"

"Y-yes."

"Then he died the same way a lot of people have been dying, even though they appeared to have escaped the *pika-don*."

"But why?"

The doctor shook his head and began to walk away. "I don't know," he muttered.

About the same time Gen's rescuer died, a man who would enter history as the survivor nearest the hypocenter arrived with the same symptoms Gen had decided he must now keep his mother from noticing. When the sky opened up, Eizo Nomura was located literally within shouting distance of the Hiroshima Dome, in the basement of the city's Rationing Union Hall. Even underground, he became aware of the flash—and the whole room simultaneously thumped.

Mr. Nomura clawed his way out of the cave-in, emerging onto ground that was barely more than 100 meters (328 feet, or one city

During the first minute after Moment Zero, on ground surfaces that had been heated to several times the boiling point of water, fire worms that chased Eizo Nomura and the Sasaki family into the water began rising like summoned spirits from the graves of buildings already destroyed by the bomb. (CRP)

block) from the absolute hypocenter. He stood on pavement hot enough to burn through the soles of his shoes, feeling as if the earth had disappeared from him and he had been placed in a strange new land. His guess was only half wrong. Nomura's little corner of planet Earth had in fact disappeared, and much of it was placed in the stratosphere. And so it came to pass that one small patch of Hiroshima real estate was transformed into something so strange and unprecedented that in the future the foundations of the Rationing Union Hall would become the site of a "rest house," near the center of the city's Peace Memorial Park.

When Nomura dusted himself off and looked up, the sky was black with smoke, and sparks seemed to be raining down from everywhere. On his side of the Motoyasu Bridge, he had found no one and nothing still alive, unless waterspouts and the serpent-like motions of the fire worms could be considered the actions of something brought to life. To Mr. Nomura, they moved and behaved like sentient creatures, advancing with giant slithering strides from the opposite riverbank and chasing him away from the bridge and under the water, where he held his breath until he was in agony. When finally he surfaced and cleared his lungs, and flung the hair and water from his eyes, the worms were moving away and he felt a measure of triumph at having survived; but he was also beginning to feel the first effects of radiation sickness, creeping up inside of him and starting to gnaw, like bites from a thousand little rats' teeth.

After two days, there were few doctors and nurses well enough to help Mr. Nomura, or anyone else. All of the medicines were gone, and there were no working microscopes with which the medics could begin to make a crude diagnostic guess at the nature of the disease that had sickened Nomura and Gen, and killed Sir.

The building Nomura eventually came to was located only 1,500 meters from the hypocenter. Most of its second floor had splashed away and burned. The lower floor was still marginally intact, having been, to one degree or another, shock-cocooned behind Hiroshima Castle. One of the directors, Dr. Michihiko Hachiya, was now a patient in his own hospital.

Dr. Hachiya had been one of the ant-walkers Isao Kita had observed from the weather station. On the first day, he wandered burned and battered and naked through updrafts and downdrafts so violent that sheets of metal roofing hummed and twirled above his head, and pieces of flaming trees whirled out of the sky like fiery swallows. The doctor vaguely remembered seeing birds dying on the ground at his bare feet, with their wings and feathers scorched. And he vividly recalled following a row of people who, like him, were naked—and he had wondered absently what force of nature had deprived them of their clothes.

The physician remembered little else about the past forty-eight hours. For most of his missing time, he had been drifting in and out of fever and sleep. On the afternoon of August 8, he wanted nothing more in the world than to get off the floor and start helping the other patients, but the chief of surgery, Dr. Kutsube, said, "You are too impatient. You should be thankful that you are going to live."

It had not occurred to him that he might have come close to death.

"Was I that bad off?" Hachiya asked.

"We were all worried about you," Kutsube replied, and explained that he had lost a lot of blood and suffered forty wounds. Mr. Iguchi, the ambulance driver, had rigged a makeshift operating room by scavenging unbroken lights and connecting them to one of several still-functioning truck batteries. In this manner, Dr. Hachiya and as many as sixty other patients—including the "miracle survivor" Eizo Nomura—had been and would continue to be treated, until the last battery was drained. As Kutsube brought Hachiya up to date on events of the past two days, the doctor-turned-patient noticed that the surgeon's hands were badly burned.

A noise outside the window drew their attention to a patient Dr. Kutsube had neglected to mention.

From time to time during his long and fitful sleep, Hachiya remembered hearing him stumbling about the garden. Hachiya looked out through a shattered window whose steel frame appeared to have been uprooted from its bed. The patient bumped his nose against the broken frame.

"Has he been fed?" Hachiya asked.

"Don't worry, Doctor," came the reply. "There are plenty of potato leaves in the garden, so I don't think he'll be hungry."

The patient happened to be a horse, who was burned along one whole side of his body, and who seemed to have been simultaneously blinded by the *pika* (the flash). He had come staggering to the front gate about the same time as Dr. Hachiya, and Dr. Kutsube explained that he did not have the heart to turn the poor creature away, so he was sheltered in the garden, outside the doctor's window.

For Hachiya, the horse was not only a distantly remembered companion but a constant one as well. Companionship had meant a lot to him whenever he awoke in the night and recalled what he saw along the ant trail and fell into despair. At first, he felt lonely. He would write later that "it was an animal loneliness. I became part of the darkness of the night. There were no radios, no electric lights, not even a candle in the room. The only light that came to me was reflected in the flickering shadows made by the burning city. The only sounds were the groans and sobs of the burn victims."

In the midst of such loneliness, Hachiya always heard the blind horse bumping against a wall and pawing at leaves.

By now the patient had already eaten most of the doctor's potato leaves. The garden was once a tennis court, but the war effort had required every available piece of land to be converted into a so-called victory garden. Hachiya became infamous throughout the hospital for breeding strawberries and potato plants that produced huge, lush leaves, but yielded dwarf, peanut-size strawberries and strawberry-size potatoes.

Dr. Hachiya lifted his head and asked, "Don't you think we should dig up the potatoes? They must be quite big by now."

Dr. Kutsube and his nurse Kado laughed, and for a moment (albeit only for a moment), misery was forgotten.

When Dr. Kutsube began to explain how patients were succumbing to vomiting and diarrhea, and how not even plumbing was available and the battery-powered operating room was just about finished—and how the army was bringing no food to the hospital—a new reality began to bite down. It bit down with all the force of sudden realization and mortality: Dr. Hachiya's constant companion had become the only source of protein any of the patients would be able to count on, for many days to come.

HANAKO ITO AND HER HUSBAND, Akio, had waited for the firestorm to weaken before venturing into central Hiroshima, where their son Hiroshi had attended the highest-ranked school in the province. The school was a desert of ashes and cracked bricks. Its only recognizable landmark was an Olympic-size swimming pool, into which more than two hundred people had fled, seeking shelter from the flames. Their bodies were boiled and bloated. Their faces appeared to have been roasted before the boiling began.

By the time Charles Sweeney learned he was going to have to do this again, and drove into the night searching for a priest, Mr. and Mrs. Ito had seen enough. Corpses—none of them identifiable—were being dragged from the pool and stacked for pyres by soldiers who moved to and fro in stunned silence. Clinging to her husband's hand, Hanako followed a set of trolley tracks toward home, her only light the growing numbers of mass-grave funeral pyres on either side of the road. Firelight guided her, and something the color of moonlight.

"Between the pyres, we could see trails of silvery phosphorous weaving all about," wrote one witness. "They looked for all the world like the spirits of the dead in the old storybooks."

Hanako believed they might be the ghosts of Hiroshima searching for their loved ones, and she wondered if little Hiroshi might come looking for her in this way. When she arrived in the eastern hill country, however, she found her son alive, though quite exhausted from the ordeal.

"I was chased by the fire," he explained, "and I had to cover my ears because I could hear people crying for help behind me." As he told the story of the fire worms and the black rain, Hiroshi was stricken by chills and vomiting. A doctor was called to the house but he could not diagnose any known disease, and it did not seem to matter because by midnight the boy's appetite began to return and by the morning of August 8 he was feeling well enough to assist his brother's fifth-grade class in a new assignment from the Association of Homeland Security.

The Itos' town was among the few that did not turn all the non-resident survivors back toward Hiroshima. Instead, trucks and horse-drawn carts were being sent westward beyond the Kaidaichi train wreck to bring Hiroshima's injured to the local school. Though the Truman announcement was kept secret from the town, Tsugio Ito knew from the appalling size of the August 6 cloud, and from the blast that broke windows nearly thirteen kilometers away, that he and his brother Hiroshi were witness to an unusual bomb. The flash burns and the de-gloving injuries of the people arriving in the trucks confirmed its uniqueness beyond dispute.

By the afternoon of the second day after the bomb, 360 survivors filled the tiny classrooms. Homeland Security assigned children to heal the injured, but provided no ointments or medication. A local farmer offered thinly sliced cucumbers and advised the children to apply them to burns—*cucumber Band-Aids for* pika-don *wounds*, Tsugio thought bitterly. It seemed a completely hopeless assignment. Some of the people were hemorrhaging and losing their hair and were certainly dying; and Tsugio felt a jolt of fright when Hiroshi removed his work hat and most of his hair came away clinging to the straw weave.

But it can't be THAT bad, Tsugio told himself. His brother had suffered none of the burns that appeared to be killing the other survivors; and after all, when the day's work at the school was finished, Hiroshi felt well enough to play ball; and he was not vomiting like the others; and his appetite was holding up well. And he would be dead by the second week of September.

"YOU MUST REMEMBER," Susumu Tsuno told Drs. Koyano and Akizuki, "you must never forget that the reason I am alive to tell you this is because the atomic bomb gives you time to get under cover. If you see the flash, you'll have maybe three seconds to duck and roll and seek cover before the blast wave strikes."

The dean of the Nagasaki College Hospital had run straight to the school from the Hiroshima train on a self-assigned mission of warning and preparation. What seemed to horrify him above all else were the intense heat waves—which, even if the bomb did allow three seconds to duck and cover, tended to burn anyone standing under the flash.

"Whatever you do," Tsuno warned, "you must not just stand still, looking around. The burns of those who immediately dove facedown to the ground, and into shade behind walls or in ditches, were comparatively mild."

Tsuno went on to describe, in a lesson his listeners were sure to remember and heed, how a man who had been sitting at a trolley stop, reading a newspaper, survived with a pattern of burns indicating that white paper reflected the glare of the *pika* and protected his face and the upper part of his body—and his thumbs—though his fingers, curling around the front of the paper, were seared and fused together. The man happened to be wearing black suit pants, and they absorbed the light, with the dye heating up and burning the fibers deep into his groin and his legs.

Dr. Tsuno reported numerous instances of women and children wearing patterned clothing, sometimes displaying decorative flowers on white cloth. The dark flowers were now branded permanently onto their skin.

As a precaution, he advised the students to wear white clothing and white, wide-rimmed hats, and to hang white sheets in all of the hospital's windows. The dean was describing how ordinary sheets of calligraphy paper, being hung in a window by a teacher, were substantial enough to protect the teacher's face from the flash. As his lesson neared its end, wrapped up as a warning, a student known to Akizuki only as "young Mr. Fujii from the theological school," entered the room.

"Given what I have seen of this new bomb," Tsuno concluded, "I feel sure it won't be enough as an air-raid precaution for you to simply be on alert when you hear enemy planes approaching. You must all—and you students in particular—be more on your guard than ever before and prepare for the worst."

As Dr. Tsuno spoke, his own agitation increased, and seemed to become contagious. "What had been a city," he said, "is now a prairie, baked reddish-yellow." His voice cracked when he related the story of a little girl who had tried to help a man calling out to her for water. Sitting against a wooden column, he begged her to help him stand up and walk down to the river. The entire side of his body facing her had been flash-burned black. The wood behind him was also burned black, and when she grabbed the man's hand and helped him to stand up, she saw that his perfectly clean shadow was etched behind him on the wood, like a pale image on a photographic negative.

"This was only a little less than two kilometers away from the center of the flash," Dean Tsuno explained, adding that he would not have believed the tale the girl had told, had he not seen such horrors with his own eyes.

At this same radius from the *pika*, a castor bush's leaves and branches had completely disintegrated near the ruins of the Meiji Bridge. The telephone pole behind the bush had been flash-burned from light brown to charcoal black—and yet every point and crevice of the vanished leaves lived on as a light-brown shadow against the black. The trunk of the castor plant still existed, albeit as a blackened nub of blown-apart wood. Nearer to Hiroshima Castle—which was "simply gone"—Dr. Tsuno crossed the Misasa Bridge, and there he saw a bicycle leaning against the bridge railing, with its carbonized, partly skeletonized rider still upon it. Trying to make sense of the inexplicable, Tsuno said he had searched for the man's shadow, but could not find it.

At this point, the theology student ran out of the room, and Dr. Akizuki ran after him. The student's girlfriend and her father lived in Hiroshima. Rage and fear were taking control of him—because, until now he had believed the official announcement from Tokyo. Officially, the city had suffered "slight damage" by a new weapon and several people had been killed.

"Slight damage?" he cried out to Dr. Akizuki. "According to what we have just heard, at least fifteen kilometers square have been burned to the ground!"

Dr. Akizuki understood at once what the student was planning. "No," he said. "You must stay away from that place."

"As long as the trains are still running in that direction, I've got to try. Until this moment all we really knew was that no news was coming out of that area. I've got to find out what's happened to her."

Akizuki tried to dissuade him, warning that several cities along the rail lines had been firebombed only the night before, and that he could be killed along the route north if the firebombings continued tonight. But the young man set off toward the rail station with a rucksack on his back, and Dr. Akizuki would record later, "No one knew how fortune smiled on him that afternoon, as he left Nagasaki to go to Hiroshima."

He would also record that, as one of the few surviving doctors in the Nagasaki region, his first tasks were fated to involve triage, which amounted essentially to mercy killing. The hospital was located barely more than 1,600 meters from the hypocenter of a detonation three times more powerful than the previous atomic bomb. Here and there, random shock-cocoon effects were going to diverge around hills, leaving perimeter concrete walls and multiple floors of the hospital mysteriously intact. Just the same, 42 professional physicians, 206 office workers, 109 nurses, and 535 students were about to be lost.

Dr. Akizuki would always attribute his own survival, and the survival of many others, to the warnings from Dean Tsuno.

The dean, he learned later, did not die in the hospital. At Moment

Zero, he would be relating his cautionary tale to military authorities at Prefectorate Command Headquarters, almost 1,500 meters nearer the hypocenter. In fewer than twenty-four hours, Dean Tsuno was fated to survive in a second shock cocoon, close enough this time to receive a lethal dose of radiation from the *pika*. Impossibly, while Tsuno was given a few more days in which to live, people fifteen meters from him (barely more than 49 feet away), throughout the outer rooms of the very same wooden building, were fated to be literally vaporized, becoming part of the radioactive fallout that Akizuki and the other survivors would inhale.

PREFECT TAKEJIRO NISHIOKA WANTED, for himself, nothing more than to be with his family, before Nagasaki suffered the same destruction he had seen in Hiroshima. Yet in spite of his desire to see his wife and child, a sense of duty sent him directly from the Nagasaki train station to the office of Governor Nagano.

Up to that point in time, on the afternoon of August 8, the governor had been told only that a new bomb had been involved in the loss of contact with Hiroshima, which was due largely to some disruptive pulse effect on radios and transmission lines. The bomb was said to have killed several hundred people and damaged some buildings as well as the power grid. The American president's threats of massive destruction, according to Governor Nagano's top military advisors, had been grossly exaggerated. And then Prefect Nishioka came rushing into the office, describing tornadoes of fire rising from a horizon-spanning sea of flames . . . and large trees felled by the blast at a radius of several kilometers . . . steel-reinforced buildings and bridges uprooted and flattened.

The governor asked him if he was describing something he actually saw, or rumors told to him.

"I saw it," Nishioka said. "Everybody on the train with me saw it, and they're telling everybody about it."

The governor seemed more concerned, in that moment, with the spread of the story than with the actual facts behind it; and when Nishioka recognized this, he begged Nagano's word that he would not be quoted. Spreading "bad stories" and "rumors of defeat" were treasonable offenses that threatened not only the prefect with military retribution but his entire family as well.

Nagano gave Nishioka his oath that he would not tell, and proved himself a liar the moment the prefect stepped out the door. He immediately assembled the police and the government executives and related what the prefect revealed to him. Each of them took the cue from the tone of Governor Nagano's voice and from the expression on his face, and responded with a sense of fear and a need for preparation, rather than an old indoctrinated reflex to retaliate against the messenger.

In years to come, the prefect would regret that death-dealing censorship protocols had forced him to confine his report to the governor's ears alone. Nishioka would grow prematurely old, knowing that had he been allowed to publish what he and Dean Tsuno already knew in the newspaper that he owned, uncounted thousands of lives might have been saved.

From the governor's office, Prefect Nishioka went directly to the site he had selected to shelter the largest generators and printing presses and the greatest national treasures. With him were the executives of the Prefectural police and the chief of the *Tokko*, Japan's special plainclothes military police. Temporarily, vital equipment and treasures would be stored at the governor's private shelter. This was to be the final, virtually impregnable Crisis Command Center. A broad tunnel was to be dug, allowing heavy equipment to be trucked into a cavern beneath the hill of the Gokoku Shrine. The site was located just outside the coming hypocenter, in a region where rebounding compression waves were going to converge and echo with such force that not a single foundation stone would remain in place to suggest where the shrine had been; even the original geography of the hill would be rendered unfamiliar.

Nishioka arranged to meet again at the shrine with equipment ready—promptly at eleven o'clock on the following morning, August 9.

Radiation sickness intervened, and kept the prefect from his appointment with destiny. All his life, he had been healthy. Now, out of nowhere—out of the deep, impersonal nowhere—nausea and debilitating fatigue, and a feeling that he was being flayed from inside, seized total control over him. He remembered the miniature volcanic plumes that had sprouted near Field Marshal Hata's house, and how he understood even then that he should have given the plumes a wide berth, but he had walked through them anyway.

Sitting down on the ground now and rolling up his pants, he cursed himself. Just beneath the skin, Nishioka's legs had sprouted dark blue, starlike spots, tinged with yellow on the edges—as if he had suddenly developed something that was a next of kin to hemophilia.

That quickly, his only directive became to simply head home and get his family away from this place. He did not think he could travel very far, but he did not have far to go. *Home* was within walking distance of the Gokoku Shrine, near the Roman Catholic Cathedral of Maria.

"God! Where were you?" Mrs. Nishioka asked, when she saw how ashen and sickly—and even how filthy—her husband had become.

"I've been in the city of corpses," he answered. "Now, don't ask anything more. Just follow my instructions if you want to live."

The prefect ordered his wife to leave at once with their child to the village of Uzen, about two hours away by car. He filled the car's tank with the last of the family's gasoline (which he had been hoarding for more than three months), and he refused to let her pack any belongings. Uzen was less than a town—nothing more than a hamlet and shrine in the middle of a national park, and this suited the prefect just fine. There was only enough gasoline for a one-way trip, and this too was satisfactory. No one would target a national park, and two hours by car, one way, had to be far enough from Nagasaki.

"Go. Go now and don't look back!" he commanded. The prefect's wife had never seen him so close to losing his composure. Mrs. Nishioka, who was Christian, was reminded suddenly of Lot's instructions to his own wife.

AKIRA IWANAGA, THE SHIP DESIGNER from Hiroshima, had disembarked the prefect's train at a town called Isahaya, some 29 kilometers northeast of Nagasaki. Akira's parents lived in Isahaya, and as the train came near, he was feeling too ill to travel on to the Mitsubishi shipyards. He decided to spend the remainder of the day and the coming night at his parents' house, hoping that after a little rest, he would awake feeling better. As the afternoon wore on, he discovered that this was a vain hope. The pains in his abdomen were growing worse, and while it became possible to believe he might pass out from the sheer intensity of the pain and attain something *like* sleep, he realized that refreshing sleep was simply out of the question.

Tsutomu Yamaguchi was feeling no better than Akira or the prefect. His burned arm and face were swelling, stinging, and itching mercilessly when he reached Nagasaki Station. About the time Prefect Nishioka discovered the bleeding under his skin, Yamaguchi stumbled into the Mitsubishi Company's hospital, seeking treatment. The moment he mentioned Hiroshima, three doctors came rushing to his aid, including a former classmate named Sato.

His old friend was clearly curious about a survivor of the weapon, but it bothered Yamaguchi that Sato did not recognize his face until he identified himself. The shipbuilder suddenly realized that his wounds must look even worse than they felt.

Sato took Yamaguchi straightaway to an operating room, gave him a shot of morphine, and began cutting away the layers of dead skin. The doctor was honest with him, describing the flesh below the "dead layer" as "bright, raw red—like whale meat." He applied oils to the wounds and bandaged them, then gave him two extra doses of morphine to take home, advising that they would be necessary for sleep. Neither man quite understood at the time that Sato had just stepped into history, as the first doctor to treat an atomic bomb victim in Nagasaki.

When Yamaguchi walked outside, the afternoon sun, though it had begun to climb down in the sky, burned his skin wherever it was exposed. His friend gave him a light linen sheet to act as a sun-block on the way home, which explained in part why his mother let out a shriek as he approached the house, and called him "Ghost!"

While he was being treated by Sato, stories from the Hiroshima train had spread quickly through the Nagasaki region, and Yamaguchi's parents began to prepare their minds for reception of the idea that he might be dead. And then their son appeared with half his face hidden by bandages and his feet hidden by a white sheet draped over him like a Roman toga.

In Japanese mythology, ghosts did not have feet.

"Have you got feet?" his mother asked timidly.

Yamaguchi lifted the sheet, and reassured her that he did indeed have feet and was not the ghost of her son. His wife, Hisako, came running from the back of the house and took him by his one good hand, and kissed him as if nothing at all had happened to his face.

Yamaguchi forgot his pain and did not believe he would be needing Sato's morphine tonight. Hisako announced that they now had a new house of their own, which she had bought with some of their savings and which he had not yet seen. The little frame house was barely more than a half-hour's walk from his parents' home, and Yamaguchi's mother insisted on babysitting little Katsutoshi for the night, urging them to go over the threshold alone. He made the trek falteringly but happily, propped up by Hisako's shoulder.

The place was small, but beautifully crafted from hardwood. There was even a balcony built for two, from which Yamaguchi and his wife could look across the river and see the Maria Cathedral in the Urakami hills—and, not very far below it, the arch of the Sano Shrine.

AFTER SENDING HIS WIFE and child away to the Unzen forest, Prefect Nishioka gathered as many critical papers as he could carry from his office, asked his men to pour some gasoline into a small army truck, and set off for Unzen. About 33 kilometers out, both the gas supply and his health gave out. Throwing open the driver's side door, he fell to his knees and began vomiting thick bile flecked with hundreds of little black blood clots. The prefect pulled himself to his feet and, through faltering painful strides, walked the remaining kilometer to an old-style bed-and-breakfast house overlooking the sea.

I'm dying, he thought. And then he pushed the thought away. He would not let himself die until he saw his wife and child again. He hoped Unzen was far enough away for them, but he was unsure. His own condition was proof enough that one did not have to be so near an atomic bomb as to be directly injured by it, to be poisoned by it. The only certainty in his mind was that Hiroshima was not the end, and that Nagasaki would be next.

ON TINIAN, Charles Sweeney learned at an afternoon briefing that the Kokura Army Arsenal would be the next target. Kokura was surrounded by antiaircraft batteries, and was one of the few sites remaining where command of the air was not guaranteed. A hornet's nest of airstrips and intercept fighters still existed there.

In the unlikely event, given current weather conditions, that excessive cloud cover obscured Kokura, then Nagasaki would become the secondary target.

Sweeney hoped the target would be Kokura. After more than a week of intensive study, he knew the streets and buildings in both places as well as he knew the layout of his own hometown. Nagasaki and its neighboring town of Urakami lay in the middle of a steep valley. According to Alvarez, maximum blast and rebound effects in the Nagasaki region could be achieved only by detonation high above the flat landscape downriver of the Mitsubishi torpedo factories and submarine support facilities. The commercial and residential districts of downtown Nagasaki were also located in this same maximum effect zone; and by everything Sweeney knew, the civilian casualties would be even higher in Nagasaki than in Hiroshima.

And so Sweeney firmed a resolve to give it everything he could, to drop his package on Kokura. He had doubts, however, that the bomb would get that far. Sweeney was familiar with the fusing malfunctions that, had they occurred in a live plutonium-supplied bomb, would have unleashed the fury of a thousand suns right below the belly of a B-29. He hoped that Alvarez's team had finally solved the problem.

The plutonium bomb was so many orders of magnitude more complicated than Hiroshima's uranium device that it could not be armed in flight and had to be made live before it was hoisted up through the bomb-bay doors.

Four kinds of detonators had already been installed—with two fuses of each kind, leaving nothing to chance. The two air-pressure sensors were set to trigger their fuses at 1,890 feet. The two time-bomb fuses would fire forty-three seconds after the bomb was re-leased, at which point it would have dropped from 30,000 feet to about 1,890 feet. The two radar fuses would be attached to a device that pinged the ground with radio waves and timed the echoes, down to an altitude of 1,890 feet. If the first three pairs of detonators failed and the bomb continued to fall below 1,890 feet, the last two detona-tors, located in the nose of the machine, would implode the plutonium core and set the chain reaction in motion within one hundred-millionth of a second, before the impact itself could damage the bomb.

The two final, last-resort triggers were what worried Charles Sweeney. A single hard bump on a runway could incinerate the entire island.

He was considering this, underneath the bomb itself, when Admi-ral William Purnell came up behind him and asked, "Son, do you know how much that bomb cost?"

"No, sir," Sweeney replied.

"Two billion dollars," Purnell stated.

"Well," Sweeney said, and let out a slight whistle, "that's a lot of money, Admiral."

"And do you know how much your airplane costs?"

"Slightly more than half a million dollars, sir."

The admiral nodded sternly, and said, "I'd suggest you keep those relative values in mind for this mission."

THE LAST TRAIN to reach Nagasaki was now departing Hiroshima Station. Master kite-maker Morimoto and three of his helpers—Doi, Shinji, and Masao—were traveling together in the same car. All four of them had survived Hiroshima without any visible injuries, but Morimoto was trying to fend off a persistent nausea and Doi was drenched in perspiration—yet at the same time he complained about intermittent chills.

In another part of the train, a survivor named Kuniyoshi Sato was sitting across from a pale figure who, much like Doi, was sweat-ing profusely. Kuniyoshi would record more than two decades later that the anonymous fellow traveler was holding a cloth-covered bowl on his lap, and this he jealously guarded, as if it were filled with gold.

"What are you holding, there?" Kuniyoshi asked.

"I married just last month," the stranger replied. "But my wife died. I want to take her home to her parents." And then, after a pause, the man lifted the cover from his bowl.

"See? Do you want to look inside?" He spoke these words in a tone that also said, *See? This is what you get for sticking your nose into other people's lives.*

The bowl was filled with scraps of human bone. And, though the train was very crowded and it seemed very unlikely that Kuniyoshi would be able to find another seat, he stood and hurried away. Kuniyoshi never did learn the name of the man with the bowl of bones, but there would be little doubt among future historians that this was Kenshi Hirata.

Behind Kenshi, Kuniyoshi, and the kite-makers, rescue crews were now moving from the countryside into Hiroshima, more and more of them each passing hour.

At the Communications Hospital, a doctor named Minoru Fujii passed through with a team he had assembled in the suburbs. En route to another field hospital, Dr. Fujii left behind a crate of ointments and bandages and enough food for two days. Any other Wednesday, two days' supplies would not mean very much, but today they were everything. Given the increasing incidence of what appeared to be flu-like symptoms and a contagious anorexia, Dr. Hachiya believed the food supply might last four or five days. It seemed to him that the horse in the garden (the hospital's nutritional safety net) now had a reprieve, if only a fleeting one. The Communications Hospital, like the Hiroshima Dome and the Fukuya Department Store, stood apart from the landscape, crying out for attention. For acres and acres in every direction, this region of the city was a prairie that sprouted no grass and whose rocks were wind-scoured bricks and roof tiles. In the midst of this, the hospital was like a lone outcrop of bedrock, and also like a magnet. And so, all but inevitably, the building drew a gang of soldiers to its entrance. Guns drawn, they demanded bandages and food for the Second General Army. Four days later, when he felt well enough to write, Dr. Hachiya would record in his diary that the thugs had left behind

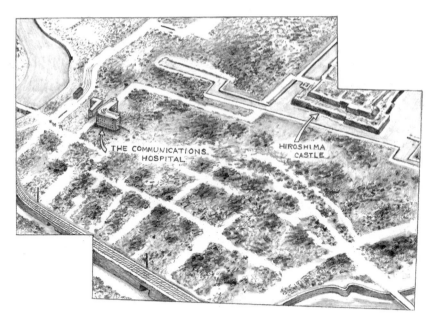

The Communications Hospital complex was shadow-shielded from the bomb's compression wave (radiating from the direction of Hiroshima Castle), after the castle and its ramparts absorbed and disrupted a significant fraction of the wave's force. Dr. Hachiya's rescue team made its base of operations in the smaller of the two buildings—which was shielded behind the larger, more heavily damaged building. The Misasa Bridge is visible in the lower right corner. The rail line in the lower left is the same line that ran across the river to the Hachiya and Sasaki homes. (Patricia Wynne)

essentially nothing for the treatment and feeding of more than eighty patients.

Dr. Hachiya, though he seemed to be the only member of his staff to still possess a healthy appetite and feel as if he were getting stronger, was not yet well enough to get out of bed and to be walking around visiting patients. In fact, the other doctors loudly forbade the former ant-walker from trying to move. So he took reports instead, serendipitously recording history.

None of the patients had any appetite. One by one they had developed symptoms ranging from migraine headaches and chills to profuse sweating, bleeding under the skin, and bouts of severe vomiting.

By now, vomiting was turning into dry heaves, and many of the patients were reporting shooting pains in their lower spines. Often the pains spread to the area of the kidneys.

What alarmed Hachiya most was that many of these patients—with the whites of their eyes now turning bright red from subsurface bleeding and with the skin on their faces displaying brilliant starlike speckles of red—had not been battered or burned at all by the *pika-don*. Several of the apparently uninjured did not seem to know any longer exactly where they were.

Hachiya's friend Koyama cursed the soldiers who had looted the last of the antibiotics, but Dr. Hachiya was beginning to suspect that conventional drugs would have no effect on the illness. The symptoms were consistent with severe hemorrhaging throughout the body. There were diseases known from Africa and New Guinea that caused people to bleed out, and which were immune to antibiotics and sulfa drugs. Hachiya began to worry that the Americans had followed the *pika-don* with disease warfare, and the thought of this filled him with dread.

As reports progressed from sickness to sudden death among the afflicted, a doctor who had been treating blast victims brought Hachiya the gift of a brief distraction from worries about bio-weapons.

"Doctor, do you think a girl could still see if the blast pulled her eye from its socket?" He asked this in a completely matter-of-fact way; and in years to come, Dr. Hachiya would marvel at how quickly human minds adapted, rendering even the unbelievable commonplace.

In the same, matter-of-fact fashion, Hachiya asked, "Was the optic nerve still attached?"

"I think so," the physician said. "She held the palm of her hand against her cheek and the eye was resting in her palm and she insisted she could see me—and I can swear to you that her pupil was staring right at me."

On an ordinary day, in an ordinary place, Hachiya would have been chilled to the bone. But today his mind shifted easily into speculation about how the girl's brain might have tried to deal with the problem of constructing a three-dimensional picture from such a distorted binocular view.

This train of thought was interrupted by more horrifying concerns. Dr. Koyama reported that the patients were becoming too weak to walk away from their floor mats and leave the building to relieve themselves of urine and feces. More than half of them were now lying in pools of watery, bloodstained feces—which explained, Dr. Hachiya thought, why the building was beginning to smell like a charnel house filling slowly with sewage.

The most alarming part of Dr. Koyama's report involved two male patients who had shown some improvement in the morning but who over the course of only a single hour had become dramatically worse. The red spots under their skin expanded to massive bruises, turning their faces purple. And then, long after the previous day's vomiting had emptied their stomachs down to the level of ineffective dry heaves, their mouths began bringing up fresh arterial blood. Dr. Hachiya guessed that something was breaking down the capillaries and blood vessels while something else drastically reduced the blood's ability to clot, as if the bone marrow had begun to die. By the time the men vomited their first mouthfuls of blood, their kidneys and vast regions of their spines and brains must have begun bleeding from the inside and shutting down, following the bone marrow into death.

As Dr. Koyama told it, one of them rolled onto his side and vomited more than two liters of blood; and then the other produced a sound like a long, long sheet of silk ripping—the sound of his dead, oxygen-starved intestinal lining pulling away and being extruded onto the floor through his bowels—or rather, what was left of his bowels.

"Neither of these men had been injured at all by the *pika-don*," Dr. Koyama said, over and over. "Not at all!"

Dr. Hachiya was convinced now that he was dealing with a contagious and possibly weaponized disease, in which case there was no choice but to make sure his people cremated the dead quickly, and isolated the infected. Dr. Koyama, as the new provisional deputy director, was assigned the task of setting up the isolation ward. With the help of suburban rescue and recovery workers who were drawn to the only standing building in the neighborhood, he was able to construct what amounted to a crude, open-air and partly tented-over pavilion beyond the south side of the hospital. What they were doing probably was not worth very much, Dr. Hachiya would record later, but it helped his morale to think they were doing *something*.

The next step was to get all of the still-uninfected patients and staff into fresh air and away from the contamination hazard of bloody diarrhea in the ground-floor corridors. The upper floor had splashed and burned during the attack and no longer had a roof, but it seemed a far better option than remaining below.

Dr. Hachiya was carried on a stretcher to a new second-floor home, where almost all of the walls had disappeared, but where rows of twisted and charred bedframes still stood mysteriously in place.

One might complain about the soot and ashes, Hachiya observed, but he had probably never lived in a hospital ward so nearly free of bacteria as this one, sterilized by blast and flame.

NANCY CANTWELL HAD already undergone the first of several name changes. She was born Namsun Koh, and as a young Korean nurse inducted into a Japanese military hospital, she had suffered less than most under the prevailing racial arrogance of the times; yet she had suffered. The conquered Koreans were generally regarded as an inferior slave caste. The work details assigned to Namsun were exceedingly strenuous, but she had impressed a head nurse with her commitment to working even harder, saying, "Because I certainly won't die of the work."

The nurse transferred Namsun to a new hospital in the suburbs of Hiroshima, and gave her a new, Japanese-sounding name: Minami.

The hospital was surrounded by tall hills, and by parkland that had been converted to farmland. During the months leading up to the bombing, all food shipments were suspended and an order came down from the military, dictating that the hospital would have to "live off the land." Minami and the rest of the medical staff doubled up their workload, and became farmers and caregivers for wounded and tuberculosis-infected soldiers. Most of their patients were the latter. It seemed strange to Minami that fewer and fewer military personnel appeared to be coming home with wounds. The majority of the beds were occupied by elderly veterans who had become ill. It occurred to her that perhaps the war was becoming more deadly to soldiers than anyone admitted.

The problem with trying to grow food at a hospital during the approach of war's end was that seed was becoming scarce. Corn and tomatoes had been off the menu for months. Fortunately, potatoes could be made to bud and multiply easily enough, and for all of her hard work Minami was occasionally given two potatoes from her crop. She was learning now that constant hunger could make even the small and the ordinary seem huge. Minami would recall more than sixty years later that few things could ever taste so wonderful as a simple potato, before or since.

Up till the first week of August 1945, the patients had been steadily weakening and dying even without the added hazard of black rain and radioactive fallout. Dr. Minoru Fujii, who by now had become Minami's mentor, explained that the three key elements in the treatment of tuberculosis were rest, fresh air, and good nutrition. Of these three, nutrition was the cornerstone. In desperation, during the final weeks leading up to August 6, Dr. Fujii contrived a plan to drain a pond in the park adjacent to the hospital. The blueprints for his trenching operation were simple but exhausting, though they had the benefit of having worked. Hundreds of carp and catfish were trapped, dying and baking in the mud. Cleaned, salted, and sun-dried, they supplied the necessary nutrients during the last week of July and into the first week of August—with a little left over for the rescue mission to Hiroshima. Up to the time of "the great fish kill," the patients who were strong enough to leave their beds sneaked away into the countryside at night to dig up radish leaves and soft plant roots, which they cooked in salted water with a small amount of potato-and-rice porridge. One patient claimed credit for a recipe that included soup nutrients derived from the hospital's "mouser." He had strained juice from hairballs vomited by the cat.

Having already known such hunger, and despite knowing that it would likely return again, the staff and the patients decided to pack nearly half of their remaining fish and potato reserve (which did not amount to very much), and let Dr. Fujii bring it with him to the stricken city. The army's theft, from the Communications Hospital, of even a small donation of food was therefore a far greater loss than even Dr. Hachiya could have guessed.

On the evening of August 8, Dr. Fujii brought Minami and the rest of his team to the ruins of the Motokawa Elementary School, where a new makeshift hospital had been set up in a now roofless gymnasium. They found hundreds of burned, bleeding, and mostly naked survivors crowded all the way out to the school's gates. Conditions at the new hospital were much worse than at the Communications Hospital. Volunteer groups from suburban towns were overwhelmed by what they saw and smelled, and they had begun to wander around like ant-walkers, not knowing what to do.

Dr. Fujii supposed that the words to describe what he found must exist somewhere, in some dictionary, in some language, but he would never be able to find them. When he saw the wounds for the first time, he thought he might lose his bearings completely. *This will help no one*, he warned himself, and he made a decision to harden his heart. Fujii allowed himself precisely five minutes to stand in the midst of it, and to be utterly horrified by it; and then, when his watch ticked off the three-hundredth second, he was able to numb his sensibilities, and take command, and call the rest of his medics to work.

Minami seemed as stunned as anyone else, but Dr. Fujii saw that she was coming out of it faster than the rest. He went to her directly, and propped her up with an old proverb: "They say that a hunter does not see the mountain."

Dr. Fujii did not know exactly what the words meant and he was glad that Minami never asked him. All he knew for sure was that the proverb seemed somehow appropriate, and it worked.

His first action was to circulate instructions for triage, by which only those patients most likely to be helped by whatever medical aid was available would be treated. This meant that those who seemed likely to die within forty-eight hours would be left alone. The vast majority fell into the most likely to die category.

Even those patients who seemed to have a chance at survival could be given little more medical care than bowls of rice and water. The only medicines available for the treatment of burns and gashes were a few stitching kits, and Mercurochrome for sterilization. A mixture of zinc oxide powder and oil could be applied to burns. Any thoughts of surgery were simply not in the equation.

Minami was not sure she could tell who would survive and who would not. She simply moved from patient to patient, following a Buddhist philosophy of trying to shine a little light wherever she could. She rubbed the zinc-and-oil mixture onto the faces of flash-burn victims whose features were so swollen that there was no way to tell male from female just by looking at them.

As sunset approached, vast quantities of food were brought into the gymnasium. The sudden contrast between the makeshift hospital and the Communications Hospital just a few hundred meters away became extreme. No one could understand at first where all the white rice, fresh vegetables, peaches, and boxes of fish and chicken were coming from. "Important people" came with them, and then the medics realized that a wealthy family from outside the city had discovered relatives alive in the gymnasium. They were literally trucking in supplies. For a while, Minami was angered that veterans in a town just over the hills had been trying to squeeze nutrition from cat vomit while such reserves of high-quality food existed nearby. She wasn't the type, however, to let her anger seethe for very long. Nor was she the type to, as she believed the Americans phrased it, "look a gift toss in the mouth." So she helped herself to some rice and meat and walked out to the front gate.

Her appetite did not last very long. There were still a few ant people wandering about; although by now there were not enough of them to form long lines, so most wandered aimlessly in twos or threes, or alone. The last of the ant-walkers displayed open sores on whatever side of their bodies had been exposed to the flash, where the skin had been almost instantly roasted and then blasted away. Often the skin was so completely flayed that the musculature of the arms and legs became exposed. They were bleeding a watery substance from the muscles themselves, dripping trails of it as they walked.

Dr. Fujii explained that the higher functioning of the outer regions of the walkers' brains must already have died, erasing *who* they had been and leaving behind only an animal-like core instinct to continue walking blindly ahead. He advised Minami to stop looking at them and return to the gym, but she stayed outside a little while longer anyway, until she observed enough to know that they could no longer be conscious of pain and that the watery substance flowing so freely out of their bodies eventually stopped them dead in their tracks with dehydration.

The sights inside the gym were scarcely less distressing.

Dr. Fujii showed Minami a technique—newly invented—for washing hundreds of maggots from a wound by squirting saline solution under peeled-back and dying skin. Fujii and the other physicians expressed great fear of the maggot infestations and instructed everyone to either flush them away or remove them one by one with tweezers. Minami was mortified to find the very air filling with swarms of flies. She discovered that each patient had grown a kilogram or more of maggots. Many of these creatures were direct descendants of parents who had dodged the flash effects during those first few milliseconds of the *pika*. Minami found it impossible to believe that writhing carpets of fly larvae could come to life under the skin of human beings. The sudden abundance of human protein in Hiroshima, she judged, was causing the white worms to grow rapidly.

Minami wanted to cry and vomit; but she remembered Dr. Fujii's advice, hardened her heart, and removed the maggots, cleansed the burns, applied disinfectant, and painted the skin and any exposed muscle with the zinc-oil mixture.

What Minami and Dr. Fujii could not know—what few people in all the world would understand until America's Food and Drug Administration formally classified fly larvae as "medical devices" in 2007—was that Hiroshima's plague of maggots probably delivered more healing than harm. Although the city's adult flies often carried bacterial infection as they flitted from decaying bodies to patients whose immune systems were already weakened by radiation, the eggs they laid on and in the wounds were unleashing one of nature's most efficient cleanup crews. The white worms were, like all carrion feeders, very fussy eaters. They shunned living flesh, liquefying and digesting only dead and bacteria-permeated tissue. Already, American military surgeons were noticing that Okinawa survivors with maggot-infested wounds were faring better than similarly wounded soldiers without the infestation. They learned also that it was almost impossible to wash out all of the maggots, for each creature removed seemed to be replaced within hours by ten more from newly hatched eggs. And then the surgeons discovered that infested limbs scheduled for amputation no longer stank of putrefactive bacteria and gangrene and had begun to heal.

About three hours after sunset, Minami left the lair of the white worm to stretch her muscles, straighten her spine, and take a breath of reasonably fresh air.

From the front gate, she could see that some of the distant buildings were still burning, and that mass grave funeral pyres were being lit near and far. A light, misty rain began to fall, and with it came the blue fireflies. Before sunrise on August 9, hundreds of other rescuers and survivors would witness the same "firefly" phenomenon. The worst of the radiation had already passed; and so, even in the context of twenty-first-century physics, no known effect of the bomb would be able to adequately account for the brilliant blue fireballs darting like phosphorus through the air.

"They simply appeared here and there in the dark," Minami would recall. "They were not solid; they were more like fire moving through the air, disappearing and reappearing. They were neither exactly flame-like nor wisp-like. They were more like points of light, like fireflies—only bigger. One would dart away and another would reappear in another place; or perhaps it was the same one darting away and reappearing. There was no way to be sure. What I was sure about is simply this: they were not appearing where the fires were burning. These were something else. They appeared everywhere and shot away to nowhere."

Appearing anywhere made sense to Minami. The blue sparks were moving busily to and fro over the ruins of the entire city, and Minami knew by now that people died and were still dying everywhere.

Even the ant-walking water bleeders had not filled her with a fright such as she knew the night of August 8, while standing all alone in the dark, in what used to be the city center of Hiroshima. Minami let out a groan, held her head low, and sat down hard on the damp earth, drawing her knees in tight against her chest and shivering. She had never been so frightened before, and even though she would be shot in Korea and would live to see American Airlines

Flight 11 pass over her head in Hell's Kitchen, on its way to the killing of a favorite student on September 11, 2001—even these events would be incapable of putting such fright into her ever again.

Hiroshima was a city of ghosts. That was how Minami would remember this night. She had stepped from the lair of the white worm into the domain of the blue fireflies.

KENSHI HIRATA ALMOST DOZED off, but a sudden bump in the train tracks and a bright flash outside his window snapped him to full alertness. Off to one side, an orange glow began blooming against the sky, spreading there, brightening. The city of Yahata was dying under what he guessed to be at least a fifty-strong B-29 raid.

He thought of Setsuko.

Kenshi's intestines still did not feel quite right, and he noticed bleeding under the skin of his fingers—and though he felt weak and achy, he was afraid that if he dozed off he would drop the bowl of precious bones lying on his lap.

Two additional swarms of night-raiders helped him to keep sleep at bay. En route to Nagasaki, he witnessed the firebombings of two more cities: Tobata and Yawata. The latter introduced a new FUBAR factor into the Alvarez equation, guaranteeing that tomorrow, Kenshi Hirata's and Charles Sweeney's paths would converge a second time.

FOR YEARS TO COME, Dr. Hachiya would be awakened about 2:00 a.m. by the same recurring nightmare. He found himself in a great city—larger than Tokyo—a city where buildings stood a half-kilometer high. At daybreak, towers of all shapes and sizes gleamed like mica, and by noon they were only ashes and smoke, and twisted steel. All around him, the city was heaped with decomposing bodies, all of whom were looking at Hachiya pleadingly. He saw an eye sitting in the palm of a girl's hand—and high above another city whose towers dwarfed the tallest skyscrapers of his day, the eye blinked, then opened again as a huge fireball.

About two o'clock in the morning, on August 9, the physician awoke to the odor of burning sardines. For a moment he wondered what could cause such a smell, and then he remembered where he was. Looking down from the splashed and charred second floor of his hospital, he could discern several fires scattered about the ruins, all the way to the most distant hills. In the beginning, the fires were mostly burning rubble, but not anymore. Toward Nigitsu an especially large blaze rivaled the fire worms of August 6. There, the dead were being burned by the hundreds. To suddenly realize that Hiroshima had become a city of funeral pyres made Hachiya shudder.

Near the center of the city, the Dome and one or two of its concrete neighbors—having somehow been left standing by the *pika-don*—were still afire on the inside. In a city that no longer had street lighting, they made eerie silhouettes against the night sky. These glowing ruins and the blazing pyres—and the occasional flashes of blue phosphorescence—set Dr. Michihiko Hachiya to wondering if Pompeii had looked like this on that last night. And it occurred to him that there were not nearly as many dead in Pompeii, as in Hiroshima tonight.

6

KAITEN AND THE FAITHFUL ELEPHANTS

Now that President Truman had announced the atomic bomb's existence to the world, the veil of secrecy began to disintegrate. Along with the scientists assigned to Charles Sweeney's plane was an observer from the *New York Times*; and because, as a civilian, he was not familiar with the squadron's never-ending variation on the theme of musical chairs, for more than two decades history books would record the plane that dropped the bomb on Nagasaki as *Great Artiste*.

The plane that actually dropped the bomb was typically under the command of Fred Bock, and he had named her *Bock's Car*, after himself. Both *Great Artiste* and *Bock's Car* were identified only by their numbers, without the usual names and artwork painted on their sides; and each had been modified in specific ways: one to monitor the world's largest bomb, the other to drop it. Logically, no one was going to switch tons of specialized equipment from one plane to another when pilots Charles Sweeney and Fred Bock switched planes. No one told the reporter about the switch; so logically, when he was assigned to climb into a plane filled with scientists under the command of Fred Bock, he concluded that the scientific instrument plane was Bock's own *Bock's Car* and that the bomb carrier was Sweeney's plane, the one called *Great Artiste*.

At 2:00 a.m., Charles Sweeney strapped himself into the cockpit of *Bock's Car*, and began running through his preflight systems check with co-pilot Don Albury and flight engineer John Kuharek. Sweeney was about to start the engines when his flight engineer leaned forward and said, "We have a problem. The fuel in our reserve tank in the rear bomb-bay bladder isn't pumping. We've got six hundred gallons of fuel trapped back there."

"Any idea what the problem *is?*" Sweeney asked. "Could it be instruments?" he suggested hopefully.

The engineer replied that checking and double-checking had proved his gauges to be giving accurate readings—which meant that the only means of correcting the problem involved replacing a pump.

Sweeney ran some quick calculations through his head. George Marquart had already taken a weather plane to the primary target of Kokura. The forecast called for clear skies, but not for very long. A band of rain and mist was expected to move in from the Pacific and might linger for several days. Indeed, most of Japan's large south island might become clouded over for a week or more—and then the cyclone season would be coming along in full swing.

Sweeney called an "All Stop," unlatched his shoulder straps, and climbed down the nosewheel ladder. Paul Tibbets was already waiting under the wing when Sweeney emerged. Their discussion was all about mathematics, crisp and unsympathetic.

Fully fueled, *Bock's Car* carried 7,000 gallons, including 1,000 gallons in two reserve bladders—600 gallons of which were now trapped. If their primary target became clouded over and they had to fly extra miles from Kokura to Nagasaki—or if anything else caused them to consume extra fuel—the plane would not be coming home. Replacing the pump would take hours and might scrub the mission for days if clouds began moving over the targets—and then again, the cyclone season was looming straight ahead. Transferring the bomb to another plane would be even more time-consuming and was out of the question because its contact fuses were live.

If he left now, Sweeney would probably beat the weather window, but he would still have to fly at 17,000 feet to stay above the turbulence of a Pacific storm front, which would consume more fuel than if he flew at the optimal altitude of 8,000 feet. Due to a design plan that had never considered this situation, the 600 gallons of trapped fuel could not be drained without fixing the faulty pump. So *Bock's Car* would be obliged to lift and carry—in addition to a plutonium bomb far heavier than the Hiroshima device—600 gallons of extra mass, causing the plane to consume more fuel just to carry the "dead" fuel.

"It's your call," Sweeney's commander said.

The math told Sweeney that he could certainly fly 2,000 miles (or 3,200 kilometers) to the target and return to Tinian, so long as none of the snafus that tended to intervene in even the best of plans caused target changes or other delays.

"To hell with it, boss," Sweeney said. "We're going." And so Charles Sweeney strapped himself into his leather seat for a second time this night. Less than ten minutes later, and only slightly behind schedule, he lifted off from Runway A. The clock ticked forward to 2:56 a.m., Tinian time; 1:56 a.m., Kokura and Nagasaki time.

DR. PAUL NAGAI, like Dr. Hachiya, was now a patient in his own hospital, but for a very different reason. The cancer diagnosed only several months before had begun to spread throughout his body; and as his closest colleagues put it when they tried to assess how long he had to live, "Sometimes people at this stage can remain reasonably active for six months. Sometimes they can survive for up to three years. And sometimes they fool us all."

"I hope to fool you," Paul said. He hoped so, but he really did not believe it likely. Tonight he did not even have the strength to walk down the hill to his home and be with his wife. He simply crashed at his job on a spare hospital bed. To judge from a daily assessment of his own strength, the deterioration was progressing steadily and even seemed to be gaining speed. The physician supposed that he would come through the remainder of the summer and through autumn as well, into what was promising to be a short winter.

About 3:00 a.m., Dr. Nagai awoke from uneasy dreams and found that he could not go back to sleep—which was unusual, since the advancing cancer tended to leave him wanting to do almost nothing except sleep.

He went to a window and looked down upon the town of Urakami, from the hill of Nagasaki Medical Complex. The wartime blackouts now hid a river valley of more than a quarter-million people from view, but in the glow of the stars alone, with his eyes properly night-adapted, he was able to locate his house, where his wife, Midori, was doubtless sleeping peacefully and above the covers.

Three a.m. became four and four became five, and still Dr. Nagai could not sleep. Lying in bed and watching the first hints of daylight gathering in the eastern sky, he thought about the number of patients he would have to visit today; and the more he thought about lost sleep and the job to be done, the more impossible sleep became.

Nor was it possible to escape the nightmare that had snapped him awake in the first place. An eye opened up, somewhere in the jungles of the night, and it was searching for him. The doctor-turned-patient tried to dismiss the horror as a fever dream brought about by a natural and instinctive fear of the cancer that was growing inside of him. There was a rational explanation, therefore, for what gave the illusion of being a deep interior alarm bell, warning that a horror worse than cancer was coming this way.

AT 6:00 A.M., Nagasaki time, *Bock's Car*'s master alarm warning lights began signaling that the fail-safes, designed to prevent the bomb from detonating inside the plane, were neither safe nor unfailing. Apparently, plutonium was very unfriendly to electrical systems.

Lieutenant Philip Barnes looked up from his black box (the fuse-monitoring device connected to the bomb) and called out to Sweeney, "We have a master alarm."

"Repeat that," Sweeney called back, wanting to make sure he had heard correctly.

Commander Fred Ashworth confirmed Barnes's observation that the red warning light on the fuse monitor had started flashing. If this warning, like the fuel warning, was accurate, then a multi-kiloton nuclear weapon's firing circuits were closing and one or more detonation fuses were about to pull the trigger. In all of three seconds, Sweeney ran the fusing checklist through his mind. If either of the two contact fuses in the bomb's nose were self-activating, he and his crew would already be a false sunrise over the Pacific, about to register on Japan's seismographs. If the barometric or radar fuses were involved, they would be fine unless *Bock's Car* fell below 1,890 feet . . . and unless the altimeters were giving the fuses faulty readings. Again, he'd already be ions and gamma rays if the latter case were true. This left the timing fuse—in which case Barnes and Ashworth had less than forty seconds remaining to solve the problem.

Oh, sweet suffering Lord on ice skates . . .

During the next two seconds, with his mind racing at maximum overdrive, Sweeney considered all two options: jettison the bomb and hope to escape the blast, or pray that it was not the timing fuse and hope that even if it was, his weaponeers could find the problem and fix it in a half-minute. He had no intention of jettisoning the weapon. The admiral's lesson about the relative values of the bomb and the plane now seemed sickeningly prophetic. If worse ever came to absolute worst and the plane became flacked full of holes and was bleeding fuel from dead engines, Sweeney had already resolved himself to bail his crew out while he and Kermit Beahan dove *Bock's Car* into Japan, aiming for a fuel depot or, if no other target existed, a cow in a rice paddy.

Sweeney doubted it would ever come down to that. He had faith in his men, his plane, and himself. Behind him, Phil Barnes already had the bomb's hatch open and was giving the maze of wires, circuits, and switches one of history's most rapid inspections. With more than seven seconds to spare (as the timing fuse measured time), Barnes determined that the timer was not involved. A few moments later, he traced the source of the problem to a false-positive warning and corrected it.

"False alarm," Barnes called forward. "None of the firing circuits were closed."

Good. I'm breathing again, Sweeney thought. His voiced reply was a whispered, "Oh, Lord."

* * *

FOURTEEN-YEAR-OLD HAJIME IWANAGA had been awakened with a stomachache about 3:00 a.m. and never did get back to sleep again. Now his work at the school was sure to suffer, although school was not really a place of higher learning anymore. The school was in fact now attached to the Mitsubishi Torpedo Works, and instead of calligraphy and mathematics, students were being recruited to the factory's tool-and-die presses.

During the past week, Hajime and two of his friends—who, like him, were of small stature for their age—were offered the honor of one day working the torpedoes themselves. The "work" involved manual controls for the torpedo guidance system, with the worker lying prone and sealed inside. Adolescent boys were the preferred guidance systems, because the torpedoes—which were actually minisubs modified into guided bombs—allowed for a maximum shoulder width of only 55 centimeters (about 22 inches).

These days, the veteran submarine I-58 was typically equipped with four of the special *Kaiten* torpedoes, each of them resembling a cross between a midget submarine and a long bomb. The *Kaiten* represented the undersea equivalent of the "divine wind," or kamikaze raiders.

At 11:40 on the night of July 29, torpedoes launched from the I-58 tore open all the watertight compartments of the American battle cruiser *Indianapolis*, three days after it delivered the core components of the Hiroshima bomb. "*Indie*" became historic for two other reasons: for history's worst-known feeding frenzy of sharks upon humans, and for being the last American capital–named ship sunk during the Second World War. Presently, the I-58 was returning to port, with a request for four new *Kaiten*.

Hajime, like the rest of the students, had grown up knowing nothing except indoctrination to all-out war. Though not yet old enough to truly understand the meaning of death, he was nonetheless prepared to die for his emperor. He was taught to be a proud and daring soldier in a holy war that would attain a sure peace. The Americans, the British, and the Chinese were lower than animals—a nameless, faceless "them," barely suitable as slaves. Only Japan's late-great German and Italian allies could be considered human. The Japanese were the chosen children of the gods. So the *Kaiten* volunteers were taught, and so they believed.*

Like other children of his age, and in this time and this place, Hajime trusted what the officers who came to the armaments factory told him—never doubting their instructions, even when told that the special mission for which he would be training was to be kept secret from his mother, his sister, and his teacher. He had been chosen by the Emperor himself, he was told.

When the chosen showed signs of fear, they were reminded of all that the zookeepers in Tokyo had been willing to suffer, to prove their love and dedication to the Emperor. The tale of the faithful elephants was already legend—at once horrible and wonderfully patriotic. To a later generation it would become a legend about the cruelty and foolishness of war, but presently it was taught as an example of war's glory. To the would-be *Kaiten* children, the recent and unprecedented agony of the zookeepers, demonstrated by great action and not just by empty words, was testament to the lesson that one must be ready to suffer whatever was necessary for the greater good of Japan.

The testament had its beginnings in wartime food shortages. When nightly firebombings of refineries, depots, and transportation centers brought severe rationing to the entire country, the army quickly put Tokyo's Ueno Zoo at the bottom of the food and fuel priority list, cutting off all supplies for the animals, instantly. Somewhere along the chain of command, someone remembered that body parts from some of the animals themselves—and especially from bears, tigers, and cobras—were highly sought as medicinal folk remedies, sometimes worth their weight in gold. By command of the army, the animals' caregivers were forced to put all except the zoo's three performing elephants to death, by a combination of gunshots, sword thrusts, and

* The young age of some *Kaiten* workers was not, at this point in history, unique to Japan. One of the last German submarines sunk during the war (off the south shore of Long Island, New York), turned out, when it was explored during the 1980s, to contain the skulls of crew members as young as 14. In Philadelphia, Italian immigrant boys were permitted to enlist for combat positions at 17, and a few entered the service as young as 16. On British ships, the legal age of entry into military service during World War II was 15, and occasionally as young as 14. Throughout most of the twentieth century, adolescence was rarely recognized as a distinct age group, separate from adulthood.

lethal doses of sedatives. Those carcasses judged to be valuable were carted away by the army. The rest were dragged to the city dump.

Military planners had a special, propagandistic fate in mind for the zookeepers and their elephants. The field marshal understood that elephants, being among the most intelligent of animals, developed strong bonds with their trainers and caregivers. Soldiers had observed firsthand that the bond was mutual and ran deep.

The zookeepers were denied guns and swords and every other relatively humane means of euthanizing their elephants. Next, they were ordered to live in the zoo with their animals, and watch them starve to death.

The smallest of the elephants, whom they had named John, died after seventeen days. As the starving began, the zookeepers were allowed to grow potatoes for their own nourishment, and from day to day they offered the two surviving elephants—Tonky and Wanly— portions of their own meager rations—though an occasional sweet potato was to an elephant as a raindrop is to the sea. At best, their mercy only prolonged the agony. And the field marshal saw, and understood. The trainers and the caregivers were told that their sacrifice was small compared to what soldiers on the outer islands had recently suffered: "For this is what it means to be a true son of the Emperor."

By callous mathematical certainty, the rule of three held sway: Men and elephants could live for three minutes without air, up to three days without water, three weeks without food.

As the third week came and went, Tonky and Wanly's ears began to appear too large for their bodies—and, as one of the zookeepers would later describe it, whenever he approached the cage with water, his two friends would stand up on their hind legs with their trunks held high, their still-loving eyes seeming to beg, "Please give us something to eat."

By then, the zookeepers were themselves succumbing to grave hunger. And still, when they believed the soldiers were not watching, they gave freely of their own rations, until their ribs began to show and their clothes became too large for their bodies.

The elephants' primary trainer, it was said, loved them as if they were his own children. More than two weeks after John died, the trainer found Tonky and Wanly dead in their cage, with their trunks stretched high against a horizontal cross bar, seeming to have died trying to perform their famous, crowd-pleasing bonzai trick. "Faithful for all eternity," as the *Kaiten* officers told it: "Faithful to the friend who might reward them again with food, as he used to reward them every day, before the enemy invaded Iwo Jima and Okinawa."

The trainer sat down on the concrete floor and lovingly caressed the dead elephants' trunks and legs. He had no more tears left in him, but a later generation would relate how this did not matter, because in the Ueno Zoo, it was believed that even the rocks shed tears that day.

The moral of the story, as told to Hajime, was that he must be ready to sacrifice anything to help bring the war to an end. A generation later, he and the other children of the bombs would tell an altogether different cautionary tale—of how they trusted without question what adults said, what the government said, and what the men in uniform told them the highest levels of government had meant to say.

"But what's most important," Hajime and his fellow students would endeavor to teach, "is that we must question as well as trust."

ALLIED PRISON CAMP Number 17 was located 63 kilometers northeast of Nagasaki, on the opposite side of Ariake Bay. On August 6, Corporal Dale Frantz had observed a strange cloud penetrating the stratosphere in the direction opposite Nagasaki—237 kilometers away, 145 miles northeast, in the direction of Hiroshima. The cloud must already have risen more than 10 kilometers when he first noticed it, and the strange shape continued to build high and fast. Fellow prisoner Earl Bryant also saw the cloud. He watched its cap turn pallid white, tinged with a pinkish glow. A narrow column followed the mushroom cap into the heavens, but the column was black and appeared to be made of smoke and lightning.

On the morning of August 9, about the time Lieutenant Barnes was clearing master alarm warnings aboard *Bock's Car*, the prisoners of Camp 17 were already working 439 meters underground in Omuta district's condemned Fukuoka coal mine. Bryant and Frantz had been working the mine for almost two years, but they were by no means holders of the endurance record. Clarence Graham, now twenty-five years old, displayed a strange mixture of strong muscles and emaciation, and appeared to be at least twice his actual age. He was captured on the island of Corregidor in May of 1942, and had been surviving as a slave miner a year longer than anyone else.

Nearly a half-kilometer down, the atmosphere was filled with dust from the unusually soft coal. The pumps brought down only enough fresh air to minimally sustain life, so the cave atmosphere was stagnant and hot. Water pumps barely kept pace with underground seepage. The streams of ankle-deep and knee-deep water provided Clarence Graham and the other miners with their only source of refreshment. They could splash the sweat and dust from their brows, and drinking the black seepage washed the coal from their throats, held dehydration at bay, and even allowed them to stave off some small measure of hunger by filling their stomachs with water. Clarence had survived longer than anyone else on account of not yet having been crushed during a cave-in and by keeping his wits about him. If a man developed a reputation for staying quiet, never looking his captors in the eye, and working hard, he was usually permitted to live long enough to be worked to death on a near-starvation diet. His main task involved engineering huge piles of slate into pyramid-like pillars that held up the ceilings of the caves wherever they began to weaken—which was pretty much everywhere. On twelve-hour rock-moving shifts, he lived on three bowls of rice per day, sometimes coughing up so much black phlegm that the pain in his lungs never abated and he had to take off his loincloth and dip it into the stream and wrap it around his face so he could breathe.

Clarence knew he had to keep his mind focused on seeing his family again, lest he raise a shovel, curse a guard in the face, and go after him, as others had done: suicide by armed guard.

From the world above, only the Japanese equivalent of buck privates were actually sent into the caves with the prisoners. The officers knew that death underground reached out from many directions, so they stayed above, while their underling Morlock caste took its fear and frustration out on the prey. *Shit rolls downhill*, Clarence reminded himself, *and we're at the bottom of that hill.*

Whenever a new shift of workers shambled into the tunnels, the old shift would ask, "What's new topside?" For two years, the answer had been either "Nothing" or made-up rumors about the approach of war's end. Today, the answer was, "Nothing. Same old bullshit—*except* that something's got them stirred up like hornets, and they've decided to stop feeding us."

On August 9, Clarence Graham's crew emerged into daylight about an hour after the replacement shift began work. He and the other arrivals from the night shift were ordered to line up and stand at attention under the rising sun. They were given no food, and an officer announced that they would be given no water, either. Anyone who spoke or who fell, or who made any sound at all, would have his head cut off immediately.

"Because of Hiroshima," an officer shouted, "the Emperor has commanded that you shall work without food until he decides that you do not have to work anymore."

Clarence was hot, but he supposed that the sun would not burn him too badly today. A bank of clouds was drifting in from the east, offering shade. Some twenty or thirty miles away in the direction of Kokura, a silvery glint caught his eye. *One of ours*, he guessed, *mapping and gathering weather reports*. As a distant siren whooped and hooted, and the power plant shut down the mine's water pumps, Clarence wondered, *Why don't the planes stop joyriding and just come here and do something?*

Clarence did not own a wristwatch, but he guessed from the angle of the sun that it was almost eight o'clock.

AT 7:45 A.M., the next weather plane reached Kokura and *Bock's Car* reached its rendezvous point, 30,000 feet above the island of Yakushima. *Great Artiste* appeared on Charles Sweeney's starboard wing, but the photographic plane, *Big Stink*, was nowhere to be seen. Fifteen minutes and 125 gallons of fuel later, the third plane still appeared to be lost. By coded signal, two distant weather planes called out, "C-1" and "C-2/10-2." Though morning haze had been anticipated at both targets, Kokura was clear, and only about two-tenths cloud cover could be expected at the secondary target.

This was the first snippet of good news Sweeney had received through the entire mission, and it soon began to look as if it would be his last.

At 8:30, after thirty minutes more of circling for rendezvous—and after another precious 250 gallons of fuel were consumed—Sweeney scanned the empty sky one last time, then told his co-pilot and bombardier, "That's it. We can't wait any longer." Maintaining radio silence, he wiggled *Bock's Car*'s wings, signaling to *Great Artiste* that they were to depart the rendezvous point and proceed to the primary target.

The missing photographic plane was circling almost two miles too high, and over the wrong point on the earth's surface. At nine o'clock, *Big Stink* broke radio silence and called out to Tinian Base: "Has Sweeney aborted?" The pilot's voice was sharp and stressed, and the message came through as "Sweeney aborted."

On Tinian, the against-protocol breach of radio silence, followed by no further transmissions, could be interpreted only as a sign that something had gone very wrong with Sweeney's plane. The most likely scenario was that *Bock's Car* had been shot down, or was just barely limping along somewhere between Yakushima and Kokura. Those who knew Sweeney understood that in a crisis, rather than bring home a wounded plane on the verge of crashing with an atomic bomb's impact fuses armed he would ditch the weapon over the nearest military target he could find, on a return path that would take him over Yakushima toward an emergency landing on Iwo Jima. All of Tinian's air-sea search-and-rescue resources were therefore realigned along Sweeney's newer, more apparent return route—which, by a life-and-death margin of hundreds of miles, was now more apparent than real.

If *Bock's Car* ran out of fuel and actually did have to ditch in the ocean, all the rescue ships and planes were presently being sent in the wrong direction.

IN NAGASAKI, GOVERNOR NAGANO was still skeptical about Prefect Nishioka's descriptions of Hiroshima. What stopped him from dismissing the report as a gross exaggeration was that he knew the prefect to be unflappable almost to a fault. In the end, he weighed logic against incredulity. If the prefect's description was indeed accurate and he took no extra precautions to protect his family and his staff, the result could be catastrophic. If he took action and nothing happened, then no real harm was done and he could punish the prefect later for spreading false rumors.

On a hill overlooking Nagasaki Harbor on one side and the suburb of Urakami on the other, a multichambered tunnel wide enough to accommodate two trucks side by side had been excavated with great haste during the previous two months. Power generators and air-filtration systems equipped with the newest lithium-hydroxide carbon dioxide scrubbers had already been in place for more than two weeks. An outer blast door of steel-reinforced concrete and asbestos rendered the tunnel system so airtight that it might just as well have been a submarine, sealed inside a mountain and resistant even against a hurricane of fire.

Great works of art were now sheltered deep within. All that remained to be installed were beds, food supplies, and the rest of Prefect Nishioka's printing presses.

While *Bock's Car* and *Great Artiste* closed the distance between Yakushima and Kokura, Nagano brought his family into the shelter with everything they could carry. Then he called in his administrators and officers from the Regional Air Defense Ministry to assess the situation and to plan the day's work details accordingly. The official word from Tokyo was to expect nothing serious but to remain on guard. Officially, everything was under control.

Governor Nagano was not so sure. If the prefect's description was even half accurate, very little was under control.

The governor called the meeting to order and had just begun to describe what he was told about Hiroshima when the mayor of a town called Sasebo came running into the shelter, stammering about urgent news.

"Is this how you present yourself to your governor?" Nagano shouted. And then, after a pause, he noticed that the man's clothes were soggy with sweat, and realized that there must be a good reason why he looked like a vagrant.

Nagano walked up to the mayor, and asked him gently, "Where were you?"

The mayor stared fiercely into his eyes and replied, "I am in hell."

MORE THAN TWO KILOMETERS upriver, Dr. Tatsuichiro Akizuki had just begun his examination of several outpatients, including Paul Nagai. Despite a night of fitful sleep, Dr. Nagai insisted he was feeling well enough to carry on with his duties. Akizuki approved. Both men shared a belief that the best defense against sitting down in a worry chair and letting an affliction dominate one's life was to have a job that kept the afflicted engaged in thoughts about everyone except himself.

Akizuki left Nagai with the outpatients and was walking toward a second ward when another B-29 weather plane approached, breaking over the airwaves with a call of "C-2/10-4," which meant: "Four-tenths cloud cover, secondary target." Simultaneously, a siren let out a long, continuous wail signaling "Yellow Alert," which meant: "The enemy are on their way. Prepare to take cover."

Dr. Akizuki hurried from room to room, warning patients to stay away from the windows. Under Yellow Alert, all doctors were to drop whatever they were doing and proceed immediately to basement shelters. Akizuki went to a window instead, looking for B-29s. There were none to be seen; and the siren stopped, then blasted out the signal for all clear, Status Green. This was the second false alarm in as many hours. The sky appeared to be clouding over a little, which would have made the planes difficult to see; but other than that, there seemed to be no cause for concern. Indeed, a buildup of clouds was cause for the opposite of concern. Formations of B-29s did not like to drop bombs, day or night, when targets were clouded over. Rainy days were always known to be the safest.

It was hot outside and the humidity was steadily rising. *It looks like rain*, Dr. Akizuki told himself; so he was humming cheerfully as he walked downstairs to the consulting room. When he entered, he found Dr. Yoshioka performing an emergency pneumo-thorax operation on a patient. She was about ten minutes into the procedure.

"You ought to stop working when the air-raid warning goes off," Akizuki said, trying to sound stern.

"Thank you," she replied, "but there were so many patients waiting."

Dr. Akizuki did not believe it was possible, but Dr. Yoshioka looked even more tired than Dr. Nagai. Lately, even the streetcar service seemed to be running out of power, so she had begun walking the more than five kilometers across Nagasaki, starting out every day just after dawn, toward a shift that would not end for at least twelve hours.

"Have you eaten today?" Akizuki asked.

"Later," she replied.

"No, *now*," Akizuki insisted. "Doctor's orders. I'll help you finish up here; and then I want you to go upstairs and take a rest. I'll carry on for a while in your place."

"Well . . . thank you," she said, and smiled. "But how long is a while?"

"As long as you need," said Akizuki. "I guess we'll just have to see."

AT 9:45 A.M., Kokura lay directly ahead. Charles Sweeney set course for the final bomb run and was about to hand the controls over to bombardier Kermit Beahan when Beahan suddenly yelled, "I can't see it! I can't see it! There's smoke obscuring the target."

Between the time that George Marquart had radioed his last "C-1" weather report and the moment of final approach, the wind had shifted. Below, and now directly upwind of the Kokura arsenal, the town of Yawata was still in the same condition Kenshi Hirata had observed from his train the night before—burning out of control. The arsenal was completely hidden beneath a sheet of thick, oily smoke.

Sweeney yelled into the intercom, "No drop. Repeat, no drop."

A single pass-and-drop would have left Sweeney with just enough fuel to make a try for Tinian. If he had to circle thirty miles out for a second pass and then divert to his secondary target, even the nearest base at Okinawa would soon be beyond reach.

Sweeney banked sharply to port and began a long, southward arc to a return approach, with *Great Artiste* following close behind. That's when the first flak shells began bursting on all sides. Tail gunner Pappy DeHart reported that the detonations were targeting wide; but the gunners on the ground were setting their altitude fuses perfectly—"almost to the inch."

"Roger that, Pappy," Sweeney replied. Through trial-and-error settings, gunners were now "crawling" the flak toward him, slowly zeroing in on the target. Throughout the month of July, and leading up to the August 6 bombing, the ruse Joseph Fuoco had been part of worked out quite well. Most of the enemy observers and gunners were eased into a false sense of security about two or three B-29s traveling together and dropping no bombs, as if they had strayed off course from their main squadrons or were just taking weather and reconnaissance reports. Clearly, a deception that had worked one time for Hiroshima was not going to work a second time for Kokura.

Charles Sweeney would recall later that he was now doing something a bomber pilot in a pressurized aircraft at 30,000 feet—vulnerable to being popped by flak bombs like a rubber balloon—rarely if ever did: he was making a second run on a hotly defended target. Second runs gave antiaircraft gunners second chances. Sweeney knew that if *Bock's Car* popped, the contact fuses would surely detonate the bomb during that first, all-important hundred-millionth of a second. He was not certain that a twenty- or thirty-kiloton explosion at 30,000 feet could reach all the way to the ground and take out the arsenal. *But even if it doesn't kill them down there*, he mused, *it will sure as hell give them something to think about.*

Sweeney resolved to give Kokura a second try. It wasn't only the added fuel consumption of a Nagasaki detour that firmed his resolve. His secondary target was much wider than the Kokura arsenal. Between Nagasaki and the suburb of Urakami lay more than a quarter-million civilian souls. So he climbed *Bock's Car* up another quarter-mile, hoping to ride above the gunners' latest altitude settings, but Pappy called excitedly from the tail: "Damned flak is right on our ass and getting closer!"

"Forget it, Pappy," Sweeney said evenly. "We're on a bomb run." But the second approach revealed more smoke blowing over the target than during the first approach. This time, the flak bursts were close enough to make the floor jump. Sweeney decided to take her up another fifth of a mile to throw the gunners off track again, even though the thinner air would put a higher tax on dwindling fuel reserves. He wheeled around into another very long arc and began plotting a third approach from a different angle, gambling on the slim hope that from a new angle they might find a hole in the smoke screen. But the third run was no more successful than the first two, and the flak was beginning to home in even nearer. This time, there were actual clanging sounds as well as floor jolts, and Pappy began to wonder, *How the hell did I get into this fine mess?*

"You can relax, guys," Sweeney announced. "It's time to leave all of this behind. We're going for the secondary."

Sweeney wagged his wings for *Great Artiste* and led the way south. A minute later, flight engineer Kuharek leaned forward and said, "I'm afraid our fuel situation has reached critical."

"Define critical."

"We have enough to reach Nagasaki and make just a single run. But we won't make it to Okinawa. We're going to fall short by at least fifty miles."

"Do you have any more good news of that sort?" Sweeney asked, and Ed Buckley, his radar operator, replied over the intercom:

"Fighters below and coming up to meet us!"

It sounded to Sweeney like the old sick joke about the doctor who says, "Bad news and good news. I'm sorry to report we amputated the wrong leg. But don't worry, the other one is getting better."

Sweeney's sharp turn southward had caught Fred Bock by surprise. He was flying *Great Artiste* through flak, starboard and only slightly aft of *Bock's Car* when the turn occurred. *Great Artiste* was now on the portside wing and a little farther behind. Looking to starboard and not seeing Bock's plane where he expected it to be, Sweeney called out to the gunners' positions, "Where's Bock?"

The FUBAR factor intervened—again. An elbow or a clipboard had struck the selector button. Instead of speaking to his crew over the intercom, "Where's Bock?" was broadcast for hundreds of miles in every direction.

Immediately, a return call came from the long-lost pilot of *Big Stink*—"Chuck? Is that you, Chuck? Where the hell are you?"

At the moment, Sweeney did not know who he wanted to kick harder—himself for hitting the wrong switch, or the captain of *Big Stink*, who evidently expected him to broadcast who he was and exactly where he was to the whole empire.

He made sure the selector button was set for intercom, bit hard into his lower lip, and directed his navigator to plot a "straight-line" course from Kokura to Nagasaki.

During the flak runs, Navigator Jim Van Pelt had completed the calculations and was ready with a precise compass heading. "But of course," he added quickly, "this route will take us right over the Kyushu fighter fields."

As Sweeney saw it, he had no other choice. If he swung more than fifty miles westward over the sea, and then added another sixty miles by swinging southeast toward Nagasaki, the fuel situation would become doubly critical. A direct, southeast line of flight was the sole option. Jim was right about the hazards of the overland route. Even though *Bock's Car* and *Great Artiste* were now beyond the range of Kokura flak and had quickly left the fighters behind, the enemy was, if anything, smart. For anyone watching from the ground, the planes' contrails pointed like twin compass needles toward their destination. Sweeney tried to comfort himself with the calculations of experts— who had assured each crew that, given the greater speed of the B-29s, the best that a Japanese Zero could hope for was a single pass and less than one second of actual firing time. *But no*, he reminded himself, *how often have we seen those experts actually flying inside the planes they claim to have designed so well that we need no guns to defend ourselves?*

"We can't avoid Kyushu, Jim," Sweeney said, and chose the direct route. He was short 600 gallons from the moment of takeoff; and now, the hour and a half of extra flight time over Yakushima Island and Kokura had put him another 750 gallons behind. At Nagasaki he would have enough fuel for no more than a single flyby if he hoped to ditch anywhere near the American-controlled waters of Okinawa. Considering all the other little gremlins that had been sticking their prying hands into this mission, Sweeney supposed that even with less than a second's firing time, perhaps this would be some Zero's lucky day.

He almost asked the forbidden question—and caught himself, holding the question back. Then, looking more than a hundred miles ahead, he observed a silvery-white sea of cumulus clouds marching toward the target area. That's when Sweeney finally lost his grip on the question's reins. He turned to his co-pilot, and unleashed what was never to be uttered by submariners or airmen: "Can any other goddamned thing go wrong?"

KENSHI HIRATA REACHED his parents' home, on what was to become the shadow side of a tall hill, about the same time Charles Sweeney asked the wrong question. Seconds later, flight engineers aboard *Bock's Car* and *Great Artiste* reported that a ground station in the direction of Nagasaki had begun pinging the planes with radar. Less than an hour now separated them from Moment Zero, and barely more than 3.3 kilometers separated Kenshi from the next hypocenter.

As he approached the steps, his parents came running through the door with tears in their eyes. At that same moment, an air-raid siren began to signal what was likely just another in a seemingly endless series of false alarms. False or not, Kenshi was not taking any chances. Mindful that a second flash might appear, he told his parents to come inside with him quickly and to stay away from the windows.

Kenshi's father was shocked at the sight of him—pale, with shaking hands, and with perspiration running down his cheeks, his chest, and his legs. He looked like a man half starved to death.

"Have you eaten?" his mother asked.

"Not hungry," he said. "I can't seem to keep anything down." He cradled the wedding bowl to his chest and rocked it gently, and his father bowed his head.

"I knew you were alive," Mrs. Hirata said. "Even when no more word was coming out of Hiroshima, I knew you were still in this world."

"And Setsuko?" his father asked, almost at a whisper.

Kenshi lifted the bowl and bent his head down toward its rim, and kissed it. "This is all that's left of her," he replied.

"We already knew this," his mother said.

"How can that be?"

"Because early this morning," she explained, "Setsuko's mother arrived at our door with the news. She knew her daughter was dead in Hiroshima because Setsuko has been visiting her in dreams."

His mother's words brought no comfort, only more agitation. He remembered how, when the *pika-don* came to Hiroshima, a woman's voice had cried out in his brain and had made him stay under cover while everyone else stood up and was either grievously injured or killed. At first, he had thought it might have been his grandmother's spirit—then he thought, later, that it must have been Setsuko, urging him to live. Now he knew it was her. *Knew* it.

Kenshi held back his tears, stood, and said to his father, "We must go at once to Setsuko's parents, with this bowl, and bring her home."

When they stepped outside, though only a few minutes had passed, the day had become noticeably drearier. Thick clouds now covered more than half the sky.

The air-raid siren wound down and blasted the all-clear signal. *Another false alarm*, Kenshi reassured himself. The Hiroshima blast had come out of a perfectly blue and clear sky. Dreary days were good news, in these times. The Americans never dropped bombs if they could not see the ground. Everyone knew this, and took it for a fact.

Passing a Buddhist shrine, Kenshi and his father heard a radio playing loudly. For some reason, everyone who possessed a functioning radio these days delighted in cranking up the decibels for the whole neighborhood to hear. Someone only a little farther down the road was also booming out the same station. Presently, an announcer broke into the music to tell his listeners that several B-29s had been deterred from their attempt on Kokura and were presumed either shot down or headed out to sea. Consequently, the air-raid warnings for Kokura and the Saga Prefecture in the north and the Yellow Alert for Nagasaki were being lifted.

As Kenshi walked, the cloud cover thickened quickly, and his stomach spasms abated ever so slightly. He believed that he might even be able to drink a little water now, and to keep it down. All he needed was a little breathing space. All he needed was for Nagasaki to be safe today.

SHIP DESIGNER AKIRA Iwanaga had arrived from Hiroshima at his parents' house on August 8. They lived a safe distance from Nagasaki, near the hot springs of Obama.

Sickness had continued to keep him safe in bed through the night, but in the morning he awoke feeling a little better and had even regained some of his appetite. So he boarded a train at the local station and caught the last connecting segment between Hiroshima and Nagasaki.

In a different compartment on the very same train, one of Morimoto's military kite-makers, Masao Komatsu, was also returning from Hiroshima to Nagasaki. On August 6, he had gone to a warehouse to collect supplies for the day's work and was drawn outside by a roar that sounded like a B-29 on the verge of crashing straight down on top of him. At a distance of three kilometers from the hypocenter, Masao was shadow-shielded from the flash and completely cocooned from the blast. The warehouse splashed completely apart on one side, but his skin was struck only by a wave of very hot air. He did not burn. He did not even become sick.

About the time Kenshi arrived home, Masao and Akira were approaching Nagasaki's outer suburbs. Masao was feeling well enough to finish the last of his biscuits. Akira, though he had awakened at his parents' home feeling a little refreshed, quickly lost his appetite again, and his strength, too. Deep in Akira's tissues, the rays and the black rain continued to do their work. He had slumped down in his seat and fallen into a deep but dreamless sleep.

AKIRA'S FELLOW SHIP designer and friend, Yamaguchi, was already at work. Although still feeling pain from his burns and barely able to drag himself out of bed even with his wife's help, he remained obedient to an order to present a full report about Hiroshima at the headquarters of the Mitsubishi Industrial Combine.

"Orders are orders," he told Hisako. "That's the beginning and the end of it."

At the conference room, still bandaged and bleeding, he told the executives and engineers about the woman in the black mompe—and how anyone wearing dark clothing near the flash zone had been simultaneously grilled and flayed. He told them how even a harmless twig could be propelled with bone-piercing force.

"This piercing hazard goes doubly for flying glass," Yamaguchi warned. "If a similar device should explode here, at the instant you see the flash, you must seek any shelter available, even if all you can do is duck behind a desk or a chair." He then ordered his colleagues to open every window in the room.

"This is beyond common sense," a section chief interrupted. "The damage to Hiroshima is nothing like this hoax you are trying to weave. How can one bomb turn out such energy to destroy an entire city? You are an engineer. Calculate it!"

"I already have," Yamaguchi said flatly, motioning with his one good hand toward his left arm and the left side of his face, covered with bandages.

"Exactly," the section chief said. "You were injured, Yamaguchi. Your brain was not working properly."

Outside the windows, a siren came suddenly to life again.

PREFECT NISHIOKA STILL had only one goal: to join his wife and child in the imagined safety of the Unzen national park. He was able to get a special services taxi sent to him at a station near the town of Isahaya. The dispatcher's instructions from headquarters were to return with the prefect directly to Nagasaki, but Nishioka saved the driver's life with the words, "New plan."

"You mean, we're not going to Nagasaki?" the driver asked.

"We're going to Unzen," the prefect said.

"But that's—that's way off in the opposite direction."

"I understand," he explained, and added that his new orders included a detour to Unzen.

Once again, Nishioka did not get very far. Sickness stopped him in Akira's neighborhood, in the resort town of Obama, overlooking

Ariake Bay. As he stood beside the car, wiping vomit from his lips and trying to recover his strength, a wide break in the clouds revealed a contrail very high up, reaching eleven kilometers or more. He saw twin glints of silver at the head of the contrail—meaning not one, but two B-29s, scratching a vapor trail across the heavens, traveling wing to wing. They were pointed like an arrowhead toward Nagasaki, only thirty-three kilometers away.

ALMOST AS IF NOTHING at all out of the ordinary were happening, the officer whom Ichiro Miyato was assigned to relieve stood away from the radar screen, rubbed his eyes, and offered Miyato the chair. Normally, the two "techies" liked to talk about shop or girls between shifts, but not this morning. Both of them had been worn down by a very difficult seventy-two hours of doubled-up schedules. Whenever relieved from their ten-hour screen watches, they were trucking new equipment to bomb-resistant tunnels—which, when completed, would provide retractable and more powerful radar installations that in theory could detect the invading American ships and planes at distances out to 1,000 kilometers.

Miyato could easily see that all his friend wanted to do was get out of the room and go to sleep. Looking at a blip coming down from the direction of Obama, he made a try at conversation anyway.

"What have you got?" Miyato asked.

"Only another false alarm," came the reply. He scarcely bothered to look back, as he put on a hat and left the South Kyushu compound. Miyato supposed that the intensifying schedule and the atmosphere of defeat were enough to fray the nerves of anyone, but he had expected better. At the end of the previous shift, his friend looked so exhausted that this time Miyato decided to relieve him at 10:40 a.m., even though his tour was scheduled to begin at eleven.

Miyato took his seat and watched the blip notch down from the north with the next two sweeps of the radar beam. This was nothing new to him. Surveillance planes were now joyriding all over the region, triggering at least three false alerts this very morning and generating an increasingly deadly complacency about air-raid sirens. Miyato did not want to be responsible for calling in another false Yellow Alert, so he made a note in the log book, recorded the time as 10:45, and adjusted the scanning frequencies. On the next sweep, the object looked vaguely like an echo from two separate blips, but on a subsequent sweep he could not be sure. The intruder was now putting out interference—pinging back at Miyato with its own radar.

He picked up the phone to Command Headquarters.

"What do you see?" a voice on the other end said.

"Looks like a lone B-San running radar," Miyato replied. "My guess is that it's mapping. Altitude above 10,000 meters—probably above fighter range."

"Thank you," the voice said, and hung up. Like most conversations these days, the person at the other end spoke with a curious mixture of politeness, boredom, and resignation.

Several sweeps later, Miyato noticed that the object appeared to be holding to a straight-line path. He plotted the vector and lifted the phone again.

"What do you see?" the same voice said.

"If they stay on present heading, their course will take them straight to you. It should pass directly over Nagasaki in about ten minutes. You may want to take countermeasures."

Putting the phone on speaker mode to free his hands, Miyato adjusted the scan and tried to resolve the blip more clearly; but it was interfering again, using its own radar. He poured himself a cup of tea and waited for a response. Six sweeps, two sips, and it was still following a straight-line heading. Miyato was expecting another polite "Thank you" and hang-up. He knew almost to a certainty that no interceptors would be sent. The Boeing B-29 was too high, and there simply wasn't enough reserve fuel to waste in a futile attempt to bring down a lone "stray"; and there did not even appear to be enough time.

The response Miyato received was not what he had anticipated. Two clearly agitated men were speaking in the background, and the polite voice asked, "Are you certain that you are tracking only a single plane? Is there any possibility that they are really two or three, flying in a very close formation?"

"I *did* note an anomaly about ten minutes ago. For a moment, it looked as if I might have been tracking two planes."

"Hold on!" the voice said, and cupped a hand over the phone so Miyato could not hear anything of what was being said. The blip remained on its beeline to Nagasaki. The city was only 25 kilometers from Miyato. Thirty seconds more passed, and the object inched closer to Command Headquarters.

The voice came back, more with sad resignation this time than with detached politeness: "Any change?"

"Negative. It's still on a firm heading for Nagasaki. I'm going to scan the frequencies again and see if I can get a clearer resolution of—"

"No! Keep this line open!"

"I've got you on speaker!" Miyato said, a little more sternly than was necessary. And then, more politely, he added, "I just need to keep both hands free for the radar."

"Understood," the resigned voice said, and then began to say something else but cut his words short, as if to leave unsaid, *You really don't understand.* In later years, it would occur to Miyato that what the anonymous voice actually wanted to say was, *Please stay with me. Please.*

FIFTEEN-YEAR-OLD MICHIE was about to be saved by a refusal to think like everyone else in her class and to join them in dismissing the latest air-raid alert, like the ones that preceded it, as just another false alarm.

At 10:55 a.m., Michie was located only 600 meters (or six blocks) from the hypocenter of a detonation that would be nearly three times worse than Hiroshima. When the school day's second preliminary, condition Yellow Alert sounded, her teacher ordered all of the students out of the classroom and into the tunnels that Governor Nagano's people had dug into the side of a hill, behind the playing fields and bamboo gardens of the schoolyard.

Michie's teacher never underestimated the seriousness of an alert. She hollered for the girls to *run* for the shelter, following slowly to make sure no child was left behind. Like the captain of a foundering ship, the teacher was unwilling to seek escape for herself until everyone else was safely away ahead of her. But most of Michie's friends

shuffled along through the field, talking quietly among themselves and even stopping to look around, as they marched a city block closer to the approaching hypocenter.

Only Michie and a half-dozen others actually ran to the tunnel. As usual, she entered ahead of the rest of her class.

Seven-year-old Emiko Fukahori would be saved by the same reflex. She was playing with her best friend, Sumi-chan, in a bamboo grove nearby. The grove was a favorite neighborhood gathering place for families. Sumi-chan's mother had spread a straw mat on the ground and commenced with her usual restful routine of needlework while the children played tag among the tall reeds.

Emiko was totally absorbed in a hide-and-seek chase with Sumi-chan and three other children when the siren began to howl. She stopped and scanned the skies, and through a clearing in the north she observed a distant glittering speck.

"Enemy plane!" Emiko shouted.

"It can't be an attack," Sumi-chan's mother called back, "because it's only a *preliminary* air-raid warning."

"No!" Emiko screamed. "Bad plane! *Bad plane!*" And she broke into a sprint toward one of the tunnels.

"I'll race you!" Sumi-chan shouted, and immediately outpaced her. Another child followed; then five others, shrieking and laughing. Sumi-chan's mother put down her knitting and also began to follow.

On August 9, 1945, the difference between life and death was often deter-mined by actions taken during the last few seconds before the flash. By a mar-gin of seconds, Michie Hattori would survive in one of the tunnels behind her school while several of her friends, seen walking toward the tunnels or sitting on benches outside, disappeared with much of Nagasaki's Urakami district. (Patricia Wynne)

After all, what point was there in setting a bad example during an alert? If a week or a month from now, something genuinely bad ap-proached, then demonstrating that it was okay to sit outside the shelter—should children copy such behavior—could mean all the difference in the world to them. The line between the slow and the saved, the quick and the dead, was a cheerless bisector. Razor sharp, it divided sister from friend and mother from daughter with reptilian indifference.

BARELY MORE THAN A kilometer from the school and the bamboo grove, Hajime Iwanaga, the boy who would be a *Kaiten* driver, was swimming with a classmate in the Urakami River. Being a *Kaiten* trainee had its privileges. The volunteers ate better food than the other children; and they were encouraged to take exercise breaks from work in the Mitsubishi torpedo factory. Typically, these breaks involved water sports, including contests to see which child would be first to succeed in holding his breath for more than two and a half minutes underwater.

The two boys were about a half hour into their morning break when a siren announced the approach of the *Kaiten* program's end. Looking around, they observed through an opening in the clouds what Hajime's friend believed to be "a very brave plane, flying alone over enemy territory."

Hajime did not agree. "No," he called out, "friendly plane," then dove under the water, grabbed onto some eel grass anchored to the bottom, and began to hold his breath for as long as he could.

AT FIRST, CHARLES SWEENEY did not want to believe what his eyes were seeing. Were he a more superstitious man, he would have blamed this latest serving of bad luck on having asked the forbidden question. Nagasaki was now obscured by more than 80 percent cloud cover.

On the heels of this unhappy realization, flight engineer Kuharek reconfirmed for Sweeney that *Bock's Car* would be down to flying on vapors in little more than a half hour. Only 300 gallons of fuel remained. This meant only enough flight time for a through-and-through, single-bomb run, followed by a short dash to a ditching in friendly waters. Sweeney called Navy Commander Fred Ashworth forward. He was the weapons expert, officially in charge of the bomb itself. Officially, Sweeney was only in charge of the plane.

"Here's the story, Commander," Sweeney began, summing it up as fast as he could. "If we can't drop on the first run and if we have to circle back for a second try, we might be forced to crash-land on the ground in Japan. The rule book calls for getting a visual fix on the target or we can't drop. If we don't get a visual on the first run and then depart, our best scenario is probably losing the bomb and the plane and the crew when we crash in the ocean."

"That's if we go by the book," Ashworth said.

"By the book," Sweeney acknowledged. "So, let's say *to hell with the book*, and with its 'no-win' scenario, and let's put a little faith in the new imaging radar. I'll personally guarantee we come within . . . well—within a few hundred feet of the target."

"You mean, maybe within a half-mile?"

"Let's be a little real here, okay? With this thing, a miss is as good as a mile."

"I don't know, Chuck," Ashworth said.

"It's better than losing it in the ocean, isn't it?"

Ashworth nodded, and asked cautiously, "Are you sure of the accuracy?"

"I'll take full responsibility for this," Sweeney said.

"Okay, then. Let's go for it."

There was no time for discussion with the navigator or the bombardier. Sweeney had confidence that they knew exactly what to do. Jim Van Pelt checked his navigational figures and Ed Buckley monitored the outlines of the city on his radar scope, inviting verification from Van Pelt. Buckley then called out the headings and precise closure rates to bombardier Kermit Beahan, who fed the data into the world's first portable computer—which weighed almost as much as a Jeep and was connected directly to the bombsight.

The outlines of the city were fuzzy at the edges, but the river and the rail lines were reasonably easy to see, and all three men were confident that the machines would work. Just the same, Beahan continued searching for a break in the cloud cover.

"You own it," Sweeney announced, and turned command of the plane and its payload over to his bombardier.

"I've got it! I've got it!" Beahan suddenly shouted. He wasn't acknowledging control of the plane, but rather a hole in the cloud cover that was yawning open near the Mitsubishi armament factories in the industrial valley. The hole was more than two kilometers upriver of the assigned aiming point—almost into the wrong town, with much of Nagasaki now shielded behind low hills. It looked to Sweeney as if the suburb of Urakami, and not Nagasaki proper, was going to be Ground Zero. Beahan locked on to the oval outline of the Urakami racetrack as a reference point and fed whatever last-minute course adjustments could be made into Sweeney's indicator panel.

Thirty seconds from release, the tone signal was activated, the bomb-bay doors snapped open, and *Great Artiste*, flying nearby and ready to drop its three monitoring cylinders, simultaneously opened its own bomb-bay doors.

The tone fell silent and *Bock's Car* lurched upward, suddenly five tons lighter.

"Bomb's away," Beahan announced, and then quickly corrected himself: "*Bomb* away."

7

A VAPOR IN THE HEAVENS

Three hundred kilometers away in Hiroshima, Dr. Hachiya lay on his back on a charred bedframe, looking up into a cloudy sky and wondering what alarm had shaken him awake. Something deep-rooted and instinctive crept out of Hachiya's subconscious, filling him with a strange belief that thousands of voices had just cried out.

Glancing down at the Hiroshima wilderness and trying to determine the direction of the sun, he guessed that it was about 11:00 a.m. No one was calling out from the prairie in alarm, or making any other noises. Central Hiroshima was as silent as a tomb—which, essentially, it was.

The night before, once Hachiya had come to accept the city as another Pompeii, he became ever so slightly less restless, and was able to snatch two or three hours' sleep at a time. Shortly before sunrise, he dozed off, and slept until awakened about nine o'clock by a surprise visit from an old schoolmate, Mr. Okamoto of the Communications Ministry. Three days earlier, Okamoto almost became part of the ash and debris in Hiroshima Castle's foundations—and it should have ended for him that way, if not for a near-fatal reaction to a bee sting 40 kilometers away, in the town of Kure.

"That bee saved your life," Hachiya had said; and as the two men laughed about a strange swerve of fate, the doctor realized he could sit up without pain.

After his friend left, he waited until none of the other medical staff were watching and tried to stand, but the stitches began to pull at his shoulders and hips, and he was obliged to lie down again, crestfallen and exhausted. He had slept from then until now.

Why, he wondered, did he feel as if a spectral hand had suddenly reached out and shaken him awake? Dr. Hachiya did not believe in the motility of consciousness—or in anything like the meaning nurse Minami and the rest of Dr. Fujii's crew had taken from the blue fireflies—and yet, for an instant, a bone-chilling sense of dread stole into him, and seemed intent on staying.

The same hand that shook Hachiya awake grabbed all four legs of his bed and shook again, and the doctor began to laugh at himself, and to calm down. When all was said and done, it registered as a most gentle shaking: *A baby sine wave quivering through soft earth*, Hachiya told himself. *Richter 2; Richter 3 or 4, at most.*

The shaking continued for several seconds more, dislodging little drifts of soot that had been lying for days on a blackened pipe overhead.

Richter 3 or 4, he told himself again. *It's just an earthquake, nothing more.* Then, from 183 miles away in the south, a low rumbling roar reverberated through the heavens, building to a loud crack that definitely was not the sound of an earthquake.

Hachiya drew a deep breath, held it wistfully, and expelled it in a sigh.

ICHIO MIYATO'S RADAR station was located almost halfway between Clarence Graham's prison camp and Ground Zero. At 11:02 a.m., Miyato had just told the anonymous controlled voice at Command Headquarters, "The object should be over Nagasaki now—" when his radar screen overloaded and went completely blank. Simultaneously, the wires inside the speaker phone were seared. During a chip of time in which the telephone at the other end of the line began to vaporize, the many kilometers of intervening wire swept up some small measure of the *pika*'s electromagnetic pulse, and conveyed the

surge toward Miyato at light speed. Had he been holding the telephone receiver to his ear, both he and the officer at the other end of
the line would have died at precisely the same instant, though they
were more than 25 kilometers apart.

At a radius of 63 kilometers, Clarence Graham could not tell
where the flash came from. It arrived as an all-encompassing brightness, filling the whole sky and then only slowly beginning to fade.
The energy released by the Hiroshima bomb was not quite equivalent to 10 kilotons of TNT. The Nagasaki bomb blazed forth at
greater than 22 kilometers, and nearer to 28–30 kilotons; so even at
Clarence Graham's distance of 38 miles, it loomed large—first with
stinging bright light; then, many seconds later, with a great tremor in
the ground. The airburst arrived almost a half-minute after the
tremor—manifesting as a strong wind that came from the direction
of Nagasaki. And, following the first wind, there came a second hot,
hot wind—"terribly hot," Graham would recall, "hotter than direct
sun on your face." And next came a brief lull, as if a typhoon had now
passed overhead and the prisoners were standing in the calm of its
eye—and, just like the rapid passing of a typhoon's eye wall, a strong
blast struck suddenly from the opposite direction, rushing backward
toward Nagasaki. The third wind was so strong that it toppled some
of the weaker prisoners.

Clarence remained standing—perplexed; but he observed that
one of the prison guards seemed to know what was happening, and
more, to understand it. The huge dome of a rising sun appeared over
the hills in the southwest; and this single guard glared as if analyzing
the fireball, as it turned white and ascended on a column of smoke.

All of the guards except this one stood in awed and confused silence. The one who understood—the one Clarence had listed among
the most sadistic in the camp—offered a prisoner water and a ration
of food, and said, "You and I are now friends."

You've got to be fucking kidding, Clarence told himself. And he
wondered what the guard really understood about the fire in the sky.

THIRTY KILOMETERS NEARER THE hypocenter, at a radius of nearly
twenty miles, Prefect Nishioka covered his face from the flash—and

still, when he opened his eyes several seconds later, the golden-white ball rising above the city was so brilliant he was forced to close his eyes again.

"Don't look at it!" he shouted to his driver, and to anyone else who would listen. "Get under shelter—right away!"

Glancing back, the prefect saw, on the surface of the water, a spreading white arc racing toward him from across the bay. Behind the expanding arc, the entire sea surface was turning white. Nishioka estimated that the people of Obama had about fifteen seconds.

"Hurry!" he hollered one last time. Shock waves traveled much faster through rock than through air, so he did not have to shout his orders a third time. The ground itself was already booming, frightening everyone into immediate action. A half-dozen men ran ahead of the prefect and dove into a well-protected space behind a bus. Nishioka's driver fell in on top of him—followed by a hammerhead of compressed air that smashed windows and almost tipped the bus on its side. Nishioka kept his head down through the lull and the back-blast, which pulled the bus in the opposite direction and nearly toppled a house. When he looked again, most of the cumulus clouds that had been there a minute before were gone, and the atomic cloud was now towering more than sixteen kilometers over the city—the color of a muddy white cloth mixed with splashes of fresh blood.

He did not believe that anything could grow so tall, in only a few seconds.

"Shall we continue to Unzen?" the driver asked.

"No," the prefect replied, suddenly no longer aware of how sick he had been feeling. "We must go back to Nagasaki."

"OH, NO—NOT AGAIN," Kenshi cried out to his father.

This time, he actually heard one of the planes straining to turn around and fly away from the bomb, sounding at one point as if it were flying straight at him. Once again, he was slightly more than three kilometers away from the center of the explosion, owing to the fact that the home of Setsuko's parents—located dead center between several key military targets and therefore near the original aiming point of Sweeney's bomb—had been obscured by clouds during the critical three minutes of *Bock's Car*'s final targeting maneuver.

At the moment of the bomb's release, the puffy white clouds that covered most of the river valley were pulling apart on the opposite side of Kompira Hill, above Urakami Stadium. Instead of Kenshi's witnessing his second nuclear explosion from beneath the actual aiming point, the target had shifted abruptly, almost two miles up-river, away from Kompira's southern ridge and central Nagasaki.

The first time, distance combined with a voice in his head and an instinct to stay away from the windows until the blast wave passed had kept Kenshi alive. This time—in the presence of a bomb three times worse—what saved Kenshi was not so much a matter of distance and response as the shielding provided by Kompira Hill. Despite the greater fury of the plutonium device, Kenshi found the blast and roar "not so terrible as in Hiroshima." He would not be aware for some time to come how a small mountain (standing only 366 meters high) had shadow-shielded him from the heat rays and shock-cocooned him from the blast. Not very far from where Kenshi and his father stood, at the same radius from the hypocenter—and all within those same few seconds—people down in the shipyard were simultaneously flash-grilled, uplifted, shotgunned by flying glass, and hurled through walls. On the other side of Kompira Hill, almost everyone who witnessed the *pika* was either grievously grilled or dead.

Walking through a neighborhood that if not for a cloud bank would have been located deep within the circle of Ground Zero, Kenshi was buffeted by a harsh wind and saw only a few roof tiles loosened. And after the wind had passed, dragonflies still flitted about, seemingly unshaken. *But the bones*—little Setsuko's bones, to which he had made offerings of flowers and rice and which he had held close to his chest for most of two days—the bomb had ripped the cover from Kenshi's wedding bowl and flung the bones out of his hands.

"All this way," Kenshi said to his father, weeping. "All this way, and her bones are scattered who knows where—and to what purpose?"

There *was* no purpose. No dignity in it, either, Kenshi told himself. No purpose. No dignity. No purpose.

Except, Setsuko might have said, *to bear witness.*

ONLY ONCE BEFORE had more than a hundred thousand voices cried out together in startled surprise. Half of them yelled again. The other half ceased to be.

The bombing survey photographs—and hence the history books—would record much of the Nagasaki shoreline's architecture standing intact, and this would help to create for many the false impression that the Nagasaki bomb was not so bad as the Hiroshima bomb. The most enduring photographs of Ground Zero, including those showing a Catholic church, the Yosē Girls' School, and the Mitsubishi Steelworks—all reduced to protruding nubs of structural bone on an otherwise featureless plain—would memorialize Urakami, not Nagasaki.

Despite Charles Sweeney's guarantee to Commander Ashworth, the bomb missed Nagasaki and obliterated the district next door. It opened in the hot, overcast sky above Matsuyama, the riverfront section of Urakami. The blast rebounded against the valley walls on either side of the Urakami River the way a shotgun blast is focused down the barrel of a gun. Ground Zero, the zone where everything was essentially leveled, ran 3.2 kilometers upriver and an equal two miles south; and it spread just under a half kilometer (or nearly six city blocks) east and west of either bank. On the other side of a valley wall, not very far from Kenshi Hirata's neighborhood, Dr. Paul Nagai's four-year-old daughter Kayano was playing in the village of Koba. She survived in a shadow-shielded eddy, behind a small mountain called Kawabira, which completely blocked the flash and the wind radiating out of Urakami.

Kayano's older brother Makoto had taken her down to a local stream for a swim with a cousin and some of the neighborhood children. After the *pika* (the flash) and the *don* (the blast), the grass on Kayano's side of the valley, in the shadow of the mountain, remained green and virtually unruffled. Viewed from high above, Kayano's cocoon survived as one of several islands of green in a sea of desiccated brown leaves and gray ash. Yet very soon, her cocoon was to experience a strange rain of yellow oil, and the stream would not run clear again for a very long time.

The light, when it came, was completely silhouetted by the mountain, making the peak look black against streamers of bright red. Then, on the heels of the red, came a flash of blue. "The red was bright enough to stun a person," Kayano's cousin Fujie would recall—but once the heat ray and the compression waves had squeezed the nearest clouds out of existence, the blue was no longer filtered out and blazed forth bright enough to cause a slight sunburn, even behind the mountain's shadow.

Both flashes—the red and the blue—came within the first half-second. During that same part of a second, directly opposite the sheltered side of the stream—outside the shadow of Mount Kawabira and directly in the glow of the bomb—rooftops and chickens and clothing sent up vertical columns of smoke. People on the stream's far side, just like people caught outdoors throughout Hiroshima and in downtown Urakami, became like ants smoldering under the focused sunbeam of some diabolical schoolboy's magnifying glass. As the glare faded, the grayish-black columns of smoke rose three meters or more, over the monk's robes, the child's mompe, the gardener's hat, the refugee's rags. Chickens running away from gardens and lawns sent up more erratic columns—until, after three or four seconds, the shock wave crested the hill, overflew Kayano's head, and slammed down on the far side.

The little stream in the center of the ravine seemed to divide Kayano's world in two: one side normal and alive and still inhabited by butterflies, the other side strange and terrible, populated only by dead or unconscious people and blackened, twitching chickens.

Looking directly overhead, little Kayano saw "from the other side of the big green mountain a giant tree rising into the sky." A tree made of fire, she recalled. "First it was all red but then it began to be different colors—oh, so bright! The tree made my eyes hurt. And just then, my brother came running up from [the protected side of] the stream. He was all excited and he said, 'My goodness! What was that? That plane must have crashed into the sun!' Sure enough, the sun was no longer shining. I looked up at it through that awful cloud and it was the color of a dead thing."

And then the ravine became suddenly dark, and cold. Astonishingly cold, and as black as night. Things began falling out of the cloud—impossible things: flurries of burning paper . . . a door frame . . . a singed cat that hissed, and ran away . . . the hood of a fire truck . . . and farther afield the head of a woman who seemed still alive. There wasn't even a sign of bleeding. A gold tooth gleamed in her wide-open mouth. Then the raindrops came, as wide as pearls, and greasy.

Kayano's brother took her by the hand and led her behind a sasanqua tree. "There were pumpkins—and lots of pretty strawberries all around," she would write years later. But Kayano did not feel like eating strawberries. Ever again. Not after the head and the cat and the oily, yellowish-black rain.

AT APPROXIMATELY THIS same radius, Dr. Nagai's friend Takami-san was one of the people Kayano saw on the "wrong side" of the stream. Outside the mountain's shadow shield, he left a shadow of his own, as a patch of unburned grass.

Even at a distance of nearly 9 kilometers (almost 4.5 miles), one whole side of Takami-san's body was severely "sunburned" by the *pika*. He lived for barely a week, but it was not the heat ray that killed him. Before the boy died, Dr. Nagai recorded that he was succumbing to an unknown source of intense radiation. Nagai believed that either some metallic object had been simultaneously irradiated and hurled into the sky or that something from the bomb itself had rained down upon the young man; for he had lived long enough to describe strange fireballs rocketing straight down at him from the direction of the *pika*. Takami-san was returning to the neighborhood stream with his cow when the flash came. The cow saw it, too, and lifted her head. Takami-san felt nothing at first and happened to be facing away from the light. He saw the cow burst into flames, and then realized that silent white balls of fire seemed to be raining down upon both of them. Two or three had struck the cow, killing her instantly. One struck Takami-san's foot, all but burning it off.

Dr. Nagai noted in his medical log that it did not seem to matter that the boy was located at a reasonably safe distance from the *pika-don* when the strange balls of light came after him. There were several such cases and Nagai recorded that even if the fireballs grazed the extremities of the hands and feet, everyone touched by them succumbed quickly to symptoms of radiation poisoning.

BARELY MORE THAN two kilometers closer to the hypocenter, the train carrying Masao the kite-maker and Akira the shipbuilder had just passed Urakami's Michinoo Station when Masao heard the familiar strains of a propeller-driven B-29 trying so hard to get away from something that it dove perilously close to splattering in pieces through the sound barrier.

"Get down!" he shouted to the other passengers, rolling to the floor and saving the lives of many who followed his example.

During the next twenty or thirty seconds, the plane slowly faded into the distance. A man laughed and stood up. Then another. And another.

"Stay down," Masao warned. "It's a new kind of bomb. When the flash comes, you need to—"

The entire car was bathed in a stark, silent white light. Masao's hands were covering his eyes and ears, but he felt the hair on an exposed eyebrow sizzle and curl up. By now, almost everyone was heeding his warning, but some who were still standing, and who had not covered their eyes, fell victim to an involuntary reflex to look in the direction of the flash. Their retinas began to scorch even before a secondary reflex—shortcutting through a nerve arc faster than the actual pain of the scorch—tried to stop them from looking.

The cries of pain from those still standing shocked Akira out of his radiation-induced sleep. Because he had seen this awful thing before, he was hiding under his seat long ahead of the airburst. He and Masao counted off five seconds or more, between the *pika* and the *don*. Those passengers who had not responded to Masao's warning, and who stood with their eyes burned, were shotgunned from waist to head by fragmenting windows traveling at more than half the speed of sound.

The train's conductor was one of those who had looked directly at the *pika*, and who was now completely blind. If there was any saving grace at all, to keep Masao's and Akira's train from reenacting Hiroshima's occurrence at Kaidaichi Ridge, it was that this time the dead-man's switch remained operational, and brought the train to a stop as soon as the conductor removed his hands from the controls.

A conductor's assistant came stumbling through Akira's car, urging passengers to evacuate the train and take shelter in the woods nearby. The man's face was a scarlet stew.

A half kilometer nearer the hypocenter, but shadowed behind (and inside) a hill, Governor Nagano and his entourage survived without even being scratched. The mayor of Sasebo was summarizing what the commander of Hiroshima's Naval Station had reported when the shelter's electric lights failed. Nagano was ready to order start-up of the emergency generators when it seemed to him that the doors to the shelter were suddenly pulled open and far more light than he was about to call for came streaming in, accompanied by what sounded like either several very large planes or a multi-ton bomb crashing very nearby.

When Nagano stepped outside, he saw the shelter's construction workers gathered on a steep hill and looking toward Urakami. The hill's contours and its position had placed the workers and everything in their vicinity off to one side of a shotgun's barrel, instead of positioning them like fleas inside the barrel. A tremendous pall of smoke was rising over the valley walls from the direction of Urakami, but as the governor climbed toward the workers, the hill allowed a view only of lower Nagasaki—which appeared to be standing unharmed. Glancing back, Nagano was surprised to see that his house had suffered no damage at all. Not a single window appeared to have been cracked, and all the flowerpots on either side of the front steps were still in place.

The *pika-don* effect had been bright and noisy, and what Nagano saw and heard in the shelter seemed consistent with what Prefect Nishioka had described about a new weapon used against Hiroshima. Yet Nishioka's conviction that Nagasaki would be the next city destroyed by an atomic bomb seemed both anticlimactic and

puzzling when the governor looked around and saw his administrative quarters and the region he administered surviving essentially
unchanged.

Nagano was beginning to suspect that the prefect's story about
square kilometer after square kilometer of buildings blown down
had been exaggerated. And then he reached the workers on the crest
of the ridge, and saw much of Urakami transformed into a giant crematorium, where a mountain of flame appeared to be growing out of
the earth. The mountain was slowly rotating, creating a vortex of
fresh, inrushing air to supply itself with oxygen. As the flames rose,
convection effects drew gales in from both ends of the valley—force-
feeding the firestorm.

By some accounts the fire mountain, acting more like an actual
hurricane of flame than a mere column or pyre, was unable to draw
in enough oxygen to sustain runaway growth. At times, it seemed to
stall and even to flare out, sending forth great waves of black suffo-
cating fumes.

On a side of the storm opposite Governor Nagano's hilltop vantage point, only 850 meters (or almost 10 blocks) from the center of
the blast and not very far from the tunnels in which Michie and
Emiko had taken shelter, junior high school student Tamotsu Eguchi
had just crawled out from under the debris of his school. Looking up,
he beheld the outer skirt of a cyclone whose flame and smoke surged
almost to the altitude of a small seaplane that had apparently strayed
way in the wrong direction, and seemed on the verge of falling like a
dead bird.

What most mystified Tamotsu was the realization that, given his
close proximity to whatever had flattened his school and created the
wall of flame, and given that the school building was wooden, the
wood itself had never caught fire. He appeared to have been near
the center of a great wind that had blown out all of the fires nearby.
On opposite sides of the blown-down school—upriver and downriver—at least two giant cyclones of fire were trying to be born. One
had begun to suffocate and was collapsing into a sea of smoke. But
near the outer wall of the still-living storm, burning objects several
meters across were being uprooted and carried skyward. When the
skirt of the monster stalled and its flames appeared occasionally to

be snuffed out, Tamotsu was able to catch clear glimpses of the wreckage as it fell to earth: the upper portion of a trolley car . . . the roof of a house . . . the tail end of a small boat, shooting out its own flames as it tumbled end over end.

AT MOMENT ZERO, seven-year-old Emiko had been only the second child out of the bamboo garden and into the shelter. Located near the 600-meter mark, where the light from the bomb lanced the earth at an angle of almost exactly 45 degrees, she raced inside just a few steps behind her friend Sumi-chan. A third child—laughing loudly and almost close enough to tag Emiko on the back—was caught in the glare and all but ceased to exist. Glancing over her shoulder, Sumi-chan thought the third child looked like a beautiful sculpture in her final instant, outlined by a blue atomic aurora. Emiko also flashed with the radiance of a solar corona. She felt an intense heat touching her shoulders and her neck, even though she and Sumi-chan were deep in the shadows of the tunnel.

When she and Sumi-chan stepped outside again, they found their friends seared and literally stamped into the ground. Some were still breathing, but they quickly died one after another. Emiko forgot that her home should have been visible across the now missing bamboo grove. Sumi-chan was just beginning to register—though not with complete understanding—the fact that her mother had disappeared. Neither child had begun to surmise the possibility that they were now orphaned.

Only Emiko's older brother had survived long enough to come looking for them. Shielded outdoors from both the flash and the blast, the sky-shine effect had pierced him. Soon, he would start suffering nosebleeds. Believing himself lucky to have escaped the bomb without any serious burns, he was fated to vomit up disintegrating chunks of his own tongue, along with the lining of his stomach. The final bleeding out would be so extreme that it was to be recalled a generation later that the boy's corpse contained no blood at all.

Emiko's mother had been running an errand more than two kilometers beyond the hypocenter when the storm began. Her sister and younger brother were with her in the end; and Emiko would soon learn from a kindly, radiation-doomed uncle that her last two siblings died weeping over her mother's body.

Emiko and her friend looked up at the storm. Vast, radiant, and indifferent, it swelled and stalled, and tried to rear up again. For all the storm's fury, the children's world seemed eerily silent.

Thinking of her whole world, and not just of her family or herself, Emiko began to believe that she and Sumi-chan were the only ones left alive.

Not very far away, at the entrance to another tunnel, Michie Hattori was now coming to a similar belief. She had been standing inside the shelter, calling for the other fifteen-year-olds to hurry and join her when the brightest light she had ever seen blazed through the clouds and into the cave, flashing down violet and then bleaching even the back of the cave a brilliant, brilliant white. Though she was safely inside, the light itself, reflecting off ground and atmosphere, blasted Michie with a great heat. In the next second, the *pika* seemed to flash more dimly, shifting canary yellow and sapphire pink, and through that crevice in time, Michie thought she saw her classmates "skeletonizing," as if the rays were so bright that one could actually see them shining through clothing and flesh, and silhouetting bones. The girls' clothing and skin had begun bursting into flames when the airburst reached down and scattered them like bowling pins. Michie believed she saw nothing for a while after that. The same powerful wind that beat down upon her friends shotgunned her toward the rear of the tunnel; then in an instant, just before she would otherwise have been smashed against the back wall, the wind reversed direction and drew her out through the tunnel's entrance.

Though shielded from direct exposure to the flash, the heated air had singed Michie's hands and face before it pulled her out of the tunnel and rose to join the fireball. Once she looked around she realized that most of her classmates were barely more than shivering corpses. The skeletons she had seen silhouetted through the light were still clothed in flesh, though there was very little life left in any of them.

The strange horrors Dean Tsuno witnessed in Hiroshima were now manifesting for the children of the shelter. One of the older girls pleaded to Michie, "Come, help me to get away from here."

Unable to think of anything else to do, Michie reached down and pulled her up by one hand; but the girl seemed to lose her grip and she fell slowly to the ground. Michie was still holding her class-mate's hand—or what appeared to be all the skin of her hand and arm, down to the elbow. Like a long glove, the charred and blast-loosened skin had pulled away. Michie could see the girl's shadow imprinted where she had been sitting and talking with someone when the *pika* came.

About the time the shadow girl died, the only other classmate to make it into the tunnel ahead of the heat ray walked up behind Michie and suggested, "I think we should go back to the school."

Her name was Fumiko, and she seemed transfixed by the roiling black clouds overhead and the bright flames off to one side. The clouds were so dark that they blocked out the sun like a total eclipse, rendering the wall of flame the only real source of illumination.

"*Shigoku*," Fumiko called it, which meant hell. She could not take her eyes away from the objects falling out of the sky and whirl-ing aloft into the cyclone of fire. Exploded houses and all of their contents had gone spiraling up. A whole library of burning books came flapping down across the hundred-meter desert that now sepa-rated the shelter from the school. The bow section of a fishing boat came crashing down amid the books and was quickly followed by what Michie at first believed to be several sets of bars from the Urakami prison.

Fumiko corrected her: "They must be animal cages from the zoo."

Bars from hell, Michie thought. This was the closest she ever wanted to come to *shigoku*.

Save for the strange meteors, the route to the school was flat and empty. Michie began to accept the idea that sunflower gardens could be ironed into the ground and turned black in an instant, and that buildings could disappear. "Weren't there houses here when we went to the shelter?"

Fumiko did not answer. She ran about thirty meters ahead into the smoke and gloom, and began calling excitedly for Michie to fol-low. She was pointing toward a large black reptile that appeared to be waddling toward them on its belly from the direction of another fallen cage.

"See!" Fumiko said. "I told you they were cages from the zoo. The alligator has escaped."

This did not make sense to Michie. All the zoos had been closed and there were no longer any animals in them. The alligator did not seem to know this and lay in their path to the school anyway. Fumiko hefted a broken piece of concrete in one hand and approached with caution, raising the rock above her head and ready to throw it at the animal's head if it did not allow them to peacefully pass it by.

Fumiko's footsteps stopped abruptly, and she started screaming. The face looking up at her from the alligator's body was human. No clothes or hair were visible—nothing except large, scale-like burns that resembled the alligator-skin pattern on burned wood. Fumiko's screams prevented Michie from hearing what the face was trying to say. She could only see that it appeared to be begging for something— probably water, Michie guessed later.

The head fell forward, facedown in the dirt and the piles of smoldering books. The alligator man did not move again. One minute later Fumiko dropped the rock and fell to her knees, still shrieking. Michie knelt down beside her.

WHERE JOSÉ MATSOU SURVIVED, not even alligator people still stirred. At eleven o'clock, she had been part of a bucket brigade assigned to remove water from a newly dug air-raid tunnel, 185 meters (or approximately two blocks) from the hypocenter, on land that was eventually to be named Nagasaki Peace Park.

Survival in a basement beneath the bomb or in a steel-reinforced building, or in a multi-storied house, was just barely possible in Hiroshima. In Urakami, a great deal more shielding was required. At the instant of the *pika-don*, José was working deeper inside the tunnel than the other fifty-two women in her brigade. Six meters of overlying dirt combined with fifty meters of tunnel protected her from more than 98 percent of the prompt radiation effects. Along the tunnel's length, the intervening water, carbon, and iron in the bodies of the other women blocked off and attenuated the rest. In addition to becoming radiation shielding, those women nearest the tunnel entrance became natural dampers against much of the heat that was trying to reach in toward José.

Death came to them within one two-hundredth of a second, and two-tenths of a second after that all the soft tissues in their bodies became incandescent gas. Vaporizing brain matter and blood tried to escape through the eyeless sockets of a woman's skull as jets of black steam, but the sudden rise of pressure was so great that the skull exploded from the inside.

What happened during the next tenth of a second probably saved José's life—by a very slim margin, if the large oak tree standing near a tennis court overhead served history correctly. At precisely the instant that a combination of steam pressure from the tunnel entrance and the first impact of the lower hemisphere of the bomb's shock bubble sent a wave of dense air shooting toward the back of the tunnel, the blast rippled down the tree trunk's sides from directly above. The trunk, though stripped of its branches and seared to a depth of several centimeters, remained sufficiently intact to indicate that once the deadly precursor waves began bunching together and surging outward in every direction, the very center of the impacting hemisphere was back-blasted skyward. Still within a time frame of milliseconds, the shock bubble began to deform and implode; the back-blast from the ground began to form the stem of the fireball and the tree's shredded branch stumps were raked upward as the forces that initially shot down against the trunk and the hypocenter suddenly reversed direction.

Inside the tunnel, the steam jets and the rapid rise in air pressure instantly killed twenty or thirty more of the women standing between José and the entrance; and if not for the almost simultaneous vacuum effect outside, the rear wall of the tunnel would have become, for José, an insider's view of a pipe bomb. And yet, though the jets of steam were drawn out of the cave almost the moment they burst toward her, José suffered blistering burns and was knocked instantly unconscious. She would remain asleep in the back of the tunnel for three days, until a rescuer found her still breathing, and carried her on his back to the ruins of a Urakami hospital.

José's husband had been on the surface at 11:02 a.m., assigned by the military to work on a larger shelter designed by Prefect Nishioka. He had surely died nearby. In the building to which he had been sent, not a single stone still lay upon another stone that was not thrown down.

José had married a stone mason–carpenter, one of the hardest workers she would ever know. When she joined his church and became a Catholic, she remained true to her unconventional side and chose a male apostle's name for herself—José, in honor of Jesus' brother, who was adopted by a carpenter.

Just as unconventionally, the once-orphaned José honored her parents' memory by keeping her maiden name in marriage. Her husband, Zenkichi Kawaguchi, had always been exceptionally kind and considerate to her; so as soon as she was well, she would make a Hirata-like journey to the hypocenter, searching for any trace of him. When none was found, she would place a sample of soil from the hill above her shelter in a small container, and she would convince two Jesuit priests to hold a funeral service without a body. Then, until her death in 1975, José would keep Zenkichi's picture with her always, along with a vial of constantly half-lifing Urakami dust.

CADET KOMATSU WAS STATIONED ten minutes' flying time from Urakami when the naval air base at Sasebo was rocked by shock waves. A false sunrise in the direction of Nagasaki meant only one thing to him: the Truman announcement was not an exaggeration, and this was another Hiroshima.

Komatsu and two of his friends boarded a seaplane and flew toward the target for a close-up view of the cloud. The flight was unauthorized and in direct disobedience of orders, but as almost anyone who could fly a plane was being "volunteered" to kamikaze duty, Komatsu asked his friends, "What can they do? Kill us?" He would tell future historians that he, fellow cadet Tomimura, and Chief Petty Officer Umeda suspected that the war might soon be over, and this could be their last chance to "sky surf" an atomic cloud.

Komatsu's friends laughed at his joke about their "last chance," and the story they lived to tell arose from a remarkable combination of initiative and luck, mixed with mid-morning alcohol and the Japanese equivalent of the words, "I double-dog dare you."

By 11:15 a.m., their plane emerged through clouds on one side of the Urakami Valley and Komatsu saw a broad pillar of black smoke looming straight ahead. He was flying at a height of three kilometers—and from this 10,000-foot vantage point, the top of the "mushroom" already towered more than nine kilometers overhead. The cap was a massive storm on a stem—swelling up and fading slowly from an orange-red ring to a ball of white vapor.

Komatsu banked hard to port and began to circle the mushroom's stem, little bothered by large objects falling out of the cloud—a whole section of roof sweeping by like a giant fly swatter, a crate trailing what looked for all the world like a swarm of tennis rackets, the saucer-shaped lid of a water tower, and endless streamers of burning paper.

Everything below was boiling dust. The men's moods alternated abruptly between wonder and horror, laughter and tears. They could see nothing of Urakami or upper Nagasaki through the churning fog. At twenty of twelve, Komatsu announced, "We've circled long enough," and decided to ride into the cloud. Adding spice to the danger of his adventure, Komatsu slid the cockpit window open and extended his gloved hand outside. Dust burned through the leather like a blast of live steam and within two seconds he had pulled his hand in and sealed the window again, but it was too late.

The world outside had gone completely dark and the cabin was now filled with yellowish-brown mist; and Komatsu's glove was covered with sticky black matter. In the co-pilot's seat, Tomimura's eyes were suddenly burning and he could barely see the control panel. No more than five seconds after Komatsu burned his hand, the engine overheated and began to sputter. The air intakes were sucking in tremendous quantities of dust, along with something like burned twig fragments mixed with a hot, gluey liquid. By the time the plane burst into daylight again several seconds later, Umeda was already vomiting. Tomimura opened his window and cleared the heat and dust out of the cabin, fighting off his own sudden surge of nausea.

By now the engine was beginning to make noises like a vacuum cleaner sucking up chunks of taffy-coated glass, and Komatsu felt the plane dying in his hands. Fortunately, he was flying a seaplane—easy to control even in a glide with a dying engine.

Fighting off his own onset of nausea and weakness, Komatsu descended around one side of the mushroom stem in a long arc. Taking advantage of a fire-induced updraft, Komatsu was able to gain enough altitude to aim the plane toward a landing in the bay before his engine "gave up the ghost." He had hoped to stay aloft long enough to take photographs, but the heat of the Urakami updraft forced him to veer off and set down as quickly as possible.

As soon as the pontoons touched water and the plane came to a stop, they dove in and washed the gluey, stinging dust off their bodies. As if to prove that human bodies were not machines, each responded differently to whatever poisonous isotopes had entered the plane, exposing them each equally. Umeda seemed to recover after vomiting blood and descending into a short-lived delirium. He would die of leukemia two years later. Tomimura would die of leukemia in 1964. Cadet Komatsu would survive into the 1970s, with a burn on one hand that never healed.

BOCK'S CAR WAS long gone by the time Komatsu rode into the cloud at 11:40 a.m.

At 11:01, the bomb-bay doors had snapped shut and Sweeney took the B-29 into a steep 155-degree turn to port, diving along a northeasterly Tibbets trajectory. By now Sweeney had become somewhat addicted to the time-dilation illusion that accompanied high-adrenaline situations. He never ceased to be fascinated by the sense of a single second stretching out to whole minutes—or to occasionally be tricked by the effect. The expected detonation seemed never to come; and Sweeney was beginning to wonder if he had dropped a dud when, 42 seconds after the bomb-bay door closed, the entire horizon was bathed from behind in a super-brilliant burst of light, far more intense than the Hiroshima flash. Then, even in a state of suspended time, the shock of heated air recoiling from the *pika* seemed to come very quickly, striking with unexpected force. At Hiroshima, Sweeney had experienced four distinct shock waves of rapidly diminishing fury, while Joseph Fuoco, though evidently closer to the bomb in *Necessary Evil,* had noticed barely any shock waves. But here, each shock was like a flak bomb bursting right outside the windows—and at least five of them came one after another, with equal force.

After Charles Sweeney completed his turn and the last of the shock waves died away, he looked back. The top of the plume was rising much faster than at Hiroshima—alive with those strange purple and orange hues, colors whose brilliance he had seen only once before and hoped he would never see again. The cloud continued to accelerate upward after it passed Sweeney at 30,000 feet, and it continued shooting up to at least 45,000 feet, almost to the edge of space. The Nagasaki cloud seemed more intense, more angry.

Sweeney's flight engineer reported that *Bock's Car* had just under 300 gallons of fuel remaining and was 350 miles away from Okinawa, the nearest gas station and landing field in the neighborhood. The math was depressingly simple: using approximately one gallon per mile, they would fall fifty miles short of Okinawa, splashing down on water about the same time as Komatsu's plane.

Despite the fuel shortage, Sweeney continued to bank to one side, to allow his bombardier to begin writing an assessment of the strike.

Sweeney, who knew every street and railway yard of the valley, made his own quick assessment. The center of the mushroom's stalk was rising over the Urakami district, with a terrific firestorm breaking out on one side. The high slopes along one whole face of the valley appeared to be aflame, while the center of downtown Nagasaki, sheltered behind a ridge of hills separating the Urakami Valley from the coastal plain, looked as if it might have survived. This outcome was fine with Sweeney. The focus of the impact, though considerably northward of the original aiming point, was still concentrated near enough to the Morimachi industrial plants, the Mitsubishi steelworks, the Mitsubishi shipworks, and the Mitsubishi torpedo factory. There was no doubt in the pilot's mind that, in a single stroke, the name Mitsubishi had been stricken down forever.

"FRIENDLY PLANE!" HAJIME had called out as *Bock's Car* approached. Then he dove under the water in a contest with another *Kaiten* boy to see who could hold his breath longer. At Moment

Zero, they happened to be swimming near the Mitsubishi torpedo factory. Conserving energy by holding on to river-bottom eel grass instead of kicking with his arms and legs to stay down and fight the currents, Hajime found the first forty seconds quite easy, and believed he might hold out for a minute and a half longer, when the *pika* erupted.

Even under more than two meters of muddy water, with his eyelids instantly snapping shut, the flash was dazzlingly bright. Because water was not packed with large heavy nuclei that could be chipped and accelerated—and even the occasionally accelerated oxygen ion could not travel very far through the liquid shield—a few feet of water provided better shielding against gamma rays and neutrons than lead or steel. If one had to be caught near the hypocenter of a nuclear explosion, then underwater was definitely the right place to be. His only injury—caused by the apparent lensing effect of a ripple on the water's surface—had focused a narrow shaft of light onto his left shoulder, leaving a permanent brand on his skin.

His ears ringing, Hajime surfaced into a world very different from the one he had left only a minute or two earlier. His friend was nowhere to be seen—and it would occur to him later that if the other boy had surfaced ahead of the *pika*, then he was simply gone.

The shore was covered with smoke, obscuring the schoolhouse and the Mitsubishi building, both of which had been simultaneously stamped flat along one side and ballooned grotesquely out of shape on the other side. The sky above was absolutely black, and from the center of the river two spheres of greenish-black flame were suddenly streaking directly at Hajime over the water's surface. Each was about the size of a baseball. On their way to the shore, the fireballs parted on either side of him and disappeared.

He did not need to see much more to send him splashing and then wading toward the riverbank. As he reached knee-deep water, a shower of huge oily raindrops came and went. More dark green, incandescent spheres also came and went. One of them struck a dead animal or a bundle of rags, set it afire, and disintegrated.

While the oily rain and the green fire passed, a rank smell came to Hajime and did not go away—a smell like squid and sweet pork, coming from near and far. Hajime realized that it must have been the people who were making that smell—the alligator-skinned people who were running toward the water and toward him—the dozens of them coming out of that same dark place where the green fire must have been born. He did not want to look, and yet he could not take his eyes away from them. They were at once utterly obscene and utterly fantastic, terrifying and yet at the same time spellbinding.

Hajime's journey along the riverbank—whether deeper into Ground Zero or farther out, he could not tell—should have been totally unforgettable. Yet four weeks later it would come to him only in flashes of memory. Some of the alligator men, as they staggered knee-deep into the water, literally fell apart—disintegrating before young Hajime's eyes. One man who did not make it to the river lay on his back, puffing up as if he were being inflated, or steamed, from the inside. His stomach burst open and instead of blood, black fire came out of him.

Hajime could not guess what the black fire might actually be, and years later, none of the scientists he spoke with could tell him what he saw. One would suggest that perhaps events were misremembered in both sequence and detail, and that a body bloating in the heat days later (and not right after the *pika-don*, as Hajime seemed to remember it) sent forth a swarm of black flies and not tongues of black fire. Among themselves, a few scientists would give the Hajime phenomena at least some probability of being vivid hallucinations brought about by concussion. That a multi-kiloton shock wave traveling underwater along a radius of not quite one kilometer could provide a sufficiently powerful blow to the head seemed beyond serious dispute. And yet, strange balls of light had been witnessed by nurse Minami and more than a dozen others who were with her in Hiroshima. Dr. Nagai's friend and his cow were fatally wounded by fireballs more than eight kilometers from the bomb, and Prefect Nishioka had been sickened by ominous flaming "candles" that fell out of the Hiroshima cloud. The large raindrops, the shadow people, and the disintegrating alligator people had been witnessed by multiple survivors in both cities, along with many other strange and inexplicable events.

· · ·

INSIDE THE MITSUBISHI torpedo factory, Sachiko Masaki was shock-cocooned. Hajime's age, she had been assigned to precision finishing work on the smallest parts of the torpedoes, including the *Kaiten* controls. Under a childhood of indoctrination, Sachiko's highest goal was to die a hero for her emperor—and her greatest regret was that girls were allowed to build and test equipment for the *Kaiten* torpedoes, but never to steer the controls and become Kaiten themselves.

The Mitsubishi factory stretched nearly a half kilometer—more than four city blocks—along the Urakami riverbank. Sachiko and her teacher Komaichi were located approximately three city blocks farther from the hypocenter than Hajime, in a section of the building that ballooned out and burst like a ripe grape, while Hajime's section was squashed. Sachiko and Komaichi perceived two distinct flashes, the second one blazing much brighter than the first, accompanied by enveloping waves of heat and ear-popping pressure. The steel and concrete sub-ceiling did not live up to its bomb-resistant label, but as the walls burst outward and flew away and as the ceiling frame came down almost to floor level, it performed a serendipitous function of all but stopping the heat ray, and absorbing much of the gamma-ray surge. Turbines and torpedo stands kept the ceiling from falling to the level of Sachiko's head. During that critical, three- or four-second period, she felt wind roaring in her ears and had a strange sensation of floating gently in midair.

When Sachiko regained her bearings, Komaichi appeared to be in a daze. Everyone else was gone—with the rest of the factory. It was beyond Sachiko's ability to take in the disappearance.

"We should go to the protection of the tunnel factory," Kamaichi said, and Sachiko agreed. As it turned out, the imagined safety of the tunnels was precisely that—imagined. With the electric pumps immobilized, they were filling quickly with groundwater. And the enemy was coming out of them. American, Australian, and Javanese prisoners had been assigned to dig the tunnels—and they, too, appeared to have been cocooned.

"There are more of them than there are of us," Komaichi observed.

"I think I should go home now," Sachiko said, and Komaichi nodded agreement and ran away.

When her older brother came searching for her, Sachiko was smeared with oil from the factory and with the blood of the disappeared, but she had escaped with only a few minor bruises and with none of the characteristic nausea of Ground Zero survivors. This was her brother's second experience of the atomic bomb. Three days earlier, the elder Masaki was stationed at Etajima Island's Naval Academy when, before his eyes, all of Hiroshima "went into the sky like the smoke of a furnace." He returned to Nagasaki on Kenshi Hirata's train, with friends whose entire families were lost in the firestorms of August 6. One had identified the foundations of his mother's house and his mother's half-melted wristwatch, and nothing else. All of them had been ill since August 7. Sachiko's brother appeared to be dying from a scratch on his hand that would not stop bleeding.

After the two Masaki siblings and Hajime abandoned the Mitsubishi plant, only the prisoners still stirred within. Beyond the tunnel they had been building, and outside of a few smaller shock cocoons here and there, everyone else was dead. The POWs decided to hunker down among the wrecked torpedoes and turbines of Ground Zero, hoping that the local military commanders, if any of them remained alive, now had much more important matters on their minds than hunting down escaped prisoners.

A HALF HOUR after the explosion, Michie Hattori was still in *shigoku*. It would seem to her later an absurd thing to have done in the aftermath of a nuclear attack, but she separated from her friend Fumiko and went into the battered remnants of her school, searching for her books. All Michie could think about was how her parents had spent every spare coin they could scrape together to pay for those books. In a building that had been half squashed and splashed, she found her schoolbooks intact. Looking around the rest of the neighborhood, it occurred to her that the center supports of the school were the only landmark structures that might be called, even by exaggeration, "somewhat intact." That books could survive—

somehow still stacked in the same order in which she had left them—seemed all the more miraculous.

Strapping her schoolbooks on her back, Michie set out in the direction she believed to be home. She rubbed her eyes repeatedly, not only because of the hot smoke but because the landscape through which she walked defied imagination. Electric poles and wires had become a crazy network of cobwebs, spun over collapsed houses that, along block after block, appeared to have been squashed and kicked about by stampeding giants. Along one side of a ridge, a huge flowing debris field had been deposited by a wave of dust and compressed air that crested like water, crashed, then abruptly retreated. At the top of the heap, leaking something thick and foul-smelling, a train of tanker cars lay sprawled, wheels pointed up at the sky, like a dead worm bleeding poison.

Farther uphill, about an hour's walk beyond the place where the air seemed to have flowed liquid, a second ridge of land was more natural-appearing and familiar. Standing some thirty meters high and forming a natural wall that paralleled the Urakami River, the ridge had acted as a flash shield and blast barrier between the flattened school and the little valley containing Michie's neighborhood. Buildings nearly a kilometer and a half farther downriver no longer existed, yet when Michie climbed a saddleback atop the ridge and looked down, a perfectly cocooned world met her eyes.

In the glen below, all the grass had remained green. Clothing still hung unburned and undisturbed from undamaged laundry lines, and not a single door or roof tile appeared to have been dislodged. People were riding bicycles along the main street. Among them, a lone truck moved along at a leisurely pace as if nothing at all out of the ordinary had occurred. Michie walked back to look down the other side of the ridge to convince herself that her journey through the wasteland had not been a dream.

Following a path that led down to her neighborhood, Michie asked people she met on the street if they knew what had happened. Most did not want to walk to the top of the ridge and see it for themselves. Hearing was enough. Others like Michie had come down the path and told them about the column of fire and the disappearance of almost everything between the ridge and Urakami. They did not know what had happened, only that it was something terrible. Michie told them about the flattened school and the alligator man, then hurried home.

At 11:02 a.m., Michie's parents had been at work in a small neighborhood factory, assembling munitions for fighter planes. They saw a flash through the windows and they felt the room shake, but the glass in the windows remained unbroken, so everyone shrugged off the event as an earthquake and continued working. Eventually, the factory manager returned with news that only the factory and their own town in the bottom of the glen still existed—everything outside had been destroyed.

The manager released Michie's mother and father to go over the ridge in search of their daughter. There were no landmarks leading to the school, and the cyclone of flames was throwing off so much whirling debris and black smoke that they could not continue into Urakami. Slicked with soot and sweat, they turned back, and arrived home only a few minutes before Michie.

"Do you have feet?" her joyful father asked, as he caught sight of Michie. It was the first time she ever saw him cry. Long before she reached the ridge and saw the town, Michie had counted her parents among the lost. And from the moment her parents crossed the ridge and looked down in the direction of the school, they had counted her among the ghosts of Urakami.

GOVERNOR NAGANO'S SENSE of anticlimax and well-being did not last any longer than it took him to climb up from his shock-cocooned mansion and crest the hill that had sheltered him. He understood now that Prefect Nishioka had not exaggerated Hiroshima. Not by a gnat's breath. Just as he had warned, Urakami was transformed into a manifestation of hell on earth. Impenetrable black dust hugged the ground—and, off to one side, the rotating mass of fire and smoke reared up higher than the Pyramids. Somewhere near the heart of the storm, one of the army's major communications hubs must by now have become clouds of ash.

From the far side of the cyclone, the head of the Urakami Council called in a report to the governor through one of the few still-functioning police radios. The flames seemed to be throwing up a wall of static, but with many repeats, the full picture was coming in. Hundreds—perhaps thousands of people—burned by the flash were fleeing into the mountains behind the medical school, and the stream of the wounded was becoming a flood of the dying.

"They have been coming in droves," a stenographer recorded. "They are all begging for help and water when they arrive. They grab on to your legs and they can't walk. Is the Prefectural Office aware of this situation?"

Another report described the scattered dead and the dying in an area between the firestorm and a town that stood apart from the rest of the landscape—like an oasis in a desert.

"In the desert," the caller said, "there was a young woman, about twenty years old, lying facedown and calling for water—just, 'Water . . . water . . .' in a voice so small it was like a mosquito humming."

"How many fatalities are you estimating?" Nagano demanded.

"In the hills below the Medical College . . . I believe we're looking at fifty thousand dead in Urakami alone."

Nagano had already prepared a telegram to Tokyo reporting his own estimated total of 20,000—and it would be sent before Nagano could correct his estimate. In time, the initial estimate would be used to corroborate an official low-mortality statistic favored by General MacArthur's investigators.

But Urakami was not a statistic.

"*Fifty thousand?*" Governor Nagano was practically wailing over the airwaves. "What are the police doing? Where are the fire brigades?"

"Most—" and the caller broke off in a wash of static.

"Repeat?" the governor called. He just did not seem to understand. "Why haven't the police and the local administrators been sent to see what's going on?"

"Most of them are dead," came the reply. "And those who are still alive can't go into the middle of a fire."

"Who's in charge over there?" the governor asked.

The obvious reply was "Aren't you?" but the caller kept the snipe to himself and said, "We've got turmoil erupting—with everyone looking for doctors, nurses, and police. The hospitals on this side are burning and the doctors are evacuating the patients. Forget about fighting the fires or policing the area. We're going to need doctors, nurses, and medicine."

The initial shock-state appeared to be passing, and the governor seemed to regain control of himself. "The situation is understood," Nagano assured the caller. "I've decided to order the head of the health department to mobilize all the doctors and nurses on this side into a medical team that will head into your area."

At approximately the time that would normally have marked the governor's late lunch schedule, an assistant informed him that the local health minister appeared to be missing in action.

"Then, has anyone seen Prefect Nishioka?" Nagano asked. It seemed incomprehensible to him that the prefect would not have come to the mansion and taken his assigned post in the shelter by now. As far as Nagano could tell, Prefect Nishioka had never in his life been late for anything.

IN THE HILLY suburb of Isahaya, Nishioka and his driver encountered the first refugees streaming away from the city. Ant-walking alligators. At first they took his thoughts back to Hiroshima, and then he realized that he was fully ten kilometers from the center of the storm. He was almost as far away from the hypocenter in Urakami as Harlem and the Bronx are from the lower tip of Manhattan. This *pika-don* appeared to be worse than the one in Hiroshima. The alligator people said so, without saying a word. The prefect knew that they could not have walked very far from the places in which they had been injured. Many were now eyeless and faceless—with their heads transformed into blackened alligator hides displaying red holes, indicating mouths.

The alligator people did not scream. Their mouths could not form the sounds. The noise they made was worse than screaming. They uttered a continuous murmur—like locusts on a midsummer night. One man, staggering on charred stumps of legs, was carrying a dead baby upside down. Its diapers and legs were burned even blacker than the clouds from Urakami.

Millions of tons of dust had been hoisted into the crown of the mushroom, and the ashes were spreading across the heavens like ink poured into water. Objects still dropped out of the cloud—little black flecks of wood, concrete grit pinging against the windshield, a pebble, a wisdom tooth.

"What is this?" the driver asked.

"Fallout," the prefect said. *Radioactive fallout*, he emphasized for himself, and left unsaid.

Elsewhere, almost everything Nishioka had said the day before was saving lives. His observation that people in Hiroshima who were even minimally sheltered had a good chance of surviving the *pika-don* had been passed on by the governor to the district police chief, who passed this advice on to his thirteen-year-old son as a stern instruction.

At 11:02 a.m., the chief's son had been standing outside his middle school with three friends, near a street called Daikoku-Machi, on the fringe of Ground Zero. On this particular morning, his father sent him to school wearing a white, wide-rimmed hat. He feared his father's displeasure more than embarrassment, so without any fuss he wore the embarrassing hat and the long white pants. When the flash cut across the sky, the boy responded instinctively to a duck-and-cover maneuver, practiced before breakfast—over and over, until he performed it perfectly for his father, in under a half-second. Just as quickly, he ducked and rolled into a gully-like "shrapnel shelter," cut into the pavement. He hollered as he ducked, calling for his friends to dive in with him. Only one obeyed, rolling in practically on top of the boy. The other two stood, watching the *pika* grow into a shock bubble—and they were never seen again.

Another saved by a witness to Hiroshima was Dr. Tatsuichiro Akizuki. Dean Tsuno had described a monstrous flash-and-bang, brought about by a single plane that dove earthward before the flash. This warning sign was very different from the steady drone produced by an approaching fleet of firebombers—which allowed up to two or three minutes to take cover. Tsuno advised that the sound of a single plane's engines straining would provide only a few seconds' advance warning.

At 11:01 a.m., Dr. Akizuki had just struck a pneumo-thorax

needle into the side of a tuberculosis patient, when he became aware
of an extremely sharp low sound, like a B-29 diving toward earth.

"What's that?" an assistant said. "The all-clear has sounded,
hasn't it?"

"Get down!" Akizuki hollered, withdrawing the needle and dropping to the floor. Seconds later, the hypocenter was created, almost
1.4 kilometers away. Urakami's medical college and St. Francis Hospital were located high on a hill that became, after a fashion, the
barrel of the valley's shotgun effect. The building's roof and many of
the outer walls were stripped away and not a single window survived, but this was a shock-cocoon effect, compared to the seething
hell below in the river valley. After the searing flash, the ceiling
crashed down like a tidal wave. Akizuki and his assistant stood
amazed at having survived the concrete and plaster tsunami without
wounds. The patient had not been so lucky. He took a direct shot in
the head from a spray of glass and concrete.

The rest of the patients did not come toward Akizuki and the
nurse. Instead they ran away, fleeing the hospital as if chased by de-
mons, covering their bloodstained faces with their hands as they ran
for the imagined safety of the highest hill.

Most of them were looking back as they ran; and when finally
Akizuki looked toward what they appeared to be fleeing, he saw the
southwestern sky turned every bit as dark as coal; and below
the black veil, over the surface of the earth, hung a strange fog
that—as the dust cleared little by little—rooted him to the spot
with horror.

The fog was fire.

Dr. Akizuki was among the few who lived to see, and to tell, how
the Urakami cyclone formed: "To say that everything burned is not
enough. It seemed as if Earth itself emitted fire and smoke, flames
that writhed up and erupted from underground. The sky was dark,
the ground was scarlet."

And then, as he watched, a crimson-and-yellow-flecked figure
rose up from the ocean of flame and tried to become a mountain. It
seemed to Akizuki, and to many others who saw it that morning,
that the whole world was dying and they with it.

When Dr. Paul Nagai looked down from the hospital and saw the cyclone, he, too, thought about the end of the world. Yet, as a man who had taken a Christian name when he was baptized and confirmed, it became an end foretold for thousands of years, from the time of Daniel. To Nagai, the dizzying display in the valley was the brink of the beginning, and a warning—not of things that had to be, but he hoped only an antidote against what might be. He did not want to believe that he was witnessing the world to come. A Jesuit teacher had said as much after Osaka burned. He told the little-known story of Jesus and James, in which James learned that even when a fate was foretold by prophecy, there really was no fate except that which people made. The Jesuit had explained Jesus' lesson in a more modern vernacular: "And the Lord said, 'Children, do you remember that part about *love one another*? Don't make me have to come down there and smack you—because it will be pale horses and pale riders, and it will be really bad.'"

Dr. Nagai did not believe it was merely a coincidence that the hospital and Urakami Cathedral overlooked the place where Saint Paul Miki—the samurai who became a Jesuit—was crucified with twenty-five of his followers in 1597. Dr. Nagai wondered if what might seem to most people to be a mere accident of history—the convergence of hypocenter and crucifixion—was a reminder to all humanity that though everything about man except man's way of thinking had changed, if his way of thinking did not change, then indeed all of this was prologue to the way the world ends.

ON THE FRONT lawn of the hospital, Dr. Akizuki was discovering that the ground must have been briefly heated to at least the boiling point of water. The grasses—and the leaves of all the vegetables—were flattened, scorched, and smoldering. Most of the people who were working in the garden had their backs turned toward the *pika* when it flashed red, and they must have involuntarily turned their heads in time to behold the full fury of the blue flash—before they had time to realize they must not turn around and look. The gardeners' backs were scorched raw by the heat rays. Their faces were burned within those same first three seconds. And they were blind.

At first, Dr. Akizuki wanted to run away, but when he looked up, he saw fires beginning to spread little by little through the ruins of the hospital's uppermost floor. For a moment, he thought it a bit odd that the roof was the first part of the building to catch fire. And then, in the next moment, he thought of Dr. Yoshioka. She was up there somewhere. And he had *sent* her there.

When he ran inside and climbed the stairs, Akizuki found several Jesuit brothers from the local chapel already assisting in the evacuation. During the next ten minutes, the brothers and the staff, along with several of the uninjured patients, helped Akizuki to evacuate everyone from the building.

As the empty hospital burned, taking almost all of the medicine and equipment with it, someone called out Akizuki's name, shouting over the roar of flames, "Please come quickly, sir!"

He followed the man to a hill behind the hospital, where one of the brothers had carried Dr. Yoshioka on his back.

"She is about to die from loss of blood," said Nurse Tsuyako, quietly reproaching Dr. Akizuki for being so long in coming.

A gauze cloth had been wrapped so many times around Yoshioka's head that only one eye peered out at Akizuki as he took her pulse and checked the bandages.

"I don't think you're in any danger," Akizuki said, not sure he was telling the truth. "Your pulse is strong, you're not too pale—and the bandages have stopped the bleeding."

"Have you found out anything about your mother?" Dr. Yoshioka asked.

"No," he said, with polite resignation. "She's probably been burned." Looking toward the cyclone of flames, he could not make a good guess at the precise location of his mother's house. As he watched, people began moving up the hill toward him, groaning and murmuring for help. The ant-walkers' faces were like masks, and the physician felt as if he were watching a procession of ghosts—as in a dream he recalled from childhood. But this was worse. With the hospital now sending up flurries of sparks, there was no medicine except what the staff had grabbed on the way out. There was not even a roof under which to shelter the wounded. Akizuki felt that he could be of no help without medical supplies, and he really did want to run away, but he decided that even if it became impossible to provide much actual treatment, sometimes the comfort of a medic's presence or just a caring human hand could be enough to keep a patient's will to live alight. Once he heard the people's pleas for help, he could not leave them.

As the stream of survivors from the valley increased in number, the groans and murmurs grew in strength, sounding to Dr. Akizuki like a prophecy from the Buddhist scriptures: "re-echoing everywhere, as if Earth itself were in pain."

SHIP DESIGNER YAMAGUCHI'S SECTION chief was still explaining how he did not believe an atomic bomb could possibly work, when the second *pika* concluded the argument in Yamaguchi's favor. At a distance of three kilometers, some 10,200 feet downriver of the hypocenter, the heat that burst into the room was so great that, this time, Yamaguchi believed he was gone.

Once more, he was standing on the edge of Ground Zero. All around him, all wooden structures and almost all light steel-frame buildings were flattened by the blast. Within this zone, even exposed concrete could be briefly ignited to produce a secondary flash of limelight. Here and there aluminum burned like rocket fuel. Anyone standing outdoors unshielded was safely beyond the range of lethal gamma-ray dosing—but this condition was rendered irrelevant by the instant lethality of the blast wave and the heat ray.

During the critical first three seconds, Yamaguchi's arguments were instantly recalled, and his listeners dove under tables and behind door frames. In the end, Yamaguchi's section chief did exactly what Yamaguchi had said he should do if he saw the bright flash, and he survived with almost no injuries—in a room that, unlike the rest of the building, appeared to have been cocooned between diverging shock waves. Somehow, in a hilly region where during a period of about six seconds shock fronts were actively rebounding and converging with bone-granulating force, a wave bearing down upon Yamaguchi's location parted harmlessly around an adjacent stairwell, like water shunted to either side of a boat's prow. The wave appeared to have carried away everything and everyone except Yamaguchi's conference room, and the people there with him. Even the superheated air seemed only to have eddied around the outside of the office, before retreating backward toward Urakami and following the fireball into the sky. Before they collapsed into smoke and dust, multiple floors of concrete and steel had provided their own added layer of protection by absorbing the heat and the gamma rays, but Yamaguchi still felt a renewed sensation of heat throughout his body— followed by a chill and nausea.

He ran down through a broken stairwell that no longer had walls, through a once familiar hallway with no ceiling into a neighboring building that was now a field. The only familiar structure was an old steel-and-concrete watchtower that used to be a lighthouse.

Like Yamaguchi and his colleagues, the tower appeared to have been inexplicably spared, though its steel door was almost hot enough to burn his fingers when he pulled it open. For the first time he became aware that his burns from Hiroshima were now fully exposed to the increasingly powerful gusts of smoke and wind. Though the precursor wave had bounced and diverged as it burst through the Mitsubishi office building, the gale that came with it had blown off all of his bandages and even de-gloved much of the skin beneath.

The tower's lookout was still at his post. Evidently, he had been watching either the B-29 or the bomb itself through powerful binoculars. His face was a mask of blackened alligator skin, but his brain took the brunt of it. The binoculars had focused the heat ray into twin beams that must have burned through both eyes and almost to the far side of the man's skull—all within one small part of a millisecond. The engineer merely shrugged at another new horror and looked out from the top of the lighthouse, trying to find home.

In home's direction, everything had been kicked sideways and seared—then something evidently came through and snuffed out the fires that should now have been burning there. The ground appeared to have been scratched and raked, as if by the devil's talons.

The engineer discovered that one side of his house was a curiously intact box, filled with raked table and chair parts, and balcony splinters—all of it sheathed in a veneer of black carbon. The rest was ruin. As Kenshi had done in Hiroshima, Yamaguchi now dug frantically for his wife, Hisako, and their year-old son—and eventually he came upon curled ribbons of flesh, clearly belonging to a baby. But

the bomb's effects seemed to go hand in hand with the random de-
viations of human routines. Sometimes Yamaguchi attributed the
fortune and misfortune in his life to a path planted for him by God.
Other times he believed that what appeared to be destiny only appeared so, and really happened "just because."

Yamaguchi soon found Hisako and little Katsutoshi alive. After
he left for work on the morning of the second bomb, a cousin's wife
came to visit Hisako, bringing along her own baby. Hisako had offered tea and stepped out for what was only to have been a brief
errand prior to her afternoon-through-evening shift, directing the
expansion of a Mitsubishi tunnel. Her husband's injuries from Hiroshima sent Hisako along a path she would not otherwise have taken.
She would normally have been at home, preparing lunch for relatives before setting off for work. As the critical split second approached, Mrs. Yamaguchi walked away to visit an herbal pharmacist
who knew something about treating burns. Like most first-time
mothers, endearingly overcautious Hisako tended to take Katsutoshi
everywhere with her—even when relatives were at home willing to
babysit. When the final air-raid alert sounded, Hisako's mission
to find a remedy for her husband's burns had altered her normal
routine and brought her to the Mitsubishi shelter ahead of schedule.
She and Katsutoshi were inside a tunnel when the fires came—and
fortunately, the fires themselves ignited far away.

Sometimes it worked out. "Sometimes by God's will," Yamaguchi
liked to believe, "and maybe sometimes, just because."

DR. NAGAI'S FIRST THOUGHT, after the blast wave had passed through
the hospital, was gratitude to still be taking in air and able to think
clearly, and to walk. His next thought was of his position as an officer of the Rescue Committee. Looking downhill, toward central
Urakami, he knew that his wife lay somewhere under the flames. He
would learn much later that a sister who last saw her had urged Midori Nagai to spend the rest of the day in what was to become the
shadow-shielded cottage, near the stream where little Kayano and
Makoto were playing at 11:02 a.m. His wife had declined, explaining that the cancer was making Paul sicker than usual lately; so she

wanted to make a nutritious lunch for him and bring it to the hospital. Paul Nagai would eventually discover that she must in fact have died in the midst of preparing something for him. Mixed in with her bones were cooking utensils—mashed flat, then melted.

Dr. Paul Nagai had begun the morning with about six months of life left to him, but four years later, haunted by survivor's guilt, he would write (in one of history's most starkly introspective memoirs) that in choosing to stay near the hospital after the *pika-don* instead of trying to return home to his wife, he had discharged his responsibility. "What will be my reward," he wondered, "in the eyes of Makoto and Kayano when they are grown?"

Believing that he would soon die from his cancer, Dr. Nagai's initial guiding instinct was to be remembered as a hero. Distraught over the disappearance of Urakami and his wife, he forced himself to control his emotions and direct the evacuation of patients from his end of the hospital. He was fully conscious of seeking posthumous praise, of wanting to be recognized as someone who rescued people from a burning building without showing any private feelings.

From Paul Nagai's perspective, the students, the nurses, and the Jesuit brothers were not driven by such vanity. They kept going back into the danger zone under Nagai's sometimes draconian supervision, while he later received the praise: "The dying doctor who thought only of others."

On the fifth anniversary of the bombing, he would recall a young nurse who appeared to have received no cuts or bruises from the *pika-don* but who collapsed three times in a state of utter exhaustion, pleading for him to bear her along part of the way. Instead, he reprimanded her for showing such weakness and commanded her to stiffen her spine, and continue the work of rescue. Two days later, she was vomiting blood. On the morning of the bomb, Nagai noticed that several of the other nurses were also weakening and stumbling.

"I allowed them no help," Nagai lamented, when he understood the truth. "These girls were all far sicker than they looked—some were actually in the death agony—and, not knowing it, I made them all stand up and walk without help. I often wonder what their families would think of me now."

Those nurses and brothers who (though shaded from the heat ray) had been outdoors when the gamma rays burst toward them, or who were near the hospital's outer lobby, were irradiated with approximately one-third of a lethal dose. Even within the building's shell of steel and red brick, Nagai received up to one-fifth of a lethal dose from prompt radiation, and at least twice as much from the subsequent fallout—a total dosage that killed approximately half the people it impacted. The reason radiation struck hardest at the lining of the intestinal tract and at the bone marrow was that its disruptive effects were most pronounced against rapidly dividing cells. Cancer cells fell into this category. As the nurses sickened before Dr. Nagai's eyes, the bomb—while still causing nausea and making his skin brittle—was killing Nagai's healthy blood-producing cells and cancer cells with equal ease. Almost from the start of the first gamma-ray surge, his cancer was being driven toward remission.

Unlike Kenshi Hirata and Tsutomu Yamaguchi, Nagai did not believe God or fate had spared him merely to bear witness. He believed there was a penance to be paid as well, as if life on Earth was just some other planet's purgatory.

If not for the fact that it would have left her orphaned, Dr. Nagai would rather have died than lived to hear what happened when an aunt told his little girl that her mother was dead. Kayano was only four. She did not know what it meant. She did not cry; she simply smiled and asked, "When is Mommy coming home?"

That night, Kayano's cousin Ritsuko developed diarrhea. Cousin Takeo developed the same symptom, along with an upset stomach.

On the unburned side of the ravine, where the grass still remained green in spite of a strange rain of what looked and felt like "dead jellyfish goo"—in spite of the smoldering paper and the other objects that seemed to have no business falling out of the sky—fireflies had lived through the blast. The children saw them flying around with their reflections in the stream. Auntie Urata would recall that the fireflies, along with the scent of live grass, gave a wonderful sense of life to the air—which made it all the more impossible to believe the tragedies that were yet to unfold.

On the fifth anniversary, though only age nine, it would be clear that Kayano Nagai was being compelled to acquire wisdom beyond her years. "Cousin Ritsuko died," she would record for a memorial memoir. "Before she died, she coughed up a lot of blood. Her sweat was blood. Cousin Takeo also coughed up a lot of blood and he died, too."

It would never escape Kayano's notice that the war had begun on the Feast of the Immaculate Conception, December 8 (the day of the Pearl Harbor bombing on Japan's side of the International Date Line). It ended the day Ritsuko died, August 15. *How many cruel swords must have pierced the Holy Mother's heart all this time*, Kayano wondered.

"I can remember when I was little, but mostly bad things," Kayano would tell history. "The year I was born, the war began. The whole time I was little there were air raids all the time. It was awful but anyhow I had my mommy there, so it was nice; I was so happy. I saw the atomic bomb. I was four then. The atomic bomb was the last thing that happened during the war and no more bad things have happened since then; but I don't have my mommy anymore. So even if it isn't bad anymore, I'm not happy."

8

THREADS

About the same time Cadet Komatsu flew into the cloud's radioactive stem and Michie Hattori made her acquaintance with the alligator man, Charles Sweeney was coming to terms with the depressing mathematics of his situation, and with another of Paul Tibbets's "bonehead" maneuvers.

From Nagasaki to Okinawa was 350 miles. After the bombing run, *Bock's Car* and *Great Artiste* had risen from 20,000 to 30,000 feet for a quick high-altitude reconnaissance of the target, and also to stay above and ahead of ascending fighters. At this starting point for the voyage home, Sweeney's engines were burning approximately one gallon of fuel per mile. He was starting out with only 300 gallons. To conserve fuel, he needed to reduce altitude and get down to more richly oxygenated air. In addition, he could throttle the propellers back from the by-the-book speed of 2,000 rpm to 1,800 rpm. This would save a little more fuel but not a significantly large amount, by Sweeney's math. So he decided to throttle back to 1,600 rpm, which would unfortunately reduce the necessary inflow of lubrication and the levels of cooling needed to keep the engines in good condition. This decision was all but guaranteed to damage all four engines, but they would be much more thoroughly ruined by a crash on salt water and could therefore be considered expendable.

The throttle-down reduced *Bock's Car*'s speed by a hundred miles per hour. Sweeney was now consuming 300 instead of 500 gallons per hour, but he would still drop into the sea fifteen minutes and several miles short of his destination.

Sweeney hoped that Tibbets's boneheaded theory might just make up the difference. Tibbets's name for the theory was "flying the staircase." Accordingly, with velocity and power settings being equal, a gradual step-down-and-level-out, step-down-again-and-level-out-again descent would give the aircraft a brief, temporary acceleration with each down-step, without using any extra fuel. Theoretically, Sweeney would be able to milk a few extra miles out of the remaining fuel reserve. *And in practice?* the pilot wondered. Starting out from 30,000 feet, Sweeney believed he had plenty of time to find out; so he began his climb down the stairs, trusting the mathematics of Paul Tibbets and Isaac Newton to do most of the driving.

Fifteen minutes out from Okinawa and over the original estimated crash point, the fuel supply, though down to barely more than a dozen gallons, was still providing food for the engines. Sweeney gave thanks to Tibbets, Newton, and the Lord when finally the island came into view. Unfortunately, America's closest airfield to Japan was also its busiest. Even ten minutes out, Sweeney could see signs of air traffic over every runway.

"Yontan. Yontan tower!" Sweeney called out to a receiver who seemed too busy to answer. "This is Dimples 77. Mayday! Mayday! Over."

"All gauges now reading empty," Kuharek called forward, and immediately after he said this, Number 4—the starboard outboard engine—shut down.

"Increase power to Number Three," Sweeney called back.

The revving up of Number 3 steadied *Bock's Car*'s starboard wing, but if by now any outcome was at all certain, it was that the only way to land was along a straight-in glide path. Being waved off by a flight controller to a "circle-round-and-try-again" landing was not an option.

Sweeney told Van Pelt to fire the red and green emergency flares, signaling *Aircraft out of fuel.* He backed this up with another call of, "Mayday! Mayday! Dimples 77." Streamers of red and green were now trailing behind *Bock's Car*, and Sweeney could hear the control towers talking to the other planes as if nothing unusual were on the horizon.

"Are they blind as well as deaf?" Sweeney shouted to his crew—and then, into the mike, "Mayday! Mayday! I'm calling any goddamned tower in Okinawa!"

Not even static came back. Sweeney put down the landing gear and yelled back to Van Pelt, "Fire off every damned flare we have on board!"

"All of them?"

"*All* of them! Do it now!"

Seconds later, the flares were bursting on all sides—reds, blues, and greens; purple and sparkling white stars. Van Pelt was signaling, *Aircraft out of fuel! Aircraft crashed on water, over here! Prepare for incoming crash! Aircraft on fire! Dead and wounded aboard!*

Sweeney imagined that *Bock's Car* must now look like the Fourth of July, barreling in fast.

"Who *is* that jackass?" called a weary air traffic controller.

At least now I have their attention, Sweeney thought, as planes began swerving out of his path, allowing him to pound down onto the nearest runway with only two of the four engines still sucking in air and providing thrust.

No fewer than ten seconds after Sweeney came to a stop, emergency vehicles were at *Bock's Car*'s side. One of them began spraying down the engines, though clearly nothing appeared to be burning. A medic poked his head up through the nosewheel door and asked, "Where are the dead and wounded?"

Sweeney flipped a thumb over his shoulder, indicating the north and the direction of Nagasaki. "Back there," he said, and said nothing more on the subject. He was a long way from Tinian Air Base, and even if President Truman had already spilled the beans and announced the bomb's existence, everyone aboard *Bock's Car* understood without being told, that they were to say nothing to anyone about where they had been, where they were going, or what they had done.

As an order came in from Admiral Purnell on Tinian for the ground crews on Okinawa to give Sweeney everything he needed for the next leg of his journey, and as the hours ticked by, the response from Tokyo continued to be a desert of silence.

Could their actual response to two atomic bombs be contemptuous indifference? Sweeney wondered. *Could that possibly be true?*

It certainly appeared so. Instead of news about a Japanese surrender, the headline story on Armed Forces Radio was all about the Russian invasion of Japanese-occupied China, followed in second place by the discovery of "lost" archival recordings of the late Glenn Miller's "Caribbean Clipper" and "Little Brown Jug."

Sweeney was the only member of his crew who knew that the plutonium cores of the next two atomic bombs would not exist for another month or more. He would record in his memoirs that this thought left him colder than any other. The gap between bombs might convince overlords in the Imperial Palace that if the country could absorb two atomic blasts and regroup, then this new horror—just like the conventional firebombings—could be fought through and survived.

Jesus . . . , Sweeney said to himself. *If only we had another bomb that could be dropped tomorrow or the day after, then Tokyo would believe we were able to load them one after another like shotgun shells. And then they'd surely surrender and stop the madness. But this? This?*

The delay of a whole month would communicate only one lesson: Truman was playing poker and the vast nuclear arsenal did not really exist. And the tragic irony of it was that when the next bombs became available in a few weeks, Sweeney would have to fly more of these missions. At least three more of them, he guessed.

Just what the hell must they be thinking back there in the Emperor's Palace?

AS HIS CONTEMPORARIES TOLD it, "Nero fiddled while Rome burned."

During the passage of nearly two thousand years, those words had never been more apt. Field Marshal Shunroku Hata, who had missed his meeting with Prefect Nishioka but had survived the fires of Hiroshima and arrived in Tokyo with only flash burns on one side of his face, insisted with Dr. Sagane that the Americans possessed only enough nuclear material for the delivery of two atomic bombs.

"They appear now to have used both of them," Hata said. "They have now done the worst that they can do."

Foreign Minister Shigenori Togo and physicist Yoshio Nishina pressed again, as politely as possible, to plead to the Emperor for a decision.

War Minister Korechika Anami seemed to have stopped worrying altogether and was actually learning to embrace the bomb. Having heard descriptions of the atomic cloud blooming into the stratosphere like a radiant flower, he waxed poetic and said, "Would it not be wondrous for this whole nation to be destroyed like a beautiful flower?"

The self-styled warrior poet's lesson to young kamikaze and Kaiten had been much the same. He taught them that their destiny was war—"to fall for the Emperor like petals from a flower." In several days, following revelations that he knew of and was now considering fellowship in a military coup against the Emperor, aimed at eliminating all possibility of surrender, Anami would commit ritual suicide after treating his friends to sake, showing them two of his "death poems," and lamenting, "Oh, what a poet the world is losing."

Presently, Anami was refusing to tolerate the foreign minister's phrase, "The war situation grows more unfavorable for us every hour." Togo was forced to rephrase his words, "The war situation has developed not necessarily to Japan's advantage."

General Yoshijiro Umezu assured Anami that antiaircraft countermeasures concentrated against two or three planes traveling alone should be able to repel an atomic attack.

"And what if they should have another atomic bomb already in waiting on one of the islands?" Foreign Minister Togo broke in. "And what if they know that we have learned by now to beware especially of only two or three planes? Do you not believe they are smart enough to hide one bomb among a fleet of fifty B-29 raiders? Or a hundred? And how are we to shoot them all down?"

For a moment, it seemed to Togo that War Minister Anami had no answer; but with cheeks flushing red and glistening with tears, he said, "I am quite sure we could inflict great casualties on the enemy;

and even if we fail in the attempt, our hundred million people are ready to die for honor, glorifying the deeds of the Japanese in recorded history."

General Umezu agreed, and announced, "We must fight on with courage and find life in death. It is the only way we can honor so many brave men who have already died for the Emperor."

And for what? Dr. Nishina thought. *We honor our war dead by piling more corpses on top of them?* But as Admiral Ugaki began singing the praises of a suicide rocket-plane squadron, Nishina kept his thoughts to himself, for he could see all too clearly that standing rationally and tall at this time was a quick way to be made short—by having one's head cut off. So the physicist listened and held his tongue while the war minister and the foreign minister argued in political double-speak about whether the war was turning truly "unfavorable" or just "not necessarily desirable," while Urakami and Nagasaki burned.

FAR TO THE south of Tokyo, in the smoldering prairies of Hiroshima, Gen, the boy who was saved from a funeral pyre by a soldier known to him only as "Sir," found the hat of a dead fireman and used it to cover the telltale signs of "Disease X."

Since early morning, Gen's hair had begun falling out in large clumps. He knew that the hat was of little use; his mother was sure to notice how sick he was becoming. So Gen snuck away from the sheet-metal lean-to he had helped his mother to erect and renewed his search for food.

Beyond the foundations of Hiroshima Castle and the ruins of the Communications Hospital, Gen discovered bales of carbonized rice still standing in orderly stacks, even though the army warehouse in which they had been stacked appeared to have been lifted off the ground and carried away. Weakly and painfully, he burrowed into the bags, trying to find something still edible. Packages of sugar had become a brownish, amber-like caramel, preserving grains of blackened rice alongside some of Hiroshima's tiniest casualties—thick clusters of ants that in their final seconds of life must have raced one after another into the sweet molten lava.

Gen's mother had already told him of a scene such as this. During those last ten minutes leading up to the *pika-don*, she had observed hundreds if not thousands of ants filing out of the vegetable garden and into the house. One of the last things she heard Gen's little brother Senji say was that he had never seen so many ants.

The fossilized ants did not concern Gen. He merely filed them away in his memory and continued foraging. Below the layer of fried ants and rock candy, the rice he found ceased to be darkened by carbonization. Instead, the darkening appeared to be caused only by black rain seepage and the first growths of black mold. Below the black mold layer, he penetrated into a stratum that was merely dampened by seepage and only slightly boiled by the heat—and here, the rice seemed quite edible. Gen located some charred paint cans and filled them with as much white rice and as many slabs of candied ants as he could carry.

As he walked, Gen tasted the rice grains and the brownish-black sugar. Even with dead ants and a charcoal aftertaste, and even against persistent waves of nausea and chills, the first sugar he had tasted during a childhood of strict state-ordered rationing was delicious beyond words.

On the way home, he saw piles of bones already stacked two meters high around the army's funeral pyres. Such scenes no longer disturbed Gen. In only three days, he had become accustomed to bones and corpses. As a chip of "Hiroshima ant candy" dissolved against his tongue the first-grader learned, with a sense of grim fascination, that human bodies burned like overdone seafood. When the flames reached the dead, it seemed to him that they reared up and even sort of sat up—"just like squid on a grill."

The army's pyres would continue to burn for nearly a month.

The food Gen brought home came from an army barracks very near the hypocenter and had been deeply penetrated by black rain. Though most of the radioactive elements had been so short-lived that they faded and dissipated within hours, isotopes of iodine had a half-life of eight days and strontium-90 would still retain half of its original potency after thirty years. The much rarer and less active plutonium generated by uranium fission irradiated flesh more slowly and a little less severely than iodine-131 and strontium-90, but it had a half-life decay rate of 24,000 years.

Gen had no way of knowing at the time that the food he was carrying home to his mother was crawling with slow death.

Not even Drs. Alvarez and Urey understood yet that radioactive fallout released into a city or a stream did not merely dilute with each passing rainfall like ink spilled into water. It had a sneaky habit of concentrating inside biological systems. Gen's situation could thus be described by a frighteningly simple biological arithmetic: If three micrograms of iodine-131 were mixed with three liters of water, it could indeed be said that three micrograms of the isotope (in liquid form) had been diluted evenly through the water. However, if those same three liters of fallout-laced water were poured into a pond and passed through the living tissues of a fish, then a person monitoring the water excreted by the fish might be led to conclude that because the water coming out was less radioactive than the water that went in, a pond polluted with radioactive iodine was growing cleaner all by itself. In reality, almost all of the critical three micrograms of radioactive iodine would have been absorbed by the fish, and a person eating three fish exposed to this same condition (of three micrograms each) would likely absorb nine micrograms—concentrating most of it, like any other form of iodine, in the thyroid gland.

The same principle of absorption and concentration applied to the fallout-tainted rice and sugar Gen mined out of the ruins for his mother. Plutonium, like iodine, tended to get caught up in living systems; it concentrated in the lungs, liver, and bones, exposing surrounding cells to long-term radiation. Though the element did not even exist on Earth until humans created it, the body's chemical machinery was easily fooled into grabbing plutonium—often confusing it with calcium, iron, and other metallic vitamins and thus allowing it to migrate into the glands that produced mother's milk. Similarly, human metabolisms confused strontium-90 with calcium, and sent it to the bones and the milk glands—giving priority to the milk glands if a mother happened to be lactating.

Gen's little sister Tomoko was only three days old, born on the evening of August 6. A scarcity of food had made her mother's milk run dry; and Gen's most immediate concern had become providing good nutrition for his mother, so that she could produce milk again for little Tomoko.

The rice and the sugar worked, after a fashion, but Gen's baby sister, "crying her life out," he would recount later, "died like a candle consuming itself." The child was doomed by the air she had already breathed, doomed by the milk she was about to drink.

A FEW HOURS after lunchtime, Dr. Hachiya's horse died. The Communications Hospital now had, instead of a constant companion, a constant supply of protein that could be cooked and dried and rationed out for at least several days.

As more patients staggered up to the hospital, more and more of them were sent to the isolation pavilion.

Hachiya, meanwhile, was pleased to discover that as his appetite and health recovered, his scientific curiosity was also reviving. He and the other surviving doctors were now dividing the contaminated (or "infected") into three groups for Disease X.

1. Those with nausea, vomiting, and diarrhea who were improving.
2. Those with the same symptoms who neither improved nor worsened.
3. Those worsening with additional symptoms, including hair loss, chills, and hemorrhagic fever.

Most of those in the third group seemed to have a frightening tendency for sudden death.

From Dr. Hachiya's perspective, neither Disease X nor anything else about the atomic bomb seemed to abide by natural laws. At least two of the newcomers to the hospital had glass in their lungs. Hachiya did not believe it until a colleague brought one of the patients to him. Sitting up in his own sickbed, the physician listened through a stethoscope and heard the tiny slivers clinking together with every labored intake of breath—scores and scores of them. He could not imagine what force had caused a man to inhale so much glass, or how he had managed to stay alive in this condition.

Definitely a mystery, Dr. Hachiya decided, and tried to forget about it and get some sleep. He hoped that making his bed more comfortable would help, but his bed was little more than a nest on a scorched frame, and thickening a makeshift mattress with the spread-out pages of a binderless book was simply not enough to help him lie down and shut out all he had seen these last three days. The hours wore on and Hachiya was unable to stop thinking. Every time he began to doze off, he was immediately snapped back to full wakefulness, always hearing the endless moans from below, punctuated by the occasional scream.

One of the screams came from the wife of a doctor named Harada. The physician had died suddenly in his own isolation pavilion. Nurse Hinda, who seemed to have been in perfectly good health until the vomiting and diarrhea started, also died in the pavilion.

They gave one of the vacant beds to a little girl, newly orphaned by the bomb. The child's cries for her mother would keep Hachiya awake well into the night, until the cries died. If anyone who survived in faraway Nagasaki had possessed the power to sit for a few moments on the edge of Dr. Hachiya's bed and to look around, they would have realized, to their growing horror, that the physician was seeing and hearing their own future.

THE DEBRIS IN THE STREETS and the endless, aimless stream of alligator people stopped Prefect Nishioka's car at the inner edge of the Isahaya suburb. Eight kilometers from the Urakami hypocenter, hundreds of people lay dead before his eyes. Soldiers were already piling corpses in the nearest open space, turning a primary school playground into a makeshift crematorium.

The prefect's car was equipped with one of the city's few functioning radios. A government broadcaster tried to assure the nation that Tokyo was aware of the problem in Nagasaki. The minister of war then acknowledged an attack on civilians with a new type of bomb that had caused "some damage" to the city, along with more than a hundred casualties. Later in the day, Tokyo would revise the official figure to about 500 souls.

More than three times nearer the hypocenter than Prefect Nishioka, master kite-maker Morimoto had survived with only two of his family members still alive. He would not have survived at all, if not for the cloud banks that had shifted the target away from his house and nearly 2.5 kilometers farther north, toward Urakami Stadium. Even so, two of the kite-maker's relatives were missing in Hiroshima, and now eight more were lost in Urakami. One of these had been working near José Matsou's husband at Prefect Nishioka's newest shelter. Now and forever, he would simply be among "the disappeared."

At Moment Zero, Morimoto was telling his wife about what he had witnessed in Hiroshima. "First, there came a blinding blue flash—"

A double flash cut his words short, blinking first red then blue and then flooding his kite shop in a stark yellow glare. Acting on sheer reflex, Morimoto grabbed his child and shoved his wife bodily down the steps into what until now had been merely a supply cellar, not a bomb shelter. Taking no chances, he pulled the heavy trap door down behind him and shielded his wife's and child's bodies with his own. Once the lid was down, thunder exploded instantly overhead.

Close! Morimoto told himself. He did not understand exactly how close, until he climbed out of the cellar. The whole top of his shop had been broken off in the middle, hauled away, and dropped on top of a house across the street. A stove was still sitting in place, with a teapot still upon it, but everything else—*everything*—appeared to have been scooped out of the building and taken up into the clouds. Envelopes with his name on them, along with shreds of singed kite paper, were presently drifting and fluttering with paper from every office building in the area, along a debris track that would spread 25 kilometers—fully 15 miles—north and east.

For all of his recent hardships, Morimoto was among the lucky ones. His shop was located in what by all appearances became a hole in both the firestorms and the radioactive downpours. Though ten in his family were now lost, Morimoto and his wife and child had suffered no burns or injuries other than the bruises sustained while tumbling into the cellar. Aside from nausea during the train ride from Hiroshima, Morimoto had escaped Disease X, and so, too, would his wife and child.

As Yamaguchi had observed, sometimes it worked out. In years to come, Shigeyoshi Morimoto would see children and even grandchildren flying his kites over a city that was fated to be symbolized by the phoenix.

MORIMOTO'S ASSISTANT, Doi, seemed to share his same improbable "fool's luck." Though he was still fighting against the chills and nausea of Hiroshima, Doi and his family, much like Dr. Nagai's two children, happened to be located on the shadow side of a mountain when the bomb exploded, 4,300 meters away, at a radius of nearly three miles.

Much like Morimoto, the apprentice kite-maker was explaining Hiroshima to his wife and daughter at the critical moment. Not anticipating immediate danger, he had let his nine-year-old son play on the grounds of a Buddhist temple next door.

"If you ever see the white flash," Doi emphasized for his wife and daughter a third and a fourth time, "you must immediately prostrate yourself on the ground. And whatever you do—*whatever* you do, do not look in the direction of the flash."

Doi's little girl became fidgety and asked if she could go down to the stream, where other children from the neighborhood were planning to bathe.

The flash interrupted her—cutting across the sky and shining through the windows as if a hundred search lamps had suddenly been aimed directly into the room.

"That's what I'm talking about!" Doi shouted. His wife jumped to her feet and began running toward the yard and the temple, but Doi tripped her to the floor and pulled his daughter down with him as the blast wave rocked the cottage, cracked windows, and punched holes through the paper sliding doors.

Like the Nagai children, Doi had no idea that on the other side of Kawabira's high ridge line lay an 80 percent kill rate and utter devastation. He found his son hiding inside the shrine's main building, a little bit shaken and staring wide-eyed at a fallen statue of the Mother of Mercy, but otherwise he was uninjured. Shock-cocooned. The only real danger appeared to be from the top half of a grandfather clock that fell out of the cloud and crashed into the shrine's yard like a meteorite. It was followed quickly by a strange hail of golf balls and tennis rackets . . . followed minutes later by a blizzard of paper.

ONLY A FEW kilometers from Doi, traveling along the scorched faces of Mounts Kawabira and Kompira, ship designer Yamaguchi's friend Akira discovered that even at a distance, the radiative heat of the Urakami cyclone did not let him approach within 1.6 kilometers (or within a mile) of the stadium and the hypocenter. Along the river-facing side of Kawabira, the foothills were pierced by five tunnels, each housing portions of Mitsubishi's aircraft and munitions works—including two ramps for catapulting some of the country's few remaining fighter planes out against the anticipated invasion by the American fleet. The workmen outside the tunnels were carbonized and even those inside appeared to have been blast-furnaced and suffocated. All of the vegetation was gone, except for the blackened trunks of trees—blown down, each of them, in the same direction.

Akira gave up the idea of reporting to the Mitsubishi office and followed in the direction the trees were pointing. He went to the top of Kawabira, hoping, if nothing else, for a chance to assess the damage from high ground. Second assistant kite-maker Masao, who had come from Hiroshima aboard the same train as Akira, and who had walked away from the same train wreck without injury, was following this same path to the top.

When the pair of double survivors crested Kawabira Hill, the clouds streaming across the sky were so dark they reduced the sunlight to barely the strength of a full moon. The far side of the valley—the part that had been located outside Kawabira's shadow and which therefore faced the full glare of the *pika*—appeared much as Akira expected it to be: severely mauled and smoldering. But people were forming bucket brigades from the stream below and all of the houses on the nearer, shadowed side, stood as if nothing had happened to them. Nothing at all.

Akira left Masao without any parting words, and began walking down toward the still-living grass and the still-flowing stream, vowing with each painful stride and with each pause to vomit that if he somehow managed to get out of this war alive, he would never go back again to Urakami or Hiroshima, to Mitsubishi or the navy.

In time, Akira's bouts of atomic bomb disease would pass, and he would live a long life in which to evolve from a designer of warships into an advocate for peace. Along with his friend Yamaguchi and an American physicist who once designed brave new bombs, he would advocate an impossible yet simple (if only symbolic) pipe dream in which countries in possession of nuclear weapons could be governed only by mothers who were still breast-feeding babies.

"IN THE END, all we can do is pray," one of the Jesuit brothers told Dr. Akizuki. Although he was Buddhist, Akizuki understood.

Presently, the black smoke rising from Urakami had nowhere to go. It was being contained by hills on either side of the valley the way the sides of a bathtub contain water. With gales being drawn in from the north and south, the only way out was to overflow the valley walls—so, mostly the smoke just accumulated overhead, shutting out the sun. The nearest and strongest source of light was the burning hospital. It blazed brightly enough to read by.

A nearby warehouse appeared to have survived reasonably undamaged. Akizuki and Nagai believed its metal roof would provide adequate shelter against the snowfall of ashes—which appeared to be irritating the lungs of Dr. Yoshioka and the other burn victims to such an extent that the open spaces of the hillside and the streets were beginning to sound like the world's largest emphysema ward.

The Jesuits helped Dr. Akizuki to spread mats on the concrete floor of the warehouse and to move Dr. Yoshioka there. Akizuki carefully removed the bandages from her face and cleaned her wounds a second time. He hoped she did not notice the pity and fear in his eyes. Splinters of glass and wood and even several twigs had been driven into Dr. Yoshioka's skin. Akizuki thanked whatever gods might be that Yoshioka's face was completely bandaged again when her mother arrived from a shadow-shielded town on the far side of the hill.

"You have done nobly," she told Dr. Akizuki, upon seeing her daughter injured and bandaged—and thankfully still alive.

Akizuki looked at the ground and shook his head, very slowly. "You don't understand," he said softly. "I am the one responsible for her injuries."

DR. PAUL NAGAI would live long enough to observe that the atomic bomb did not only crack concrete and steel. It cracked human souls with equal ease and with equal indifference.

Nagai's niece Tatsue would never forgive herself for staying with Kayano and Makoto at the shock-cocooned stream on the safe side of the mountain, after she saw the fireball rising from the direction of Urakami. Tatsue wished she could have been with her mother on the other side of Kawabira to at least provide some small comfort in her final moments. And no matter how many times Paul Nagai explained to the girl that even had such magic existed—as to allow her instantly to have been transported through a cyclone of flame to her mother's side—no matter how many times he tried to tell Tatsue that the most she could ever have hoped for was to become just one more dark spot in Urakami's drifts of gray ashes, she added her own false blame for a lack of courage to the weight of her mother's death.

On the day Urakami exploded, Tatsue's brother had escaped Saipan and managed to survive on a raft at sea with one side of his body burned and with the fingers of one hand gone. What kept him alive was the thought of returning home to see his mother and his sister alive again. He would never ask Tatsue to explain the details of their mother's death, but between the personal bond of brother and sister, the bomb had, from Moment Zero, begun radiating invisible cracks.

Even the bond between mother and child was not immune.

Tatsue would neither forget nor forgive the way her little cousin Eiko died. Never again would she refer to Eiko's mother by any name except, "Skinny Aunt."

The aunt, like Tatsue, had been shielded behind the shadows of Kawabira hill and the 366-meter peak of Kompira. Unlike Tatsue, Skinny Aunt did run to the other side, anxious to find the Urakami school where she had last seen her eight-year-old girl.

Somewhere beyond the flattened school, beyond the tangled mass of prison bars and the dead alligator man, she heard Eiko calling to her from one of the tunnels.

All of the other girls near the line of tunnel entrances appeared to have been simultaneously roasted and squashed like bugs. Most of them did not look human anymore, and neither did Eiko. Somehow her eyes had been shielded, but the rest of her face was a huge blister, and the whole front of her body was blackened alligator skin.

"My child was turned into a monster!" Skinny Aunt would tell Tatsue—over and over again, trying to explain it all away, thinking that Tatsue, if no one else, would somehow understand.

As Skinny Aunt told it, Eiko knew she was going to die; but she was so overjoyed to see her mother one last time that she seemed to revive. Tatsue believed that Skinny Aunt became afraid that the monster might survive.

"Mother!" Eiko said, "I couldn't walk any farther. I wanted to come to you. Please cover me up. I'm cold."

The mother stood, and said, "Wait a minute. I'll find something to make you warm. Just wait a minute—hold on to yourself."

And then she ran away, haunted from that moment and for the rest of her life by the image of little Eiko shivering alone in the dark, tormenting her forever with remembered cries of "Mother . . . Mother . . ."

"But Eiko was a *monster*," Skinny Aunt wanted to explain, and Tatsue would become all the more insulted by the woman's belief that she would understand.

"The real monsters," Tatsue would one day tell Uncle Paul Nagai, "they look just like us."

And perhaps the sainted ones, too, she would later relate. Hours after Skinny Aunt fled, another parent searching the shelters for a missing child found Eiko still alive and kept her warm until death came to her the following morning. Eiko lived far longer than she probably should have, calling the whole time for her mother. The stranger who cared for another's child as if it were her own gave her a Catholic burial near the ruins of Urakami Cathedral and the St. Francis Hospital, making sure little Eiko's name was recorded on a stone.

Five years later, in her memorial memoir, Tatsue would record that with the passage of time, whenever her aunt spoke about that day at all, she would "fix up" the part about how Eiko died. Each passing month, she would ask Tatsue to visit Eiko's grave for her, evidently unwilling to stand before Eiko herself.

"She kept trying to make friends with me," Tatsue would tell history. "But I [was] not to be taken in. I knew perfectly well that if such a thing ever happened again, she would desert me the way she did Eiko. So on the surface I [would] act respectfully toward her, but I really despised her. Yet who [was] I to despise her when I neglected my own mother? I despise myself. I hate myself!"

In his own memorial message, Paul Nagai would record that Skinny Aunt eventually lost all rational control of herself and began running into the streets scaring little schoolgirls—trying to push them to the ground or snatch them up. He and Tatsue had no doubt that each girl reminded her of Eiko. By this time, Tatsue's brother began abusing her with curses about his mother's death, escalating eventually to slaps and bone-cracking punches—at which point Tatsue vowed to kill him where he stood if he ever even tried to approach her again.

The fissures that formed in the hypocenter would still be present many years later. According to Paul Nagai: "But I am not talking about cracks in the ground. I am talking about the invisible chasms which appeared in the personal relationships of the survivors of that atomic wasteland. These rents in the ties of friendship and love have not closed up with the passage of time; on the contrary, they seem to be getting wider and deeper. Of all the damage that the atomic bomb did, these are by far the cruelest."

AS NIGHTFALL CAME to the hill of Kompira, Dr. Akizuki's father appeared unexpectedly alive, with his mother. Their smiling faces seemed to him like an image out of a dream.

"You've not been hurt, either!" Mrs. Akizuki said. Like many reunions that day, each had believed the other to be dead.

Dr. Akizuki's father began to describe a tour of terrors and odd wonders that began with a pre-*pika* detour to a law court in the business district of central Nagasaki. The courthouse was located behind a protective hill, more than 5 kilometers south of the Urakami hypocenter. At 11:02 a.m., the elder Akizuki saw a flash outside the windows and, several seconds later, he felt the building shake. The blast was so loud that when Mr. Akizuki stepped outside, he expected to find one whole side of the courthouse caved in by a direct hit from a conventional, half-ton bomb, but locally there did not appear to be very much damage at all and even some of the windows had survived.

Walking toward the flames and smoke of Urakami, the elder Akizuki became increasingly certain that his son could no longer be alive. No fewer than twelve square kilometers of flame forced him to detour around northern Nagasaki and south Urakami, sending him eastward along the ridges of Kawabira to the saddleback of Mount Kompira. There, atop the Kompira overlook, he watched the Urakami cyclone periodically rearing up through the sea of black smoke. For a very long time, the sight held him rooted to the ground. He had never seen or heard the like of it.

He asked the people who staggered up to the overlook what had happened and if Urakami Hospital was still standing.

Pleas for water and help were their only replies.

When Mr. Akizuki saw the hospital in flames and worked up the courage to descend toward it, he prepared his mind for the final fatherly duty of seeking young Tatsuichiro's bones. Instead, he and his wife found their son unhurt.

"And now," the elder Akizuki said, as he looked farther down the hill and saw that his house of four generations was gone, "now I ask for nothing more."

That night, father joined wife and son in the work of providing comfort to the injured. All of the medicines and dressings had either been burned or used up, so there was very little that could actually be provided by way of comfort except words, or a kind hand, or a place to rest on the lawn. The patients, the uncounted two or three hundred of them, were sleeping or weeping and bleeding under the starless sky.

As midnight approached, the cyclone weakened and collapsed into a mere lake of flames, and down there in the bottom, the black smoke began to part like the Red Sea. Noticing that the landscape was suddenly brighter at midnight than it had appeared at midday, Dr. Akizuki and his father paused and looked.

On the side of Urakami opposite the river, the ruins of several large buildings could be seen silhouetted within the flames. On this side, in the direction of the Yosē Girls' School, a tall steel frame—all that remained of an engineering school—seemed to be cooling from yellow-orange to a dull red glow when, spawning fire worms, it sagged slowly into the earth like a great ship sinking.

"Rome falls," Dr. Akizuki observed.

"What?" his father asked.

"This is how it ends," he said. "The Empire is consumed in flames.

AT APPROXIMATELY TWENTY minutes before midnight, Hirohito, the 124th Emperor of Japan, entered the conference room and sat across from Foreign Minister Togo. He was a thin, introverted, and nervous man, whose reign had begun at the age of twenty-six and had now lasted eighteen years.

The Emperor was a religious figure, said to be a direct descendant of the Sun Goddess—and now, according to Dr. Nishina and the other physicists, the Sun had touched the Earth, twice.

Togo's side of the table and Anami's side were equally deadlocked about whether to consider terms of surrender or to continue the fight. Reportedly, the debate continued for more than two hours, with each side airing the same arguments of the hour before, and the hour before that, sometimes word for word. The Emperor listened, taking it all in and quietly making notes to himself on a white pad.

Finally, about 2:10 a.m., Hirohito stood, and most of the attendees heard their bespeckled, Pharaoh-like ruler speaking to them for the first time. His voice was surprisingly human, faint and high-pitched.

Foreign Minister Togo would dictate the words to his son-in-law later that morning, wanting them to be freshly and accurately burned into history. According to Togo, the century's last emperor-as-deity announced, "I have concluded that continuing the war means destruction for the nation and a prolongation of bloodshed and cruelty in the world."

He looked past the ceiling toward the eastern sky as he spoke.

As Togo told it, Cabinet Secretary Hisatsune Sakomizu had to re-
strain himself from crying out, "We now all understand His Majes-
ty's wishes! Please do not condescend to say another word!"

"It goes without saying that it is unbearable for me to see the
brave and loyal fighting men of Japan disarmed," the Emperor said
without interruption. "It is equally unbearable that others who have
rendered me devoted service should now be punished as instigators
of the war. Nevertheless, the time has come when we must bear the
unbearable."

He looked down from the ceiling and glanced at Togo, who low-
ered his head; for tradition held that it was forbidden to look the
Emperor in the eyes.

"I now swallow my own tears," Hirohito said, and announced
his intention to give official sanction to Foreign Minister Togo's proposal to send a message to the American president, probing the enemy for their final terms of surrender.

LATER THAT MORNING, Joseph Fuoco awoke on Tinian to the news
that there was still no news from Tokyo. Apparently, the response
remained *mokusatu*, meaning "to treat with silent contempt."

After breakfast, Tibbets, Sweeney, Fuoco, and the other members
of the two missions were called to pose for group photographs in
front of their planes and then to be interviewed, in order to preserve
their thoughts and observations.

"We posed stiffly," Sweeney would recall. "And in proper military
jargon, we recited the facts: what, when, and where."

As was often the case, the mathematics of the situation were foremost in Sweeney's mind. During the three months since Truman took
office, the final advance from island to island and toward the Japanese
homeland had gained momentum. During this same brief interval,
Tokyo's own version of the "scorched earth" policy had inflicted almost half of all American casualties suffered in the Pacific throughout
the entire three and a half years since Pearl Harbor. By Sweeney's
arithmetic, the closer they came to victory, the higher the cost in
American lives. By this same arithmetic, the probability of atomic
bomb missions becoming routine by October clearly seemed too high.

Sweeney dreaded the thought of another atomic bombing. So did Joe Fuoco. Though the firebombings of Kobe, Osaka, and half of Tokyo had taken more lives, a crew member never knew if his own plane's incendiaries actually killed anyone. If death troubled him even remotely, there were about fifty other planes on each section of each raid—plenty of places to spread the blame, or hide it. Certainly, no one ever felt responsible for *all* the fires he saw below. Fuoco's way of coping was to convince himself that he was always riding the best plane in the fleet, and that his firebombs did not fail to hit the targeted oil tanks, refineries, and munitions plants. With the atomic bomb there was no pretending and there was no spreading of the blame. Hiroshima and Nagasaki were far more personal, because every death could be traced back to just a handful of men.

Luis Alvarez had feared that the weapons of mega-death would make war more impersonal, and perhaps even a little less distasteful as well. No one had anticipated that the opposite might turn out to be true. Joe Fuoco, for one, examined the photo of "his" mushroom cloud with a mixture of wonder and revulsion. "The shape of things to come," he said, and joked acidly about already missing "the good old days of the fifty B-29 raid."

He would say much later that he had been given "a glimpse of the future, up close and personal—and it ain't pretty."

Shortly before lunchtime, Fuoco received news that the White House had put out an order for a "temporary moratorium" on fire-bomb raids. Hope sprang throughout the isle of Tinian that Truman had received a response from Tokyo after all, and was giving Japan time to surrender.

Instead of firebombing, *Bad Penny* would be sent with the rest of her fleet to drop millions more of the counterfeit bills bearing warnings of surrender in the face of total destruction. The new messages were shorter and much more to the point than any that had been dropped before—"written to deliver the news like poison darts," Fuoco was told. Some of the leaflets were actually written as haiku-like paragraphs. The translations made Joseph Fuoco wince. This was as close as anyone would ever come to what death threats would look like if they were written by Edgar Allan Poe.

This time, the air force had enlisted the aid of a legendary writer of love letters from the navy, along with a recently freed survivor of a Japanese POW camp who just couldn't stop writing with hatred about his captors, their ancestors, and their descendants, and who regarded the atomic bombs as "pest control." The latter was named James Clavell and in future years he would obsess on trying to come to terms with everything he could learn about Japanese history all the way back through antiquity—then, after penning the semi-autobiographical novel *King Rat*, he would write a masterpiece called *Shogun* (though he would be more widely remembered for *The Fly*). The writer of love letters and short collections of love stories was a Quaker who, during his time in the South Pacific, had become embroiled in what was, in these days, a controversial interracial romance. Being a Quaker, James Michener was exempt from having to shoot down the Emperor's planes; so instead he offered to threaten Hirohito with nuclear annihilation. In his spare time, Michener began penning the first draft of his book about the Pacific war, which would soon evolve into the musical *South Pacific*.

While Joseph Fuoco waited and hoped for war's end, a fit of intrigue, rebellion, and suicide erupted in Tokyo and the Emperor became more cut off from the rest of the world than ever before, forced to lock himself in a hidden corner of the palace with a handful of loyal and trusted soldiers.

As Emperor Hirohito secretly recorded two copies of his surrender on phonograph records, an admiral named Ugaki, who sided with War Minister Anami and Field Marshal Hata against surrender, ordered seven bombers to be filled with all the high-level explosives they could carry on a one-way trip. Targeting Okinawa as the presumed source of the atomic bombs, Ugaki contrived a plan for a kamikaze raid, using what he believed to be the largest non-nuclear blockbuster bombs ever designed.

The admiral hoped that by this shining example he would inspire followers to continue the fight with a glorious new fleet of airplanes turned into rocket-assisted super-bombs.

By now, at Hirohito's orders, as carried out by Foreign Minister Togo, more than half of the nation's munitions factories were shutting down. As for the rockets at Ugaki's back—which in theory would have made his plane an unstoppable target during the final dive at Okinawa—the merging of rockets with a propeller-driven bomber at such short notice had already been described by the admiral's engineers as "technologically premature." The best that Admiral Ugaki could have wished for was to come through the sound barrier on final approach. With propellers hitting supersonic air on either side of his cockpit, this could not possibly have worked out as effectively as the admiral hoped.

The last word anyone heard from Ugaki was an announcement that his target was in sight and his squadron was ready to "light the candles" and streak down upon the hangars of Okinawa.

The fireworks north of the island were faint and not particularly noisy, given their distance of at least fifteen miles. U.S. military reports recorded no kamikaze raids that day or afterward—not on Okinawa, nor anywhere else.

Admiral Ugaki's planes simply flew in formation into mystery and legend, and became one of history's ghost squadrons.

THE WEATHER FRONT that caused Charles Sweeney to relocate his target the day before had shifted, bringing perfectly clear skies and promising a typically hot and humid August day.

Dr. Paul Nagai and the rest of the St. Francis medical staff had spent the night sleeping in rows on nests of ironed-down grass and scorched paper. Nagai awoke half believing that the events of the previous day were merely a nightmare, but when he looked down toward the gray wilderness in which his wife had most certainly perished, he accepted the reality that his whole world had been changed in a split second.

An old and previously senseless expression came quickly to mind, seeming all so clearly ironic and apt: "Under the talon of time, the blue ocean can turn into a mulberry field, and a forest can become a sea of ice."

Nagai's world was now a landscape of sudden, ungodly changes.

Though its steel and concrete skeleton still stood, the hospital had been gutted by fire. On the far side of the lawn, Dr. Akizuki and several of the nurses were cobbling together a kitchen range from piles of fallen bricks. They were already starting to prepare meals for the injured, using pots and sacks of only slightly scorched rice that someone had scavenged from the ruins downhill.

That the stream behind the hospital was bringing a steady supply of water for cleaning and cooking lulled the survivors into a sense of being doubly blessed. This day, the blessings just kept on coming. Akizuki and his mother were preparing a mash of "rice milk" for several orphaned babies when the hospital's carpenter called to them excitedly, urging the doctor to follow him quickly.

The carpenter led him to an underground storehouse beneath the collapsed walls of the hospital's kitchen. The air below was unbearably hot and Akizuki was certain that everything within the cave must already have been cooked or burned.

"Is this safe?" the doctor said, and began coughing. In one corner, a pile of coal for the kitchen's stoves was glowing bright red.

"Trust me," the carpenter replied, and led the way to a much cooler corner where two large wooden crates stood intact.

"You're a godsend!" Akizuki said, and surprised the carpenter with a powerful bear hug. When he first heard about Hiroshima, the carpenter began squirreling first-aid supplies down below, along with the kitchen's usual stores of coal and rice. The boxes of gauze and bandages near the tops of the crates, though slightly browned from the hot coals and the burning building, were still usable. More important, they had acted as an insulating buffer between the heat and the medicines deeper down. The two crates constituted less than a hundredth the medical supplies he needed for the patients covering the lawns and the walkways—but even with a little gauze and Mercurochrome in his hands, Dr. Akizuki's spirits soared.

When he stepped outside again, a new line of the walking wounded was advancing up the hill from the direction of Urakami. A woman had gone down to the edge of the place where the cyclone had raged and died the night before and found her husband wandering aimlessly. She explained that he had been working in one of the factories and was sheltered behind concrete when the *pika* came down from almost directly overhead.

The woman had carried him leaning on her shoulder all the way uphill. "He looks fine," she said, "but the explosion injured him somehow."

The physician examined him for signs of fractures or internal bleeding. Except for minor scrapes and bruises, the man from Ground Zero did not appear to be wounded at all, and yet he had become strangely weak and feeble, and seemed to have lost interest in everything.

Akizuki stood and looked down toward the zero point. All below spread a panorama of ridges and plains on which almost nothing stood. All of the familiar buildings had been blown over, gutted, or converted to dust. Telephone poles seemed to have fared better than buildings, although most of them were shoved over to one side. Almost none of the roads could be identified, because houses and stone fences had been lifted up and splashed across them. Wherever electricity poles still stood, sheets of scorched clothing and objects that resembled torn mattresses were suspended from their wires. Near the river, where fires still burned and columns of smoke were still rising, the iron skeletons of the Mitsubishi buildings were so twisted out of shape that they looked like fields of reeds caught in a storm.

The valley below was dead. There was no sign of any movement, by either human or beast.

After a while, Akizuki turned away from the scene, performed a quick mental inventory of the supplies remaining in his satchel, and headed off toward the warehouse in which Dr. Yoshioka lay. He had reserved a portion of his limited supply of painkillers specifically for her—still convinced, in his heart, that by sending her upstairs to eat something and to get some sleep just ahead of the *pika-don*, he had caused her injuries.

He found Dr. Yoshioka no better and no worse than she had been an hour before. Working at the most gentle pace he could manage, Akizuki added antimicrobial salves to the new dressings. As he worked, thoughts of the strangely lethargic man from Ground Zero became increasingly intrusive. He began to worry that he was missing some important detail that must not be overlooked. Dr. Nagai had mentioned to him at least two similar cases, in which nurses who came up from the foothills with no injuries at all were now violently ill.

And just once, Dr. Akizuki felt a cramp and a surge of nausea so strong that if it tarried for another two or three seconds, he believed it would have brought him to his knees.

It passed as quickly as it came and did not come again, so he explained it away as a muscle spasm, and forgot about it.

9

TESTAMENT

With the survivors now accustomed to mass pyres, a curious calm settled over Hiroshima. The normal human responses to roving black fog banks of corpse-fed flies were completely dulled. On August 10, the boy who called himself Barefoot Gen no longer felt able to react with excitement or fear, even when he beheld a river delta so glutted with bloated bodies that from that day forward whenever very low tides came to the mudflats they would appear to be sprouting fields of twig-like rib bones.

For years to come, Gen would not speak about what he had witnessed or how he responded to it. He had no choice. Soon, the MacArthur protocol would prevent anyone from speaking too loudly. And beyond official censorship, Gen was governed by an old schoolyard tale about the devil, who was said to have proclaimed, "If we catch a glimpse of hell and speak of it, we are pulled back again to hell."

Only much later would Gen reply to the devil's proclamation, telling all who would listen that if everyone remained silent and allowed hell to be forgotten, then hell would be all but guaranteed to come again.

Inside Ground Zero, on that fourth day after the bomb, there was simply no time for either emotion or reflection. Gen spent almost all the energy he could muster, mining more rice out of the destroyed army barracks. Along the path home to his mother, he saw a woman kneeling on a slab of broken concrete, hammering a charred human skull into fine powder. He paused to watch, and the woman took no notice of him as she gathered up the skull powder and sprinkled it over the wounds of a young man lying in the shade of a makeshift lean-to.

"What a strange thing to do," Gen said with detached curiosity.

The woman gave him no reply. She lifted the young man's head, pried open his mouth, and poured in a handful of the powder. The man's nose appeared to have been bleeding for at least a day or two, and all of his hair had fallen out. Even his eyebrows and eyelashes were gone, and his entire skin surface had been bruised. The mouthful of dust made him cough up a huge clot of blood.

"Excuse me," Gen said, as politely as he could, "but why are you feeding him powdered bones?"

"Putting this powder on the bruises makes them heal," she explained with an oddly flat courtesy. "And if you swallow the dust of a *pika*-man, it keeps you from dying."

"That can't be true. It sounds crazy."

"Stupid!" the woman shouted, no longer either detached or courteous. "*Hundreds* of people have been saved this way!" Then, noticing that Gen's own eyebrows were shedding hair, she offered him a handful of dust.

"No thank you," Gen said, and walked away. Farther along the path, he noticed a second woman, sprinkling dust on two burned children. Throughout the ruins, strange rumors were taking root. *Everyone wants to help the injured so badly that they'll believe almost anything*, Gen thought; and he wondered who had first come up with the idea that the bones of those touched by the *pika* could heal.

When Gen arrived home at the lean-to, he discovered (not unexpectedly) that trying to cover his baldness with a dead fireman's cap might have fooled Mother for an hour or two, but no longer.

"Tell me," she said, pulling the hat from his head, "are you in pain?"

"No," Gen said. "I feel fine, Ma."

"Are you sure? Don't lie to me."

"Really, Ma. I'm fine. Look at all the rice I'm able to find and carry."

Hugging him, and making him promise not to die, Gen's mother gave him a very strong tea she had been brewing all morning. She called it "medicine tea." It tasted absolutely awful in spite of being sweetened with a large chunk of "ant sugar," and when he told Ma to take the cup away, she insisted that drinking all of it would make him well.

When Gen finished drinking, he discovered that the entire bottom of the cup was filled with a dark, gritty mud.

"Ma?" he asked. "Is this medicine by any chance powdered bone?"

"Why, yes—how did you know?"

Gen had no response. He just took it as another strange fact of life after the *pika-don*. His mother had put more than repulsive dust in his tea, and in return, he continued to bring his mother and his baby sister more than a few buckets of rice. The amounts of residual radiation in the bones and the food were such that if Dr. Nishina or the scientists who dealt with the neutron surge on Tinian ever passed a Geiger counter over the material, their eyes would have widened with alarm and they'd have backed up a few steps. The substances were not overtly lethal. With rubber gloves and other minor precautions they could be safely handled. Yet no one who knew their true nature wanted the dust and the food on his skin or in his body.

Gen's mother still had all of her hair and seemed well, but she was already in serious trouble. In years to come, Gen would wonder if there existed a point during the feeding of poison from child to mother and mother to child, at which one more dose of radiation was reduced to mere redundancy. He supposed he might just as well ask how many angels could dance on the head of a pin.

While Gen's own symptoms of atomic bomb disease were easily seen, his mother's sickness would be hidden in progressive anemia, chronic leukemia, and bone cancer. When eventually she died and was cremated, Gen would be confronted with the mystery of a body converted entirely to ashes. Already, he had seen enough cremated bodies in Hiroshima to know that the bones, though fragile and easily crushed, still retained their original shape.

"Damn you!" Gen would shout to the bomb itself, to the minds that conceived it and the hands that gave birth to it. Though a coroner would give him many reasons why the skeleton disintegrated, Gen never doubted that radiation consumed his mother's very bones; it had continued eating away at her even after she died.

And one evening a cry went out to the impassive stars: "Give them back! Give me back my mother's bones!"

DUST AND SMOKE blew straight across Hiroshima Castle's foundations and through the Communications Hospital. The sun was almost down to touching the hills now, and even though it still had a way to go before actually reaching the horizon, the smoldering ruins and the funeral pyres and the dust were tinting it gold, almost orange. The lensing effect of the polluted atmosphere gave the ruins a ghost-image aspect, even in broad daylight.

That same afternoon of August 10, as Gen's mother fed him a strange brew of bone dust, a girl named Shoda, much like the once comatose Gen, seemed to be recovering some of her strength in the isolation ward for Disease X sufferers. Dr. Hachiya, the former ant-walker, thought that any improvement among these people was a reason for raised spirits. In his worst nightmares, he had imagined a biological weapon that eventually killed everyone it infected. The report of someone actually making a dramatic recovery now made Hachiya more determined to get out of bed—even if the sutures did pull at his skin. His friend Dr. Hinoi brought a cane and helped him downstairs to the isolation pavilion where the girl lay. On the way down, they both found their eyes drawn constantly toward the hypocenter.

"Aren't you curious?" Hachiya asked.

"About what?"

"About what's in there. What does it really look like, up close?"

"I've been giving that a lot of thought," said Hinoi. "I'm not really sure I want to know. And yet . . ."

"And yet, what?"

"I have a bike that still works—and I have to make a visit tomorrow to an army supply barge docked near the gutted bank building. I was thinking, perhaps if you're feeling up to it—"

"Then it's a deal," Hachiya said. He would have Hinoi remove the stitches early in the morning, and after their errand to the supply barge was done, they would mount, by way of detour, an expedition to the hypocenter.

When Hachiya reached the isolation pavilion, with thoughts of exploration and despair vying for first place in his mind, hope came racing toward the finish line in the form of a girl named Shoda whose pulse was strong, whose nose had stopped bleeding, and whose appetite was returning. Shoda returned a weak smile to Hachiya, and for the first time since the *pika-don*, he felt a sense of what might be called happiness.

Don't worry, he told himself a moment later, *it won't last*. As indeed it could not, once he took his first hard look at the other patients in the pavilion. On first hearing that a girl's health had improved enormously and that there were no new deaths to report today, Dr. Hachiya had allowed himself to believe that the worst was over. But when he saw the evidence of fresh bloody urine on virtually every mat, he understood that Hinoi and the other medics were reporting only a fleeting respite.

Two women complained of having balls stuck in their throats. Hachiya and Hinoi helped them to cough up golf ball–sized clots of blood and phlegm. As Shoda looked on, parasitic roundworms came out of their mouths.

Hachiya jumped to his feet, pulling two stitches.

"I've seen this before!" Hinoi said. "But it happens only when people are already dead. Only when the flesh begins to decay and can no longer support them do parasites abandon their hosts."

Dr. Hachiya glanced over at Shoda and asked Hinoi to move her at once out of the pavilion and into open air. Shoda nodded in grateful agreement. As she stood, one of the dying women emitted a strangled cry and suddenly spat an amazing wad of red phlegm and white worms onto the floor.

"Doctor?" Shoda whispered, trying to keep her gag reflexes under control.

"Yes," Hachiya said.

"I wonder if there is an operation that removes memories."

• • •

NEAR THE SOUTHERN fringe of Urakami's Ground Zero, ship de-signer Yamaguchi, his wife, Hisako, and his child were among the few creatures still moving, though Mr. Yamaguchi was becoming increasingly lethargic and depressed.

The engineer's side of his brain told him, logically, to be grateful that his burns from Hiroshima had sent his wife along an improba-ble path to shelter. Nevertheless, Yamaguchi's heart told him that his siblings were dead. His cousins were dead. A cousin's wife and their infant child lay dead in his own home.

Hisako's family had been worse than decimated. Yamaguchi and little Katsutoshi were all she had left, and Yamaguchi began to fear that even this would not last. A tunnel had become their only home, and as Yamaguchi's depression grew, his left arm and one whole side of his face had begun to swell like balloons inflating, turning purple and quite painful. The burns on his arms became gangrenous and started sprouting nests of fly larvae, at which point Yamaguchi passed out and could not be roused awake.

Hisako tried to remove the maggots but someone who seemed to know something about medicine arrived at the cave and insisted that she leave the maggots living in her husband's skin. The idea sounded to Hisako like an old wives' tale; but she put her faith in the visitor and decided that, even if it was only a myth, if it healed her husband's burns and he recovered, she would believe in it. She helped the new-comer feed her semiconscious husband concoctions made from dried rose hips and any other sources of vitamin C that could be found, and she was instructed to cook him helpings of liver from any animal— even from rats, if they could be found. She became convinced, over time, that had she taken Mr. Yamaguchi to one of the woefully over-whelmed and undersupplied first-aid centers in central Nagasaki, he would surely have died.

Little by little the blisters stopped discharging blood, and the maggots, hour by hour, removed dead and gangrenous flesh until Hisako believed the bones in her husband's arms might soon be ex-posed.

The visitor had sprinkled a powder of crushed grape seeds and talcum on the wounds to dry them out and prevent further infection. He also suggested attaching live leeches to the still-living flesh that surrounded the worst of the burns, explaining to Hisako that leeches would keep blood circulating through her husband's wounded hands, and prevent his fingers from dying and having to be amputated.

It would all have been dismissed as witchcraft by her ship designer husband, but he was semicomatose and now under the advice of the only house-calling doctor in town, so Hisako obeyed the "witch doctor" and spent uncounted hours searching for leeches and gagging on the bitter mineral water given her by the visitor. The concoction reeked of chalk and something mixed with miso that tasted how iodine smelled. In years to come, Hisako would leave physicians perplexed with assertions that, except for irritability and brief bouts of vomiting, she and the baby did not get sick at all during their stay in a tunnel on the edge of a radioactive no-man's land. And except for permanent, swelling-induced deafness in one ear, Yamaguchi would make a full and equally perplexing recovery.

The strange visitor Hisako would forever regard as her guardian angel refused her offers of thanks and devotion and, like most true heroes, simply walked away from history's stage.

MORE THAN TWENTY-FOUR HOURS had passed, and yet none of the additional doctors and medical supplies promised by Governor Nagano arrived at or near St. Francis Hospital. After the initial contact over a police radio, about lunchtime the day before, no more news appeared to be coming across the ridge from the governor's mansion.

When Prefect Nishioka arrived at Nagano's office, the governor appeared to be walking around in a state of shock. Nishioka learned that Nagano had been existing in a semi-trance state from the moment the initial estimates climbed from 50,000 presumed dead to more than 75,000—with at least another 75,000 severely wounded or near death.

The prefect had struggled for nearly a full day and night through rubble and through a second dose of radiation to cross through fields of fallout and reach the governor's headquarters, only to be immediately upbraided for being late. After this, the governor paced back and forth wordlessly while his chief of foreign affairs yelled in Nishioka's face about all the staff he and the governor had lost, blaming the prefect for not warning everyone about what he had seen in Hiroshima.

"If I had done as I wished and published a pamphlet about Hiroshima," Nishioka said in his own defense, "then you fine gentlemen would have been the first to accuse me of spreading wild rumors and I could have been shot for treason."

"If it were up to me, I'd shoot you now," Chief Nakamura said, "except for the fact that your hide isn't worth the cost of the bullets."

The prefect vomited a thick yellow mouthful of bile at the foreign affairs chief's feet. Before either man could step back, a second mouthful came up, mixed with blackened speckles of blood.

"What's wrong with you?" the chief demanded.

"I think we call it radiation poisoning," the prefect said, and added, "I think I'll go to my wife, now."

"You can't leave!" the governor yelled.

"I'm probably dead already," Prefect Nishioka announced, and he thought about the black-stained leaves he had observed in the governor's garden. "Just one last thing, though. Was there a fall of black rain here, yesterday?"

"Yes. And black dust, too."

"Then I suppose we shall all be in the same boat soon," the prefect said, and left.

WHEN DR. NAGAI FINALLY WENT down from the St. Francis medical outpost into his neighborhood, he found two of his neighbors arguing over a pile of charred human remains, located midway between the foundations of their houses. All the clothing and most of the musculature had been burned away on the bodies and a wedding band gave no clues to identity because it was now little more than a melted and re-solidified pool of gold. Both men were shouting that the body was that of his own wife. A third neighbor joined in, pointing out that Mr. Tanaka's wife had been "kind of heavyset," and he tried to determine from the diameter of a black stain in the gray ash whether a larger than normal amount of human body fat had been cooked into the ground. He could not tell one way or the other, and neither could Dr. Nagai—who continued his journey downhill, hoping that such an argument would not erupt over his beloved Midori.

Less than halfway home, Paul Nagai stumbled and almost passed out. He stood and stumbled a second time, and a little farther downhill he met his aunt Matsu, who kept him from falling a third time and told him, "You don't want to go down there."

"Why?"

"Because the people you'll meet are going crazy," Auntie Matsu warned. "They are like animals after a forest fire—dangerous and half scared to death, fighting over anything and willing to do petty little bits of evil."

Leading him back uphill, Auntie described arguments over broken bits of dinnerware turning suddenly bloody, but what seemed to bother her most was an encounter with a young woman who returned home to find her grandmother uninjured and who was singing to herself cheerfully as she washed singed, flower-patterned clothes in black well water and hung them out to dry.

"I'm so happy," the strange woman had said. "I never thought Grandma and I were such especially good people, but it's only by God's special grace that we weren't killed." Then, looking out across the center of Urakami, she announced, "Those people who were burned to death—they must have made God angry, mustn't they? They must have provoked him to wrath."

"You mean, like my baby cousin Kimiyo?" Auntie Matsu said. It seemed to her that such civilized ideas as "Judge not" and "Love thy neighbor as thyself"—in which Auntie always believed—had been lost and now belonged to an older world.

Dr. Nagai heard that by nightfall of August 10, the strange young woman collapsed and began to suffer nosebleeds. By midnight, she would die very old.

AT DAWN ON AUGUST 11, a wealthy citizen of Nagasaki arrived at St. Francis, bringing fresh white rice for his mother and for a hundred other patients, along with gleeful rumors for Dr. Akizuki—"Doctor, I hear that we have recaptured Okinawa, and dropped America's own atomic bombs on Washington and New York."

"Even if it were true," Akizuki said, "I would never rejoice over that kind of story, I swear it. Hasn't enough been lost? Is useless reciprocal killing all that we have left?"

The man went home for more supplies, and he would never speak to Dr. Akizuki again about winning a nuclear war.

MUCH AS NO NEWS except that carried by survivors was going out of the two cities, little real information was coming in. At Hiroshima's Communications Hospital, on the sunny, unusually windy morning of August 11, Dr. Hachiya heard rumors about Admiral Ugaki's victorious attack on Okinawa before he received confirmation that the earth tremor he felt two mornings before was in fact Nagasaki dying.

Dawn had also brought news that more people appeared to be coming down with the mysterious hemorrhagic fever; several women in the isolation tent had died during the night. Hachiya believed he was beginning to feel the first flu-like symptoms, and wondered if he might now himself be one of the infected.

"I might as well see what's happened out there before I die," Hachiya told Dr. Hinoi, and he asked his friend to remove all of the remaining stitches from his wounds and set out with him on the expedition they had discussed the day before.

"You mean, right now?"

Hachiya nodded.

"Well, and why not?" Hinoi said, and shrugged. "I woke up today with a bit of the gastroenteritis myself . . . if that's what we're deciding to call it this morning. We might as well go while we're still guaranteed to have the strength."

"Or before the excursion becomes two men on a bike with bloody diarrhea," Hachiya said, and tried to force a laugh. Hinoi stared toward the distant Dome and ignored the joke. He was all business now, mapping the route in his head, revising in accordance to the dictates of roads and debris piles. The path to the army's medical barge looked simple enough. Their starting point was already within

Ground Zero, and buildings tended to be stamped more flatly into the ground here than on the landscape Dr. Nagai had tried to navigate in the hills of Urakami. In central Hiroshima, the streets were clearly visible and in most places seemed not to have been hit from the sides by avalanches of debris.

As Hinoi and Hachiya progressed, the most consistent obstacles they encountered turned out to be downed trolley wires and their supporting cables—which had to be negotiated at regular intervals, two or three times along each city block. These pauses gave Dr. Hachiya opportunities to inspect the ruins on both sides of the road. Most of the buildings had been squashed like wicker baskets stepped on by elephants. Some had burned after they were squashed. Others were simply ground down to pulp and grit. Chips from tile walls and bathtubs were localized in some of the debris piles, indicating where bathrooms had been. Fragments of crockery pointed toward kitchens, and shards distinguished by patterns of finely wrought cloisonné reminded Hachiya when they were passing through a wealthy neighborhood. The occasional burned or broken toy always brought him back to darker realities.

"Damage to the city was far worse than I had imagined," Dr. Hachiya would record, which said much about what he had seen and touched during the expedition. From atop the Communications Hospital, he had looked across the hypocenter and had imagined quite a lot.

One of the largest mansions in town must have been completely carried away by the updrafts and the fire worms; for instead of being hammered into the earth, the house appeared to have been lifted off the ground like a box and hauled away. The first-floor landing of a magnificent oak stairway was deeply charred, but otherwise it still stood perfectly in place with its handrails undisturbed—in the middle of the neighborhood of Komachi, where everything else had disappeared.

Mrs. Nagahashi, a famous musician, had lived in this most modern house in all of Japan, designed by her late husband during a kinder decade, with input from the American architect Frank Lloyd Wright. On either side of two grand pianos, built-in cabinets stood floor to ceiling, bearing an entire library of 78-rpm records.

The westernized house was considered treasonous by most of the neighbors, and in time of war, even the mere playing of music was frowned upon—more so, playing the instruments and songs of the barbarians. But even during hard times, Mrs. Nagahashi insisted on teaching the neighborhood children how to play the piano. According to her only known surviving student, Seki Chieko, who had been away with her family on the day the *pika-don* came, Mrs. Nagahashi's desire to teach music grew noticeably stronger after her son, who once had a promising musical career of his own, was killed in the battle for Tinian and the other outlying islands.

Like the stairway and the two charcoal pianos, everything else on the mansion's ground floor was somehow still in place, exactly where it had been at 8:15 a.m. on August 6. Behind a mound of small black drum cans that turned out to be stacks of records fused together, soldiers had found Mrs. Nagahashi in front of a Buddhist altar. She looked like a praying mantis—*carbonized*—and no one who saw the mantis woman could escape the realization that she must have been praying at the moment of the *pika*.

When he returned to the Communications Hospital, Dr. Hachiya was too tense to follow Hinoi's orders and go straight to bed. He resumed something akin to making normal visits to the patients, walking around in a filthy torn shirt, with fresh stitch holes slicked in sweat and grime. He looked and felt like a snail with a beard, and he realized he was beginning to *like* the feel and the smell of his own filth.

Even when night came and exhaustion finally sent him upstairs, all Hachiya could think about were the broken toys and the army's funeral pyres burning under the cold stars while Mrs. Nagahashi still prayed. He paced the upper floor of the ruined hospital, paused from time to time to lie down on his bed frame for a few minutes, then paced again. As dawn approached, a great wind began to blow, blotting out Hachiya's view of the city behind a translucent lens of dust and filth. The gusts knocked plaster and chips of concrete from the hospital's few remaining walls.

"This I enjoyed," Hachiya would later record. "And I seemed to lose all restraint. It suited my mood."

A new day had begun.

• • •

MICHIE HATTORI, the shock-cocooned Urakami schoolgirl who returned home to discover her whole neighborhood miraculously cocooned behind a tall ridge, was drafted along with her parents and everyone else on her block into the rescue and recovery effort. By the morning of August 12, the effort was reduced mostly to the collection of bodies for a makeshift morgue on the blackened side of the ridge, which became a temporary holding pen of sorts until Michie and the other children could gather enough wood for a funeral pyre.

Almost all of the survivors who came from the blackened side were dead within a day or two. With the exception of Michie, everyone else who walked away from the center of the explosion appeared to have been exposed to something that burned them from the inside, and few of these were expected to live for very much longer.

A woman who had survived with the pattern of her kimono tattooed by the *pika* onto her skin died suddenly after vomiting up what appeared to be part of her stomach. An army officer assigned Michie to carry the body to the wood pile. *Maruta*, he had called the corpse—referring equally to the timbers and the dead people as "logs." And as the skin of a *maruta* woman tore off in Michie's hands, and as the flames were finally ignited and huge clouds of flies swarmed around the hot perimeter, Michie could scarcely believe that only a week before she would have been horrified by a paper cut on her finger.

Less than an hour's walk uphill and to the northwest of Michie's town, the world seemed even more wretched to Dr. Akizuki. He glanced reproachfully at the sun; for it had risen as if nothing at all untoward were happening down here on Earth. Its serenity seemed only to intensify his gloom.

The governor's promised relief from an army "medical patrol" had just arrived three days late, accomplishing little more than to inoculate Drs. Akizuki and Nagai against hopefulness. Just when they began to think it was safe to suppose their situation had bottomed out and could not get much worse, something always seemed to sneak up from behind with the message that neither of them quite understood how deep the bottom could be.

Paul Nagai's aunt Matsu had warned everyone about troglodytes in the lower hills who appeared to be losing their minds. Now Akizuki and Nagai believed they were in danger of losing theirs.

The army medical patrol trucks dropped off thirty additional burn victims whose gums had started bleeding, as well as their noses and bowels. Some were actually weeping blood. The patrol leader said, "They're losing blood like this because they must have breathed some poisonous gas. They are also sick to their stomachs. Find out what's causing it."

"All of our equipment is destroyed," Akizuki explained. "We do not have a single microscope still working. How are we supposed to discover what is causing these symptoms, much less to cure them?"

"You're doctors, aren't you? It's your job," the leader said, then helped himself and his crew to more than half of the medical outpost's boiled and potted drinking water, in addition to much of the remaining food supply.

If not for the fact that Dr. Yoshioka and the other patients needed him, and if not for knowing that it would have been the immediate death of him, Akizuki believed he had enough anger-fed strength to decapitate the army's local group leader with a single swipe of a shovel.

After the patrol left, Akizuki agreed with Dr. Nagai to give himself precisely five minutes to seethe with hatred and fear, and then to dust himself off and accomplish with what few supplies remained whatever he could, until he could not.

And so, with barely more than a few pounds of gauze and a bottle of iodine, he set off on his rounds, while the nurses and medical students grew progressively weaker and one by one became patients themselves. In a seemingly opposite and equal reaction, some of the patients became nurses and interns.

Mysteriously, most of the mild TB cases were feeling well enough to assist Akizuki and Nagai in their grueling schedules. Like the previously ailing Dr. Nagai, their health seemed actually to be improving, albeit by small steps. Akizuki noticed that those TB patients who had been particularly heavy smokers also seemed to be more resilient against Disease X. He chalked it up to a Darwinian natural selection effect: were their bodies not built especially well in the first place, they probably would not have survived TB long enough to see the *pika-don*.

In the afternoon, using a rice steamer as a sterilizing apparatus, with unraveled silk thread for stitches and two TB patients for assistants, Dr. Akizuki converted a burned-out library into an operating room and tried his best to repair Dr. Yoshioka's face. He found new pieces of glass coming to the skin surface between her cheek and the bridge of her nose—and another close to her eye.

The blast wave had struck the windows almost horizontally, and two or three particularly fast slivers evidently went all the way through Dr. Yoshioka's cheeks, burying themselves inside her tongue. Another shard had penetrated her blouse and her chest, embedding itself in a rib. He removed it with a dull knife and tweezers, while one of the patients held a candle and a broken mirror to provide something approximating a close-up lighting system.

In total, Dr. Akizuki managed to extract seven pieces of glass over the course of an hour, at which point Dr. Yoshioka could endure the pain and exhaustion no more. He stitched a gash through a breast and another between an eye and the bridge of her nose. The laceration through Yoshioka's upper lip yawned so wide that the assistants could not bear to watch. A large sliver of glass still remained in her lower jaw, overlooked. Glass shrapnel was particularly cruel, for even had the hospital's X-ray machine remained functional, glass would not have shown up on the films the way metal shrapnel revealed itself and would have eluded detection.

Early the next morning, those patients who were feeling able—among them the recovering TB cases—began wandering down toward the deeper, flatter ruins: first in search of their loved ones, and then in search of useful implements that might have survived. By now there were few thoughts of rescue in lower Urakami. Theirs was strictly a recovery operation.

Those who were able to find anything reminiscent of their exploded and carbonized homes turned over every fragment of roof tile—though when they reported to Dr. Akizuki what they had found, it seemed only by an act of imagination that any of them could have believed they uncovered their actual homes. All of the roof tiles in the realm of the fire mountain were broken into fragments smaller than hen's eggs. Most were heavily granulated and pitted by the fires. As Akizuki recorded it, once the roof fragments were pushed aside, the searchers descended into narrow strata of wall plaster and ashes, sometimes studded with fragments of bone. Though most of the radiation had by now dissipated, what fractionally remained still carried a substantial jolt, especially for people already dosed to varying degrees, and especially in the area around the hypocenter.

Those TB patients who had felt well on the third day and who did not have relatives missing near the hypocenter continued to regain their health. Those who descended into the foothills in search of loved ones returned with radioactive dust on their skin, and in their lungs—which began to work in concert with the usual shocks to the immune system that accompanied the inhalation of alkaline concrete dust and gypsum-based plaster.

In his medical reports, Dr. Akizuki was eventually to call the Urakami dust "death sand." That night, however, neither Akizuki nor anyone else at or near the St. Francis Hospital campsite had any idea of a new danger that could neither be seen nor felt. Only much later would it be known to them that breezes coming up the hill brought radioactive particles as well as relief from heat and humidity. Only much later would Drs. Akizuki and Nagai understand that the returning searchers who distributed boiled rice to the patients through the night of August 13 were already very sick men. As they served dinner, their clothes shed "death sand" the way cats shed dander and hair. The radioactive particles mixed impartially with diced pumkins and apples—which the searchers stirred into everyone's miso soup.

ON TINIAN, CHARLES SWEENEY and Joseph Fuoco had seen the promising news of August 10 come and go with no word of the indicated surrender offer from Japan actually coming through. The moratorium against bombing with anything worse than the harsh writing of Clavell and Michener had continued through the nights of August 11 and 12 and through the afternoon of Dr. Akizuki's searchers from the TB ward.

On the evening of August 13, President Truman authorized General George Marshall to resume firebombings against Japan. During the predawn hours of August 14, Marshall ordered essentially the launch of every one of the more than 2,500 aircraft within striking range of Japan. Among the few exceptions were *Enola Gay* and *Bock's Car* (the latter because three of its engines were "mostly fried" and needed complete overhauls). *Great Artiste* was also held back, because all of the scientific monitoring devices were still aboard and might be needed if further atomic bomb missions became necessary in September and October. Sweeney headed back aboard *Straight Flush*, with Joseph Fuoco in the photographic plane, escorting what was, in all essentials except a working core, the third atomic bomb-run on Japan.

Like *Enola Gay* and *Bock's Car*, *Straight Flush* had been modified to carry a single, pumpkin-shaped bomb loaded with a multi-ton explosive charge of Torpex (with a slightly reconfigured detonation sequence, designed to produce a preshaped blast ring capable of cutting through anything located at ground level). On this flight, the crews were honing the skills acquired during the previous two atomic bomb runs. The *Straight Flush* pumpkin was the most powerful non-nuclear explosive ever dropped from a plane, but as Sweeney would recall, though it possessed exactly the same casing and machinery he had dropped over Urakami, "This time, it contained neither the secrets nor the horrors of the universe."

Straight Flush's target was the Toyota Motor Works at Koromo. No flak came up and no fighters, and, though *Straight Flush* was reportedly among the last of the 2,000 B-29s to release its load, this time no smoke from preceding raids obscured the target. Sweeney's bombardier reported that the "pumpkin" detonated within 200 feet of its aiming point; and the pilot concluded that, just like Mitsubishi at Urakami, the name Toyota had been erased from history forever.

IN HIROSHIMA, Dr. Hachiya's morning rounds were interrupted by air-raid alarms from the river barges. In everyone's mind was the same thought: *Could the* pika *come again, after all that we have been through?* The August 6 flash had caught everyone completely by surprise. Hachiya realized that he was now shaking with fear, and as the drone of B-29 engines descended upon the wasteland, he sought the protection of a broad, steel-reinforced concrete pillar. A large squadron was approaching Hiroshima Bay from the south. At any instant, the physician expected another great flash overhead. But he cut short his own feelings of panic and made a decision that if death were to strike this hospital again, then his final moment would be with the patients, and not cringing behind a pillar.

The planes—at least two whole squadrons of them, one after another—passed noisily overhead without dropping anything. Then, suddenly, tremors began coming through the hospital's floor and seconds later Hachiya could hear the distinctive distant detonations from stream after stream of blockbuster bombs carpeting the ground in the northwest. He concluded that the planes must be targeting the naval air base at Iwakuni.

At first, Hachiya felt extremely lucky to have been spared a second time, but it occurred to him that luck had nothing to do with it. There was simply nothing left in Hiroshima worth bombing.

In a lean-to beyond the hospital, Barefoot Gen's baby sister had ceased crying and, strangest of all, had begun refusing her mother's milk. As Gen would recall it, "Little Tomoko seemed to be quietly sleeping all the time—a baby ominously too well behaved."

Not even the squadrons clamoring overhead and the subsequent shaking of the earth roused Tomoko to cries of alarm. When he saw the B-29s, Gen did not think about another *pika*. He raised a clenched fist at them, believing they had come to gloat. There had been rumors from the outside about defeat, and about inevitable surrender.

"Tell me why now, this talk of surrender?" Gen's mother had said. "Why not before?"

Less than a kilometer away, a thirty-two-year-old poet named Kurihara was asking the same questions as she carried from the foundations of her home a radioactive memento of human bone fragments stuck together like candies in melted glass. One day, she resolved, the memento should be displayed in a museum, where all humanity could come and witness its destiny, and vow to avoid it.

The bones in the glass had been flash-fossilized so quickly that some of them were still white. Kurihara was now adding frightening quantities of her own blood to the memento, from a nosebleed that seemed to be worsening each passing hour.

Somehow, her blood seemed apt. She thought of the Emperor's red and white flag—which up until now had represented the Rising Sun. But presently, the red of the Rising Sun became people's blood, and its background of white became people's bones.

"The people have spilled their blood and exposed their bones," Kurihara said, raising her own clenched fist against the sky—"because of the flag of blood and bones."

In Tokyo, Foreign Minister Togo received reconnaissance reports that the United States fleet was moving in right behind the bombers. The Empire's spotter planes had evidently been allowed to observe the fleet and return without being fired upon. What they reported was not merely a fleet but an armada that seemed to put the record-breaking Normandy invasion in the minor leagues: supply ships of every size and configuration, destroyers, cruisers of indescribable variety, and several aircraft carriers. The ships were grouped in formations five across and twenty deep.

War Minister Anami refused to believe that the armada meant defeat and, along with Field Marshal Hata, General Shizuichi Tanaka, and a major named Hatanaka, he insisted that an all-out bombing raid on the convoy "might make the Americans rethink their actions." They amazed Togo, speaking as if none of them had attended the Imperial conference of August 9, as if even were their heads chopped off and lying upon the floor, they would somehow be able to bite the toes of their enemies and continue the fight.

A general named Mori was ordered by Hatanaka to join him in sealing the palace grounds and preventing the broadcast of Emperor Hirohito's declaration of surrender. When Mori refused, he and his aide were shot and hacked to pieces. Major Hatanaka next conspired to seize control of the nation's radio studios, hoping to replace the Emperor's pre-recorded broadcast with an announcement of his own. Hatanaka still regarded the Emperor as a sacred figure who could not be harmed, but everyone else was fair game.

Meanwhile, General Tanaka and his staff received and compiled reports of air raids that appeared to be taking place virtually everywhere. By lunchtime, the general had confirmed to his own satisfaction that the approaching armada—which Anami insisted on dismissing as "only a phantom fleet of rumors"—did indeed exist and was driving straight toward Tokyo. At this point, Tanaka withdrew his support for the military coup, and Hatanaka, along with several other leading rebels, ended his life by suicide on the palace lawn.

Throughout the long hours of the failed rebellion, all members of the Emperor's staff were marked for summary execution and Hirohito himself was, in effect, held under house arrest.

Unable to locate and destroy either of the Emperor's two recorded declarations of the surrender, and with generals loyal to Hirohito quickly regaining control of Tokyo's radio stations, Anami wrote, "I apologize to the Emperor for my great crime," and wandered off to write his last poems, get drunk, and slit his stomach open with a ceremonial blade. Many years would pass before the people of Japan learned what had actually transpired as the morning of August 14 dissolved into an incomparable spasm of denial, assassination, and suicide. But rumors hatched and took flight everywhere—and about everything.

KAZUSHIGE ITO WAS NOT YET BORN on the day Hiroshima died. As his father would tell it, Kazushige's twelve-year-old uncle Hiroshi had emerged perfectly unharmed from a school on the fringe of Ground Zero, where almost everyone else had been burned and crushed. Following a set of railroad tracks homeward to the eastern hill country, he was helped by a stranger who offered his own rice ration, and whose actions matched Prefect Nishioka's description of an encounter with a "sole survivor" schoolboy, near a railroad station. By the time the boy returned home, the rest of the Ito family was already counting him among the dead, but he had been so thoroughly shock-cocooned that there was not a scratch anywhere on his body, and even his clothes seemed perfectly intact.

Locally, he became known as "the miracle boy."

Kazushige Ito's father, Tsugio, himself only a boy, recalled that during the first days following the explosion, his older brother seemed well enough to take him fishing and to participate in a victorious game of baseball against a rival neighborhood team. In reality—and all too often—atomic bomb survivors were not quite as they appeared.

The burning from within started on or about August 14, at the beginning of the Buddhist Week of the Dead. One moment the two Ito brothers were playing, and in the next the older boy fell to his knees, grabbing his stomach as if stabbed. By evening, the stricken child's mother found it difficult to go near him and began to shrink away from her own son. They all shrank away, because on each exhaled breath, there came a stench that reminded family members of a corpse already lying on the ground for several days. The normal bacteria of decay were eating the Ito child's lungs and his throat, while his tongue—bloated and purple and hot—stank of rotting meat even as he still moved and tried to speak.

Finally, Tsugio's brother Hiroshi let out a bone-chilling howl. Foam and blood flecked his lips and, just as suddenly as he had sickened from the "death sand" and the rays, the miracle boy lay back and died.

Meanwhile, in the blackened shell of Hiroshima's Communications Hospital, Dr. Hachiya had heard stories about people who were outside a house at the moment of the *pika* and who were shadowed from the heat ray. And yet, though escaping without any burns, they sickened and died while people who were inside the house, though severely injured by collapsing beams, were still alive. If the rumors about the bomb releasing a poison gas or of the Americans following the bomb with a biological weapon were true, then the people who crawled from inside the house should have been infected or gassed just as easily as those who were standing outside, Hachiya concluded. Whatever killed the people who were outside had to involve a very short-lived exposure hazard to something that had largely evaporated by the time the people trapped within pushed their way out to the surface. The more Hachiya thought about it, the more confused he became.

A visit from a navy captain who had come to Hiroshima on a medical barge brought an end to the confusion. "The *pika* itself appears to be the source of some dreadful disease," Captain Fujihara explained. "The navy has begun studying more than thirty cases, and though not a doctor myself, I can still tell you without doubt that in each case, white blood cell counts have been crashing."

"You've *got* to get me a microscope," Hachiya said.

"I'm sorry," the captain replied. "We have only one on the barge and we're working with a cracked lens." Apologetically, he opened a briefcase and, instead of medical equipment, presented the doctor with a bottle of whiskey and several packs of cigarettes. "This isn't much," he said, "but these things may actually be even harder to find than microscopes."

I'd rather have the microscopes, Hachiya thought of saying, but offered his thanks instead.

After the captain left, Hachiya lit a cigarette and began sifting through the shattered remnants of the hospital's half-dozen Bausch and Lomb scopes, hoping to cobble together at least one marginally useful piece of equipment. The effort was doomed from the start. Not a single oil emersion lens had survived as anything more than a flattened brass cylinder and glass converted once again to sand. He estimated that the blast wave must have been traveling at a speed of 200 meters—or two city blocks—per second when it struck them.

He remembered that one of the Communications Bureau's district managers had kept a microscope locked in his safe. The office holding the safe was a bunker, sheathed in reinforced concrete. It made no difference. When Hachiya found the bunker, it was shattered like a broken basket. The wind from the bomb had turned the safe completely around and smashed the steel door off its hinges. The microscope was so utterly destroyed that the doctor began to appreciate more than ever before the improbability of his own survival on that first day of the *pika-don*.

Dr. Hachiya's second visitor of the afternoon would remind him again of improbability and mortality—and, though bringing gifts, would accidentally fill him with remorse for having lost all sense of self and joined the ant-walkers that day.

Mr. Sasaki lived across the street from Hachiya, near the Misasa Bridge. He came to the hospital bearing freshwater *ayu* fish for the patients and the staff.

"How is your family?" Hachiya asked.

Mr. Sasaki explained that it had taken him several days to find them, because when the *pika* flared out, he was running an errand to one of Prefect Nishioka's suburban offices. Indoors, and at a distance well beyond the blast radius and the heat ray, he escaped without injury. Even from a safe distance, upriver and in the hill country, he could see that his neighborhood was "under the mushroom's stem." Sasaki navigated his bicycle through debris-strewn streets and found his home and Dr. Hachiya's reduced to knee-deep piles of ash. Fortunately, Shigeo Sasaki's family had traveled upriver with other survivors from the neighborhood. He found them, mud-soaked and looking hungry, about the time the tremors from Nagasaki reached Hiroshima.

"Little Sadako keeps talking about the bright light," Mr. Sasaki said. The child was only two, but not yet nor ever would she forget the false sunrise and the great wind. Sadako's five-year-old brother Masahiro and Mrs. Sasaki were bruised and shaken but safe. They had survived the picket of fire worms that advanced into the river and became waterspouts. They had even survived the rain of oil without suffering any symptoms of what Dr. Hachiya was now coming to call "atomic bomb disease."

"Were they inside the house during the *pika-don*, or outside?" Dr. Hachiya asked.

"Inside," Mr. Sasaki replied, and Hachiya sighed with relief. "That's how they got bruised," Sasaki continued. "They were bounced around inside, and when they fled into the street, though the house seemed intact, it just sort of leaned slowly over to one side. And then, as the flames and the confusion grew worse, they got separated from my mother and she was lost."

"*What?*"

"They never did see her again."

For all the horrors Hachiya had seen and experienced during the past week, the death of Mr. Sasaki's kindly mother felt like one punch too many in the stomach. From what Hachiya was able to learn, little Sadako's grandmother was burned to death as the firestorm developed, and like others caught in the maelstrom, there was little that anyone could do to save her. But Hachiya had been *right there* when the fires started—and he remembered, vaguely, seeing the

Sasaki house leaning to one side before it began to fall apart, just as Mr. Sasaki had described it.

From the moment of hearing that his friend's mother had been injured and killed only steps away from him, it did not matter to Hachiya that he had emerged from the ruins of his own house, bleeding and confused, into a world turned suddenly and violently unfamiliar. All that mattered was that instead of helping his neighbor he had joined the nearest ant trail.

Not that Mr. Sasaki, who was every bit as kindly as his mother, would ever say a word of reproach against him. Instead, he would continue to bring whatever food he could spare for his neighbor, and for those under his care. Yet from that moment, the first sting of survivor's guilt began to work its poison in Hachiya's heart, and he would never be able to meet Sadako or her father without being brought back to the picture of himself as the sort of person who became an ant-walker in a time of dire need. His only hope of avoiding the pain was to avoid *them*. It was the beginning of what Dr. Nagai of Urakami was already coming to recognize as one of those invisible cracks made by the atomic bomb—a crack between neighbors and friends, although they would never talk about it.

"I have one more thing for you," Mr. Sasaki said. "News from the prefect's office. This is not rumor. It comes direct through Foreign Minister Togo. An important radio broadcast is announced for tomorrow."

"What can it be?"

Neither man wanted to speculate, but both supposed that War Minister Anami was about to announce the advance of enemy fleets toward the homeland's shores. He would presumably order every man, woman, and child to fight against the Americans to Japan's own extinction—using cleavers, knives, and sharpened bamboo sticks.

For a while, Hachiya could put thoughts of ant-walker guilt aside in favor of thankfulness for being without electricity. *We have no radio*, he told himself, and realized that living empty-handed in the Stone Age actually gave him a freedom of spirit and action he had not known since the war began.

· · ·

ON THE MORNING of August 15, Gen awoke feeling strong enough to enlarge his mother's lean-to into one of the first corrugated zinc houses in what was to become the Hiroshima prairie's first shantytown.

On the way home from his rice-mining operation, one of Gen's new neighbors told him that a truck from the Communications Bureau had come through and dropped a radio off at Dr. Hachiya's hospital. When Gen arrived at the hospital steps, someone had already hooked the radio to an all but completely dead car battery and the lawn of the Communications Hospital was humming and crackling with fading static. A distant voice said, "We have resolved to pave the way for a grand peace for all generations to come, by enduring the unendurable and suffering the insufferable."

Gen did not hear this. All that came through clearly, before the battery failed, were the words "enduring the unendurable."

The hospital's electrician, who had been standing with his ear close to the speaker, announced that what everyone had just heard was the Emperor's own voice, and that he had just said the war was over.

"Who won?" someone asked.

"He said we must bear the unbearable," the electrician replied; and then, looking around, he added, "Who do you *think* won?"

GEN'S BABY SISTER, whom he had named Tomoko because the word meant "friend," was clearly dying.

Gen's father was dead.

Presently, some of the isotopes absorbed in Ma's bones were being stealthily removed and rerouted to her milk glands, but they had already done their work and stem cells in her bone marrow, ravaged by chromosomal dislocations, were beginning to divide wrongly in a march toward eventual chaos and death.

Gen's older sister was dead.

Gen's little brother Senji was dead.

On the night of the surrender, a boy only a year or two younger than Gen, drawn by the scent of food, snuck under one of the sheet metal slats on the side of the makeshift house and tried to flee with a jar of freshly mined rice.

Gen noticed a gentle, shadowy movement under the slat, jumped up, and moments later was wrestling on the broken concrete outside the shack. Finally, Gen wrapped his legs around the boy's waist; and as his mother emerged from the shack hollering for him to stop and as the light from her lantern struck the boy's face, Gen drew back his fist to strike the thief, then drew his breath in astonishment.

"*Senji?*"

Gen let out a scream and lurched to his feet, almost knocking the lantern out of Ma's hand.

"You look just like Senji," Ma said, taking a step toward him.

"Whoever Senji is, I'm *not* him," the boy said, squirming a step backward and getting ready to jump to his feet and run.

"You look like a twin of my little brother," Gen tried to explain.

"Well, I'm not him. Okay? Can I go now?"

"Of course you're not Senji," Ma said, as calmly and gently as she could. *I saw him die,* she left unemphasized, for Gen's benefit.

"I'm sorry I stole your food," the boy said, letting Ma help him to his feet. "My name is Ryuta Kondo." Apologizing again, he tried to explain the hunger that had been gnawing at him for three days until at last he believed he lost his appetite. And then he smelled cooked rice, and he could not control himself. "But God says it's not a sin to steal food if you're really, really hungry."

"Ryuta, where is your family?" Ma asked.

Clenching his jaw, he answered, "They were all killed in the explosion." Ryuta's parents had lived in Dr. Hachiya's neighborhood, near the Misasa Bridge and the Sasaki family. He alone crawled out from beneath the wreckage of the house, only to discover that something flat and sharp had guillotined his mother's legs at the knees. She bled to death before he could run to a neighboring house and seek help. Ryuta's father appeared to have been simultaneously burned and impaled. An uncle, who at first seemed to be running toward Ryuta in answer to pleas for help, continued running past him as if he neither saw nor heard anything, leaving an eerily large splash of blood behind each passing step and a loud click ahead of each splash. The uncle's feet had been severed, and he was trying to run on his shin-bones. His stilted jog continued for quite some distance into the smoking wasteland, where Ryuta's "stilt-runner" uncle likely became the "tap dancer" who, as he passed them by, struck horror into the families of Sumiko Kirihara and Sadako Sasaki.

Gen listened to Ryuta's story impassively, as if all horrors could now be ignored as background noise—which, in fact, they could. Gen was preoccupied with other thoughts.

"You look *exactly* like my little brother," Gen said again.

"I'm not him!" the boy yelled, taking a resentful step backward. "I'm Ryuta!"

Gen said nothing. He simply looked at Ryuta apologetically, then went into the shack and came out with a half-eaten rice ball. "Here," he said. "You can have the rest of my dinner, if you want it."

"You mean, you'd *give* it to me?"

"Sure."

And before Gen could quite hand it over, the boy had taken a huge gulp out of the rice ball. He then tried to swallow the rest of it in a second gulp that almost choked him.

"What are you doing?" Gen asked. "You'll get sick."

Ryuta swallowed hard and said, "I didn't want you to take it back."

"I wouldn't do that," Gen assured.

"Why should I believe you?"

Ma knelt down, until her head was level with Ryuta's. "Where have you been living since the explosion, Ryuta?"

"Out here, mostly."

"Well, if you're still hungry, you're welcome to finish my rice, too."

"You really mean that?"

"Of course I do."

Ma watched Ryuta gulp down the second rice ball as fast as the first. It shocked and amazed her. Little Senji had also been in the habit of gulping his food, as if he actually feared that someone might snatch it away from him before he had a chance to swallow.

Gen brought out a dented copper cooking pot and offered Ryuta a spoon to scrape out any last remnants of crisped rice. He dropped the spoon, put his head right inside the pot, and began licking the sides. "Just like Senji used to do," Gen whispered.

Ma tried to explain to Gen, and perhaps to herself, "I've heard it said, Gen, that everyone in the world has five doubles. Yet, *that one of them* seems to have found us by accident is remarkable. Somehow, it's as if he were sent here."

Gen watched Ryuta licking all the way to the bottom of the upturned pot, seeking out every last trace of flavor. "Ma," he said. "Are you thinking what I'm thinking?"

"I am. But we're having such a difficult time feeding ourselves—" and she watched the copper pot become a huge helmet over Ryuta's head. "But still, if Senji were alive, it's what he would want us to do."

"So, it's all right, then?"

Ryuta did not hear the question. His entire head and now one of his shoulders had disappeared into the pot. When at last he rolled it onto the ground and announced that he almost didn't feel hungry anymore—"almost"—he noticed that Gen and his mother were staring at him with very strange expressions on their faces. At first, he interpreted the expressions as meaning he had offended them somehow and was about to be wrestled to the ground again by Gen. Then he remembered his manners.

"Thank you!" Ryuta said quickly. "I'm so sorry. I should have said *thank you*."

He received the same stare, from both of them.

"What did I do?"

"Nothing," Ma said. "Ryuta, we've been wondering. Would you like to have a home again?"

"You mean, stay here?" he asked hopefully.

"Yeah," Gen said.

The boy looked scared, as if in the next moment Gen might say, "Only kidding," and send him away again into the wilderness. He began talking about his shortcomings and trying to explain why they really weren't so bad: "I know I'm little and I can't work very hard and be much help, but I can give you back rubs. Daddy always said I was a good back-rubber." And he went straight to Ma's shoulders, pinching all the right nerves in all the wrong places.

"That's very kind of you," Ma said, "but you don't have to work hard. We're not asking for anything from you in return, Ryuta. You'll just be one of the family."

"Really?"

Ma nodded, and gently stroked his head. A tiny clump of hair came out in her fingers. It did not matter. Ryuta, who had not believed he would ever feel happy about anything again, was crying with joy.

AT DAWN, DR. HACHIYA AWOKE to learn that three more of his staff were incapacitated by the new disease. The wife of the late Communications Bureau chief, who had come to the hospital volunteering her services as a nurse, now barely had a pulse. The entire inside of her mouth was a mass of hemorrhaging tissue. Her tongue and tonsils were decaying meat.

In another bed lay Mrs. Hamada. She had been exposed in a single-story wooden house about one kilometer from the hypocenter. Within minutes she had begun vomiting and felt unbelievably thirsty, as if suddenly burned deep inside. Yet by the day of the surrender she felt completely recovered and was able to volunteer at the hospital. And now, only a day later, she had awakened to the discovery that a lot of hair was lying on her pillow. As soon as she put a hand to her head, the rest of her hair began falling out in great quantities with no resistance whatsoever. Then she noticed that the skin on her arms had become extraordinarily dry and fragile, overnight. When Dr. Hachiya examined her, he found signs of extensive hemorrhage under the skin. In a matter of hours, Mrs. Hamada had gone from being completely recovered to "condition critical."

Mr. Hirohata had also been feeling better lately, following some initial post-*pika* discomfort. At a radius of just under 400 meters (1,312 feet), he was much nearer the hypocenter than Mrs. Hamada, but he explained to Dr. Hachiya that he was located in one of the thicker, concrete reinforced portions of the Telephone Bureau Building when the flash came, and thus did he manage to walk away when everyone else was instantly blown apart or carbonized.

"Doctor?" Mr. Hirohata asked. "Is there any reason why my hair should be falling out and why I should feel so weak?"

"I don't believe you need to worry," Hachiya said. "You have been through an unprecedented stress—and, on top of that, you have tried to work night and day here, keeping the rest of us alive."

A gentle rain began to fall, and Hachiya knew that soon the ceilings would be dripping and every bed would be damp tonight.

"Stop worrying so much," Hachiya emphasized for his patient.

Mr. Hirohata decided to follow the doctor's orders—to stay absolutely quiet in bed and to drink all of the nourishing fluids that the nurses gave him. He smiled, confident that his health would return, and he, along with Mrs. Hamada and the bureau chief's wife—would be dead by the time the first microscope arrived.

About August 20, Hachiya's team confirmed that radiation, and not a biological weapon or some unknown gas, had been the cause of Disease X. Days later than had (grudgingly) been promised by the navy, Hachiya's much-desired microscope was delivered. Many in the hospital were found to have white blood cell counts of about 2,000—far below the normal range of 6,000 to 8,000. Only Dr. Hachiya's range seemed to be hovering above 3,000. Some patients had counts of only 500; and one, with a count of 200, appeared to be dying from a full-body onslaught of the bacteria that normally broke decaying matter into soil and fertilizer.

Hachiya quickly realized that the isolation pavilion had been folly. Though strange new infections were appearing—including putrefaction while still alive—the diseases came from within, not without. According to a memo dispatched from the Omura Naval Hospital, autopsies began to reveal bone marrow so thoroughly irradiated that occasionally it had been reduced to a yellow, bile-like fluid. With immune systems rendered essentially nonexistent, bacteria that did not normally attack human flesh until after death started to take root. In many cases, bone marrow death manifested as a hemorrhagic fever that spread to all the internal organs; and in such cases the blood did not coagulate even seven hours after death. The blood platelets, along with their clotting agents, were simply gone.

Other patients fell prey to signs and symptoms no one had seen before. Two men examined at Omura died from something that liquefied their brains and spinal cords. An infectious amoeba appeared to have been involved, a species against which human immune systems had long ago developed natural defenses. The occurrence of so many opportunistic infections was so rare that it would not be seen again until the AIDS outbreak of the 1980s.

At the Omura Naval Hospital, Dr. Hachiya's colleague Shiotsuki had been examining patients from Nagasaki and Urakami since the night of August 9. The first of them were sent by train to his 800-bed facility, located 19 kilometers from the hypocenter. Even at this distance, all the windows on the side of the naval hospital opposite the direction of the blast were broken, and all the trees on the mountainsides facing the *pika* had been so desiccated by the rays that their leaves were now brown, as if touched by an early autumn. Dr. Shiotsuki reported that the browning effect on the leaves extended 80 kilometers (almost 50 miles) in every direction from Urakami Stadium. Had all the leaves been dry to begin with, the resulting firestorm would have reached typhoon dimensions, at a diameter of 160 kilometers. Near St. Francis Hospital, if the eye wall became truly cyclonic and self-sustaining, the horizontal flames could easily have roared supersonic.

By August 20, Dr. Shiotsuki's medical dispatches were becoming filled with peculiar and often perplexing observations. He noticed that patients who were carrying lunch pails or wearing wristwatches and gold wedding bands, or who were in any other way in direct skin contact with metallic objects at Moment Zero, were literally branded where the metal touched skin and were almost certain to show symptoms of radiation sickness. The brandings were consistent with a hazard from the far end of the spectrum, opposite the very short wavelength gamma rays: a flash of microwaves. Metal will intercept microwaves and heat up to skin-searing temperatures. Under the *pika*, parts of Nagasaki appeared to have become a microwave oven. Dr. Shiotsuki also noted that though patients wearing white often escaped *pika* burns, and one patient wearing a black-and-white striped shirt had actually received "burn tattoos" patterned in vertical stripes, these phenomena seemed to apply only at a radius beyond two kilometers. Nearer the hypocenter and the stadium, wearing white or black became a moot point.

By now, at Omura, many of the young women who had volunteered to come with the train from Nagasaki to nurse the injured were beginning to show the first signs of disease. As had occurred at St. Francis and in the Communications Hospital, overwhelmed by sudden fatigue, fever, and chills, they collapsed and became patients in the very same wards they had tended as nurses.

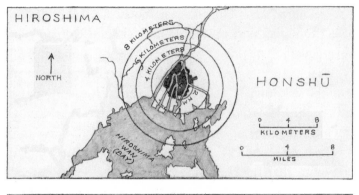

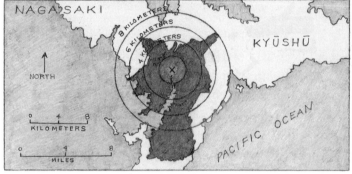

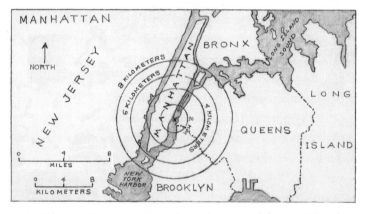

The chief difference between the scale and range of fires in Hiroshima and Nagasaki was due to the much greater strength of the Nagasaki bomb, which flash-desiccated leaves and caused them to wilt at a distance of 80 kilometers. Had the Nagasaki weapon been detonated over New York City during an autumn drought or over California during the dry season, it could have created a hurricane of fire a hundred miles in diameter. (Patricia Wynne)

"There was no need to explain to them what was happening," Dr. Shiotsuki would record in 1974, shortly before his death from leukemia at age fifty-four. "We already had reports of widespread sickness in Hiroshima. We knew what was to come."

They died. Every one of them.

"Dressed in baggy mompe trousers and overalls made out of shabby material," Shiotsuki said in a belated epitaph, "the volunteer girls were far removed from beauty in any ordinary sense of the word. And yet to my mind they were incomparably more beautiful physically and spiritually than the girls who strut down the street today in blue jeans or fashionable dresses. They were the girls who, as soon as they realized they were going to die, left their beds and used their remaining strength to nurse others. I wish that just once I could have seen those girls dressed up in today's elegant high fashions; but they were given a sentence of death with the end of the war just moments away, never to know that such prosperity would ever come to Japan."

Dr. Shiotsuki's own battle against atomic bomb disease began about the time Dr. Hachiya lifted the isolation protocol at the Communications Hospital, fourteen days after the Hiroshima explosion, eleven days after Nagasaki, and five days after Gen and his mother invited Ryuta to live in their shack. His white blood cell count had diminished dangerously, by about half its normal value—despite being located nineteen kilometers from the hypocenter and away from the prevailing path of wind-driven fallout. The only explanation was high-level exposure to radioactivity from the patients themselves, whose clothing and skin and even their breath must have been emitting particles of freshly irradiated dust when they arrived on the night of August 9. During the first forty-eight hours, the radioactivity they were shedding had doubtless invaded Dr. Shiotsuki's lungs, blood, and bone marrow.

As the days passed, Shiotsuki's white blood cell count climbed back again toward normal, then continued to climb upward. Two weeks after the train arrived from Nagasaki, Shiotsuki's concern was not about too few white cells, but about far too many of them. This was the beginning of his progression toward chronic bone marrow disease. The date was August 24.

That evening, in Tokyo, General Shizuichi Tanaka surveyed the American fleet in the harbor. Tanaka had received reports of British planes flying over Hiroshima and Nagasaki, as if on a gruesome sightseeing tour. The surrender was scheduled to be officially signed on September 2. Tanaka, who on August 14 had withdrawn his support for the rebellion that would have prevented the Emperor's broadcast, did not wish to see the play's final act. After drinking tea with his aide, the general laid his sword down beside his cap, gloves, and six pre-addressed letters. Then, wrapping a cloth around the top of his head to reduce blood spatter, and aligning his chair in a direction that would prevent matter from the exit wound from smearing the six envelopes, he shot himself.

DESPITE ANAMI'S AND Tanaka's passing, government bureaucratic snafus continued to function as usual. On August 25, a truck bearing gifts from the Imperial Army's Engineering Corps arrived at Hiroshima's Communications Hospital. The soldiers delivered four broken chairs, three battered desks, two cooking pots, one potbelly stove, and no food or coal. A second truck brought five large crates, each stuffed almost to overflowing with runway signal flags and life preservers. Dr. Hachiya's patients distributed the life preservers among themselves for use as pillows, while the children seemed to enjoy waving the flags.

Mr. Sasaki arranged for a third truck to be sent, bringing fish and cartons of cigarettes—the latter now being worth more than money. Indeed, cigarettes had quickly taken over as the new medium of currency. Dr. Hachiya cherished the flavor of tobacco, but he decided to hold on to the currency for as long as possible by taking only a few puffs at a time from a cigarette and then putting it away to smoke just a little more, just a little later.

During one of his cigarette breaks, Hachiya stepped outside for a breath of fresh air and encountered the first dog he had seen in nearly twenty days. Immediately nicknamed Woebegone, Hachiya noticed that the poor mongrel was carrying a bit of rotting potato in its mouth. *What a pitiful sight*, he thought, *to see a dog, by nature a meat eater, reduced to scavenging vegetable scraps.*

Most of the animal's hair was gone, so Hachiya made a diagnosis that Woebegone was suffering from radiation injury.

Somehow, this emaciated figure, trudging along with his hips bent, tail down, and hair gone, seemed symbolic.

"Let loose the dogs of war indeed!" the doctor said, startling the animal.

Above and behind him, someone shouted with excitement at the sighting of yellow electrical wires being strung in a direction generally headed toward the hospital. An army engineer arrived and announced that in a few days, Hachiya would have a telephone, and a few days after that, an electric light.

As evening approached, rainwater glistened on the walls for the third day in a row. Throughout the building and in the former isolation pavilion, clothing and bedding were sprouting black mold. And so, inevitably, pnemonia began making its opportunistic rounds from one radiation-weakened immune system to another. By the morning of August 26, four more patients lay dead.

THE DEATH RATE was accelerating in the Urakami hills. Drs. Akizuki and Nagai attended regularly scheduled bonfires of corpses in the hospital's yard. Nagai's health appeared to be steadily improving to such an extent that he and three nurses had been making wide-ranging house calls in the hills. But Akizuki's hair was thinning and he was having difficulty keeping food down. He wondered if he, himself, might be found on a pyre in a few more days. Living and dying in Ground Zero, Akizuki realized, was a matter of fate—in which the dividing line between the man being cremated and the doctor cremating him was misty and vague and entirely up to chance.

He was coming to regard radiation sickness as an insidious and omnipotent spirit that plucked out the survivors' hair and sucked out their blood.

From the hospital down to the ruins of the Yosē Girls' School and the stadium, a pattern of death was beginning to emerge. The latest influx of patients had seemed well when they descended into the ruins and started erecting shantytowns. They had invented a new term—"the mines of the city"—which referred to articles of value buried under the piles of debris. The miners living lower down the hill, near the stadium and the hypocenter, were the first to suffer and die during the second, late-August, outbreak of radiation sickness. Dr. Akizuki was able to chart "the shadow of death," as it moved like a slowly rising tide, steadily uphill. Miners homesteading in the valley and the foothills began to be carried up to the hospital on the backs of family members who were dwelling higher along the path. Then a family of miners a hundred meters farther uphill sickened and were carried up; then a family forty meters higher; and so on, and so on.

Dr. Akizuki named the widening advance of the disease his "concentric circles of death." He imagined that it was only a matter of time before the invisible death clouds ascended to St. Francis. The incoming tide was only about fifty meters below the hospital's front yard when the rains came, building slowly from the first of September into a tropical downpour by the second, bringing the sound of rolling thunder above and the roar of newly formed waterfalls below.

By midnight September 2, the rain descended in such torrents that when Akizuki stepped outside, it drove into his face, blinding him with the sting of rushing water. It soaked him instantly, and tore his shirtsleeves. He held on to a broken concrete pillar to steady himself—while behind, in a shattered building whose ground floor was now a rising creek, the injured and their caregivers gathered in bunches of ten and fifteen, huddling together like small birds in a nest.

"Haven't they suffered enough?" Dr. Akizuki shouted at the sky. Lightning blazed out like scores of flashbulbs . . . or baby *pikas*. It was a new kind of hell: flayed by fire, they were now to be tormented by water.

"Don't punish them this way!" Akizuki cried. "What do you want? Who are you? Haven't you done enough?"

Akizuki was thinking of the Catholic sisters and brothers who had come to help, only to become sick themselves, and now were shivering like half-drowned animals. As a Buddhist, it was difficult for him to believe with the Jesuits or with Dr. Nagai that tragedy and senseless evil were part of a divine plan.

"Why is it that you have to suffer like this?" he had asked Sister Mizoguchi, only a day before she vomited up a long strip of her own flesh and died. "Why this, for someone like you, who has done nothing but good? It isn't right!"

"I believe in providence," she had replied weakly—and then said, with a smile: "It's the will of God."

"Then God damn your providence!" the doctor now cried out to the storm, and against the universe itself.

He stayed up through the night, trying to calm the patients and cursing the storm. And in the morning, a double rainbow appeared in the sky. The higher of the two was of a brightness rarely seen in Nagasaki; and the lower apparition was of a kind never seen. It lay within a deep layer of mist, an unusual pearly color but clearly bow-shaped—a *white* rainbow.

"Something's happened," Akizuki said to Nurse Murai. "I feel there's a change in the air—I'm sure of it." He took a deep breath and for the first time in nearly a month Akizuki felt refreshed. The constant feeling of weakness and nausea had begun to disappear in spite of a stressful night without sleep. *The world has changed,* he thought.

Though Akizuki did not have access to a Geiger counter, he was certain that if he checked he would find something different about the ground as well as the air. The rain had washed the lingering, dusty fallout deep into the ground or out to sea. The very deluge he had cursed through the night was now proving to be a merciful act of . . . *Providence,* Dr. Akizuki half believed.

From that very morning, it seemed, goose grass had begun sprouting in the wasteland. A similar storm struck Hiroshima, followed by the same multiple rainbow phenomenon, followed by wildflowers blooming out of season—so many that it appeared to some witnesses that two thousand B-29s had flown over the city dropping flower seeds instead of bombs.

Shoda Shinoe, the girl who had asked the doctors if an operation existed that could remove memories, seemed to have recovered her full strength after the rains. When she located the ruins of her school, she found evening primroses growing out of every cracked brick and every fissure in the concrete. Wild blue chrysanthemums were everywhere else. In the playground, flower stalks had erupted between ribs and through the eyeless sockets of skulls—dozens and scores and hundreds of skulls. The majority of them were little; and Shoda guessed that all of the larger bones must have belonged to her teachers.

AS THE TWO cities came into bloom, an American navy surgeon and a Chinese interpreter arrived at St. Francis. Dr. Akizuki emerged from the far side of a brick pile and startled them.

The interpreter reached for his pistol but quickly relaxed, once he looked the doctor up and down and summed him up as looking no more dangerous than "the mayor of Hobo Village."

By contrast to Akizuki, who except for the storm had lived unshowered for nearly a month, the American's clothes were starched and clean, and he appeared to resemble a much taller version of the young and dashing romantic comedy star Vincent Price. Akizuki had been expecting Boris Karloff or Bela Lugosi.

The navy surgeon seemed appalled at the primitive conditions that prevailed on the hillside. He pointed across the hypocenter toward first-aid tents that were being erected five kilometers away, in north central Nagasaki. "You should take your people there," he advised.

Considering the condition of his patients, it seemed to Akizuki that three miles—which was a little more than the distance across Manhattan Island—might just as well be a march to Tokyo.

"If you would be so kind as to provide us with adequate medicines," Akizuki said, "my colleagues and I would like to stay here and continue with our treatment of these people."

The American looked around the burned-out ruin and sighed, then began to examine the patients. At first, they cringed, but when reassured by Akizuki that he would do them no harm, they began to relax. The newcomer quickly discovered a type of bomb injury that had not been apparent before.

"Most of them have had the optic nerves of their retinas damaged by the A-bomb's flash," the American said. "Their corneas have also been damaged, and they're infected."

They were losing their eyesight, the American concluded, and he pressed again, "You should send them to the first-aid station in the city center."

The patients weren't healthy enough to make the journey even if they weren't going blind, Akizuki explained.

"Well," the Vincent Price look-alike said, "the roads are all out and we have no large trucks to spare for an evacuation. But we do have penicillin and other vital supplies at the station. You should go there tomorrow and see what you can acquire."

All things considered, Akizuki was both surprised and impressed by the man who had climbed through the rubble and up the hill to examine the injured. He was much relieved that High Command's warnings about a world of rape and doom awaiting a defeated Japan seemed not to be materializing.

This was not to say, however, that everything was suddenly golden splendor. The pharmacist at the first-aid station looked at Dr. Akizuki's clothes and almost dismissed him outright as a vagrant in search of black market drugs. When the doctor explained that an American navy officer had advised him to obtain antibiotics for the Urakami hospital, the pharmacist said, "Send your patients here."

After further explanation of the conditions at St. Francis, the pharmacist released a small amount of medicine, along with vitamin B and strong doses of vitamin C, in accordance with a radiation treatment protocol proposed by Dr. Nagai that—until such supplies had begun running out at the hospital—appeared to have brought some improvement to borderline cases, including Nagai and Akizuki themselves. The penicillin, however, was withheld, and the release of each subsequent package of vitamins seemed to require two or three treks across the hypocenter.

As Dr. Akizuki recorded it, "After the American officer's visit, our wrecked hospital, standing on the fringe of the devastated area, slipped from the minds of those who came to investigate the damage done by the atomic bomb. It went unprovided with the new drugs and the help that they could bring. Those who came to see what had become of Nagasaki after the A-bomb explosion visited the intact buildings of Nagasaki proper and stopped near the vanished stadium, and they never found out what was happening on the hill that overlooked the hypocenter."

And so it came to pass that the most visible of the city's radiation cases became all but invisible. A committee of American and British scientific investigators met in Japan on September 11, and immediately proposed a detailed zoological survey, meter-square by meter-square, of excavation points at various distances from the hypocenter, to determine whether radiation effects produced harmful mutations in multiple generations of insects. Officially, the September 11 Committee was under General MacArthur's jurisdiction, and he did not want much about the atomic bombings to become known. The zoological survey was cut short almost as soon as it began. Instead, earthworms were sampled from the ground beneath Urakami's St. Maria Cathedral and the demolished hospitals nearby. Radiation effects were determined by amputating the tenth segments from the caudal ends of several Ground Zero worms and observing the regeneration of their heads. The regeneration process appeared to occur without evident abnormalities—which absence of evidence was interpreted as evidence of absence, in terms of lingering radiation effects in human populations exposed to the bomb. A proposal from committee scientists to extend the worm study to an examination of actual human subjects being treated nearby, in Dr. Akizuki's hospital, languished indefinitely in MacArthur-esque limbo.

About this time, Charles Sweeney returned to the city and led his team members to the place where a tennis court had stood, in what he calculated to be the location of the exact hypocenter. Very few people were on the prairie and in the foothills. Looking straight up into the blue sky, where at 1,890 feet the plutonium fist struck forth, Sweeney tried to form an image of what it must have been like to be standing on this spot at that moment. And he offered to his friends a simple prayer—"that ours shall be the last such mission ever flown." Later, Joseph Fuoco seconded "Sweeney's emotion."

As he looked about, Sweeney's gaze paused for a moment at a distant hillside, on which stood the scorched, red-brick walls of St. Francis Hospital.

BY THE TIME Shoda Shinoe found her teachers and Charles Sweeney found his hypocenter, Mrs. Matsuda had discovered the foundations of her home. It lay within three blocks of the Hirata house and the Morimotos' Hiroshima mansion, and almost within sniper's range of the Hiroshima Dome. Her boy Toshihiko had come wandering out of the region with a leafy pattern of black burns along one side of his body. The boy was located at a range in which the white shirt he was wearing became barely more relevant (in terms of protection from flash burns) than the garden walls that shielded him from the blast. The white cotton had browned instantly, and Toshihiko's shadow—along with the shadows of vanished pumpkin vines and rows of hanging bean plants—left their ghostly imprints on the wall. The boy appeared to be reaching down for something when the flash came.

Historians would wrongly presume that all of Hiroshima's shadow people were vaporized by the *pika* and met instant, painless death. This was rarely the case. Only in the immediate vicinity of the Dome and the "T" Bridge was this universally true. Farther out from the hypocenter, the same flash that seared skin also seared paint and wood. Against overwhelming odds, young Toshihiko was able to walk away from Ground Zero toward the wrecked school where Minami saw the blue fireflies. She and Dr. Fujii believed that since more than 60 percent of the boy's body had been shadowed from the flash and remained completely unburned, he might survive—and that was the hell of it. Toshihiko Matsuda should have survived, but upon him had fallen the gamma rays—upon him and through him. His bones soaked up gamma radiation and neutrons, and the DNA within his marrow writhed and snapped so violently that the body's ever-vigilant DNA repair systems would have been unable to cope with the scale of the damage even if the repair systems were not themselves damaged.

Though Toshihiko's aunts and anyone else who had been inside the house were killed when the blast crushed the two-story building to the height of a man's chest, Toshihiko appeared to Dr. Fujii to be another "miracle boy," having narrowly escaped while everyone around him died. But the rays had done their work, and the miracle boy had only a little while left to live.

Triaged as likely to survive with medical attention, he and several others among the moderately injured were sent with Minami and four nurses on the back of a flatbed truck to the veterans' hospital in the suburbs.

The discovery that Toshihiko's mother had been conscripted to do military work outside the city and had also survived brought new life to his eyes, but after a week his wounds refused to heal, and without any warning at all, he fell into a deep slumber and died.

Now his mother returned to the place where the horror began. Here, the circularity of the "total destruction zone" could be seen clearly. Except for the Dome, the frame of the Sumitomo Bank, and the odd water tank sticking out of the earth, the landscape swept away flat in every direction to a ring of concrete ruins, approximately equidistant from Mrs. Matsuda's home. The grayish-brown debris field was interrupted by newly emerged sprawls of goose grass and wildflowers.

Like Gen reaching down for a coin in the schoolyard, Mrs. Matsuda's son appeared to have been kneeling and handling something on the ground at Moment Zero. The part of him caught in the flash and projected onto a garden wall said so. Only the lower half of the wall still remained to tell the tale, but it was enough. Leaves and vines all but surrounded him, as he bent down to lay a hand upon a pumpkin or to pull out a weed. When the bomb flashed above Toshihiko, the leaves on the vines must surely have been shifting in the morning breeze—but the points of each of them were so sharply defined that the image had, without doubt, been created faster than a leaf could respond to wind.

Throughout both Hiroshima and Urakami, for miles around, asphalt and paint bleached under the light; wood charred—and, on every wall still standing, shadowed window frames, telephone poles, trees, clotheslines, and even people indicated the directions of the flashes and pointed unerringly toward each city's hypocenter.

The phenomenon was exactly analogous to what happens when a wristwatch protects a tiny patch of skin from sunburn and leaves behind a shadow image of the watch and band. The difference was a matter of degree. The Hiroshima and Nagasaki shadows were formed much more quickly, and with greater ferocity.

Though more than 60 percent of Toshihiko's body had been shielded from the flash—and mercifully, his face was kept in shadow

by his hat—in the end it made no difference. Near the Sumitomo
Bank and the outer fringe of the hypocenter, the gamma rays had
recolored fragments of clear glass in beautiful hues of violet. Certain
diamonds, were they present, would have turned blue, green, or red.

Digging below the strewn-field of roof tiles and the ashes of her
home, Toshihiko's mother came across six misshapen beads of
glass—her son's toy marbles. Either the *pika*, or the fire worms that
came afterward, or some combination of both, had melted them into
greenish, semi-transparent blobs.

Sixty-three years later, Nenkai Aoyama would feel the weight of
time and improbability in the heft of two melted marbles that once
belonged to "a kid down the block." Nenkai's home had been even
closer to the hypocenter than Toshihiko's. At age seventeen, Nenkai
was a conscript assigned to a construction project, about two kilometers downriver from home. It was important work, he was told—
"in preparation for the final defense of Japan."

At 7:00 a.m. on August 6, he had not quite finished breakfast
when his mother told him that he must hurry, even though he could
easily cover the distance between home and his work detail with time
to spare.

"Go, hurry!" his mother said, all but pushing him out the door.

"Bye," he said, perplexed.

This was the last conversation Nenkai had with his mother. His
house was part of a Buddhist temple, located immediately next door
to the Hiroshima Dome. The hemisphere of compressed air that shot
down the sides of the Dome's tower appeared to have struck the stone
and wood temple from above and from the sides. After the fires had
died away and Nenkai returned to the hypocenter as its nearest surviving resident, he was unable to find even a trace of his home's foundations. Everything was gone. He could not imagine how to begin
looking for his mother.

Across the river, under the very spot over which Hiroshima's Memorial Museum would one day stand, Mrs. Shigeko was luckier than
Nenkai, after a fashion. Returning from the countryside to a hypocenter radius of five city blocks, she found her son Shigeru.

She was all alone now. One son had been taken into the navy from
junior high school, and her husband was drafted into the army at age

fifty. On the day of the *pika-don*, eleven-year-old Shigeru was all Mrs. Shigeko had left.

In Hiroshima—as throughout the rest of Japan—junior high school wasn't exactly school anymore, and in preparation for the final battle, the spring semester was extended through July and August. After the firebombings of Kobe, Osaka, and Tokyo, the army had confiscated homes along rows of whole city blocks throughout Hiroshima, and had conscripted junior high school students to assist in knocking down houses along makeshift firebreaks and hauling away the wood for military recycling.

On the last morning she saw him, Shigeru's mother had prepared for him a lunch of soy paste and barley, mixed with two spoonfuls of rice, sealed in a little tin lunch box with his name inscribed.

"Shigeru, if the firebombers come," she said, giving a last bit of motherly advice, "crouch down on the ground as fast as you can."

"Got it," he had replied, and then rode happily away on his bicycle.

At the place where he died, just a short walk across one of the wrecked bridges on either side of the Dome, and downriver along the shore road, the bones of Shigeru and his classmates lay where they fell—or, more precisely, where their little bodies had been pressed into the ground.

Shigeru's lunch box, with his name still upon it, was blackened and crushed flat. One corner jutted out through a broken cage of ribs . . . tiny ribs. His mother pried open the cover and found the food inside converted to blackened carbon, like her son's flesh. Yet, like every fossil, the carbonized meal told a story.

"Oh, Shigeru," his mother cried out to history. "You died before you could even eat your lunch."

10

LEGACY: TO FOLD A THOUSAND PAPER CRANES

Within minutes, if not seconds, people were changed. As the skies darkened beneath the spreading Urakami cloud, fires became Dr. Paul Nagai's sole light source. He saw a colleague dancing and singing wildly atop the hospital's dormitory building. Half of the dorm's roof was already being swallowed by flames, and as the wall of fire gathered strength and crept toward the man, his singing turned to loud laughter.

The man clearly needed saving, but the heat was intensifying so quickly that anyone running into the dorm and trying to find the stairs would never find a way out. Neither Paul Nagai nor anyone else who saw the dancer dared advance toward the blaze. Instead, they backed away from it. They could not advance even as the young colleague— out of his mind with fear, or with denial, or both—danced directly into the flames. His singing and laughter became a long scream that lasted nearly fifteen seconds, and Nagai backed up several more steps, quickening the pace of his retreat.

"Doctor . . . Doctor, what shall I do?"

Dr. Nagai all but backed into the woman, nearly knocking her over as she pleaded from extremis for him to treat her little boy's wounds. When Nagai turned to face the young mother, he backed away in another direction, without any words at all.

"Help me!" the woman cried.

She did not seem to understand that her child no longer had a head.

Dr. Nagai recalled that those who survived the atomic bomb were, in general, the people who ignored others crying out in extremis or who stayed away from the flames, even when patients and colleagues shrieked from within them: "Those of us who stayed where we were, those of us who took refuge in the hills behind the hospital when the fires began to spread and close in, happened to escape alive. In short, those who survived the bomb were, if not merely lucky, in a greater or lesser degree selfish, self-centered—guided by instinct and not by civilization. And we know it, we who have survived."

Buildings could be repaired, Nagai observed. Hypocenters could be covered up with gardens and memorial sculptures, but visitors to the rebuilt cities would never understand or even be aware that there existed a spiritual wreckage. From that first summer of the bombs, Dr. Paul Nagai suspected that this worst wreckage of all would pass like an invisible virus through multiple generations, and that none who remembered could ever be fully recovered.

"We who have seen and survived know what the atomic bomb can do," Nagai called out to futurity. "We carry deep in our hearts, every one of us, stubborn, unhealing wounds. When we are alone, we brood upon them; and when we see our neighbors we are again reminded of the wounds, theirs as well as ours."

NORTH, IN HIROSHIMA, Dr. Hachiya and Mr. Sasaki understood Nagai's lament. Before the bomb, they were neighbors and best friends. The family histories of both men would record that Mr. Sasaki made multiple trips between the hill country and Hiroshima's Ground Zero, bringing food down to Dr. Hachiya and his patients at the Communications Hospital. And yet Mr. Sasaki's son Masahiro would note that after the age of five or six, though his family would always be within walking distance of Dr. Hachiya, he did not recall ever seeing him again.

In his diary, Dr. Hachiya wrote, "When [Shigeo Sasaki's] house collapsed . . . I had just reached the street in flight from [the wreckage of my own] home. Mr. Sasaki's mother was killed but [the rest of his family] escaped. If I had not been injured, I might have saved his mother because their house collapsed at my feet. . . . [This is] a sorrow without surcease."

In Hachiya's mind, it did not seem to matter that when he climbed out through the battered walls of his house, his wounds were near lethal and he emerged so completely disoriented that he became one of the city's ant-walkers. By any standard of common sense if not by emotion, he should henceforth have held himself blameless. No one who knew even this small fraction of Hachiya's story would have censured him. Nonetheless, whenever he met Mr. Sasaki or his wife and their two children on the street, he was reminded of little Sadako's grandmother. His only escape from remembrance lay in silent retreat and avoidance.

This was precisely what Dr. Nagai of Urakami meant when he said the bomb had created "cracks," or "fissures," between families and neighbors. History would record that not only did Mr. Sasaki never utter a word of complaint or reproach against his friend, he never gave reproach a thought. And yet a gulf yawned open between two neighbors. And the saddest cut of all was that there had never existed a basis for reproach in the first place; but the wound seemed beyond healing, and Dr. Hachiya would carry an undeserved guilt, quietly, to his grave. The physician never learned the truth. He thoroughly avoided the subject, and never asked.

On that day, during the minutes leading up to 8:15 a.m. and Moment Zero, Masahiro Sasaki had left his mother and his little sister Sadako at the breakfast table—running off to the backyard garden, where he commenced to play. That's where he saw two of the three airplanes. Decades later, when more was known about how events unfolded during the bombing, and in what sequence, Masahiro would come to realize that the reason he survived was that he did not see Luis Alvarez's instrument packages falling from *Great Artiste* and sprouting parachutes. He saw only the planes before his mother called him inside. Others who had watched the parachutes from this same radius, between the Misasa Bridge and the main rail line, at a distance of 1.9 kilometers, received approximately 7R from the gamma surge and neutron spray. At a 1.2-mile radius, 7R amounted to not quite 2 percent of a lethal radiation dose, but in household gardens and on the Sasaki neighborhood's streets, people were simultaneously blinded and seared by the heat ray.

As it turned out, and as random chance would have it, Sadako saved her brother from the flash. The two-year-old had not finished the last two or three spoonfuls of rice and fish gruel. Not wanting to leave anything to waste, Mrs. Sasaki called Masahiro inside to finish his sister's breakfast. For Masahiro, the margin separating his mother's call away from the *pika* was frighteningly small. He believed he escaped flash burns and death by less than ten seconds: "That's how fast it came—only the *pika* [the flash], with no *don* [no bang]."

Masahiro did not remember any sounds, either from the blast or from the planes that preceded it. It seemed impossible to him, but the *pika* and the cracking of thick wooden beams happened in utter silence.

Sadako remembered only the flash, and Masahiro remembered stepping out into a world in which all the other houses had burst open or were flattened. Already, the first fire worms were hatching out. The worms grew with astonishing rapidity, and the family fled three blocks east to the waterfront, all four of them—five-year-old Masahiro, Mrs. Sasaki with little Sadako in her arms, and Grandmother leading the way.

About the time the Sasakis reached the river, Dr. Hachiya had just burrowed into fresh air through the fragmenting splinters of his home, just in time to see the Sasaki house leaning and creaking toward him and falling literally at his feet. This was the beginning of the silent gulf between friends, of questions unasked, and of an unspoken guilt. Dr. Hachiya could never erase from his mind the image of Shigeo Sasaki's mother trapped inside the collapsed house. Nor could he free himself from the possibility that, as a doctor, he might have been able to help. What Hachiya never learned was that his friend's mother was not even in the vicinity. At the moment the house fell, she happened to be alive and perfectly unharmed, more than 200 meters away at the river's edge. She had remained at the waterfront for at least several minutes after the physician staggered away and joined the ant-walkers.

Masahiro Sasaki remembered that, even at a distance, the

spreading tornadoes and multistoried waves of fire made his face feel sunburned. A group of men were trying to launch a half-destroyed boat, loading it with women and children as fast as they could, while they bailed and pushed.

"Anyone else?" one of the men called, motioning for people to climb into the boat immediately. Those gathered nearest the gunwales should not have needed more encouragement to jump in and row away, but the manifestations of the bomb confused them. Not more than fifty meters away, a waterspout came ashore and flung whole families to the ground. Tearing away their clothes, it strode inland and, shedding dozens of tons of water, it metamorphosed into an ordinary whirlwind, then into a fire worm.

Grandmother assisted her daughter-in-law Fujiko into the boat and passed the two children to her, then looked around and hesitated.

"You go," she commanded. "I must return to the house."

"You can't!" Fujiko cried.

"Look around you!" Grandmother said. On both sides of the river, and as far as Fujiko Sasaki could see upriver and downriver, a full-scale firestorm was trying to be born.

"All the food in the city is about to be burned," Grandmother continued. "We have tins of rice in the house. You'll need them to survive."

"No. It's too dangerous to go back."

"Go out to the center of the river and wait for me," Grandmother told the men in charge of the boat. "Row back and pick me up when I return with food."

"No!" Fujiko yelled, but the men pushed the boat through the mud and sand into deeper water and jumped aboard. Then, about three minutes after Grandmother ran under a train trestle and followed the nearest street westward toward home, whirlwinds of sparks and flames bunched together and stalked after her.

Masahiro remembered seeing monstrous walls of fire roaring to life along both shores. From the direction of home, he saw people burned. Many ran into the water, still in flames. Oddly, once the flames were doused and it seemed to the boy that the people were finally safe, most of them stopped moving.

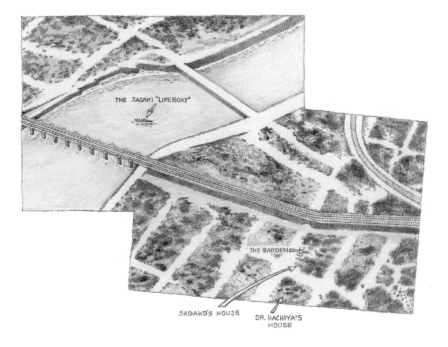

THE SASAKI "LIFEBOAT"

THE GARDEN

SADAKO'S HOUSE   DR. HACHIYA'S
                   HOUSE

Grandmother never returned from the fire, and Masahiro knew for a certainty that he would never see her again. Throughout the city, aboveground cisterns had been constructed specifically for the use of neighborhood fire brigades. Days later, when survivors returned to the Ground Zero fringe zones, they found every one of the concrete cisterns with at least two or three roasted bodies inside. Grandmother was one of the people in the cisterns. In the end, during their final seconds of life, men had ushered women and children into the hoped-for safety of the water tubs and stayed outside as the approaching firestorm threatened to submerge everyone in a lake of flames. Those inside the cisterns—usually children clinging to each other, or women embracing children—were given perhaps a precious minute more of life. None of them lived any longer than they could hold their heads under the water. When they surfaced, their eyes were seared from their skulls and they inhaled pure fire into their lungs.

In the boat, little Masahiro tried to help the men to bail water. All around, the river began to fill with bodies, more than ten thousand of them in the region of the Misasa Bridge, southward toward the

"T" Bridge and the Dome. Soon a score of survivors were clinging to the sides of the boat, while half-carbonized people continued to run or stagger into the river and die, until the water's surface became a logjam of corpses. The water flowed red with the blood of the dead and the dying, until the rain came—thick and black.

The very center of the black rain's path ran near the Misasa Bridge and the railway trestle—right where the Sasaki family struggled in open air in a Hiroshima lifeboat. The heat from the firestorm made Masahiro and little Sadako thirsty, and they eagerly licked the rainwater from their lips.

By the time the rains fell upon farms thirty kilometers downwind, more than an hour had passed and the worst of the bomb-generated isotopes were decayed almost out of existence. Yet even at such safe distances, cows that ate grass where the black rain had fallen experienced varying degrees of hair loss and developed a severe, sometimes fatal bovine diarrhea. Its impact appeared to be magnified in young calves.

The dose received by Sadako and Masahiro and by everyone else in their lifeboat was unknown orders of magnitude worse.

AT FIRST, Dr. Nagai had fallen into despair over the incineration of his university, his wife, his hospital, his students, and all of his research.

"However," he wrote in his memoirs, "the feeling of despair did not last, because I found a new purpose and a new hope—in a disease that had never existed before: atomic bomb disease. I had to research this new mystery. When this was decided, my dark depressed heart was filled with hope and courage. My spirit as a doctor surged. My body regained energy and I stood up."

Dr. Nagai and his nurses began traveling up to twenty kilometers a day, beyond the fringes of the fire and blast zones, bringing cans of peaches and the strange-sounding advice not to wash away the maggots that were living in gangrenous wounds. Nagai's team became known for a distinctive theory that shoring up the immune systems of irradiated survivors by extracting vitamins from liver (even from rat liver), and by seeking out all known sources of vitamin C and vitamin B, gave the injured an increased likelihood of survival.

Throughout the suburbs, wherever the oily rains had fallen, Nagai became famous as "the maggots, liver, and peaches doctor."

Nagai's little girl Kayano recalled that when her father first arrived from Urakami, he brought a can of peaches recovered from a reasonably intact supply shelter. To Kayano, he looked very severe and worn out in spite of his curiously recovered strength. Her father's head was wrapped in bandages—each stained black and red with varying stages of drying blood. His face looked pale and filthy, and yet his eyes were shining.

Kayano and Makoto excitedly showed him places in the valley where the ground and the plants were stained with dark residue from the rain of jelly and oil that had fallen on the day of the *pika-don*.

"Do not touch those places where the dark rain has fallen and dried!" he warned the children. Paul Nagai sensed, already, that the rain from the *pika-don* was bad.

"Yes, my father *did* look rather severe," Kayano remembered. "Then he brought the can of peaches from his pocket. He did not eat them himself. He saved them only for us."

In a shelter on the far side of Ground Zero, Mr. Yamaguchi had remained, at best, only semiconscious after reuniting with his wife and child. Twigs were still embedded in his skin from the Hiroshima blast, and a pebble had gone into his arm like a bullet. In Mitsubishi's Nagasaki office, he experienced partial de-gloving of an arm and the exposed muscle surface collected a sampling of all the debris that had whirlwinded through the room.

Yamaguchi's flesh was badly infected by the time the unknown "witch doctor" arrived and told Hisako not to remove the maggots. He also left a can of peaches and spoke about vitamin sources in the weed-covered hills nearby. The members of his team did not leave their names or accept thanks—and, though Hisako was never able to confirm it for him, Mr. Yamaguchi would always believe that his mysterious rescuer was his old basketball buddy Dr. Nagai, or the people who worked for him. There were not many other candidates.

Most of the doctors in the area were killed, and Nagai's remedies were, if nothing else, distinctive.

By the time Dr. Nagai and the hospital's carpenter unearthed the last crate of canned peaches, rumors and theories began circulating about the death of the land itself. People were starting to believe that no creature would grow and survive in Urakami for seventy-five years.

"I'm already a short-timer," Nagai told his friend Akizuki, declaring that the cancer alone (though it had ceased troubling him and his hair was growing long while other people's hair continued to fall out) must already have shortened his life. "I've decided," he announced, "to build a scientific research station down in the ruins, and to place myself there as a laboratory rat."

By then, in the aftermath of the September storms, poor Dr. Akizuki's white blood cell count had dropped to half the normal level and he was beginning to hemorrhage under the skin. Even in the midst of post-deluge improvements, the vicious cycles persisted. The people who nursed Akizuki on a diet of liver and canned peaches collapsed with high fever as he recovered his strength and began feeling well enough to make rounds again. The cared-for Dr. Akizuki became the caregiver of his caregivers. Finally, Nagai collapsed—from "extreme exhaustion," according to Nagai's self-diagnosis, but Akizuki reminded him that any physician who practiced self-diagnosis had a fool as a patient and a fool for a doctor.

Akizuki suspected that persistent radiation had caused Nagai's eventual collapse and concluded that everyone who lived in or near the hills was doomed. Though the scorched limbs on the trees were sending forth new leaves, Akizuki recorded in his notes that the "abnormally bright" splashes of green under the setting sun and against the clouds seemed to him to be harbingers of death rather than signs of life.

Dr. Paul (Takashi) Nagai did not see it the same way. The ever-thickening growths of grass that had followed the September floods and the appearance of tiger beetles and cabbage butterflies among the grasses and the leaves hinted to Nagai that the seventy-five-year theory was wrong and that the hills would come alive again, quickly. He began to believe that if humanity somehow managed to destroy itself utterly, nature would cover up all of civilization's mistakes in only a decade or two, spreading whole forests up the avenues and through the ruins.

From sheet metal debris and pieces of scrap wood hauled down from the demolished medical center, Nagai built himself a hut, 600 meters from the hypocenter, in the footprint of his home's foundations. The single-room structure was located steps away from the very patch of earth on which he found his wife's rosary with its glass beads melted.

Moving downhill into the zone of Dr. Akizuki's "concentric circles of death" and becoming the first permanent settler of Urakami, was not merely a scientific exploration for Nagai but an exploration of faith as well.

As a young student, he once rented a room in the house of a family whose members had been active in Nagasaki's underground Christian movement from the time of Shogun Tokugawa's 1614 purge through the execution of the Christian leader Kichizo in 1856. Nagai married the landlord's daughter Midori—who was a direct descendant of Kichizo. His post-holocaust hut was erected over the ancestral home of Urakami's Christian underground and overlooked the site where Shogun Tokugawa had ordered the crucifixion of the Jesuits.

Mrs. Nagai's influence, and the influence of her multigenerational creed of "Love your neighbor as yourself," had once brought the doctor close to court-martial, just as, presently, it brought him closer to hypocenter radiation. As a medical army lieutenant stationed in occupied China for nearly three years, he had provided treatment to Imperial shock troops, then to Chinese civilians, and finally to a wounded Chinese soldier. "When making a diagnosis," he said in his defense, "I would not take nationality into consideration."

If not for the unlikely circumstance that one of his commanders had ancestors in the Urakami underground, Nagai's story would have ended in death and obscurity in China. Instead, he was sent back to Urakami, where he discovered that deteriorating wartime conditions had left many residents impoverished, ill-fed, and in declining health. What Nagai learned in China came back with him: "When making a diagnosis and offering aid," he told his staff, "we should not take an ability to pay into consideration."

Thus it came as no surprise to Akizuki or to anyone else who knew Nagai that during the first autumn after the bomb he christened himself a laboratory rat, moved downhill into the forbidden zone, and grew his hair as long as Einstein's.

He named his hut *Nyokodo*—the "As Yourself" hermitage.

When he raised his roof and sealed it against the rain, ants were already at work, excavating tiny pebbles and carbonized chips of bone. Fifty meters in every direction, the ants flourished.

In the land between Nyokodo and the hypocenter, and for an equal distance opposite the zero point, everyone had been killed except two children and a woman, all of whom happened to be shielded within Prefect Nishioka's tunnels.

By October 1945, even the "miners of the town" had fled the forbidden inner circles of Ground Zero. Nagai recorded that the plant growth continued to thicken and that the growing populations of insects were soon joined by mice, and finally by birds. His notebooks also memorialized flash burns on tree trunks out to a distance of 10 kilometers (about 6.4 miles), adding that, beyond Ground Zero, whatever grass and trees grew within two to seven kilometers—"all were irradiated at the time of the explosion and were scorched red or crisped brown." Even the shadow-shielded sides of distant hills were not spared. In the little valley where Kayano and Makoto now lived, all the unscorched leaves that had been stained by the black rain withered and died.

Dr. Nagai examined two farmers who, at a distance of nearly 17 kilometers (10 miles), had cut down some wood stained with black rain and carried it on their shoulders, a day after the explosion. The next day, their arms and shoulders broke out in an itching red rash. Mosquito bites oozed pus and were very slow to heal. Their white blood cell counts were still abnormal two months later, but their overall health appeared to be slowly improving.

It seemed clear to Nagai that the effect of radiation on the human body was more violent at the beginning. As autumn gave way to winter, he wrote, "I myself sleep in a small hut with icicles hanging on the walls and roof and with snow filtering in. I have only a thin blanket to protect me. And yet I have not contracted pneumonia, or even so much as a cold. Even if I get an injury or a scratch (as when bitten by a spider), I myself have no fear of infection or pus developing in the wounds."

Soon, even the swelling of Nagai's face, and the painful abdominal bloating effects brought about by his cancer, appeared to have gone into complete remission. The Japanese and American "bombing survey" scientists who visited him one morning were quick to report to their supervisors that the radiological effects had dissipated and that, in at least one case, might even have enhanced a survivor's health. As jokes about the health benefits of being bitten by radioactive spiders flourished, the MacArthur Commission chose to ignore Nagai's loudly voiced conclusion that had this been Tucson, Arizona, instead of the Urakami River valley, the radioactive dust would have lingered for a decade or more on every breeze, instead of being washed down the hills and out to sea by a typhoon.

("Don't eat clams till late next year," Nagai had advised everyone.)

No one in authority seemed to be listening to anything except what they specifically wanted to hear. Everything else became irrelevant. And so, inevitably, when combined with a bombing survey laboratory study that revealed Urakami earthworms to be developing normally, Nagai's results were misused to achieve a preconceived conclusion poorly disguised as science: "A city cannot be obliterated wholly by the atomic bomb. It is not so fearful. It is just another weapon, with greater physical effects than those which preceded it."

"Greater physical effects!" Dr. Akizuki raged (in a letter from the time of the commission's conclusion). "Do they really wish to make all of us who have been injured or killed by the fallout simply nonexistent?"

For Nagai's part, he was still quite frightened by the radiation effects of these new bombs. But he alone seemed equally concerned that the American, British, and Japanese scientists who visited the ruins neither understood nor attempted to investigate "what this weapon does to the heart and conscience and mind of someone who survives."

Nagai's friend Akizuki was an example of this—a thoroughly decent man plunged instantly into a cycle of remorse and rage. Akizuki could no longer face Dr. Yoshioka because he felt responsible for her exposure to the blast; and as the first winter approached its midpoint, he spoke often of wanting to cave in the back of a "stingy" American pharmacist's head with a shovel.

"They are ignoring us out here!" Akizuki said during a visit to Nyokodo. "They ask us nothing, and they send us nothing."

"We should not hate the people who seem bent upon ignoring us or hurting us," Nagai responded. "I have named this place *Nyokodo* because the ancient prophets—Buddah and Jesus, Hillel and Mohammad—each, near the ends of their human journeys, said essentially the same thing: 'Love others as you love yourself.'"

"That does not help at this kind of time."

"But it *does*," Nagai insisted. "This blame reflex of yours is quite natural. Yet we, more than perhaps any other people on earth, must come to understand and to teach that the need to strike back at someone is wrong thinking and can lead to nothing good. Do you not understand that the power of the atom was a *gift*, planted in the universe at the very beginning?"

If the gift is handled properly, Nagai tried to explain, each man is given the key to the universe—"a key that may one day throw open the doors to the planets, and the stars beyond." And yet, somehow this same key had been fashioned in such a manner that it could also unlock the gates of hell.

Motioning toward the hypocenter, Akizuki asked, "You call *this* a gift from God?"

"I do not mean that this destruction is a gift. What happened here is a message of hope, and a warning. It was, in a manner of speaking, a pentecostal apocalypse."

"I think your brain is going soft from living down here," Akizuki said.

Nagai returned his friend a laugh, and emphasized, "What happened here . . . is simply what happened. It becomes what it is. And now we must go forth and overcome the instinct for finger-pointing. We must learn to be guided by civilization and not by instinct, by mercy and not by the old tribal, territorial drumbeats. Why else do you think we have survived—we of Nagasaki?"

"I don't know. Just lucky, I guess. Or maybe just unlucky."

"Exactly the latter, I think. Does it not occur to you that those who were taken instantly or who died during those first days were perhaps the lucky ones? Even if what comes after death is merely infinite dreamless sleep, aren't they less tormented than those of us who live to grieve and to carry a survivor's scars? Perhaps those who disappeared were simply taken, and those of us who were supposedly 'saved' failed our entrance exam into heaven and were left behind because we are *meant* to stay."

"To what purpose?"

"To learn, and to teach."

Dr. Akizuki looked to the place where a melted rosary and Midori Nagai's bones had been found. Mrs. Nagai was evidently among the instantly taken. Akizuki shook his head. "I'm sorry, friend. But God had nothing to do with this. *People* did this."

"Indeed we did. We all let the words, 'Who takes a knife will die by a knife,' go through one ear and out the other. We took the greatest knowledge that science could provide and, lacking wisdom, we human beings busily made warships, torpedoes, and now atomic bombs. God did not twist and pervert nature's gifts. We did."

Akizuki shook his head again, drew Nagai's door shut, and left, angry and confused. He wanted to punch his friend for suggesting that the bombing of his city was somehow ordained by a compassionate god.

That night Dr. Nagai wrote a wish, which he hoped would prophesy the longest strategic peace the world had ever known:

"Nuclear war ended in Nagasaki.

"Nagasaki is the period.

"Peace starts from Nagasaki."

HAD THE CHAIN of *Bock's Car* misfortunes not placed the Nagasaki gamma-ray burst at precisely the right distance from Dr. Nagai, the apparent remission of his cancer might not have occurred, and his voice would soon have disappeared from history. Had the uranium bomb not been compromised by the Tinian accident, the outer fringe of Hiroshima's Ground Zero would have extended far beyond Tsutomu Yamaguchi and, instead of being grievously injured, he would have ceased to exist. Located at Yamaguchi's same radius from the

Hiroshima hypocenter, the Sasakis and Dr. Hachiya would also have become silenced voices, lost to history.

Yamaguchi's curious distinction of being twice bombed and having twice survived was improbable by a figure that needed to be squared or cubed, and not merely doubled. If cloud cover had not conspired with a desperate fuel shortfall to shift *Bock's Car's* target from Nagasaki proper to the district next door, Mr. Yamaguchi would have been located directly under the bomb.

An improbable swerving of history had dictated that Sadako Sasaki and her neighbor would bear witness. Another apparently reset Dr. Nagai's life clock. *Two* unlikely swerves, one after another, had made Yamaguchi the bomb's most spectacular survivor. No one else, not even the other double survivors, had been so directly exposed to the effects of a nuclear explosion—twice.

"On August 9," Yamaguchi recalled, "the devil's column of fire stood even taller than before, as if mocking me with laughter because I thought I had escaped with my life from Hiroshima to Nagasaki. I felt as though it were a sentient beast that had literally chased me down."

Mr. Yamaguchi's wife tended to his wounds for nearly three days without sleeping, struggling to keep him alive. In Hiroshima, his skin and even the muscles in one arm had been penetrated by glassy buckshot, air-blasted across a potato field from office windows more than a city block away. In Nagasaki, three days later, bits of mahogany flew away from office furnishings and pierced the same wounded arm, like poison darts. Nonetheless, Dr. Nagai's odd ideas about maggots, fruit, and lightly cooked liver seemed to be working, though it was difficult for Hisako to keep the chickens under control. They were continually seeking out her semiconscious husband, and from time to time he remembered being awakened by the hungry birds.

"Behave yourself," Hisako warned, "or my husband will have your liver."

And it seemed that every time Hisako turned her back on the chickens, one or two of them managed to sneak past her. They went to Mr. Yamaguchi directly and began pecking and plucking the maggots out of his wounds. One of them apparently bit too deep, and a half-conscious hand reached out, still with enough strength to crush its neck. Hisako made the bird's liver into a very strong, iron-rich porridge.

The Yamaguchis were living with four or five other families, inside the very same tunnel Hisako had been building for the Mitsubishi offices, under the governor's and the prefect's "Emergency Preparedness Protocol."

Aside from feeding the chickens, the next thing Mr. Yamaguchi clearly remembered was awakening in a dark cave one afternoon to the sound of two-dozen people weeping. They were listening to a radio on August 15, and the Emperor's voice had just announced the surrender.

The tunnel itself was all the evidence anyone really needed to know that the war had been clearly perceived, by those in charge, to be drawing toward its final battle. Even before Hiroshima, Yamaguchi had begun anticipating the fall of Japan; so he went back to sleep, and continued to bleed from his nose and his bowels.

During the next week, soldiers were sent, under orders from the deputy governor, to assist survivors from the Mitsubishi offices. By then, all surviving engineers who knew anything about ships or steam-catapulted planes, about submarines or bomb shelter construction, were of keen interest to the American occupation's scientists and engineers. The soldiers, under the advice of Professor Shirabe and Dr. Nagai's house-calling nurses, brought a rich supply of tangerines and cans of peaches.

As Nagai had predicted, once Hisako began feeding her husband substantial quantities of fruit, Yamaguchi's health improved to such extent that by the first week of September he was able to return with Hisako and Katsutoshito to their half-exploded house, and to begin thinking about reconstruction. Nonetheless, he was still a long way from being able to make effective repairs. Even if the house had not been cracked and scorched by the *pika* ("Oh, that's bad," Hisako said), he was not up to the task. Even the saving grace of having the flames blown out by a great wind ("Oh, that's good," Hisako said), this, too, left Mr. Yamaguchi overwhelmed; for even had the same, fire-snuffing wind not blown the house in two and bounced it off its foundations ("Oh, that's awful . . ."), he did not feel like working, even though repairing the roof was a straightforward engineering problem.

"I was quite able physically, and in terms of basic knowledge," he recalled. "But now, spiritually, I wasn't really quite human anymore. I moved around, day by day, like a machine, and not like a husband or a father at all."

When the September storms came, he and Hisako hid under umbrellas in the house. Hisako laughed. Yamaguchi did not—*could* not. He began to think that his soul, if not his life, had been ended by the two bombs. And then he began to think about the fate of Father Simcho of Urakami. Simcho had left before the bomb, to a place called Auschwitz.

Simcho was a preacher who came with the Jesuits from France and gave aid to widows and orphaned children—and, wherever possible, arranged adoptions. By 1942, Simcho and the other French missionaries began to draw suspicion from the military (partly based on accusations that their church had been decorated with "secret society" chevrons, triangles, and circles). They were eventually "ejected" as spies.

"Not merely ejected," Yamaguchi learned. He inquired into what happened to Simcho in Auschwitz and heard that a man in the concentration camp had been accused of stealing and hoarding food. The man was going to be either hanged with piano wire as an example to others or "sent to the gas."

"Father Simcho made a remarkable decision," Yamaguchi later taught all who were willing to listen. "He actually took the position of a man accused by the Germans of stealing loaves of bread from them. The accused man had a family out there, somewhere beyond the prison walls. Simcho had no family; so he confessed to a theft he did not commit, so that children might have their father."

With Simcho on his mind, Yamaguchi told his wife of the decision he was finally coming to: "If my life ended on August 6 and August 9, then whatever might come afterward, I should perhaps consider to be my second life?"

The white rainbow that manifested over Nagasaki in September seemed to firm Yamaguchi's resolve. What meaning was there in Simcho's example, he wondered, if someone did not remember the missionary and carry on after him, and send forth acts of human kindness in his memory, hoping that they might spread like ripples in a pond—anti-ripples, perhaps, against Dr. Akizuki's concentric circles of death.

Mr. Yamaguchi eventually walked away from engineering, especially of machines of war. As he saw it, his second life gave him only one choice: to regard himself a victim and nurture hate or to regard himself a survivor, walk in Father Simcho's path, and treat others with humanity.

And so Yamaguchi decided that his second life would be devoted to the children of Nagasaki. He became a carpenter, and then, after helping to rebuild schools along the Urakami River, he went inside the buildings and became a junior high school teacher.

MISAKO KATANI, the schoolgirl who witnessed the fire horses of Hiroshima and who would forever remember that horses could scream, also remembered her father telling her that they must flee the city. "Thank God we have relatives in Nagasaki," he had said. "We will be safe there."

"Obviously, some obscure meaning of the word *safe* not found in any dictionary of the Japanese language," Katani would tell historians, "or in any other language."

She and her father had left Hiroshima aboard the same train as Tsutomu Yamaguchi, and in fact Katani's relatives lived in the same Mitsubishi housing district as Mr. Yamaguchi, at the same distance from the Urakami hypocenter.

The house was knocked on its side, yet remained curiously intact. After this, Father decided that because the bomb had apparently missed central Nagasaki and fallen farther upriver, someone might come back to finish the job, and therefore Hiroshima—which had been mostly erased—was probably a safer place after all.

Slowly making their way north, they arrived just ahead of the September 17 typhoon and narrowly escaped death a third time. A fellow traveler, Professor Mashita of Nagasaki, was not as lucky. After surviving Urakami, he had been recruited by Drs. Nishina and Sagane to monitor radiation in Hiroshima's hypocenter. His tent was blown down and his equipment destroyed by the typhoon. When Mashita tried to shield himself from horizontal rain behind the walls of the Hiroshima Dome, loose bricks tumbled down and killed him.

"Life seems to be worth nothing more than a leaf or a straw at the mercy of the wind," wrote Dr. Akizuki, after hearing of his friend Mashita's death. "Now we have surely suffered enough. No more!"

But history was not through with the survivors. Katani's hometown house was located between the Misasa Bridge and the Dome. Even after her father saw that the fires had reduced the entire neighborhood to dust and charcoal, he was able to convince himself that Katani's mother and little sister were only "missing." There was something astonishingly contagious about the "missing" mind-set. Though everything appeared to have been stamped flat, Katani adopted the mind-set as well.

As she walked along a familiar road and recognized the location of her home, Katani yelled, "Mom! It's me!"

"But my voice wasn't reaching her," Katani recalled. "My father looked at our surroundings and said that maybe my mother was holding my little sister Tamie, and they were under the house. Even then, Father considered them to be only missing. I removed ashes and debris around an area one meter square . . . and there were the flakes [of blackened flesh]. I saw the ornate hairpin that my mother always wore. That is what at first caught my eye. I yelled, 'Mother!' And then I frantically sifted [through the flakes]. And underneath was my little sister—sheltered by Mother. Now, at last, Father accepted that his wife and child were not missing but were gone from him forever."

After that, Katani's father began to die.

And before the year was through, new beliefs emerged, about radiation exposure and atomic bomb disease—and in terms of marriage, people exposed in either of the cities (to say nothing about exposure in both) became untouchables.

Katani decided to keep her mouth shut, carrying inside of her the secret that she had experienced the atomic bomb twice. She made a further private decision to take her peculiar distinction of double survival as a symbol of improbable good luck, rather than the sign of a life somehow jinxed.

Having survived where so many others perished in every direction, Katani asked herself, "How could anything bad happen?"

Moving far from the ruins, she went to school, where she could eventually fall in love, marry, and continue her schooling. Her three children would be born dead, and dead, and dead.

ONCE HE SETTLED IN, and stayed alive, Nagai was joined by other hypocenter pioneers—who, as the winter of 1945–46 became the spring of 1946, began erecting a shantytown in the ruins, eventually redirecting a stream through makeshift aqueducts, and reintroducing a streetlight here and there, with Nagai turning one wall of his little hermitage into the first local library.

As wild daisies and clover spread across the ground, and as the first hawks began to depopulate the returning mice, Dr. Nagai noticed stabbing pains in his lower spine and in his spleen. He did not need Dr. Akizuki to tell him that his remission had been only temporary. As the land between Nyokodo and the hypocenter came back to life, so, too, did carcinogens' angels.

Nagai's new neighbors offered to build extra rooms onto his shack, but he told them that he wished to travel lightly through life, and that one room with a wall of windows and an opposite wall that shelved his books was actually all he needed.

An American chaplain paid him a visit, offering building materials and two carpenters, but Nagai served him tea and said he needed nothing more. Days later, a bishop visited and, right behind him, a beggar. Nagai welcomed them both, equally, into his "palace." Two of Nagai's former students turned South Pacific soldiers also arrived, speaking proudly of their dream to one day rise from the ruins of Urakami with swords in hand.

To all of them, Nagai said, "If you had been here on that day and at that hour, if you had seen the hell that opened up on Earth before our eyes, if you had even a glimpse of that, you would never, never entertain the crazy thought of another war. If there is another war, atomic bombs may explode everywhere and there will be no beautiful songs of distant Earth [from other planets]—no poems, no paintings, no music, no literature, no research. Only death."

After the spring rains cleansed the hypocenter and wildflowers established dominion over the land and songbirds returned in great numbers, Dr. Paul Nagai brought his children down to Nyokodo.

One morning, he awoke to the sound of five-year-old Kayano chattering to herself in the yard. Stepping outside, Nagai found her playing house with her toys, acting out the same tea-serving game she used to play with her friends from this same neighborhood. Before her were the head of a doll, some glass bottles, plates, and part of a broken mirror, set on a table that was a scorched rock. Kayano served imaginary tea and talked with imaginary friends. All of her real friends were dead.

IN HIROSHIMA, the trains were running on schedule again, and electric lines now powered Dr. Hachiya's Communications Hospital. Though most of the bridges were still bent and fractured and navigable only by people with very good balance, the main roads had been cleared of debris and, with gasoline slowly becoming plentiful, the streets were filling up with the first traffic seen in more than two years.

The makeshift hospital where Minami saw the blue fireflies was a school again, attended by Gen and his new little brother, Ryuta Kondo. Electricity had reached the school, but most of the walls were slicked with mold and every time the weather took a turn for the worse, the children endured rainstorms indoors. Chasing down and filling in all the cracks in the steel-and-concrete roof proved to be an intractable problem for carpenters. As the compression waves passed, entire floors had moved and rippled—like swells at sea—before abruptly solidifying.

The tin-roof shantytown outside the school, now subsidized by government-appointed suppliers, provided little more comfort than the school, but it had several advantages over the makeshift dormitories near the Communications Hospital, which were built on ground still covered with the bones of Hiroshima Castle's soldiers.

Instead of skulls, the neighborhood around the school had slugs. Gen did his best to exterminate them, but they were breeding in unprecedented numbers since the bomb. They piled up in living masses around the bases of walls, around the legs of tables, and on the edges of sleeping mats. Ryuta entertained himself by plucking them off the floor with chopsticks and dropping them into a can of salt. Gen preferred killing them with hot coals from the stove. The boys' never-ending war against the slugs gave Ma a creepy feeling.

Yet even as a brotherly bond developed between Gen and Ryuta, the bomb had laid down the foundations on which the invisible cracks described by Dr. Nagai could begin to form.

Gen's spirit was already flayed by the time he and his mother found Ryuta in need of a family and made a decision to help him. And, though no one was truly to blame, the uncanny resemblance between Ryuta and Gen's lost brother sometimes caused such confusion that Ryuta felt loved only by virtue of being a convenient counterfeit replacement for Senji.

Never did the pressure become more painfully manifest than during the afternoon a neighbor who had rescued Gen's mother from the fires of August 6 actually mistook Ryuta for Senji, though he was certain that he had seen Senji die.

Angrily, Ryuta began mocking the neighbor, calling him "a stupid Korean."

More angrily than Ryuta, Gen said, "Have you forgotten what Papa told us—that the generals and the government tried to sell their war by spreading lies about the Koreans and Chinese and that we were never to be fooled by it? So, why are you making fun of Koreans, Senji?"

"I'm not Senji!"

"You say you're not, but I know you survived."

"You wandering idiot!" Ryuta shouted, and ran away. He stayed away for many days, returning hungry and unwashed, to a lonely sorrow in which he would never trust Gen to love him as an adopted brother—only as an accidental doppelganger.

In years to come, Gen would tell the story of Ryuta with at least three different endings, ranging from how it eventually turned out for them to how he wished it had turned out. Each ending underscored a gulf between brothers that persisted until atomic bomb disease intervened, and time ran out.

• • •

ALL AROUND NYOKODO and along the path down to the hypocenter burned and broken trees that appeared to be dead had continued to send up healthy green shoots.

"Another example," Nagai reiterated for Akizuki, "of how, at the very bottom, there is always the great earth."

An inspiring thought, Akizuki guessed, *if one is willing to ignore the monsters*. In a corner of Dr. Nagai's garden, a crown chrysanthemum had bloomed with its petals arranged in the flower's center, and with multiple central heads surrounding the petals. And on a scorched wall, a vine of pale ivy flourished without chlorophyll—a vine whose seeds were already spreading as far away as Tokyo.

Dr. Akizuki was no longer as concerned about the health of his

NORMAL   MALFORMED   MALFORMED

NORMAL   MALFORMED

Dr. Paul Nagai observed and recorded unusual mutations in plants growing near the Urakami hypocenter, most notably among flowers of the Persian speedwell (*top*), followed by strange new varieties of the crown chrysanthemum (*bottom*). (Patricia Wynne)

natural surroundings as about Nagai's health. His white blood cell count had reached more than four times normal and was represented by "many mitotic figures"—which defined cancer.

"I've had a good run," Nagai said. "I guess this means I must quicken my studies, and write faster."

At Akizuki's request, a microscope was delivered to Nyokodo, so Nagai could study the health of Ground Zero plants at home. As he became increasingly confined to bed, he did indeed begin writing faster; in addition to filling notebooks with biological observations, he wrote the first of thirteen books, *The Bells of Nagasaki*, which he penned between May and July of 1946.

Revisiting an earlier confrontational discussion with Akizuki, Nagai read his friend a passage from the final chapter: "'God concealed within the universe a precious sword. First the human race caught the scent of this awful treasure. Then we began to search for it. And finally we grasped it in our hands. What kind of dance will we humans perform while brandishing this two-edged sword?'"

Akizuki shook his head slowly. "No God," he sniped. "No sword planted in the universe, either. I said it before and I'll say it again: God had nothing to do with this."

"You miss the point. Whether you see God in it or not, it's either the keys to the universe for us or the fall of our civilization, if not our extinction. So, which shall it be?"

"Stop thinking so much," Akizuki said. "You need to conserve your strength."

"Oh, I think God will keep me around longer than you anticipate. You and I both know that I need to write a lot more if I'm going to pass my entrance exam."

Dr. Akizuki did not believe Nagai needed to hurry with his entrance exam to heaven, any more than he believed an invisible friend in heaven would grade the papers. By the first anniversary of the bombing, Paul Nagai's leukemia cells had doubled once again in population from their July value. Statistically speaking, he would probably be dead within considerably less than a year.

Five months later, his second book was finished and his first was coming off the press. Ten months after that—more than three months after Akizuki expected Nagai to be exploring whatever happened (or did not happen) to one's conscious existence after death—admirers of his first book began paying visits, without any warning. One of them was Helen Keller.

Nagai wrote in his journal: "She came toward me, her hand searching in the air for my hand. Finally our fingers touched and we grasped each other's hands. In an instant, I felt the warmth of her love flow through my extremities like electricity through a closed circuit."

Helen Keller explained through an interpreter that she could not see what the weapon had done to Urakami—but more than a year later, she could smell it.

"I cannot smell it," Nagai said. "But sometimes late at night I *feel* it. The lesson I take from this place is that the person who wishes for peace does not hide even a needle as a weapon. Even when driven into the need for self-defense, if you have a weapon, you are qualified to fight—maybe—but you are not qualified to pray for peace."

Akizuki wished Nagai would stop talking like this and simply return as a patient to the newly resupplied and now nearly half rebuilt hospital. "Your Nyokodo is becoming more of a tourist attraction than a home or a proper sick room, and the visitors are draining too much of your energy."

His book was indeed bringing too many visitors: parents who had lost their children and wanted revenge . . . a representative from the Vatican who wanted a message of peace; and three monks from Tibet who sought the same. And then, two polite men from a new American establishment called the Internal Revenue Service.

"What have you done, in terms of paying your tax obligation from the sales of your book?" they inquired.

"Taxes?" Nagai asked. "I only need this workplace, as you see it here. Everything else—including the money from my writing—I have given to the orphans of this city."

"But you're not allowed to do that before settling your tax obligation."

Nagai served them tea and said, "Men with wiser voices than mine have always preached that charity is the cornerstone of faith.

They tell us that if you adopt orphans into your heart, you will be the father of many children."

"Who said that?" one of the tax men asked.

"Jesus, for one example."

"Really?"

Nagai nodded, gave the men a warm smile, and told them to drink the tea because it was good for their health.

The IRS did not bother him again, but other people continued arriving at his one-room home and workplace, as Nagai's face and abdomen began to swell, and as his strength declined to only one-fifth that of a healthy man's.

"I wanted to live here with you in quiet happiness," he told Kayano and Makoto. "But now it has become impossible to fulfill that wish."

The reconstruction of railways and streetcar lines brought even greater numbers of visitors each passing month. During the day, Nagai served each of them tea and by the time the last streetcar left outer Urakami each evening, his own stomach was so full of tea that he could not sleep at night, so he stayed up writing while the children slept.

In the morning he was often too exhausted to join the children in play—Kayano and Makoto as well as orphans placed with new parents in neighboring homes. That he spent so much of his strength on others as to leave almost nothing for play pained Nagai far, far more than the advancing cancer, he told Makoto.

To Makoto, his father's guilt would become every bit as undeserved as the burden carried by Dr. Hachiya of Hiroshima. Makoto never once doubted his father's love, and he was truly thankful to him for the Nyokodo message—which he would pass forward into the next century through his own son, Tokusaburo Nagai.

"You start with an act of love or kindness to your neighbor," Tokusaburo would tell a new generation, more than sixty years later. By then a museum and library complex would surround the Nyokodo hut, in a thriving suburb whose tree-lined streets hid every trace of hypocenter scarring.

"I do not know for a fact that a spreading ripple of mutual hu-

man tenderness can overcome the darker half of human instinct,"
Tokusaburo would say. "But we need to try; because those of us who
were born afterward can scarcely understand how scary it really
was, and how important the peace is. Down this road, where the Sun
touched the Earth, there are tall office buildings and tall trees
everywhere—and if you search carefully, you will come upon a
white statue of a young girl holding a paper crane—and beyond the
statue, you'll find a dome of grass in a garden where a plaque reads
'HYPOCENTER.' All the ruins are covered up by offices and gardens; so it's easy to forget the terror and that's why I am saying, *Start
by loving your neighbors.* Start, by loving others as you love yourself. That's what Grandfather taught his children, and anyone else
who would listen."

In February 1951, five years after Dr. Akizuki had expected Paul
Nagai to be dead, his white blood cell count reached sixty-five times
the normal value. While finishing *Maiden Pass* (a history of Nagasaki's Christian community from the time of the 1870 oppression
through the destruction of Urakami Cathedral), internal bleeding in
Nagai's right shoulder left his right hand paralyzed.

Nagai dictated the last few pages to nine-year-old Kayano. Having come to regard the disappearance of Urakami's "Maria" Cathedral and its congregation on August 9, 1945, as a prophetic sacrifice,
he told Kayano, "Even if you are one of the last people on earth, you
must be against war."

When Nagai died on May 1, 1951, Dr. Akizuki was unable to
figure out what force of will had kept him alive so long. An autopsy
revealed that his blood had become all but nonfunctional years before. It was as if Akizuki's often adversarial colleague had somehow
managed to reanimate himself and walk around in a body that was
already quite dead, but to Nagai's mind, alive-seeming still.

By New Year's Day 1952, Akizuki had read everything Nagai
wrote while living in Ground Zero, and he began asking his friend's
two children to teach him everything they could remember that remained unwritten. Afterward he began to take part in honoring
Nagai's work, and he evolved, like Nagai, into a man of peace and faith.

"Well, and why not?" Akizuki said to the children of Nyokodo.

"After all, haven't scientists and Buddhists, physicians and Christians been saying very much the same thing all along to those who had ears to listen? It's just that, sometimes, we use different language. Different words."

And with such grace did Akizuki begin to live the rest of his life with one simple, Nyokodo-esque commandment: "Be kind."

IN HIROSHIMA AND BEYOND, while Nagai became crippled by his own blood and taught Akizuki how to stand, the fortunes and misfortunes of other survivors and witnesses were being altered as dramatically as Urakami's increasingly green landscape.

Eizo Nomura, who had managed somehow to walk away alive from the Rationing Bureau's basement—only one hundred meters from Hiroshima's "Atomic Dome"—was dying from a full spectrum of medical complications.

As a "prisoner of peace," nuclear physicist Yoshio Nishina continued to maintain close professional relationships with his prewar colleagues, including Luis Alvarez, Niels Bohr, and Albert Einstein, until he passed away suddenly in 1951.

Nishina's assistant Eizo Tajima had been one of the first scientists into the hypocenters of the two cities. Noticing that flash-shadows sometimes stretched out behind objects that survived the blast wave, and that they pointed like accusing fingers toward the origin of the flash, Tajima accurately determined the precise location of the Urakami hypocenter. He also excavated samples from beneath the flash point, inhaling dust that was still highly radioactive despite being mostly decayed, and sentencing himself, sooner or later, to slow death.

Paul Tibbets would outlast Tajima and Nishina, dying of natural causes in 2007, proud of *Enola Gay*'s role in history.

Field Marshal Shunroku Hata, whose survival in a Hiroshima shock cocoon led him to believe that atomic attack could easily be endured (which belief contributed to the delay of Japan's surrender) was arrested in 1945 and found guilty of atrocities as commander of 1941's Zhejiang-Jiangxi campaign, during which a quarter million unarmed Chinese civilians were killed. A further conviction arose from his commanding role in the Changiao Massacre—which brought his total to more than 300,000 civilians killed. He would outlive Dr. Nagai by eleven years and would die unrepentant.

General Seizo Arisue, chief of Japanese Military Intelligence throughout the war, used his extensive knowledge about the Soviet Union and China as leverage with General MacArthur, to become a "prisoner of peace." He was, like Dr. Nishina, allowed to live free yet under guard, instead of being confined to a three-pace by two-pace concrete cell, like Hata. Arisue was instrumental in silencing testimony by Drs. Kitano Masaji and Shiro Ishi about human experimentation in China's Unit 731 biological weapons facility, so that MacArthur's people could transfer bio-weapons technology to America's Cold War weaponeers with minimal controversy. Among Unit 731's subjects were several captured soldiers from MacArthur's own forces. Arisue and MacArthur both had decades longer to live and prosper before dying of natural causes, peacefully and in their own beds.

Foreign Minister Shigenori Togo, judged to be of no strategic postwar value to MacArthur's commission, was not fated to live as long as MacArthur or Arisue, or even Nagai. He died a prisoner in 1950, at the age of sixty-eight.

THREE YEARS AFTER Dr. Paul Nagai died, Sadako Sasaki, the two-year-old who had survived Hiroshima's fire worms and black rain in an overcrowded lifeboat, was growing up to be an unusually athletic child whose teacher Nomura began to see in her an Olympic hopeful. During interschool sports day events, fleet-footed Sadako dominated all of the speed records, and helped to pull her class relay team from its previous standing in last place into second, and then into first.

As a reward, the class won a field trip to the Miyajima Shrine Island, where eleven-year-old Sadako promptly challenged her teammates with a race to the top of Mount Misen—up the very same steps Kenshi and Setsuko Hirata had climbed in 1945, at the beginning of a marriage that lasted only ten days.

At the peak, everyone laughed when Sadako called out to her

exhausted friends, "Well, that was fun. But now I'm hungry, so when do we eat lunch?"

Another classmate cautioned that it was not safe to joke near the mountaintop, because a jealous goddess was rumored to dwell there.

Sadako looked her friend in the eye with feigned severity, and said, "We've lived in Hiroshima too long to be afraid of ghosts. Just look around you."

Fully one-third of the children in their class were survivors, and more than half of this third had lost parents and grandparents, brothers and sisters.

Sadako continued, "We've lived through the atomic bomb, you and I. Nothing else as bad can happen."

Indeed, it did not seem possible. Sadako, her mother Fujiko, and her brother Masahiro had been shock-cocooned and shadow-shielded in a region where almost everyone else died. During Joseph Fuoco's photo reconnaissance flight over Hiroshima a day after the bombing, his plane had followed the railroad tracks through Sadako's neighborhood. He remembered seeing the distinct shadow of an individual walking across the Misasa Bridge at the exact moment of the *pika*. The shadow pointed upriver, across the walkway, down the curb and onto the road surface, then across the curb of the opposite walkway. The person who cast that shadow appeared to be one of the few shadow people who could actually be named. On that very same walkway, at 8:15 a.m., Shizuko Ohara, a petite nineteen-year-old from Sadako's neighborhood, had been on her way to work and was wearing a light dress. A soldier found her and assisted her to the Communications Hospital, where she died from flash burns (and probably from exposure to black rain) at precisely the moment Dr. Hachiya felt the tremors from Nagasaki.

So how, Sadako wondered, how, after escaping Shizuko Ohara's fate herself, could anything unlucky ever happen?

The first nine years after the war had been difficult, but everything seemed gradually to have improved. During the first two years, Sadako's family had lived with relatives a hundred kilometers upriver, in the town of Miyoshi, before returning to Hiroshima in 1947. They settled near a badly damaged steel-and-concrete school with ceilings that leaked and a gymnasium that had no roof at all.

Their new house was smaller than the old one, but Father opened a hair salon in the midst of the Ground Zero settlement, less than four blocks from the school where Minami witnessed the blue fireflies.

In 1954, the roof still leaked and multiple classes were being held in a partitioned auditorium, but at least the gymnasium had a new roof. Athletic competition and practice sessions were Sadako's favorite parts of every school day.

Though her parents spoke often of a languishing economy, Sadako felt that life was good, and that even her difficult beginnings— because she had survived where so many others died—must indeed have been filled with good luck signs.

Then, in December of 1954, she began arriving home from after-school track practice complaining of being increasingly worn out. Over the course of only a few short weeks, Sadako's dinner table conversations became more and more dominated by murmurings of, "Tired . . . tired . . ." In late January, going to bed early no longer seemed to help. Gradually, she was becoming tired even at breakfast. The bad times really began gathering force in January 1955, when a new family photograph revealed by chance the first clear signs of swollen lymph nodes on one side of Sadako's neck.

That's when Father took her to a doctor for blood tests. The results were as horribly apparent as the swelling in the photograph: "an abnormally high white blood cell count . . . many mitotic figures . . . leukemia."

The doctors asked Shigeo Sasaki if his daughter had been exposed to black rain. And when he confirmed that this was indeed the case, the doctor bowed his head.

"Atomic bomb disease," he said, in a voice that cracked from having given this same diagnosis to scores and scores of other parents: the most unnatural horror of all—for parents to outlive their children.

For a little while longer, Sadako felt well enough to attend school, play jump rope with her friends, and live at home; but on February 21, 1955, she was hospitalized. The disease seemed to strike like a lightning bolt. During a span of weeks, her blood counts deteriorated to levels that had taken the late Dr. Nagai more than two years to reach. Judging from the rate of her decline, a doctor told Mr. and

Mrs. Sasaki that their daughter probably had less than a year to live, more likely only three or four months. Leukemia was not only incurable, its symptoms were all but untreatable, given even the best that 1955 medical technology could offer. The doctors told Shigeo that they could only try to reduce his daughter's fevers, administer painkillers, and provide occasional blood transfusions.

Sadako's mother was bewildered. Only seven months earlier, during an annual physical at the Atomic Bomb Casualty Commission clinic, doctors had said that both children's blood values were absolutely normal. Even now, Sadako did not look sick to Fujiko—merely a little sleepier than usual.

"No one is lovelier to a mother than her most miserable child," Fujiko Sasaki said later. When Sadako was born during the war there was rarely enough food and she had always been at least slightly underweight. Yet in spite of the hungry years, she grew to become so thoughtful and considerate an adolescent that Fujiko came to depend upon her; and in years to come, when Sadako visited Fujiko in her dreams she would always say, "Leave it to me, Mom," and Fujiko would awaken calling her daughter's name.

That first night in the hospital, Fujiko and Shigeo stayed in chairs at Sadako's bedside until sunrise. On any given night thereafter, Sadako went to sleep knowing that when she awoke in the morning, one of them would always be there. They kept back their tears for her, not wanting to make their child any more afraid than she already was—and, as Sadako slept, her mother held her hand and prayed to herself: "If a medicine that can cure this disease exists in this world, then let me borrow money for it, even if it costs ten million yen. Or, if it is possible, let me die in her place. Please, give the disease to me instead."

That same night and during many others that followed, Mr. Sasaki prayed the same prayer, while trying to form for himself a plan for something—*anything* he could do to help raise Sadako's spirits, and maybe give her a little more time. Dr. Nagai had famously reported that being close to one's family, being meditative, and receiving even the simplest "gifts of the heart" from loved ones could keep a patient's will to live intact, even when the body was saying, "It's time to give up and move on."

Shigeo and Fujiko had an idea for a gift from the heart. After the severe rationing years of the war were over, even though food became more widely available, money fell into short supply. Still, the Sasakis had dreamed of one day buying their little girl a fine, dress-up kimono. Money remained as scarce as ever, but Mr. Sasaki realized that a gift from the heart would be rendered even more powerful if, instead of buying the kimono (which was prohibitively expensive under the best of circumstances), he and Fujiko made one with their own hands. They bought silk fabric decorated with a cherry blossom pattern—and at night, while Sadako slept, Mrs. Sasaki and the rest of the family took turns at cutting and fashioning the sleeves and belt, and all the other individual parts of the kimono, which Mrs. Sasaki checked and double-checked for quality before assembling them into the completed garment.

On the day she opened the box and ran her fingers over the silk, Sadako broke into smiles and tears at the same time.

"You did too much for me," she said. "You spent too much."

Fujiko said, "Please, model it for us," and she withdrew a camera from a large bag. She also withdrew a little silk pocketbook and a pair of zori sandals—and Sadako seemed to become filled with joy and to swell with life's surge, even as she wiped tears from her eyes.

"I'm not a good daughter," Sadako told her brother Masahiro. "It's a bad situation because Mom and Dad will be having to spend so much money for my sickness."

"There was very little income for anyone in those times," Masahiro would tell history. "Even the doctors were poor. They and the nurses gave my sister everything they could—including vitamin B injections and anti-inflammatory arthritis drugs that kept the swelling of Sadako's body under some kind of control. But all of the nurses and all of the doctors could not fund the blood transfusions beyond a monthly donation of their own blood—and there were many other leukemic children in the wards.

"So, my parents had to pay people for the blood transfusions. Father was making a living by cutting hair, and in order to fund each transfusion, he would have to serve five customers. My little sister knew the situation, and told me that she would accept it and deal with it somehow. She understood that if she received a transfusion of healthy blood, she would feel better only for about ten hours; and she saw also that economically and emotionally, it must have been getting bad for us. Here lay a grade-school girl who saw that her parents wanted to help her—a girl who also seemed to know that, except for a miracle, she really could not get better. She guessed she could probably live a little while longer if she received transfusions and medicine; but she knew at the same time that her parents' support was making them poorer. Emotionally, she was being torn in two directions."

"I just have to find a way to deal with it," Sadako told her brother, repeatedly. "We have to get by, somehow."

By March 1955 Sadako's white blood cell count seemed to stabilize at about six times the normal value, but her abnormal red cell structure brought her close to the edge of oxygen starvation and made walking even short distances difficult. A severe drop in platelet counts was causing bruising from even the gentlest touch, which raised constant fears that Sadako could be killed by a hug.

In early May local schoolchildren brought a box of colorful paper cranes to the hospital's nurses, and showed them how to fold paper cranes themselves. Throughout the day, Sadako observed the staff carrying around the pieces of multicolored origami art. When her father arrived, she pointed to a paper crane someone had left at her bedside and asked, "What is it, about these paper cranes?"

"Why, someone probably sent the cranes as a wish for wellness to all the children here."

Shigeo remembered what Paul Nagai had written about the pain-relieving and potentially healing powers of concentrated, enthusiastic thought. He also knew of a legend, dating back to the 1600s and the Shogun era, about the crane, and about what it meant to fold a thousand of them; and this gave him an idea.

"Sadako-san," her father said cheerily, "there is a legend that the crane lives for a thousand years. And they say that if you fold a thousand paper cranes, putting your heart into each one, they will help you with your wish for wellness."

And so it began: Sadako's first three or four cranes were large and lopsided, and the heads did not bow down quite right. After her first twenty, they became perfectly symmetrical, although when nurses came to take blood samples, the slightest movement sent two or three pieces of origami to the floor. So Masahiro brought a long, long string to the hospital, pushed a pin through the twenty paper cranes, and threaded them together.

The first twenty averaged ten centimeters in length (about the size of a sparrow). Among them was a large silver crane, fashioned from a piece of protective paper from an X-ray plate, which had been given to Sadako by one of the doctors.

"Now I have only nine hundred and eighty left to fold," Sadako announced. The difficulty now lay in acquiring enough paper, which was expensive in these times. She traveled to other patients' rooms asking for paper wrappings from get-well cards and candies. By mid-May, more silver X-ray cranes had joined the strand. Red cellophane from medicine wrappings followed the silver cranes, in addition to any piece of colorful paper that Sadako's family, the doctors, and the nurses could scrounge from anywhere, including squares of color cut from eye-catching magazine advertisements. It became a quiet group effort, with nearly a dozen people straightening all of the wrinkles out of paper scraps and leaving them under Sadako's bed.

Sadako soon discovered that conserving paper by folding smaller cranes required a greater effort to make each fold. This suited her. By the end of May, the cranes were down to an average length of seven centimeters (almost the size of a hummingbird). Sadako's blood abnormalities were also down—from six times a normal white cell count to twice normal.

She now felt well enough to go home for a weekend; and when she returned to the hospital on Sunday evening, Sadako told the doctors, "I think I have enough strength, these days, to be a good roommate."

The nurses nodded agreement, and moved her into a double room with a junior high school girl named Kiyo, who happened to be relatively energetic and very widely read, and who introduced Sadako to all sorts of fantastic, forward-looking novels, ranging from stories about Isaac Asimov's utopian robotic societies to Ray Bradbury's *Martian Chronicles* and Arthur C. Clarke's *Childhood's End*.

The two girls began corresponding with other readers of fiction through hospital-sponsored pen pal programs—and throughout their mid-May surge of activity, Sadako still had enough reserve energy to show her father and Masahiro a continuous strand of paper cranes, and to announce, proudly, "Only five hundred and fifty to go. I'm almost halfway there!"

By this time, the cranes were shrinking to average lengths of four centimeters (still within the size range of the smallest hummingbird). "Her eyes were shining while she was folding the cranes," her mother observed, "showing that she wanted to survive by all means."

She was twelve years old now, and as May phased into June, and as the cranes continued to shrink, Sadako's white blood cell count climbed from twice the normal value to three times normal. She began to run high fevers. The progress of leukemia was very similar to the effects of prompt radiation, and yet at the same time, quite the opposite. One disease produced a deficit of white blood cells, the other produced a wealth of them. In the latter case, the enormous quantity of white cells was essentially a mutant population of wild, amoeba-like animals that absorbed nutrients from Sadako without doing their assigned jobs. Instead of defending her body from disease-causing viral and bacterial intruders, many cells were joining the other side and becoming invasive organisms in their own right. Sadako's body was at war with itself, prone to infection and to an attack by her own blood against her internal organs.

The doctors offered painkillers, but she waved the needles away. At first Masahiro thought this was because the opium-based substance was rare and expensive. He heard Sadako reiterate to her father an earlier fear: "I'm a bad child to you, aren't I? I've used up so much money being sick."

Shigeo Sasaki recalled later, "The doctors recommended that we bring her fresh juice of carrots and other vegetables. But juicing machines cost so much. We couldn't afford one and neither could the hospital—because it was listed as nonessential medical equipment and was not even regarded as medical equipment in any case. If we had owned the proper kind of juicer, we could have gotten more nutrition into Sadako even as the time approached when she would lose her appetite. Thinking about this makes me feel wretched."

"It was the cost of the morphine that made her turn away whatever comfort the painkillers might have brought," Masahiro told a relative. But even here, he eventually came to understand that he had underestimated his sister. By now he could not escape noticing that as her little body was slowly breaking down, the paper cranes continued to grow progressively smaller. By late July, after fevers began spiking so high that the doctors resorted to bathing Sadako in cold water, the cranes were down to the size of bumblebees. She had only enough energy to fold five or six per day.

In August, Sadako's white blood cell count improved to only four times normal, then to three times normal. Her crane project began to pick up pace again: fifty in a day. A hundred. *Finished.*

The thousandth crane was barely larger than a honeybee. No one knew, at this time, that Sadako had been spying on her doctors and copying their records onto a piece of paper, charting her own blood counts. A month earlier, a boy in the same pediatric ward for atomic bomb disease—a boy about her own age—died of leukemia. Sadako told her father, "It'll be me, next time."

During her low point in July, when Sadako's paper crane project had slowed down to only five or six birds per day, her blood values were almost as deadly as the boy's. No one ever mentioned to Sadako that the disease she had was leukemia, but she clearly understood. Her hand-copied record of blood values broke off after the other child died, and Sadako began a second string of paper cranes—which continued to steadily diminish in size. Soon, she could no longer fold the cranes with her fingers. No one could, as they diminished nearly half again, from the size of honeybees into the realm of the smaller varieties of houseflies. The folds became so delicate that she used sewing needles to score and shape each wing—"As if it were a prayer," Masahiro would remember.

Shigeo warned his daughter, "Soon they'll be smaller than grains of rice. If you keep up that pace, you'll wear yourself out."

Sadako said, "It's okay, Dad. I have a plan."

"The reason for this," she told her brother Masahiro, "is that I still have a hope of getting well. That's why I must put more of my heart and soul into each one. The smallest cranes are the most difficult of all to create. So, if I'm going to continue to do this thing, I'm going to put more and more of my spirit into each one."

"All of my spirit," she confided to Masahiro, as her father's prediction of cranes smaller than rice grains became prophetic, "*all* of me . . . because, in time, the smallest cranes may be all that's left of me."

On August 19, 1955, it began to look as if Sadako could hope for a miracle. Though still quite anemic, her white blood cell count was now only twice normal. She displayed for her roommate Kiyo and for her family more than a hundred miniature paper cranes on a bedside table.

"You plan to make another thousand of these?" her father asked.

"The number isn't important anymore," Sadako replied. "What matters is the act of putting all of my concentration into each crane."

On that same August afternoon, a delegation of students from China arrived at the hospital. At the reception, patients heard an unfamiliar song, sung in Japanese: "*Genbaku-O-Yurusamaji*" (Never again, the A-bomb).

"Something in that song seemed to resonate with Sadako," Kiyo remembered. "She sang it to me over and over, up on the hospital rooftop, until I learned it."

In September, climbs to the rooftop decreased in number, as Sadako's blood count climbed above twice the normal number, almost to three. Then, the count increased by another multiple of two . . . and another . . . and another.

Masahiro knew that his sister was now living with a great deal of pain. Something was spreading outward from her lower spine, and her left leg began to swell so large that the flesh was rupturing under the skin and turning purple.

"She never said the words 'it hurts,'" Masahiro recalled. "Although, when a leg swells up to one and a half times its normal size, the throbbing alone has to hurt. Yet she continued to refuse the painkillers. For a long time, I believed she did not want our parents to bear the expense. But later she gave us two reasons completely different from this. First, she believed that the dreamlike state that the morphine put her into might become permanent and kill her. Second, Sadako did not like a dream-state in which she could not feel the touch of our mother's hand. She wanted to be aware of our presence when we were in the room with her—wanted to be acutely aware of the people she loved most. She did not want to lose even a minute with us, by floating away into a painless dream."

In mid-October, Sadako's fevers reached 40.5 degrees Centigrade (105 Fahrenheit).

About October 20, a dozen paper triangles lay under her bed, each prefolded into a starter-triangle no wider than one of Sadako's fingernails. She had, by now, folded 1,600 paper cranes. Using two pins, Sadako put the largest concentration of thought yet into a reddish-violet crane barely larger than a gnat—the last one she would ever fold.

"She was fully conscious till the very end," Masahiro would record later. "And I do not believe she had any idea, that morning of October 25, that she was about to die at any moment. I remember my father waking me and explaining that a doctor had said the time was near. I remember my mother looking at all those pieces of paper on the string and asking, 'Why didn't your thousand cranes sing? Why didn't you fly?'

"But most of all, when I think of that morning in Hiroshima, I remember my sister just slipping away, suddenly and without suffering, as if drifting off to sleep. Only minutes before, I heard Father urging her to eat something, and she responded, 'Tea or rice, please.'

"A nurse brought a bowl of white rice. Sadako swallowed two spoonfuls and, smiling, she said, 'It's good.' That was it. She drifted away with those two words—'It's good.'"

During the days that followed, Fujiko and Shigeo gave many of Sadako's cranes to her classmates and teachers. A few remained with the family and the rest were placed with flowers and a childhood doll in Sadako's casket, "so she could bring them to the next world," Fujiko said.

"Before she left," Masahiro explained, "my sister and I had a one-word saying between us, just one simple word: *Omoiyari*."

Masahiro did not recall that Sadako had ever read about Paul Nagai's path to *Nyokodo*. He believed that, like many people in similar situations, they probably arrived at a similar path to enlightenment through a process of tribulation. As two witnesses to the *pika-don* who returned to their separate Ground Zeros to die, each came to a place where the life remaining in them had been reduced to a matter of weeks. Then it came down to days. And finally, to precious hours and minutes that to ordinary people meant barely more than waiting time at the train station.

Masahiro had heard it said that when a person comes to a place where he or she is reduced to nothing, that's when we begin to understand the value of all things.

When Nagai "went to zero" he came back with the ancient principle of *Nyokodo*: "Love your neighbor as yourself."

For Sadako, the lesson became *Omoiyari*, which meant: "In your heart, always think about the other person before yourself."

According to Masahiro, after Sadako wore her first and last dress-up kimono, she had imagined and defined the perfect, one-and-only future marriage for herself as one in which both husband and wife lived by the principle of *Omoiyari*, and yet neither took it for granted.

Fifty-three years later, Masahiro said, "That's what I want to pass down from her, to young people. I do not want the next generations to think only of paper cranes and a twelve-year-old girl dying from atomic bomb disease. I want them to think, in their hearts, always about the other person.

"You start *Omoiyari* from your family members, and from your friends. Sadako thought—and taught me—that if the principle of *Omoiyari* could spread even a little, into the right places, it might ease the world toward never seeing another *pika-don*."

ON A GROUND ZERO hillside, not very far from Nyokodo and the ruins of Urakami Cathedral, a sideways kick from the blast wave had cleanly severed one leg from a temple arch. And yet the stone arch still stood intact on its remaining leg—a lone sentinel, seen standing guard the day after, over a neighborhood where everything else seemed simply to have been spirited away.

During the tenth anniversary of the bombs, as Sadako taught her brother *Omoiyari* and as China sent children with a song of peace to its former enemy, the architects of Urakami laid their blueprints for multistoried apartment buildings all around the one-legged sentinel, having decided that even as new buildings towered over it, they must leave the sentinel itself untouched.

Less than a minute's walk uphill from the sentinel, trees that had been stripped of their branches and reduced to gnarled, carbonized trunks were healing (and seemingly evolving) in strange ways. From the diseased tree trunks new branches and blob-like growths of bark and green wood grew skyward, some nearly five stories tall.

In Hiroshima, camphor trees, believed to have been killed by the rays and the flames, underwent similar metamorphoses; some were transplanted from a Ground Zero cemetery to the gardens of the city's Peace Park.

As trees healed, so did the people.

In the suburbs of Nagasaki, Setsuko Hirata's parents chose to regard such changes as a tribute of their daughter's love for Kenshi and to what she would have wished for him. By 1955, love came again and Kenshi had remarried and become the father of two healthy children to whom Setsuko's parents became *Ohana*, or "godparents," under the standard of *Omoiyari* tradition. After a 1957 article identified the "Hirata twins" as the offspring of a double-survivor (and potentially contaminated), Kenshi and his family decided to retreat into obscurity, out of history's way.

Meanwhile Arai, the Hiroshima schoolteacher whose student's calligraphy was flash-stenciled onto her face, was advised that a combination of plastic surgery and custom-made makeup could erase the dark letters from her skin. Arai decided that she could not erase the very last thing a little girl had written, and she chose to keep the letters that were shadow engraved on her face until the day she died. It became her way of offering remembrance to the children who perished.

In great Hiroshima—
Dawn came blazing and roaring.
In the river floating toward me—
Was a human raft.

Thus spoke Tsutomu Yamaguchi, more than six decades afterward, when describing the raft of corpses he had used as a bridge on his way to the train that would take him home to Nagasaki.

After he dried himself off and took a seat aboard the train, a stranger placed a rice ball in his hand—a ball of fine white rice wrapped in brown paper. The man must have seen that Yamaguchi was in a terrible state. His clothes and his hands were badly burned. A strange hail of burning objects that had fallen the day before, followed by at least two brief showers of black rain, had left him feverish and too nauseous to eat.

"Thank you," Yamaguchi said, motioning for the man to take the rice back. "But you'll be needing this yourself."

"I'm getting off the train only a few stops away, and I'm told you have a long ride to Nagasaki; so please, don't be polite. Please eat it even if it feels like too much."

Mr. Yamaguchi was moved by the stranger's kindness and "humanity" in a time of such emergency and uncertainty. Such examples were not particularly common in wartime Japan—or even after the war.

During the decade that followed, as the reconstruction period began to take root, the Mitsubishi Company was retooled to build cars and washing machines and phonographs. Yamaguchi was offered the opportunity to be hired back again as a ship designer, but he explained to his former employer that he would stick by an earlier decision to remain at the schools he had helped the city to rebuild and teach the children. He learned, however, that a reason for the job offer included his total lack of long-term radiation symptoms. A new kind of discrimination had manifested. In a city where officially no long-term radiation effects existed, many of those exposed to gamma rays and fallout, and who showed any signs of fatigue, shortness of breath, rashes, and frequent infections, were fired. Increasingly, people who were experiencing illness hid the symptoms as best they could (and thus did they become asymptomatic in the Atomic Bomb Casualty Commission's database).

Hiding the symptoms proved to be especially difficult for any of the thirty people who had been gathered with Yamaguchi in the Mitsubishi office when the second bomb exploded. Though they were reasonably safe from the gamma surge, most of them had relatives in Urakami. Yamaguchi's wife and child were in a relatively safe location, not very far from the office.

The others, who had been spared from prompt radiation exposure, went searching for their families in the Urakami hypocenter, which, in terms of secondary exposure, was orders of magnitude hotter than Hiroshima's hypocenter.

When the Mitsubishi rehirings began, Yamaguchi alone was offered a job. He never met anyone from the August 9 shock cocoon after the war.

About the time Sadako folded her last paper crane, workers in Nagasaki began designing and building a permanent memorial museum. Unlike many other survivors, Mr. Yamaguchi avoided looking back over his shoulder at the past. As one of American baseball's newest fans, he took Leroy "Satchel" Paige's warning to heart: "Never look back. Something might be gaining on you."

He did, however, make occasional visits to the museum after it was completed. One day, more than a half-century after the *pika-don*, Yamaguchi saw a child from another city filming the exhibits. He walked up to the boy and asked him, "What are you going to do with this video?"

"When I go home, after vacation," the boy said, "I want to edit this together into a film, and show it to everyone in my school."

"I think what you are doing is very important," Yamaguchi said, and bowed with his two scarred hands held together, as if in prayer. He never did explain how his hands came to be burned, nor did the boy either learn or suspect that the man bowing to him was a double survivor.

Were it possible, Mr. Yamaguchi would have preferred to remain anonymous forever, living peacefully in the forested countryside beyond Nagasaki with his children and his grandson. But history had charted an altogether different destiny—"urging me," Yamaguchi recorded, "to turn a bad thing on its head, and try to bring something good from it."

The course change began when his wife, Hisako, developed cancer. Then his son Katsutoshi developed cancer and died a week short of his sixtieth birthday, in 2005. Katsutoshi appeared to be part of an emerging pattern. People who held radiation in their bodies from childhood often developed tumors by age sixty, especially if they had fled into the paths of wind-driven fallout and black rain. Adults who were exposed and survived were generally living full life spans, but the cells of growing children rapidly divided and differentiated during the exposure period; thus any chromosomal dislocations (a primary pathway to cancer), if not immediately recognized and corrected by overwhelmed DNA repair systems, were not only passed onward to developing organs, but were often copied and mass-produced.

When Mr. Yamaguchi learned that the children of Dr. Nagai had also developed cancer, he started thinking, *It may be time for me to speak up.*

Little Kayano Nagai had grown up into a brilliant and graceful young woman who studied and taught art, then moved away from Urakami and Nagasaki. She was presently dying from a late-stage cancer. Her brother Makoto had graduated from the University of Tokyo and worked as a journalist until his retirement in 1995 at age sixty. He then returned to Urakami and lived near his father's hermitage, where he expanded the library and teaching programs, until cancer overtook him in 2001.

"And when 2006 came around, I should surely have been dead," Yamaguchi told history. "Yet there I was, in my nineties and somehow still walking around after being burned by the *pika* twice.

"It's fate," he decided. "So it can't be helped. There's no use in complaining or trying too hard to make sense of it, because it becomes what it becomes."

His friends often joked, "That guy is shameless. After experiencing two atomic bombs, dying is natural, but living is lazy."

For a long time, Yamaguchi had appreciated the jokes, and laughed along with his friends. Yet after he learned what was really happening to the children of the *pika*, it became possible for him to believe that there was truth behind the old saying that one sometimes meets his destiny on the road he takes to escape it. Perhaps the time had come to shed his hard-won anonymity and to tell the story of the two cities.

"I feel that I am allowed to live for that reason," Yamaguchi told his family. "To live long enough to do what needs to be done, and say what needs to be said."

The first thing he believed he needed to say involved a reminder from the past—an old belief that if something happened two times,

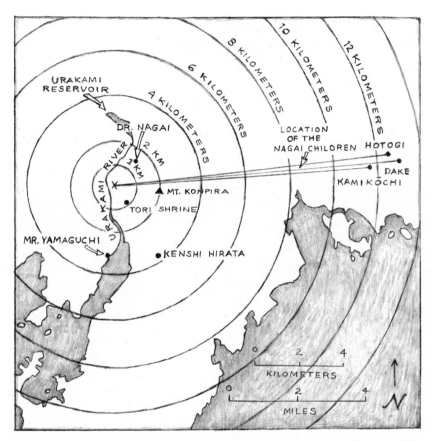

The Nagai family carried a lingering guilt, based on a belief that by bringing his two children to live with him at the hypocenter research station, Dr. Paul Nagai might have exposed them to the radiation that triggered their cancers later in life. Being near the hypocenter was not the problem, because the fallout had mostly decayed before the children arrived. However, when the fallout was fresh and "hot," prevailing winds carried the highest concentrations of black rain directly to the valley where the children had been visiting relatives. (Patricia Wynne)

there would be a third. When the government asked him if he would speak at the United Nations, he looked to the past for signposts to the future and said the core of his message would be simply this: "We cannot let an atomic bomb be used a third time."

He remembered the story of a Catholic pope, John Paul II, who visited Hiroshima and who, standing near a memorial draped with thousands of paper cranes, had remarked, "War is the work of man."

Those were the key words for Yamaguchi, to which he added later, "What this means—if we take it as truth and even if we believe we were created by natural causes—is that it is not God who created war itself; it is humans who created war. So we can stop, if we want to."

And so, for the first time in his life, Tsutomu Yamaguchi applied for a passport and traveled to New York. And it happened that a day before he gave his speech at the UN, he took a ride on a pedal-driven cab, which snapped its chain on a steep hill near Central Park, during an afternoon of record-breaking heat.

They exited the pedicab, and Yamaguchi noticed that the driver was having a difficult time trying to repair the machine, while keeping it from rolling downhill. Yamaguchi put his weight against one end of the pedicab, and said, "I'm from Japan," then asked the driver where he came from.

"Cuba," the man said quickly, as he continued struggling with the broken chain.

"Then," Yamaguchi recalled, "I noticed that he was sweating a great deal. So I pulled out my towel and wiped the sweat from his forehead. We did not speak the same language, except for a word here and there—Japan, Cuba—but I felt that in helping, there was something I could communicate. That simple act of giving him my towel—he looked so happy, to be helped by a stranger; and it brought me back to the man who had put a rice ball in my hand on the train from Hiroshima. And so it occurred to me then, and it stays with me still—this is something we can all do: simple acts of kindness."

Meeting other survivors at the UN, Yamaguchi discovered that they were, without exception, unhappy about the present and worried about the future. They seemed as much concerned about strip-mining the oceans and about spoiling Earth's soils or melting the Greenland ice sheet as about man-made wars. "Train-wrecking the ecology will also train-wreck the global economy," one said, "and a wrecked global economy is a noose around the neck of world peace—a guarantee of future wars." Another could not understand the "bio-fuel concept" of turning corn into gasoline and somehow calling the process green. "Growing food to burn it and calling this environmentally friendly?" he asked. "What can be more stupid?"

All Yamaguchi wanted to say was how he and the pedicab driver, the day before, could not speak the same language but understood each other anyway, as simply being human beings—*one and the same, all of us.*

"So, why do we fight?" Yamaguchi began. He explained to his listeners that he had asked himself this question over and over. "And I realized that maybe, even in a small way, there's something I can do. Each of you, though only a single human being, can, on your own, help us to start understanding each other. That's all it takes, small steps. That's all you need to remember. Send simple acts of kindness outward, from person to person. Send forth kindness like a contagious disease."

What could be easier? Yamaguchi wondered. What could be simpler than *Nyokodo* and *Omoiyari?*

At least a dozen in Yamaguchi's audience rolled their eyes or shook their heads.

"I realize that it may all sound too hopeful or too simplistic," he said, and paused. Then, recalling the words of the Apollo astronauts who looked back from the moon and saw Earth drifting above the mountains—*"planetary citizens,"* they had called themselves, when they fell back again to Earth—Yamaguchi continued, "Putting my faith in mutual human tenderness might sound worse than a simplistic hope—completely naive, even—but if we follow such principles, then we must emerge from the experience of war not as Japanese or American—not as Christian or Buddhist, Hindu, Muslim, or Jew—but simply as planetary citizens. We have to start somewhere. *Have to.* Because, as planetary citizens, we see things as they are, and we are not satisfied."

MASAHIRO SASAKI, when he was not meeting with other survivors, schoolchildren, or with the occasional representative from the Vatican, ran a hair salon with his wife in a quiet suburb far north of Nagasaki. Locally, he was famous for personally driving each of his customers back and forth with door-to-door car service, which was but one small manifestation of the *Omoiyari* principle.

During the summer of 2008, a scientist visited Mr. Sasaki in his salon. The visitor learned the word *Nyokodo* and he learned

Omoiyari. With Masahiro's help, he was able to pinpoint—first on a 1945 bombing survey map, and later on the actual streets of Hiroshima—the exact location of Masahiro's and Sadako's original childhood home. Thousands of bullet train passengers had been passing near the spot every day without knowing it. During the reconstruction years, the roof tiles and ashes were carted away and a parking lot was paved over the old foundations, evidently preserving them. Across the street, in the direction of Dr. Hachiya's house, a twenty-four-hour 7-Eleven store had risen from the ruins.

On the day Sadako's house was rediscovered, the scientist left flowers in a corner of the parking lot, bowed three times, and walked east toward the river. When he began filming the place between two bridges where Masahiro indicated he, Sadako, and their mother survived in a half-sunk boat, a white crane descended from the south and landed on the spot.

SHIGEO SASAKI'S FRIEND and neighbor, Michihiko Hachiya, died in 1980. His Hiroshima diary indicated that he burdened himself with the undeserved guilt of somehow causing the death of Shigeo's mother. Were he not a decent man in the first place, he would never have carried such guilt. A lesser man would not have felt anything. Thus did the bomb wound two families with Hachiya's own decency, with his loyalty to his neighbors, with his humanity. And so it came to pass that even after stories about Sadako and the thousand paper cranes began to spread throughout Japan, Masahiro could not recall that his father ever heard from Dr. Hachiya again—much as Dr. Nagai's "theory of invisible cracks" had said it would be.

In Urakami, Nagai's friend Akizuki's destiny was to die of natural causes in advanced old age in 2005. He supported Dr. Nagai's teachings until the end.

By then, in Hiroshima, Shigeo Sasaki was dead at the age of eighty-seven.

Fujiko Sasaki was dead.

Sadako's roommate Kiyo was dead.

Ryuta Kondo was dead.

Keiji Nakazawa—"Barefoot Gen"—grew up in a shantytown

The corner on which the Sasaki house stood is seen as it appeared on the morning of August 6, 1945, two days after the fires died, and during the summer of 2008. (Patricia Wynne, CRP)

between Dr. Hachiya's Communications Hospital and the school attended by Sadako and Masahiro Sasaki. Gen was often in trouble, tending to get into schoolyard brawls and to run away for days and even weeks.

"Of course I fought a lot," Gen recalled. "*Pika-don* people (called the *hibakusha*) often became untouchables. We were treated like dirt by the safer and more privileged children who began moving in from the outlands. Later in life, if a young woman's family found out we had been exposed to the bomb, we were usually not allowed to marry. Even though we had survived, we weren't really allowed to live."

During his truancies, Gen discovered comic books and uniquely styled animated films—which were in fact embryonic forms of the Manga artistic movement. Eventually, Gen became involved with the creators of *Astro Boy*, which led to the *Barefoot Gen* books and several feature-length animated films, including one based on the diaries of Dr. Akizuki.

"The *pika* and the *hibakusha* it created cannot happen again," Gen has said. "When the Americans came, they wrote our constitution, modeled on their own freedoms. But Article 9 of our constitution says: '*No Navy. No Army. No Air Force. No weapons production.*' It's an extraordinary document. No matter what, we must protect it."

All of Gen's childhood friends—at least those who were near enough to have witnessed the bomb, as he did, were dead before the turn of the century.

Satoko Matsumoto and the rest of her family were dead.

Yoshiko Mori and her son, Hiroshi, were dead.

Masuji Ibuse, the Hiroshima poet who witnessed the "crazy iris" incident, was dead.

Firefighter Yasaku Mikami was dead.

Assistant kite-maker Doi, one of Mr. Yamaguchi's fellow double survivors, suffered no known radiation effects despite the hail of bomb-flung objects from the hypocenter into his Nagasaki neighborhood, followed quickly by a light misting over by black rain. Notwithstanding Doi's apparent escape from harm, his baby girl developed blisters, swelling lymph nodes, anemia, and frequent infections. After a few years, just as it seemed the child was about to make a complete recovery, Doi's wife became ill, developed cancer, and died.

Akira Iwanaga became a clerk in the office of Nagasaki's postwar Municipal Government House, where he eventually retired in remarkably good health, then moved to the shore with his family and lived into his nineties. In 2008, he remained, along with Tsutomu Yamaguchi, one of two double survivors still known to be alive.

Hiroshima Castle in July 1945, late August 1945, and August 2009. (Patricia
Wynne)

Shoda Shinoe died of cancer in 1965.

Young Dr. Yoshioka, whose blast-lacerated face filled Dr. Akizuki with a guilt that never went away, continued to live near the
Urakami hospital complex until her death, about 1985. All around
the complex, cherry trees seared down to their roots by the bomb
came back to life, eerily turning the desert regions into restored forests and gardens.

Father Mattias never could forget the children he had left alone on
a brick tower amid the rising fire worms of Hiroshima. He descended
into severe alcohol addiction and committed suicide about 1985. The
Jesuit philosopher John MacQuitty presided over a burial on hal-
lowed ground despite his church's injunctions against such compas-
sion for suicides. "He was a good man who tried to live by a code of
kindness," MacQuitty stated. "It was Hiroshima that killed him."

Misako Katani was dead.

Masao Komatsu was dead.

Master kite-maker Morimoto was dead.

After the death of his wife, Doi fell into depression, sickened, and
died.

Prefect Takejiro Nishioka continued to suffer from radiation
symptoms during the months after Hiroshima and Nagasaki. Believing he would soon die, he signed his publishing organization's rights
over to his wife. Mrs. Nishioka vastly expanded the family's publishing earnings, then entered politics and was elected a member of the
House of Councils (Japan's equivalent of the British Parliament or
the American Senate). Mr. Nishioka retreated from politics, seemed
to recover his health, then sickened and died.

Governor Nagano was dead.

José Matsou, the closest sheltered survivor to the Urakami hypocenter, developed cancer and died.

Emiko Fukahori, one of only a handful of children to reach the
Urakami shelters in time, saw her family killed near a bamboo garden six hundred meters from the hypocenter. Because death certifi-
cates were rarely written for people whose bodies were never
found, she had difficulty proving to bureaucratic child-aid provid-
ers that she was a war orphan. At age sixteen, she was stricken
with atomic bomb–related anemia and was hospitalized about the

same time as Sadako Sasaki. Emiko recovered, continued her schooling, and spent the remainder of her life at a Catholic retreat for meditation in Osaka.

Emiko's friend Sumi-chan was dead.

Cadet Komatsu and his friends were dead.

For Dr. Masao Shiotsuki, inhaling the fresh radioactive dust and drying black rain from the clothes of patients transported to Omura Naval Hospital marked the beginning of a long-standing fight against cancer. He lost his battle in 1978.

Sumiko Kirihara, a shock-cocooned girl who lived in the same neighborhood as Sadako Sasaki, might have survived if not for the black rain. Initially, all of her family escaped alive. During the three years that followed, each of them suffered sporadic episodes of bleeding under the skin and debilitating fatigue. Sumiko developed chronic liver disease, anemia, and frighteningly high fevers. Then she and the other seven members of the Kirihara family began to die young, one by one.

Sachiko Masaki, a fellow survivor with Hajime Iwanaga at the Mitsubishi torpedo factory, died of cancer. Her mother and her sister preceded her in death.

Hajime Iwanaga was dead.

Michie Hattori, a fifteen-year-old girl who returned from a school whose surroundings had become "a graveyard with no tombstones" and discovered her own neighborhood completely shock-cocooned, moved from Nagasaki to General MacArthur's headquarters in Tokyo, where she was employed as a translator. She married an American, became Michie Hattori Bernstein, and moved to Mississippi—where she died of cancer.

Isao Kita was dead.

Ichiro Miyato, the radar man who charted the approach of Charles Sweeney's mission to Nagasaki, was still alive after the turn of the century.

Charles Sweeney was promoted to general in 1956 and became commander of the 102nd Air Defense Wing (he would die of natural causes in 2004).

Marcus McDilda, the captured American pilot who, under torture, invented an atomic bomb design that seemed feasible (based on vague and instantly made-up details about two spherical masses) was transferred to a more advanced interrogation facility near the Imperial Palace in Tokyo. Shortly afterward, his fifty fellow POWs at the secret police headquarters were beheaded. McDilda remained under constant guard and, he believed, in constant danger until August 30, 1945, when the Fourth Marine Regiment liberated the Omori prison camp on the Tokyo waterfront. He returned to the United States and lived to old age.

Physicist Ryokichi Sagane was judged a nuclear asset under the MacArthur protocol. He was moved from Tokyo to Berkeley and the nearby linear accelerator facility, where he devised programs leading up to antiproton-proton bombardment experiments.

Dr. Luis Alvarez became an advocate for peace—first for nuclear arms reduction and eventually for the abolition of nuclear weapons. When he and his son Walter stumbled upon an iridium layer spanning New Zealand and the rest of the world, they soon discovered the nuclear winter concept, etched into rocks that appeared to be synchronous with the extinction of the dinosaurs. "If we are not very careful," Alvarez said, "then the rocks will probably write our epitaph in a global dust storm of similar proportions, and we'll be as extinct as the dinosaurs one day."

Until the day he died, Alvarez harbored a deep and seething resentment for government "white-washers" from the United States and Japan who, aided by lawyer types, attempted to officially list only a dozen people in Hiroshima—and thirty cows downwind—as having been killed by radiation poisoning. Under the MacArthur protocol, atomic bomb survivors were not allowed to publish stories about their experiences; so little more than urban legends came out of the ruins. Myths about radiation-transformed mutants began to take on the mantle of oral history, and with such grace did a MacArthur-esque joke about the health benefits of radioactive spider bites, along with the curious case of Dr. Paul Nagai's remission, reach journalist Stanley Lieber, who, like James Clavell and playwright William Saroyan, had been recruited during the war as a military scribe. The atomic mythology produced in Stan Lieber an inordinate fondness for flights of abstract fantasy involving radioactive transformation. After the war he moved to New York City, anglicized his name to Stan Lee, and made his mark on cultural history by bringing to life *The Hulk, X-Men*, and, as a nod to Dr. Nagai, *Spider Man*.

Dr. Harold Urey suffered a nervous breakdown after he saw that instead of bringing an end to war the atomic bomb led to the Cold War–era mass production of nuclear weapons. As part of his recovery, Alvarez and other friends directed Urey toward solving the problems of deciphering ancient temperatures with oxygen isotopes and trying to figure out where DNA came from. With student Stanley Miller, he won the Nobel Prize for an experiment in chemical evolution. He died young, in the midst of writing a letter to a friend about the secret of life's origins.

Harold Urey's colleague Albert Einstein, whose 1939 letter to President Roosevelt triggered America's atomic bomb program, became a devoted reader of Gandhi, Nagai, and every other man of peace. Shown photographs of artifacts from Hiroshima and Nagasaki— among them a charred pocketwatch with hands frozen at 8:15 and a smashed Nagasaki clock stopped at 11:02—the physicist recalled Dr. Nagai's observation that the discovery of heaven's double-edged sword, hidden in the atom, had changed everything about the human animal except its way of thinking. To this observation, Einstein added that the subsequent nuclear arms race was heartbreak, and that indeed, though the yin-and-yang "sword and gift" had changed everything except man's way of thinking, "the solution to this problem lies in the heart of mankind. But if only I had known (in my youth, about the sword), I should have become a watchmaker." Within a decade of the first atomic bomb, Einstein was dead from heart failure.

During the decades after little Eiko's flash burns frightened her mother away, the unspoken shame of how the child died produced such pain that members of the Nagai family could only rarely bring themselves to visit her grave. Perhaps there was no stronger example of Dr. Nagai's cracks in the human spirit, created by the bomb; for by the first decade of the twenty-first century no one could remember any longer where Eiko was buried.

Little Eiko's cousin Tatsue, the last person known to have visited her grave, was dead.

Private Shigeru Shimoyama was dead.

Nobou Tetsutani was dead.

Tomotsu Eguchi was dead.

Dr. Hachiya's friends Hinoi, Koyama, and Kutsube were dead.

Mr. Fujii, the theological student who fled Nagasaki ahead of the *pika* and went searching for his girlfriend in Hiroshima, was dead.

Dr. Minoru Fujii continued to work in the suburbs of Hiroshima and kept in close contact with Minami until his death.

Minami's friends, including Nurse Reiko Owa ("I will live remembering not to waste the lives lost in the atomic bomb attack"), nurse Fujita Misako, Hiroshi Takamoya ("Please remember Hiroshima for peace"), Saito Kaneko, and Kouno Kazuko were still alive at the turn of the century.

Akiko Takakura, the Sumitomo Bank survivor, remained in Hiroshima through 2008 in anomalously good health, as did Nenkai Aoyama, whose mother disappeared without a trace at the Hiroshima Dome.

Tsugio Ito, whose brother Hiroshi decayed while still alive after escaping Hiroshima, grew up in a household where both parents survived in perfect health despite overwhelming loss and despite having ventured into a radioactive hot zone near the Misasa Bridge. Tsugio eventually married, keeping secret his status as an untouchable *hibakusha* family member. Tsugio's son Kazushige, though he grew up in a family contaminated by "death sand," showed no signs whatsoever of illness. Like Akiko Takakura, Kazushige Ito went to work for one of Japan's largest banking institutions. After receiving several promotions he was transferred in 1998 to the Fuji Bank's office in the South Tower of New York's World Trade Center—where, on September 11, 2001, almost fifty-six years to the day after Tsugio sat at the deathbed of his brother Hiroshi, his son Kazushige perished at the epicenter of his family's second ground zero.

Hanako Ito, who braved the deserts of Hiroshima's Ground Zero in search of a son already doomed by the air he had breathed, died in September 2001, as soon as she accepted the reality that her grandson Kazushige was not merely missing in New York's Ground Zero, but had died.

Mrs. Sumako Matsuyanagi remained in Hiroshima, where she lit a floating lantern and set it adrift in the river every August 6 in memory of her lost child. She continued lighting lanterns for thirty years, until she joined the boy in death.

Kuniyoshi Sato, the man who sat across from Kenshi Hirata on the train from Hiroshima, and whose curiosity about what Kenshi was carrying inside the wedding bowl was too well satisfied, was now dead.

The mother of Toshihiko Matsuda—the "marble boy" of Hiroshima—was dead.

Dean Susumu Tsuno was dead.

Mrs. Tsuno was dead.

The Tsuno children were dead.

Little Eiko's mother was brought one evening to a hospital, screaming obscenities. She vomited something black, shuddered and gasped for air, vomited again—and then she, too, was dead.

LESS THAN TEN YEARS after Hiroshima, the U.S. Air Force had tried to entice Joseph Fuoco into volunteering for the Korean War. "No thanks," he said. "I think I've done enough damage."

He married his high school sweetheart, settled into one of Long Island's Levittown houses, took a job with Grumman Aerospace Corporation, and managed to make his marriage last forever by avoiding Grumman's time-intensive, family-destroying Apollo Lunar Module Program. Later, Fuoco bought a gas station, and became a firefighter.

Minami, meanwhile, returned to Korea and in 1950 was caught up in the invasion of South Korea from the north. "If General MacArthur had not arrived at Inchon at the last minutes of September 15," Minami recalled more than a half-century later, "I would have been burned or starved to death along with so many others. My children and I would not now know the happiness we enjoy had it not been for him."

Minami escaped with a through-and-through bullet wound—entering above her right shoulder and exiting below her collarbone. After a period of time as a refugee in her own country, with the years turning even worse for her than in wartime Japan, she made her way to Germany and finally to New York University, where, aided by a key recommendation from Dr. Fujii in Hiroshima, she was employed by the New York Infirmary, on Fourteenth Street. There, she underwent another name change: from Minami to Nancy.

She added the name Cantwell when she married Larry Cantwell.

It seemed almost inevitable that she would be stuck in traffic outside the Lincoln Tunnel on the exceptionally beautiful morning of September 11, 2001. She had a firsthand view of each tower as it descended on a collapse column with a combined force of 1.6 kilotons. The only other person known to have uttered the word *Hiroshima* that morning was Joseph Fuoco. The nurse from Hiroshima and the flight engineer aboard *Necessary Evil* ended up living so near each other that Nancy could have looked east from her apartment in Manhattan and, with only a weak pair of binoculars, identified the Fuoco house.

On September 11, Joseph Fuoco was standing next to a police officer when a television camera showed the second tower bursting into flame. He knew that police and firefighters were running into the skyscrapers—and, as he watched, a grim certainty came over him.

"They've got to pull those men out," Fuoco said to the officer beside him. "Those buildings are going to collapse straight down and splash out like a fluid."

"What makes you think that?" the officer demanded.

"Because I've seen this awful thing before," the firefighter replied—and he was back in 1945, looking down again upon Hiroshima Castle and office buildings and other seemingly solid structures, splashed apart like water.

"I know how it will be," Joe Fuoco said, "because I remember Hiroshima." Joseph never really believed that he could live to see anything remotely like Hiroshima again, but now he feared that he might be witnessing the first step down a road that would reawaken the nuclear terror. "It cannot happen again," he would later record, on what turned out to be the last day of his life. "We are human beings, not animals. We should love our brothers."

Joseph Fuoco's plea sounded hauntingly like *Nyokodo* and *Omoiyari*.

Nancy Cantwell's wish sounded much the same.

"We have no choice but to be born into this world," Nancy told a gathering of young students. "Technology is constantly making the world smaller and more interconnected, whether everyone likes this or not. My grandmother always told me, 'One hand washes the other.' Whoever leads the larger nations in the future, the large countries should help the smaller countries to develop and to live in happiness. This is my wish. This is my prayer."

That there shall be no more graves of the blue fireflies.

That there shall come no more black rains.

That no loved one shall ever again know what it means to fold a thousand paper cranes.

TWENTY FLOORS HIGH on the surviving tower of 1 Liberty Plaza, in the World Trade Center "Family Room," a grieving father left a copy of Japan's constitution beneath a thousand paper cranes, highlighting the paragraph that Barefoot Gen had come to cherish. To this, the father added his own wish "for a serene world, without war and without weapons."

The bundle of paper cranes under which the constitution lay (to which a ribbon had been attached, bearing the words, "Come back to Hiroshima") was sent to the Family Room for Masahiro Sasaki's friend Tsugio Ito, who drew some small consolation from knowing that his brother Hiroshi at least died surrounded by and comforted by his family, and who regretted that his son died alone and without a trace when the disintegrating fuselage of Flight 175 passed directly through his South Tower office.

On the day Masahiro went to New York with his friend Tsugio Ito and visited the Family Room, he was introduced to 9/11 survivors as a victim of Hiroshima.

"I am a survivor, *not* a victim," Masahiro said sternly. And he discovered that many of the 9/11 families, years after the fall of the towers, still wanted revenge.

"More than five decades ago," Masahiro explained, "I was in much the same frame of mind you find yourselves in today. The difference is that I have had a half-century more to meditate upon this. During the first ten years or so, the feelings of families in all three ground zeros must have begun the same. But the important question is, what can be done for the future?"

Masahiro recalled that a scientist once told a theologian, "We are the sum of what we remember." And the theologian responded, "No. We are *how* we remember."

"All the suffering of the past means nothing," Masahiro said, "if we do not draw lessons from which to build a better world for tomorrow's child."

The big question, Masahiro said again, is, "What can we do for the future?"

He did not believe that the big question required big earth-shaking answers delivered with all the force of wide-angle shotgun blasts. A changed way of thinking needed only to go out into the world like individual pinpricks and be given barely more than a microscopic hope of reaching some person, somewhere, who might become pivotal in history ("Do I advise my commander to attack or to talk? . . . To launch or to hold back for a while?").

"I think *Omoiyari* is the best way to start," Masahiro Sasaki said. "The worst way is to call ourselves victims. To say 'victim' requires a victimizer, and the victimizer is led to blame; and that starts the *cycle* of blame. For example, if we say 'victim of Hiroshima,' the next sentence that comes up will involve Pearl Harbor and the blaming chain gets stuck all the way in the past. Then we are completely derailed from the lesson that war itself is humanity's Pandora, and that nuclear weapons are something that came out of Pandora's box."

If victimhood and blame become the lesson ("*Your country hurt me! You hurt me first!*") then we become imprisoned in the 1930s and 1940s, forever trapped by our past. Masahiro wanted to go forward with *Omoiyari*, in his thoughts and in his deeds.

"Think about the other person first," Masahiro told his listeners in America, where a separate genesis of a similar principle was already becoming known by the term "paying it forward." The essential theme went back through "as yourself"(or *Nyokodo*) to pre-biblical versions of the Golden Rule.

"Sadako understood this theme more personally and more intensely than most people ever will," Masahiro said. "And she had only enough time to begin teaching anew what most of us have so easily forgotten."

Some 9/11 survivors and their families went away from the Masahiro encounter with their way of thinking changed. Not many; for the wounds were too fresh for the majority to be moved by words. Only some were moved—just a few, in fact. But they might have been enough.

In this same year, Masahiro spoke about this same word, *Omoiyari*, in Vienna.

At the end of his talk, a boy raised his hand and asked, "Mr. Sasaki, which country dropped the atomic bomb?"

He was not expecting a question so childishly simple that it could be answered with one word. Masahiro answered, "It's been more than sixty years since the bombs were dropped. God made everyone equal. So, I forgot who dropped the bomb."

The audience, including a police officer who stood nearby, looked on in silent puzzlement. The boy, who appeared to be about eleven years old, nodded understanding and gave Masahiro a thumbs-up.

For the adults in his audience, Masahiro explained, "What I am trying to say is that it does not matter who dropped the bomb. It's not an issue. It should never be an issue for any country. It's an issue for all humanity. The important thing is that I, and Sadako, knew the feeling of *Omoiyari*—and if this principle can be taken to heart and passed down by just a few of you here in this room today, it may, in time, lessen the dangers in the world. You must overcome the sadness and come out of it by passing this simple philosophy down to the next generation. This is my wish."

Then, looking at the boy who asked the question, he said, "Children! Teach your parents."

APPENDIX: THE PEOPLE

DR. TATSUICHIRO AKIZUKI: A physician at the Urakami (Nagasaki) medical complex.

DR. LUIS ALVAREZ: American nuclear physicist. He was present on Tinian Island when an accidental neutron surge compromised the Hiroshima bomb's uranium components, and hence the weapon's maximum yield. To assure that the bomb would work, Alvarez inserted the entire world supply of polonium into the system. Along with his friend Harold Urey, Alvarez (with too high a faith in civilized thought) believed that the atomic bomb would give humanity a glimpse into the abyss and put an end to all wars.

KORECHIKA ANAMI: Minister of War, Japan. A self-styled poet-warrior who refused to accept that the atomic bomb existed or that it could signal defeat. He knew of, and would keep secret till the end, a plot to hold the Emperor under military isolation if he spoke of surrender.

NENKAI AOYAMA: Seventeen-year-old conscript whose home was closer than any other to the Hiroshima Dome and the hypocenter.

He survived only because his mother sent him away early to his work detail.

ARAI: A Hiroshima schoolteacher, exposed at a radius of 2 kilometers (1.25 miles) from the hypocenter of the explosion. The flash from the bomb, blazing through a sheet of paper Arai had been holding, burned a child's calligraphy onto her face.

GENERAL SEIZO ARISUE: One of the first people sent from the Imperial Palace, along with nuclear physicist Yoshio Nishina, to examine the damage to Hiroshima and to determine whether or not it was, as President Truman claimed, the result of an atomic bomb.

FRED ASHWORTH: U.S. Navy commander aboard *Bock's Car* during the Nagasaki mission. Pilot Charles Sweeney was in charge of the plane; Ashworth was in charge of all decisions related to the bomb.

LAVRENTI BERIA: Russia's Commissioner of State Security, in charge of Moscow's nuclear programs.

FRED BOCK: Pilot of the scientific instrument plane *Great Artiste*—and not, as history would mistakenly record it, his own *Bock's Car*—during the Nagasaki mission.

NANCY (MINAMI) CANTWELL: A Korean nurse and lifelong friend of Dr. Minoru Fujii. Joining him in the south Hiroshima rescue operation, she witnessed the last of the ant-walkers and the "grave of the blue fireflies." Born Namsun Koh, renamed Minami by the time she went to Hiroshima.

TSUITARO DOI: Assistant to master kite-maker Shigeyoshi Morimoto, Doi would become a survivor of both the Hiroshima and Nagasaki atomic bombings.

TAMOTSU EGUCHI: Junior high school student who was shielded inside the wreckage of his school from prompt radiation effects, at a radius of only 850 meters (10 blocks, or slightly more than a half mile) from the Nagasaki hypocenter.

DR. MINORU FUJII: After witnessing the explosion from a suburb of Hiroshima, Dr. Fujii assembled a rescue and treatment team and turned a destroyed school into an army field hospital.

MR. FUJII: A theological student (no relation to Dr. Fujii) who journeyed from Nagasaki to Hiroshima in search of his girlfriend.

EMIKO FUKAHORI: A seven-year-old who ran into a tunnel as the planes approached. She and her friend Sumi-chan became the only members of their group to survive. Emiko saw her entire family either killed or converted to "alligator people" 600 meters (1,968 feet) from the Nagasaki hypocenter.

JOSEPH FUOCO: Flight engineer aboard the Hiroshima mission's photographic plane, *Necessary Evil*. He also flew pre- and post-Hiroshima photographic mapping and reconnaissance missions. His last mission was with Charles Sweeney's raiders, August 14–15, 1945.

CLARENCE GRAHAM: An American POW at slave labor Camp 17, located on the outer-fringe zone of the Nagasaki blast effects, 63 kilometers (38 miles) northeast of the hypocenter, in Fukuoka Province.

DR. MICHIHIKO HACHIYA: A surviving "ant-walker" from Hiroshima. Rescued from his near-fatal wounds by colleagues at the Communications Hospital, he recovered enough strength to treat and document the first cases of radiation poisoning.

AVERELL HARRIMAN: America's ambassador to Russia at the time of the Truman announcement that the atomic bomb existed and had been used.

SHUNROKU HATA: Field Marshal of the Japanese army. Survived the Hiroshima bombing while awaiting the arrival of Prefect Nishioka from meetings with Japan's leading nuclear physicists. Hata departed Hiroshima for Tokyo and argued as an eyewitness that the nation could absorb atomic attacks and survive. The Emperor did not agree, and ended up briefly under Hata-supported house arrest.

MICHIE HATTORI: A fifteen-year-old student who survived the Nagasaki blast in a tunnel, at the same distance as Emiko Fukahori.

DR. HINOI: A friend and colleague of Dr. Hachiya. Together, they set out from the Communications Hospital to conduct a scientific exploration of the Hiroshima wilderness.

KENSHI HIRATA: Exposed to the Hiroshima bomb's blast effects at a distance of 3 kilometers (almost 2 miles), Kenshi received secondary radiation exposure when he entered the vicinity of the hypocenter, searching for his wife. On August 8, 1945, he left the Hiroshima suburbs aboard a train, carrying the bones of his wife, Setsuko, home to her parents—and toward the greatest horror of all.

MASUJI IBUSE: A poet who recorded the Hiroshima aftermath's "crazy iris" incident.

HIROSHI ITO: An honor student, age twelve, who emerged from his central Hiroshima school as one of only two known survivors.

KAZUSHIGE ITO: Hiroshi Ito's nephew. Born into a family that experienced both survival and casualty in Hiroshima, he grew up to become a casualty of the World Trade Center attack in New York. Kasushige's father, along with his friend Masahiro Sasaki, arranged to send thousands of paper cranes from the children of Hiroshima to the children of New York after 9/11, as a message of hope and healing.

AKIRA IWANAGA: A ship designer who survived the Hiroshima bomb at a distance of 3.7 kilometers (2.3 miles). Along with other essential Mitsubishi and military personnel, he was evacuated south toward Nagasaki, aboard one of two still-functioning trains able to leave Hiroshima.

HAJIME IWANAGA (no apparent relationship to Akira): A fourteen-year-old resident of Nagasaki who was being "schooled" at the Mitsubishi Torpedo Works. Being of small stature for his age, he was in training for the *Kaiten* mini-sub torpedo program and would likely have been assigned to the next I-58 submarine mission in September or October 1945. Underwater at the time of the explosion, he became one of the survivors nearest the Nagasaki hypocenter.

MISAKO KATINI: A sixteen-year-old witness to Hiroshima's "fire horses." Having escaped the inferno, Misako and her father fled toward the imagined safety of Nagasaki.

SUMIKO KIRIHARA: A fourteen-year-old neighbor of Dr. Hachiya, exposed indoors at a radius of just over 1.8 kilometers (about 1 mile). She experienced Hiroshima's waterspouts and "fire worms."

ISAO KITA: Hiroshima's chief military forecaster for the weather bureau. Kita was exposed on the side of a small mountain at a distance of 3.7 kilometers (2.3 miles) from the hypocenter. Serendipitously, he had a grandstand view of the explosion and recorded the first close-up scientific observations.

CADET KOMATSU: A pilot who exposed himself to intensely radioactive "grit" and oily rain after he, along with friends Tomimura and Umeda, stole a Japanese navy seaplane and flew directly into the stem of the mushroom cloud that formed over Nagasaki.

MASAO KOMATSU: An apprentice kite-maker in Mr. Morimoto's Hiroshima kite shop, assigned by Mitsubishi to the design and engineering of photographic reconnaissance kites for the navy. He survived Hiroshima, then decided to go home to Nagasaki.

RYUTA KONDO: A five-year-old Hiroshima orphan, unofficially adopted into the family of Keiji "Gen" Nakazawa. He lived in the same neighborhood as Dr. Hachiya.

DR. KOYAMA: A physician at Hiroshima's Communications Hospital who originally mistook radiation sickness for evidence of a post-nuclear bioweapons attack and began isolating the patients.

DR. KUTSUBE: A friend of Dr. Hachiya who worked with him at Hiroshima's Communications Hospital.

GENERAL DOUGLAS MacARTHUR: Directed plans for the final invasion and occupation of the Japanese mainland. He became the framer of Japan's postwar constitution, during a period in which he emerged as a leading antagonist against those who intended to study or write about the effects of the atomic bombs, especially in Nagasaki. He also recognized that eventual peace with Japan depended on the Emperor, a religious figure, not being put on public trial and executed by an American ad hoc tribunal.

GEORGE MARQUART: Pilot of *Necessary Evil* during the Hiroshima mission. Pilot of a weather reconnaissance scout plane during the Nagasaki mission.

SACHIKO MASAKI: A fourteen-year-old girl inducted into work at Nagasaki's Mitsubishi torpedo factory. She was shock-cocooned by heavy equipment and shadow-shielded from the gamma-ray surge by that same equipment. Sachiko survived at approximately the same radius as Hajime Iwanaga.

JOSÉ MATSOU: The survivor nearest the Nagasaki bomb. She was exposed in one of Prefect Nishioka's tunnels at a distance of 185 meters (607 feet).

TOSHIHIKO MATSUDA: The "marble boy" of Hiroshima. Exposed at a distance of approximately 600 meters (1,968 feet), his shadow was imprinted on a garden wall.

SATOKO MATSUMOTO: A young Hiroshima girl whose parents fled to the river with the Kirihara and Sasaki families. On the first night of the bomb, Satoko's neighbor turned a shower of falling stars into a chilling revelation.

SUMAKO MATSUYANAGI: Exposed near Hiroshima's Ground Zero fringe (within approximately 1.5 kilometers), Mrs. Matsuyanagi was flung unharmed into an elderly couple's home. Her two sons had been exposed in a school much closer to the hypocenter and, though appearing at first to be uninjured, began to suffer prompt radiation effects.

FATHER MATTIAS: A Catholic priest exposed in Hiroshima at a distance of 1.3 kilometers (4,200 feet). He joined Dr. Hachiya among the ant-walkers, vaguely aware that he had left three wounded children to a terrible fate.

MARCUS McDILDA: A captured American pilot who, under torture, agreed to tell his captors everything he had ever heard about the uranium bomb. Knowing absolutely nothing, but making up a design with sound mathematical intuition as he went along, he invented a system that sounded chillingly similar to the "two masses clapped together" design that had been developed by Japanese physicists.

YASAKU MIKAMI: One of only three firefighters known to have survived Hiroshima, Mikami was exposed in a tunnel at a distance of 1.9 kilometers (1.2 miles).

ICHIRO MIYATO: A radar operator who tracked *Bock's Car* and *Great Artiste* during their final approach to Nagasaki.

HIROSHI MORI: A fifth grader who told his mother, Yoshioko, of a premonition that Hiroshima was about to be destroyed.

SHIGEYOSHI MORIMOTO: Master kite-maker, recruited to make military kites, was shock-cocooned in Hiroshima beneath the thick, multistoried shielding of a cousin's mansion, in the neighborhood of

Kenshi Hirata's wife Setsuko. The Morimoto and Hirata homes were exposed within approximately 400 meters (1,312 feet) of the hypocenter. Like Kenshi Hirata, Morimoto left Hiroshima on a train bound for Nagasaki. His second exposure occurred at a relatively safer radius of 2.4 kilometers.

DR. PAUL (TAKASHI) NAGAI: A terminally ill cancer patient in his own hospital at the time of the Nagasaki bombing. After receiving a near-lethal radiation dose, his cancer went into temporary remission and, though still gravely afflicted, he lived long enough to become one of the most poetic and spiritual observers of the bomb's effects on the human mind and soul. Nagai became a key spiritual adviser in post-apocalypse Urakami and Nagasaki.

THE NAGAI FAMILY: Midori (Paul's wife, killed instantly under the Nagasaki bomb); Kayano and Makoto (the Nagai children, both of whom were exposed to black rain); and, later, Makoto's son, Tokusaburo, who carried his grandfather's teachings into the twenty-first century.

KEIJI "GEN" NAKAZAWA: A child of Hiroshima who grew up to pioneer the development of modern graphic novel art styles in Japan. Best known for the *Barefoot Gen* books, he survived and came of age in the ruins of the city, not very far from Dr. Hachiya and the Communications Hospital.

DR. YOSHIO NISHINA: A nuclear physicist and a director (with Ryokishi Sagane) of Japan's wartime nuclear weapons programs, including bomb core designs and plans for the world's first particle beam weapons (four decades ahead of the rest of the world, in 1945). At war's end, Nishina and several colleagues were targeted by the Russians for capture and by the Americans for "capture or neutralization," to prevent capture by the Russians.

TAKEJIRO NISHIOKA: A prefect who arrived in Hiroshima and experienced the atomic bombing following a meeting in Tokyo with Dr. Nishina and other leading atomic scientists. After witnessing the first blast, he fled south to evacuate his family from Nagasaki, which he was certain would be the next target.

EIZO NOMURA: The survivor nearest to the Hiroshima bomb who arrived at Dr. Hachiya's Communications Hospital. He was exposed at approximately 100 meters (328 feet) in the basement of the Rationing Union Hall.

DR. RYOKICHI SAGANE: A Japanese nuclear physicist and colleague of Dr. Nishina.

FUJIKO SASAKI: Shigeo Sasaki's wife.

MASAHIRO SASAKI: The Sasakis' son, age five on the day of the bomb. He grew up to teach his sister's message that the hope of civilization might lie in nothing more complex than "always think of the other person first."

SADAKO SASAKI: Masahiro's two-year-old sister, who, ten years later while living with the aftereffects of black rain, folded a paper crane and wrote upon its wings, "One day you will fly peace around the world."

SHIGEO SASAKI: A neighbor and close friend of Dr. Hachiya who survived in a distant suburb of Hiroshima while running an errand to one of Prefect Nishioka's offices. After entering Hiroshima's Ground Zero and discovering that everyone except his mother had been miraculously saved, he volunteered to bring food and supplies to Dr. Hachiya's Communications Hospital.

KUNIYOSHI SATO: A Hiroshima survivor who evidently shared a seat with Kenshi Hirata aboard the last train from Hiroshima to Nagasaki.

SHIGERU SHIMOYAMA: This private in the Japanese army was exposed in Hiroshima at a radius of 500 meters (1,640 feet), in an army compound north of Hiroshima Castle. "Crucified by the bomb," he later beheld "a pale horse."

SHODA SHINOE: A particularly poetic teenager under Dr. Hachiya's care.

DR. MASAO SHIOTSUKI: A colleague of Dr. Hachiya, stationed at the Omura Naval Hospital, near Nagasaki.

CHARLES SWEENEY: Pilot of the scientific observation plane *Great Artiste* (with Luis Alvarez aboard) during the Hiroshima mission. Sweeney piloted *Bock's Car* during the Nagasaki mission. Pilot of *Straight Flush* when a plutonium bomb without a core was dropped during the predawn hours of August 15, 1945.

DR. EIZO TAJIMA: A student of physicist Yoshio Nishina.

AKIKO TAKAHURA: A bank clerk in Hiroshima, exposed with her friend Asami at a radius of 250 meters (820 feet), deep within the protective steel, concrete, and granite shell of the Sumitomo Bank.

NOBUO TETSUTANI: Exposed within 1 kilometer of the Hiroshima hypocenter, Nobuo was shadow-shielded while his son, Shin, riding with his best friend on a tricycle, caught the full fury of the flash. Not wanting the children to be cremated and scattered anonymously in the army's funeral pyres, Nobuo buried Shin and Kimi with their tricycle under the ruins of his house, where they would stay, hand in hand, for forty years.

PAUL TIBBETS: Pilot of *Enola Gay*, mathematician behind the flight dynamics of atomic bomb runs.

SHIGENORI TOGO: Along with physicist Nishina, Foreign Minister Togo argued that there was no defense against nuclear weaponry and that the Emperor must consider surrender. The Emperor agreed. War Minister Anami did not.

DR. SUSUMU TSUNO: Dean of Nagasaki Medical College. On August 7, 1945, he boarded the same train from Hiroshima as Akira Iwanaga and Prefect Nishioka. He was located in a building near the hypocenter and, like most of the people who arrived aboard Akira's train, did not survive his second encounter with the atomic bomb.

YOSHIJIRO UMEZU: One of several generals at the Imperial Palace (among them Ugaki) who believed in making a last stand against nuclear attack.

BERNARD WALDMAN: Scientist/photographer at the tail gunner's position during the Hiroshima mission.

TSUTOMU YAMAGUCHI : A ship designer who worked at the Mitsubishi weapons facilities of Hiroshima and Nagasaki. Like Shigeyoshi Morimoto, he experienced both atomic bombings within "the Flatlands" as the Ground Zero regions were often called. He was saved by a shock cocoon the second time and was nursed through radiation sickness by his wife, Hisako (with help from one of Dr. Paul Nagai's rescue teams). Mr. Yamaguchi would emerge from the experience as an advocate for peace.

DR. YOSHIOKA: A good friend of Drs. Akizuki and Nagai at the Nagasaki medical complex. Highly respected, she was one of the few women in Japan actually allowed to become a doctor during the 1940s.

NOTES

For a very long time, censorship held dominion over the two cities. Governed by regulations imposed by General Douglas MacArthur's September 11 Committee (of 1945), the survivors of Hiroshima and Nagasaki were not permitted to publish anything about what they had seen or experienced.

During the decades that immediately followed, rarely did their stories get out. Notable exceptions included John Hershey's interviews with six Hiroshima survivors, published in *The New Yorker* as the August 31, 1946, issue's entire edition. Hershey's story was subsequently published as the book, *Hiroshima,** and has remained in print ever since. Like John Hershey, Dr. Paul Takashi Nagai also managed to escape censorship and to publish—just barely. Following the release of *The Bells of Nagasaki,** while he was studying the biology of the hypocenter and compiling his notes for *We of Nagasaki,** his writing attracted a brutal smear campaign. Simultaneously, Dr. Nagai received a visit from American IRS agents; but his welcoming demeanor and message of hope caused one of the agents to report that he had just met "a truly holy man." No one from the U.S. government ever bothered Dr. Nagai again.

Hiroshima (New York: Vintage, 1989); *The Bells of Nagasaki* (London: Kodansha International, 1994); *We of Nagasaki* (New York: E. P. Dutton, 1951).

Dr. Nagai's books remained relatively obscure; but John Hershey's book quickly became an international bestseller. During the birth stages of the Cold War, General MacArthur and those both below and above his command would have preferred less attention on Hiroshima and its long-term radiation effects. Beyond Hiroshima, MacArthur's people took steps to all but guarantee that a bomb three times more destructive than the one that exploded above Hiroshima's "Atomic Dome" not be remembered. Consequently, Dr. Akizuki's sense of deliberate neglect was quite real. It was no accident that Nagasaki's became the forgotten bomb.

"Nagasaki was never, strictly speaking, destroyed," George Weller, one of the first American journalists to arrive in Nagasaki Harbor, wrote in his account.* His reaction would be typical of many in those days, who saw most of lower Nagasaki's buildings standing intact, and did not know that the real center of nuclear devastation was in Urakami.

Weller was amazed to hear the stories of people who had survived near the bomb, in strange, cocoon-like bubbles, while everything around them was destroyed. The approximately two dozen cocoon incidents were told so often that Weller began to consider these unusual events to be more or less usual, which led him to conclude that perhaps nuclear explosions were not really so bad after all. At first, he did not realize that reports of remarkable survival were being deliberately sought out and fed to him, and that Ground Zero itself was being concealed from him, two miles upriver from central Nagasaki.

"What remained fascinating for me," Weller wrote in his log, "was the constant revision of my own ideas of total devastation and no-escape-from-the-bomb." In particular, the American POW survivors from the Mitsubishi torpedo factory's tunnels reinforced this belief. And so, Weller recorded that the sharpest correction of the idea of an all-pervasive doom came from these men: "Blast and ray flew harmlessly over [the prisoners'] heads. They had lain prostrate almost directly under it, and only forty claimed to have been wounded."

---

*George Weller, *First into Nagasaki: The Censored Eyewitness Dispatches on Post-Atomic Japan and Its Prisoners of War* (New York: Crown, 2006).

George Weller's more than three hundred pages of notes preserved an important oral history of American POWs who survived in
more than a dozen Japanese work camps, but his forty pages of
notes about Nagasaki were written under the handicap of having to
sneak around the harbor and finally along the valley walls for a peek
beyond the governor's undamaged mansion, avoiding General
MacArthur's censors. As it was, Weller's notes were confiscated and
classified. Later, his carbon copies were stored and replicated (in edited form) as internal military and Atomic Energy Commission
documents—and in time, they became more or less gospel. His unauthorized report, though compiled in forbidden Nagasaki, contained odd accounts filtered to him under the guise of secret
knowledge. Weller wrote about the irony of a nuclear weapon descending slowly on three parachutes—"a terminal blow riding under
a silk handkerchief."

The words were poetic, but it never happened that way. The
parachutes were really Dr. Luis Alvarez's sensor canisters, dropped
from *Great Artiste*. In like manner, Weller was informed that the
atomic bomb was simply a tactical weapon like all others, with the
exception of being able to deliver a more forceful knockout blow to
a factory, albeit with some temporary side effects on people's white
blood cell and platelet counts. The disinformation was copied by
Weller, then seized, then selectively replicated and distributed.

In 2005, Weller's son, Anthony, wrote, "My father's attitude to
what he experienced in Nagasaki was complicated, and did not grow
less so over the years—'*I lost my war in Nagasaki,*' he used to say."

A basis for this attitude was preserved in letters written by George
Weller in 1984: "Every general wants more of everything than he
has, but the difference between MacArthur and others was that he
would break windows to get it. . . . Jealous of the fact that 'his war'
of four years had been won by two bombs prepared without his
knowledge and dropped without his command, MacArthur determined to do his best to erase from history—or at least to blur as well
as censorship could—the important human lessons of radiation's effect on civilian populations."

General MacArthur was, if anything, decisive. Had *Hamlet* been
written about him, it would only have been a one-act play.

And thus did the Weller document faithfully memorialize the numbers given to the author under MacArthur's rules. As of August 30, 1945, those numbers would officially record only 19,741 deaths in Nagasaki. For a city center that had been shielded by tall hills, this statistic was technically correct for Nagasaki proper; but it was not even fractionally the truth. A couple of miles north of downtown Nagasaki, the town of Urakami was the hypocenter. There, the disappearance of more than 8,000 of the district's 20,000 Catholics alone accounted for nearly half of the official MacArthur casualty estimate. In addition to them, at least 80,000 more were killed and were excluded from MacArthur's history.

Not everyone fell in rank and became a team player in the MacArthur protocol. Risking court-martial if the general noticed, an unknown mapmaker indulged cartography as a subversive activity. On the official U.S. Strategic Bombing Survey Map, alongside the Mitsubishi torpedo factory and other military targets destroyed by the atomic bomb, he listed every church and school, including the Yosē Girls' School . . . Ouramachi Middle School . . . Nishizaka Grade School . . . Urakami's School for the Deaf and Blind.

On September 8, 1945, George Weller had spent an hour on the valley wall, looking down upon the Urakami basin from the ruins of Dr. Nagai's hospital. During the weeks between August 9 and Weller's arrival, Nagai, Akizuki, and the other doctors had recorded the emergence of a mysterious "Disease X" associated with the bomb. According to the Weller log, twenty-five American scientists were due to arrive at the bombsite on September 11, subject to MacArthur's jurisdiction. "The Japanese hope," Weller wrote, "that they will bring a solution to Disease X."

By the time the scientists arrived, Dr. Akizuki's friend Yamagami, a carpenter who survived to be strong enough to build a temporary shelter for his family near a stream below the hospital, was succumbing to a broken heart. All of his family except his four children were missing and presumed dead. Yet each of the children had escaped with only a cut or two, so there was still hope in the midst of Yamagami's pain. "But no one could know how this was only the beginning of great misery," Dr. Akizuki would eventually record. "As ten days passed, and then another ten days, the four surviving children, one after another, began to die." Dr. Tatsuichiro Akizuki published his memoir, *Nagasaki 1945: The First Full-Length Eyewitness Account of the Atomic Bomb Attack on Nagasaki*, in 1981 (London: Quartet Books).

During the first twenty-four hours after the *pika-don*, a substantial number of the medical students who found their way up to the hospital from the lower hills died in spite of having survived without being pierced by debris or suffering visible burns. During those first hours before the name *Disease X* became vernacular, all Dr. Akizuki could suppose was that their heads or internal organs had been struck by falling objects, producing fatal injuries that at first were not apparent.

Weller learned much later that the September 11 committee more or less canonized Dr. Akizuki's initial hypothesis, notwithstanding that additional evidence had caused him to quickly reject it. Officially, and for more than a decade to come, there would be no proof that people had been permanently injured or were dying from radiation-related effects. Unofficially, they existed only in obscure scientific and medical journals. Officially, those who survived with Disease X, calling themselves the *hibakusha*, were not supposed to exist. They were the target of a distinctly MacArthur-esque phrase: "An inconvenient truth."

And so it came to pass that no one from MacArthur's committee asked Drs. Akizuki or Nagai what actually transpired in the Urakami district during the first few days and weeks. None of them ever asked Tsutomu Yamaguchi or Michie Hattori. In Hiroshima, the committee failed to approach Dr. Hachiya or Dr. Fujii, the Sasaki or Ito families. Still, in time, they came forth to tell their stories. After his initial report to the Mitsubishi Company (which recorded nine double survivors, including Kenshi Hirata and military kite-maker Shigeyoshi Morimoto), Yamaguchi intentionally disappeared into obscurity until the death of his son in 2005. During those first decades, he chose obscurity even as he gained some small notoriety following journalist Robert Trumbull's compilation of the Mitsubishi report in *Nine Who Survived Hiroshima and Nagasaki* (New York: E. P. Dutton, 1957).

Approximately thirty people are known to have traveled on two trains from Hiroshima to Nagasaki and survived both atomic bombs, though most double survivors (like Prefect Nishioka) survived one or both bombs at a distance well beyond the rim of Ground Zero. Tsutomu Yamaguchi belongs to one of history's rarest minorities: people who survived in nature's shadow shields and shock cocoons within the zones of total devastation both times.

FOR ALL THE mystery and wonder that surrounds the shock cocoons of August 1945, there should never have been a need for Tsutomu Yamaguchi, Josē Matsou, or anyone else to be saved by the cocooning effect, if not for the most improbable and perhaps the most ill-placed shock cocoon of all time.

Over a year earlier, on July 20, 1944, Colonel Claus von Stauffenberg had planted a briefcase bomb in Hitler's Wolf's Lair headquarters, within a half meter of Hitler himself. The bomb detonated according to plan, shredding every piece of furniture in the room, blowing out walls and door frames, and lifting the entire roof off its mountings. Of the twenty-four people in the room with Hitler, half suffered permanent, near-fatal disability, or were killed (among these were four generals and Rear Admiral Karl-Jesco von Puttkamer). Of the remaining half, all suffered greater injury than Hitler—who, though nearest to the bomb, walked away with only scrapes and scratches, torn pants, and a maddening ringing in his ears. (The Wolf's Lair incident was described with historical precision in Herman Wouk's novel, *War and Remembrance*, published by Little, Brown in 1978.)

Extensive photography of the Wolf's Lair wreckage had already provided a permanent forensic record for physicists and explosives experts, illuminating the paradox of how people standing several meters from the bomb were maimed and killed, while Hitler survived less than a half meter from the very center of the same explosion.

A heavy table leg between Hitler and the bomb created the shock cocoon that saved his life. During an interval of only one two-hundredths of a second, before the oak cracked in half and shredded on one side, the blast wave diverged completely around the disintegrating post and passed Hitler by—carrying along splinters of wood and turning them into shrapnel. These, too, missed Hitler. Had he been standing farther away, even along the same exact vector (or direction), the cocoon-like hole in the spreading blast front would have closed to the width of a man's fist before it reached the far wall, delivering a fatal blow.

Moving the briefcase to virtually any other position in the room would probably have injured Hitler too severely to remain in command, or killed him outright. Instead, a shock cocoon formed near the bomb, wide enough to prevent the force of the explosion from reaching a target that seemed impossible to miss.

The Wolf's Lair bomb was the first step in a would-be military coup. By mid-1943, Generals Edwin Rommel and Carl-Heinrich von Stulpnagel had outlined the unbreakable mathematics that put Germany on the losing side in a war of attrition. Hitler was willing to fight until Paris and Berlin and the entire populace of Germany's territories were destroyed. Calling his policy "scorched earth," he seemed accepting of his own eventual death in defeat, so long as he could drag everyone else into the grave with him.

If not for Hitler's shock cocoon, von Stulpnagel would have called from his outpost in France for an immediate armistice with the Allied Forces on or about July 20, 1944. The Stulpnagel-Rommel plan called for placing Ludwig Beck and Carl Goerdeler in office as president and chancellor, with a mandate for Germany to surrender by the last week of July 1944 instead of May 7, 1945. Had it happened thus, the Allies would not have been distracted from the Pacific front by the Battle of the Bulge in December 1944, by Dresden in February 1945, by Berlin and the Russian advance in April 1945.

Instead, Okinawa did not fall to the Marines and the Philippines were not liberated until June of 1945. If a slab of oak had not intervened on July 20, 1944, these two key events should have occurred at least six months earlier—by January 1945, and likely as early as November 1944.

In June 1945, one month before the first atomic bomb was tested in the New Mexico desert, General MacArthur's post-Okinawa plan called for invasion of the Japanese mainland by November 1945, following the firebombing of virtually all remaining fuel reserves and shipping facilities. To judge from everything Joseph Fuoco had seen during his reconnaissance missions in July and early

August—including the utter lack of traffic in the streets and even the sight of fishing boats and patrol ships standing dead at anchor or in port, day after day in the same spots without fuel—the MacArthur plan was moving ahead precisely on schedule for an October or November landing. The mathematics of MacArthur's attrition were clear: Japan's population would be "defeated" in three to five months after landing.

In August 1945, more than 500,000 troops were already in position on Okinawa and the other outlying islands. Six million additional troops—including "Easy Company" and the Normandy, Vire, and Bulge-hardened Eighty-second Engineer Battalion—had been in training since May for the final assault. MacArthur's math had also called for the United States Mint to produce 400,000 Purple Hearts to be awarded to the anticipated wounded, and posthumously to the dead. (The medals were in fact minted, and these same Purple Hearts from the World War II surplus have been awarded through the Korean and Vietnam wars into the Iraq and Afghanistan wars.)

All of these events would have been turned backward in time six to eight months, if not for Hitler's shock cocoon. The American fleet should have invaded the Japanese mainland by May of 1945, and possibly as early as March. If the former had come to pass, then there existed better than a 50 percent probability that the war could have been ended by August. If the landing occurred in March, then the MacArthur timetable should have ended the war by the time the first atomic bomb was tested at Trinity Base, on July 16, 1945. Hiroshima and Nagasaki would never have happened.

FROM THE RUINS of Hiroshima, in spite of censorship protocols, some literary works saw publication. Among them, Dr. Michihiko Hachiya's diary, which was first published in the medical journal *Teishin Igaku*, then translated and edited under the direction of the American physician Warner Wells, who published it as *Hiroshima Diary: The Journal of a Japanese Physician, August 6–September 30, 1945* (Durham: University of North Carolina Press, 1955). Keiji Nakazawa (Barefoot Gen) wrote several graphic novel (Manga) accounts of his survival as a child of Hiroshima and was able to get them published after the censorship rules were lifted during the 1980s. Among these were *I Saw It* (San Francisco: Educomics, 1982); *The Story of Barefoot Gen* (Sanyusha, Japan, 1984); *Barefoot Gen: The Day After* (Philadelphia: New Society Publishers, 1988); and the DVD film *Barefoot Gen* (Japan, 1992), released in America by Geneon Studios and available through Amazon.com.

Nobuo Tetsutani donated his son Shin's tricycle to the Hiroshima Museum. Then, at age seventy-nine, after retiring from a career as a junior high school teacher, he began interviewing other atomic bomb survivors and assembled an archive for the museum, hoping to keep their stories alive as the population of survivors dwindles. As he expanded the archive, Mr. Tetsutani met the nurses who worked with Minami (Nancy Cantwell) at Dr. Fujii's rescue station, and he was shown three melted toy marbles that originally belonged to Toshihiko Matsuda. In 1992, Mr. Tetsutani produced the animated film *A Boy's Marbles*, and in 1995 he oversaw the publication of the children's book *Shin's Tricycle* (New York: Walker). Masuji Ibuse's story of "the crazy iris" was published in a collection with that same title (New York: Grove Press, 1985). The poems of Shoda Shinoe and Sadako Kurihara were published in *White Flash, Black Rain* (Minneapolis: Milkweed Editions, 1995).

Perhaps the most famous book to come out of Hiroshima, besides John Hershey's *Hiroshima*, is Eleanor Coerr's novella for children and young adults, *Sadako and the Thousand Paper Cranes* (New York: Putnam, 1999). The novella was not intended to be a detailed factual history and is instead based on oral traditions as they evolved among the children (and their children's children) who attended Sadako's school. Even the memorial statue in Hiroshima's Peace Park is more consistent with oral traditions of Sadako's school than with the actual history recorded within Sadako's family and by her doctors. The statue prominently displays a golden paper crane (remaining faithful to the story told by the parents of Sadako's classmates, who directed construction of the memorial), yet in reality the golden paper crane did not exist. Despite such factual imprecision, Coerr's novella is a very good introduction to the Sadako story. For a detailed account of events leading up to the construction of the memorial, see Takayuki Ishii's book, *A Thousand Paper Cranes: The*

Story of Sadako and the Children's Peace Statue (New York: Random House, 2001).

Nancy Cantwell (Minami) published the English edition of her 2006 memoir, *A Life in Three Motherlands (Japan, Korea, USA),* as a print-on-demand book, available from Vantage Press through Amazon.com. Her friends, including Nenkai Aoyama, Hitoshi Takayama, and the nurses who took care of Toshihiko Matsuda "the Marble Boy of Hiroshima," assembled essays and survivors' accounts into *Hiroshima in Memoriam and Today: A Testament of Peace in the World* (Asheville, N.C.: Baltimore Press, 2000).

NANCY CANTWELL HAD no way of knowing it at the time, but as she drove toward the Lincoln Tunnel on the morning of September 11, 2001, she acquired the historical distinction of having approached the second ground zero in her life by driving toward the birthplace of her first ground zero—a part of Manhattan called Hell's Kitchen.

Weeks later, when scientists were assisting New York City's Fire Department in developing a protocol to neutralize the effects of a terrorist "dirty bomb" (typically designed to spread radioactive cesium), they learned that the new ultra-sensitive Geiger counters supplied by the federal government were rendered useless because their sensitivity was such that they responded to trace amounts of radon gas in the granite of Manhattan's buildings—to say nothing of a lingering residue from the Manhattan Project's uranium storage facilities, located among the cattle yards and slaughterhouses of Hell's Kitchen.

In June of 1942, three years after Einstein and his colleagues alerted President Roosevelt that America might be in a race with Germany and Japan to develop an atomic bomb, Germany's attempt to sustain a controllable fission reaction depended on Werner Heisenberg's atomic bomb design. It was considered more dangerous to its designers than to their enemies. When American occupation forces captured Dr. Heisenberg in 1945, the army's embedded scientists—who had feared that a German atomic bomb was imminent—sent a memo back to the White House: "Baby not born. Mother not even pregnant."

Meanwhile, six months before 1942's German reactor failure,

under an abandoned football stadium at the University of Chicago, Enrico Fermi's team had succeeded in sustaining the world's first controllable nuclear reaction. Aroused by the implications of such success, President Roosevelt released two billion dollars in government funds for the refining and production of fissionable metals. The Manhattan Project became so secret that Vice President Truman, who would order the dropping of the atomic bombs, did not know of the project's existence until after he took office (however, the Russians had infiltrated the project almost from the start, and Stalin knew of the bomb's existence before Truman).

In early 1943, the road to Hiroshima led from Los Alamos Laboratory to Columbia University, to Hell's Kitchen. An American army colonel (code-named "Hen"), dressed in ordinary civilian clothes, was sent by Harold Urey at Columbia to the Manhattan office of a Belgian mine operator named Edgar Sengier.

As Sengier records history, "The colonel confirmed his credentials and asked me if I could help the United States to get some uranium ore from the Belgian Congo. All he would reveal was that it was crucial to the Allied cause. I asked him when he would like to have the shipment and he told me, 'Right now . . . But, of course, we'd settle for a few months from now.' So, I told him, 'I just happen to have a thousand tons of ore stored right here in New York City.' "

According to Sengier, the colonel thought he was joking, but after a ride to a ramshackle warehouse in one of the city's roughest neighborhoods, Sengier gave the colonel a bill of sale, turning the entire stockpile over to the United States government.

Edgar Sengier was by all accounts a tough, adventurous "rock hound" who lived in the Belgian Congo. In 1939, an anti-Nazi acquaintance of Niels Bohr and Enrico Fermi visited Sengier in Africa, and told him that Hitler's scientists were experimenting with uranium fission, with a view to building a nuclear bomb. Fearing a German occupation of the Congo Sengier stripped the jungle of every gram of uranium-rich pitchblende he could find. A year later he had loaded the pitchblende onto a ship and accompanied the cargo to New York. Then Sengier contacted Harold Urey at Columbia University and informed him that he had hidden a large supply of high-grade uranium ore from the Nazis. Neither the colonel nor the scientist (who would soon be working directly on the chemical separation of uranium-235 from the ore) ever imagined that a *thousand* tons of material—enough to destroy several cities—happened to already be sitting in steel drums on the floor of a straw-and-manure-slicked warehouse, nestled among the slaughterhouses and meat markets of Hell's Kitchen. This became the secret source of almost all the uranium that went into the Hiroshima bomb. Much of the remainder was used in the reactor that generated the Nagasaki bomb's plutonium.

And so, on August 6, 1945, Charles Sweeney piloted the scientific plane that documented the delivery of Sengier's uranium to Hiroshima. Three days later he flew the lead plane that dropped the miner's transmuted plutonium over Nagasaki.

In his memoir, *War's End: An Eyewitness Account of America's Last Atomic Mission* (New York: Avon-Morrow, 1997), Sweeney abided by a common courtesy code by which pilots and submariners refrained (except in the most extreme situations) from trashing the name of another pilot in public, even if disagreements or outright enmity dominated the relationship. A reader of Sweeney's book would never guess that a deep rift had developed between him and *Enola Gay*'s commander, Paul Tibbets. He had only praise for Tibbets's mathematical strategies, which had often evolved into lifesaving maneuvers.

Tibbets's behavior toward Sweeney was an altogether different story. He was quick to join General MacArthur's effort to make Sweeney and his mission fade from memory—an effort that seemed to Joseph Fuoco to be aimed largely at Tibbets's desire to magnify his own role in history while diminishing Sweeney's. In private moments, friends reported that Tibbets was occasionally horrified by what he had seen over Hiroshima, and Joe Fuoco often wondered if Tibbets's tendency to glorify his mission, which manifested as reenactments of the Hiroshima bombing at public air shows and ordering custom-designed ice-cream cakes shaped like mushroom clouds, was perhaps an equal and opposite reaction to what the bomb had done, "a thinly disguised denial of something horrible," Fuoco guessed, "perhaps even [a] pathological [reaction], which should be pitied more than despised."

Tibbets, in a 1999 letter to John Kuharek (cited by J. C. Muller at the 2005 Tinian Symposium), characterized the *Bock's Car* fuel problem and Sweeney's three flights through flak over Kokura as examples of "indecisiveness and a failure to command," and added: "Any other airplane commander would have aborted the mission after the first aborted attempt on a bomb run." In a 1999 letter to J. C. Muller, Tibbets expressed his belief that after Hiroshima and the massive firebombings elsewhere, Japan was so defeated and so close to surrender that Sweeney's bomb had become redundant if not completely irrelevant, and never needed to be dropped in the first place.

According to Joe Fuoco, in the end the grandstanding pilot of *Enola Gay* viewed the pilot of *Bock's Car* with the same level of camaraderie and affection Ahab must have reserved for Moby Dick. It looked as if even among the flight crews that dropped the atomic bombs, Dr. Nagai's cracks had a way of yawning open, in a way that did not seem possible for crews involved in the firebombings of Osaka, Kobe, and Tokyo.

SELECTED BIBLIOGRAPHY

A-Bomb After-Effects Research Council. "Guide to Treatment of Late A-Bomb Disturbances." *Journal of Japan Medical Association* 32/188 (1954); 34/676 (1955).

Akizuki, T. *Document of A-Bombed Nagasaki: Testimony of A-Bombed Doctor.* Tokyo: Kobundo, 1966; *Nagasaki 1945* trans. rev. ed. London: Quartet Books, 1981.

Anderson, R. E. "Leukemia and Related Disorders." In *The Delayed Consequence of Exposure to Ionizing Radiation: Pathology Studies at the Atomic Bomb Casualty Commission, Hiroshima and Nagasaki Symposium. Human Pathology* 2/505 (1971).

Aoki, K., et al. *Investigation of Damage to Structures by the Atomic Bombs.* In vol. 1. Japan: CRIABC, 1953.

Arakawa, E. T. "Radiation Dosimetry in Hiroshima and Nagasaki Atomic Bomb Survivors." *New England Journal of Medicine* 263/488 (1960).

Beck, J. S. P., and W. A. Meissner. "Radiation Effects of the Atomic Bomb Among the Natives of Nagasaki." *American Journal of Clinical Pathology* 6/586 (1946).

———. "Atomic Bomb Surface Burns: Some Clinical Observations Among Prisoners of War Rescued at Nagasaki." *Journal of the Indiana Medical Association* 40/515 (1947).

Belsky, J. L., and W. J. Blot. "Adult Stature in Relation to Childhood Exposure to the Atomic Bombs of Hiroshima and Nagasaki." *American Journal of Public Health* 65/489 (1975).

Bizzozero, O. J., et al. "Distribution, Incidence and Appearance Time of Radiation-Related Leukemia in Hiroshima and Nagasaki, 1946–1964." *New England Journal of Medicine* 274/1095 (1966).

Brode, H. L. "Numerical Solution of Spherical Blast Waves." *Journal of Applied Physics* 26/766 (1955).

Committee for the Compilation of Materials on Damage Caused by the Atomic Bombs in Hiroshima and Nagasaki. *The Physical, Medical, and Social Effects of the Atomic Bombings.* New York: Basic Books, 1981.

Fujita, T., et al. "Acute Effects of Atomic Bomb on Vegetable Kingdom Plants." In *Annals of the Hiroshima University A-Bomb Dead Memorial Functions Committee.* 1977.

Government Documents and Maps, U.S. Government Printing Office (GPO), Chairman's Office. *The Effects of the Atomic Bombs on Hiroshima and Nagasaki, United States Strategic Bombing Survey.* Washington, DC: June 30, 1946.

————. *Report of the British Mission to Japan on an Investigation of the Effects of the Atomic Bombs Dropped on Hiroshima and Nagasaki.* Washington, DC: 1946.

Ham, W. T. "Radiation Cataracts." *Archives of Ophthalmology* 50/618 (1953).

Harada, T. "Summary Report on Scar Keloids, Hiroshima." *Journal of the Hiroshima Medical Association* 20/199 (1967).

Harada, T., and M. Ishida. "Malignant Neoplasms Among A-Bomb Survivors in Hiroshima: First Report of the Tumor Statistical Committee." *Journal of the National Cancer Institute* 25/1253 (1960).

Harada, T., and S. Ishida. "Lung Cancer Among Atomic Bomb Survivors: Study of 114 Autopsy Cases, 1957–1972." *Journal of the Hiroshima Medical Association* 27/558 (1975).

Hirono, T., and K. Aihara. "Investigation Report on Blasts Caused by the Atomic Bombs." In vol 1. Japan: *CRIABC,* 1953.

Hiroshima District Meteorological Observatory Observation Section. "Weather Conditions of Hiroshima at the Time of the Atomic Bombing." In vol. 1. Japan: *CRIABC,* 1953.

Kimura, M., and E. Tajima. "On the Burst Point of the Atomic Bomb and the Size of the Fireball." In vol 1. Japan: *CRIABC*, 1953.

Kubo, Y. "A Study of Human Behavior Immediately After the Bombing of Hiroshima." *Japanese Journal of Psychology* 22/103 (1952).

Larkin, J. C. "Distribution of Radiation in the Atomic Bombing of Nagasaki." *American Journal of Roentgenology* 55/525 (1946).

Liebow, A. A. *Encounter With Disaster: A Medical Diary of Hiroshima, 1945.* New York: W. W. Norton, 1970.

Lifton, R. J. *Death in Life: Survivors of Hiroshima.* Durham: University of North Carolina Press, 1991.

Nakamura, K. "Survey of the Atomic Bomb Disaster in Nagasaki." In vol. 1. Japan: *CRIABC*, 1953.

Okada, K. "Biological Investigation of Atomic Bomb Disasters: Effect on Animals." In vol. 1. Japan: *CRIABC*, 1953.

Oughterson, A. W., and S. Warren. *Medical Effects of the Atomic Bomb in Japan.* New York: McGraw-Hill, 1956.

Pellegrino, C. R. *Ghosts of Vesuvius.* New York: HarperPerennial, 2004.

Sekimori et al. *Hibakusha: Survivors of Hiroshima and Nagasaki.* Tokyo: Kosei, 1986.

Shiotsuki, M. *Doctor at Nagasaki.* Tokyo: Kosei, 1987.

Timmes, J. J. "Radiation Sickness in Nagasaki: Preliminary Report." *United States Navy Medical Bulletin* 46/219 (1946).

U.S. Atomic Energy Commission. *The Effects of Nuclear Weapons.* Washington, DC: 1962.

U.S. Department of the Interior. *The Archaeology of the Atomic Bomb: Assessment of the Sunken Fleet of Operation Crossroads at Bikini and Kwajalein Atoll Lagoons.* Washington, DC: 1991.

Yuzaki, M. "Family Disintegration Due to the Atomic Bomb." *Report of the 50th Meeting of the Japan Sociological Society.* 1977.

Zeldis, L. J., et al. "Current Status of ABCC-JNIH Studies of Carcinogenesis in Hiroshima and Nagasaki." *Annals of the New York Academy of Science* 114/225 (1964).

ACKNOWLEDGMENTS

As always, I thank first and foremost my parents and my teachers, without whose cooperative efforts to help a reading disabled, ride-the-shock-wave child, I might never have grown up to read and study science, much less to explore it and write about it: John and Jane Pellegrino, Barbara and Dennis Harris, Adelle Dobie, Agnes Saunders, and Ed McGunnigle.

This project has benefited from conversations with experts and from encounters with eyewitness participants dating back three decades, almost as far back as my high school years, beginning with George Appoldt (of the FBI), who first called my attention to Tsutomu Yamaguchi, Kenshi Hirata, Arai, and the existence of double survivors. He also introduced me to the strange case of the doctor (and Private Shigeru) whose poor vision had been corrected by the overpressure from the bomb.

In approximately the order in which I met or corresponded with them about the subjects covered in this book, I am indebted to Don Peterson and Amelia Sheridan; to Harold Clayton Urey and Luis Alvarez; Father Mattias and Father John MacQuitty; James Powell (Brookhaven National Laboratory); Pierre Noyes (Stanford Linear Accelerator); Francis Crick; Senator Spark Matsunaga; Rhold Sagdeev; Father Mervyn Fernando (Subhodi Institute); Ed Bishop; Sir

Arthur C. Clarke; Frank Andrews (Carter National Observatory, New Zealand); Edward R. Harrison (Amherst College); historian Walter Lord; philosopher/author George Zebrowski; and Glen Marcus. I also owe Bill Schutt (American Museum of Natural History), Janet and Billy Schutt, Mary Leung, and the three little "Pellegrinoids," who have proved to be perfectly consistent with Masahiro Sasaki's command of "Children! Teach your parents!" It was the children who explained to me why thousands of paper cranes were sent in 2001 by the children of Japan to Ground Zero, New York, and they were also the first to call my attention to the story of Sadako and the thousand paper cranes.

Bill Schutt introduced me to the incomparable Patricia Wynne, whose artwork I have used to illustrate the book, and whose responses to each group of new chapters began to shape the direction of the narrative. I came to abide by her opinions when she thought an occasional "Pellegrinoism" needed to be dragged out onto the street and shot before it ended up on my editor's desk.

I thank Charles Sweeney and Joseph Fuoco.

Miko Hatano of the Japanese Embassy in New York was especially helpful in arranging meetings with key survivors in the two cities, and made an introduction possible with Hideo Nakamura, Hidetaka Inazuka, and Chad Deal, who had already made the identification and documentation of double survivors their personal mission. The warm hospitality of Nancy (Minami) and Larry Cantwell's family and of the other survivor families I have met will be difficult to forget. Mr. and Mrs. Hisao Maegaki both came from survivor families and grew up to build the Kamoizumi sake factory, which surrounds one of the most remarkable ancient homes I have ever seen. Masahiro Sasaki and Yoshinari [Tsugio] Ito turned out to have already formed a friendship by the time I met them, and together they helped to organize the outreach of healing from the families of Hiroshima and Nagasaki to families stricken by the 9/11 attacks on New York. For more of us than Mr. Sasaki and Mr. Ito will ever know, their outreach has meant quite a lot: *Omoiyari, Ohana,* and *Nyokodo.*

My thanks go out to Tokusaburo Nagai, to Endo Tai (a translator who happened to attend Sadako and Masahiro's school), Mr.

and Mrs. Masahiro Sasaki, Hiroshi Takayama, Tsutomu Yamaguchi, Hiroshi Fujii (son of Nancy Cantwell's mentor, Dr. Fujii), Nenkai Aoyama (and interpreter Sumie Fujii), Kazuko Kouno, Saitou, Misako Fujita, Reiko Owa, and Sigeko Wasada. Without each of these people, reconstructing the human element of what physics and forensic archaeology can reveal would not have been possible.

Special thanks also go out to editor Jack Macrae (who pointed to a few more Pellegrinoisms that needed to be revised or put out of their misery), Supurna Banerjee, Elaine Markson, Gary Johnson—and to James Cameron and Jon Landau at Lightstorm.

INDEX

ABOUT THE AUTHOR

CHARLES PELLEGRINO is co-author of the bestseller *The Jesus Family Tomb*. He is the author of nineteen books, including the *New York Times* bestseller *Her Name, Titanic*, and *Ghosts of the Titanic*, which James Cameron used as sources for his blockbuster movie *Titanic* and his 3D Imax film *Ghosts of the Abyss*. Pellegrino has a Ph.D. in paleobiology, has designed nuclear propulsion systems for space flight, and has contributed to many scientific journals, including *Science* and *Smithsonian*. He is probably best known as the scientist whose "dinosaur biomorph recipe" became the scientific basis for the *Jurassic Park* series.